ret *n*

Peugeot 505 Owners Workshop Manual

A K Legg T Eng MIMI

Models covered
All Peugeot 505 models with four-cylinder petrol
engines. Saloon, Estate and Family Estate, including
special/limited editions
1796 cc, 1971 cc, 1995 cc & 2165 cc

Does not cover Diesel or V6 engine models

(762-2T2)

ABCDE
FGHIJ
KLMNO
P

Haynes Publishing Group
Sparkford Nr Yeovil
Somerset BA22 7JJ England

Haynes Publications, Inc
861 Lawrence Drive
Newbury Park
California 91320 USA

4428

Acknowledgements
Thanks are due to the Champion Sparking Plug Company Limited, who supplied the illustrations showing spark plug conditions, to Holt Lloyd Limited who supplied the illustrations showing bodywork repair, and to Duckhams Oils, who provided lubrication data. Certain other illustrations are the copyright of Peugeot Talbot Motor Company Limited, and are used with their permission. Thanks are also due to Sykes-Pickavant, who supplied some of the workshop tools, and all the staff at Sparkford who assisted in the production of this manual.

© Haynes Publishing Group 1991

A book in the **Haynes Owners Workshop Manual Series**

Printed by J. H. Haynes & Co. Ltd., Sparkford, Nr Yeovil, Somerset BA22 7JJ, England

ISBN 0 85696 762 9

British Library Cataloguing in Publication Data
Legg, A. K. (Andrew K.) *1942-*
    Peugeot 505 (4 cyl, petrol) owners workshop manual
    1. Cars. Maintenance & repair, Amateurs' manuals
    I. Title   II. Series
    629.28'72
    ISBN 0-85696-762-9

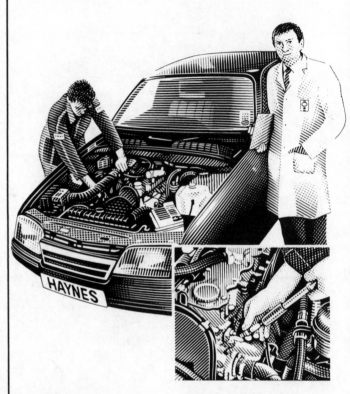

Contents

Peugeot 505 SR Saloon (1981 model)

Peugeot 505 GR Estate (1981 model)

About this manual

Its aim

The aim of this manual is to help you get the best value from your vehicle. It can do so in several ways. It can help you decide what work must be done (even should you choose to get it done by a garage), provide information on routine maintenance and servicing, and give a logical course of action and diagnosis when random faults occur. However, it is hoped that you will use the manual by tackling the work yourself. On simpler jobs it may even be quicker than booking the car into a garage and going there twice, to leave and collect it. Perhaps most important, a lot of money can be saved by avoiding the costs a garage must charge to cover its labour and overheads.

The manual has drawings and descriptions to show the function of the various components so that their layout can be understood. Then the tasks are described and photographed in a step-by-step sequence so that even a novice can do the work.

Its arrangement

The manual is divided into twelve Chapters, each covering a logical sub-division of the vehicle. The Chapters are each divided into Sections, numbered with single figures, eg 5; and the Sections into paragraphs (or sub-sections), with decimal numbers following on from the Section they are in, eg 5.1, 5.2, 5.3 etc.

It is freely illustrated, especially in those parts where there is a detailed sequence of operations to be carried out. There are two forms of illustration: figures and photographs. The figures are numbered in sequence with decimal numbers, according to their position in the Chapter – eg Fig. 6.4 is the fourth drawing/illustration in Chapter 6. Photographs carry the same number (either individually or in related groups) as the Section or sub-section to which they relate.

There is an alphabetical index at the back of the manual as well as a contents list at the front. Each Chapter is also preceded by its own individual contents list.

References to the 'left' or 'right' of the vehicle are in the sense of a person in the driver's seat facing forwards.

Unless otherwise stated, nuts and bolts are removed by turning anti-clockwise, and tightened by turning clockwise.

Vehicle manufacturers continually make changes to specifications and recommendations, and these, when notified, are incorporated into our manuals at the earliest opportunity.

Whilst every care is taken to ensure that the information in this manual is correct, no liability can be accepted by the authors or publishers for loss, damage or injury caused by any errors in, or omissions from, the information given.

Project vehicles

The vehicles used in the preparation of this manual, and appearing in many of the photographic sequences, were a 1985 model Peugeot 505 GR Saloon and a 1987 model Peugeot 505 GTI Family Estate.

Engine codes

For the sake of simplicity, the engine codes quoted in this manual may appear in a slightly-abbreviated form. It is hoped that this will not lead to confusion, but if so, refer to the list below:

XM7 = XM7A (1796 cc, overhead valve, carburettor)
XN1 = XN1 or XN1A (1971 cc, overhead valve, carburettor)
ZEJ = ZEJK (1995 cc, overhead camshaft, fuel injection)
ZDJ = ZDJL (2165 cc, overhead camshaft, fuel injection)

Introduction to the Peugeot 505

The Peugeot 505 is a sturdy well-designed car, using a proven mechanical layout with the engine in the front and rear-wheel-drive. Saloon models have a fully-independent rear suspension, whereas Estate models have a rigid rear axle and torque tube suspension.

Overhaul and repair operations are generally straightforward, with the exception of some areas of the fuel injection system and automatic transmission, which require specialised equipment.

Peugeot 505 GTI Family Estate (1987 model)

General dimensions, weights and capacities

Dimensions

Overall length:
Saloon .... 4579 mm (180.4 in)
Estate .... 4901 mm (193.1 in)
Overall width .... 1737 mm (68.4 in)
Overall height:
Saloon .... 1446 mm (57.0 in)
Estate .... 1544 mm (60.8 in)
Wheelbase:
Saloon .... 2743 mm (108.1 in)
Estate .... 2900 mm (114.3 in)
Track (front):
Saloon .... 1481 mm (58.4 in)
Estate .... 1496 mm (58.9 in)
Track (rear):
Saloon .... 1445 mm (56.9 in)
Estate .... 1450 mm (57.1 in)

Weights

Kerb weight:
Saloon – carburettor engine .... 1215 to 1235 kg (2679 to 2723 lb)
Saloon – fuel injection engine .... 1265 to 1285 kg (2789 to 2833 lb)
Estate – except Family .... 1300 to 1365 kg (2867 to 3010 lb)
Estate – Family .... 1340 to 1400 kg (2955 to 3087 lb)
Maximum towing weight (braked trailer):
Saloon .... 1300 kg (2867 lb)
Estate .... 1500 kg (3308 lb)
Maximum roof rack load:
Saloon .... 75 kg (165 lb)
Estate .... 100 kg (221 lb)

Capacities

Engine oil:
XM7 and XN1 .... 4.0 litres (7.0 pints)
ZEJ and ZDJ .... 5.0 litres (8.8 pints)
Cooling system:
Carburettor engines with manual gearbox .... 8.4 litres (14.8 pints)
Carburettor engines, with automatic transmission .... 7.3 litres (12.8 pints)
Fuel injection engines .... 7.5 litres (13.2 pints)
Fuel tank:
Pre-1984 models .... 52 litres (11.4 gallons)
1984-on models .... 70 litres (15.4 gallons)
Manual gearbox:
BA7/4 .... 1.15 litres (2.0 pints)
BA7/5 .... 1.45 litres (2.6 pints)
BA10/5 .... 1.60 litres (2.8 pints)
Automatic transmission (drain/refill):
3 HP22 .... 1.6 litres (2.8 pints)
4 HP22 .... 2.6 litres (4.6 pints)
Rear axle/final drive:
Saloon .... 1.55 litres (2.7 pints)
Estate .... 1.6 litres (2.8 pints)

Jacking, towing and wheel changing

Jacking

To avoid repetition, the procedure for raising the vehicle is not included before each relevant operation described in this manual.

To raise the front of the vehicle, position the trolley jack under the front crossmember, then support the vehicle with axle stands under the body channel sections.

To raise the rear of the vehicle, position the trolley jack under the rear suspension crossmember on Saloon models, or under the rear jacking points on Estate models. If a cradle is made to clear the rear anti-roll bar, Estate models may be raised beneath the rear axle. Position the axle stands beneath the rear crossmember (Saloon) or rear axle (Estate).

Towing

The towing eyes may be used for towing or being towed in an emergency on normal road surfaces.

When being towed, remember to unlock the steering column by switching the ignition on.

The vehicle should not be towed for more than 30 miles (50 km) on normal roads. The gear lever must be in neutral on manual gearbox models, and 'N' on automatic transmission models.

The vehicle should be towed with the rear wheels off the ground, but care must be taken not to damage the fuel tank, spare wheel carrier, and exhaust.

Wheel changing

The jack supplied with the vehicle is only suitable for wheel changing, and must not be used without supplementary supports when working under the vehicle.

To change a wheel, first chock the diagonally-opposite wheel, and apply the handbrake. Remove the jack and handle from the left- (Saloon) or right-hand (Estate) side of the luggage area. Using the handle in the slotted bolt head, turn the handle 15 turns anti-clockwise to lower the spare wheel. Unhook the carrier and remove the spare wheel. Using the handle, prise off the wheel trim. Loosen only the wheel nuts with the handle. Hook the jack in the appropriate jacking point, then raise the vehicle until the wheel is clear of the ground. Unscrew the nuts and remove the wheel. Fit the spare wheel, and tighten the nuts in diagonal sequence. Lower the jack, and finally tighten the wheel nuts. Refit the wheel trim. Fit the removed wheel in the carrier, with its outside face uppermost. Raise the carrier. Refit the jack and handle.

Towing eye

Remove the trim panel ...

... for access to the jack and handle on Saloon models

Jack and handle on Estate models

Lowering the spare wheel

Jacking point

Buying spare parts and vehicle identification numbers

Buying spare parts

Spare parts available from many sources, for example Peugeot garages, other garages and accessory shops, and motor factors. Our advice regarding spare parts is as follows.

Officially-appointed Peugeot garages – This is the best source of parts which are peculiar to your car, and are not generally available (eg complete cylinder heads, internal gearbox components, badges, interior trim etc). It is also the only place at which you should buy parts if your vehicle is still under warranty – non-Peugeot components may invalidate the warranty. To be sure of obtaining the correct parts, it will always be necessary to give the storeperson your car's vehicle identification number (VIN), and if possible, to take the 'old' part along for positive identification. Many parts are available under a factory exchange scheme – any parts returned should always be clean. It obviously makes good sense to go straight to the specialists on your car for this type of part, for they are best equipped to supply you.

Other dealers and accessory shops – These are often very good places to buy materials and components needed for the maintenance of your car (eg oil filters, spark plugs, bulbs, drivebelts, oils and grease, touch-up paint, filler paste etc). They also sell general accessories, usually have convenient opening hours, charge lower prices, and can often be found not far from home.

Motor factors – Good factors will stock all of the more important components which wear out relatively quickly (eg clutch components, pistons, valves, exhaust systems, brake pipes/seals and pads etc). Motor factors will often provide new or reconditioned components on a part exchange basis – this can save a considerable amount of money.

Vehicle identification number (VIN)

Modifications are a continuing and unpublicised process in vehicle manufacture, quite apart from major model changes. Spare parts manuals and lists are compiled upon a numerical basis, the individual vehicle numbers being essential to correct identification of the component required.

When ordering spare parts, always give as much information as possible. Quote the car model, year of manufacture, and identification numbers as appropriate.

The vehicle identification number is given on a plate located either on the engine compartment front cross panel or on the side of the right-hand front suspension tower. The serial number is also stamped directly on the body, on the right-hand side of the engine compartment.

The paint code is located on the outer edge of the left-hand front suspension tower.

The engine number is stamped above the left-hand engine mounting on overhead valve engines, or on a plate, attached to the right-hand side of the cylinder block, on overhead camshaft engines.

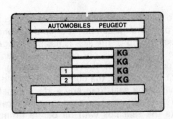

Vehicle identification plate

a   Type approval number
b   Vehicle identification number (VIN)
c   Maximum gross vehicle weight (GVW)
d   Maximum gross train weight (GTW)
e   Maximum load on front axle
f   Maximum load on rear axle
g   Identification or type code variant

General repair procedures

Whenever servicing, repair or overhaul work is carried out on the car or its components, it is necessary to observe the following procedures and instructions. This will assist in carrying out the operation efficiently and to a professional standard of workmanship.

Joint mating faces and gaskets

Where a gasket is used between the mating faces of two components, ensure that it is renewed on reassembly, and fit it dry unless otherwise stated in the repair procedure. Make sure that the mating faces are clean and dry with all traces of old gasket removed. When cleaning a joint face, use a tool which is not likely to score or damage the face, and remove any burrs or nicks with an oilstone or fine file.

Make sure that tapped holes are cleaned with a pipe cleaner, and keep them free of jointing compound if this is being used unless specifically instructed otherwise.

Ensure that all orifices, channels or pipes are clear and blow through them, preferably using compressed air.

Oil seals

Whenever an oil seal is removed from its working location, either individually or as part of an assembly, it should be renewed.

The very fine sealing lip of the seal is easily damaged and will not seal if the surface it contacts is not completely clean and free from scratches, nicks or grooves. If the original sealing surface of the component cannot be restored, the component should be renewed.

Protect the lips of the seal from any surface which may damage them in the course of fitting. Use tape or a conical sleeve where possible. Lubricate the seal lips with oil before fitting and, on dual lipped seals, fill the space between the lips with grease.

Unless otherwise stated, oil seals must be fitted with their sealing lips toward the lubricant to be sealed.

Use a tubular drift or block of wood of the appropriate size to install the seal and, if the seal housing is shouldered, drive the seal down to the shoulder. If the seal housing is unshouldered, the seal should be fitted with its face flush with the housing top face.

Screw threads and fastenings

Always ensure that a blind tapped hole is completely free from oil, grease, water or other fluid before installing the bolt or stud. Failure to do this could cause the housing to crack due to the hydraulic action of the bolt or stud as it is screwed in.

When tightening a castellated nut to accept a split pin, tighten the nut to the specified torque, where applicable, and then tighten further to the next split pin hole. Never slacken the nut to align a split pin hole unless stated in the repair procedure.

When checking or retightening a nut or bolt to a specified torque setting, slacken the nut or bolt by a quarter of a turn, and then retighten to the specified setting.

Locknuts, locktabs and washers

Any fastening which will rotate against a component or housing in the course of tightening should always have a washer between it and the relevant component or housing.

Spring or split washers should always be renewed when they are used to lock a critical component such as a big-end bearing retaining nut or bolt.

Locktabs which are folded over to retain a nut or bolt should always be renewed.

Self-locking nuts can be reused in non-critical areas, providing resistance can be felt when the locking portion passes over the bolt or stud thread.

Split pins must always be replaced with new ones of the correct size for the hole.

Special tools

Some repair procedures in this manual entail the use of special tools such as a press, two or three-legged pullers, spring compressors etc. Wherever possible, suitable readily available alternatives to the manufacturer's special tools are described, and are shown in use. In some instances, where no alternative is possible, it has been necessary to resort to the use of a manufacturer's tool and this has been done for reasons of safety as well as the efficient completion of the repair operation. Unless you are highly skilled and have a thorough understanding of the procedure described, never attempt to bypass the use of any special tool when the procedure described specifies its use. Not only is there a very great risk of personal injury, but expensive damage could be caused to the components involved.

Tools and working facilities

Introduction

A selection of good tools is a fundamental requirement for anyone contemplating the maintenance and repair of a motor vehicle. For the owner who does not possess any, their purchase will prove a considerable expense, offsetting some of the savings made by doing-it-yourself. However, provided that the tools purchased meet the relevant national safety standards and are of good quality, they will last for many years and prove an extremely worthwhile investment.

To help the average owner to decide which tools are needed to carry out the various tasks detailed in this manual, we have compiled three lists of tools under the following headings: *Maintenance and minor repair*, *Repair and overhaul*, and *Special*. The newcomer to practical mechanics should start off with the *Maintenance and minor repair* tool kit and confine himself to the simpler jobs around the vehicle. Then, as his confidence and experience grow, he can undertake more difficult tasks, buying extra tools as, and when, they are needed. In this way, a *Maintenance and minor repair* tool kit can be built-up into a *Repair and overhaul* tool kit over a considerable period of time without any major cash outlays. The experienced do-it-yourselfer will have a tool kit good enough for most repair and overhaul procedures and will add tools from the *Special* category when he feels the expense is justified by the amount of use to which these tools will be put.

It is obviously not possible to cover the subject of tools fully here. For those who wish to learn more about tools and their use there is a book entitled *How to Choose and Use Car Tools* available from the publishers of this manual.

Maintenance and minor repair tool kit

The tools given in this list should be considered as a minimum requirement if routine maintenance, servicing and minor repair operations are to be undertaken. We recommend the purchase of combination spanners (ring one end, open-ended the other); although more expensive than open-ended ones, they do give the advantages of both types of spanner.

Combination spanners - 10, 11, 12, 13, 14 & 17 mm
Adjustable spanner - 9 inch
Engine sump/gearbox/rear axle drain plug key
Spark plug spanner (with rubber insert)
Spark plug gap adjustment tool
Set of feeler gauges
Brake adjuster spanner
Brake bleed nipple spanner
Screwdriver - 4 in long x $^1/4$ in dia (flat blade)
Screwdriver - 4 in long x $^1/4$ in dia (cross blade)
Combination pliers - 6 inch
Hacksaw (junior)
Tyre pump

Tyre pressure gauge
Grease gun
Oil can
Fine emery cloth (1 sheet)
Wire brush (small)
Funnel (medium size)

Repair and overhaul tool kit

These tools are virtually essential for anyone undertaking any major repairs to a motor vehicle, and are additional to those given in the *Maintenance and minor repair* list. Included in this list is a comprehensive set of sockets. Although these are expensive they will be found invaluable as they are so versatile - particularly if various drives are included in the set. We recommend the ½ in square-drive type, as this can be used with most proprietary torque wrenches. If you cannot afford a socket set, even bought piecemeal, then inexpensive tubular box spanners are a useful alternative.

The tools in this list will occasionally need to be supplemented by tools from the *Special* list.

Sockets (or box spanners) to cover range in previous list
Reversible ratchet drive (for use with sockets)
Extension piece, 10 inch (for use with sockets)
Universal joint (for use with sockets)
Torque wrench (for use with sockets)
'Mole' wrench - 8 inch
Ball pein hammer
Soft-faced hammer, plastic or rubber
Screwdriver - 6 in long x $^5/16$ in dia (flat blade)
Screwdriver - 2 in long x $^5/16$ in dia (flat blade)
Screwdriver - $1^1/2$ in long x $^1/4$ in dia (cross blade)
Screwdriver - 3 in long x $^1/8$ in dia (electricians)
Pliers - electricians side cutters
Pliers - needle nosed
Pliers - circlip (internal and external)
Cold chisel - $^1/2$ inch
Scriber
Scraper
Centre punch
Pin punch
Hacksaw
Valve grinding tool
Steel rule/straight-edge
Allen keys (inc. splined/Torx type if necessary)
Selection of files
Wire brush (large)
Axle-stands
Jack (strong trolley or hydraulic type)

Special tools

The tools in this list are those which are not used regularly, are expensive to buy, or which need to be used in accordance with their manufacturers' instructions. Unless relatively difficult mechanical jobs are undertaken frequently, it will not be economic to buy many of these tools. Where this is the case, you could consider clubbing together with friends (or joining a motorists' club) to make a joint purchase, or borrowing the tools against a deposit from a local garage or tool hire specialist.

The following list contains only those tools and instruments freely available to the public, and not those special tools produced by the vehicle manufacturer specifically for its dealer network. You will find occasional references to these manufacturers' special tools in the text of this manual. Generally, an alternative method of doing the job without the vehicle manufacturer's special tool is given. However, sometimes, there is no alternative to using them. Where this is the case and the relevant tool cannot be bought or borrowed, you will have to entrust the work to a franchised garage.

> Valve spring compressor (where applicable)
> Piston ring compressor
> Balljoint separator
> Universal hub/bearing puller
> Impact screwdriver
> Micrometer and/or vernier gauge
> Dial gauge
> Stroboscopic timing light
> Dwell angle meter/tachometer
> Universal electrical multi-meter
> Cylinder compression gauge
> Lifting tackle
> Trolley jack
> Light with extension lead

Buying tools

For practically all tools, a tool factor is the best source since he will have a very comprehensive range compared with the average garage or accessory shop. Having said that, accessory shops often offer excellent quality tools at discount prices, so it pays to shop around.

There are plenty of good tools around at reasonable prices, but always aim to purchase items which meet the relevant national safety standards. If in doubt, ask the proprietor or manager of the shop for advice before making a purchase.

Care and maintenance of tools

Having purchased a reasonable tool kit, it is necessary to keep the tools in a clean serviceable condition. After use, always wipe off any dirt, grease and metal particles using a clean, dry cloth, before putting the tools away. Never leave them lying around after they have been used. A simple tool rack on the garage or workshop wall, for items such as screwdrivers and pliers is a good idea. Store all normal wrenches and sockets in a metal box. Any measuring instruments, gauges, meters, etc, must be carefully stored where they cannot be damaged or become rusty.

Take a little care when tools are used. Hammer heads inevitably become marked and screwdrivers lose the keen edge on their blades from time to time. A little timely attention with emery cloth or a file will soon restore items like this to a good serviceable finish.

Working facilities

Not to be forgotten when discussing tools, is the workshop itself. If anything more than routine maintenance is to be carried out, some form of suitable working area becomes essential.

It is appreciated that many an owner mechanic is forced by circumstances to remove an engine or similar item, without the benefit of a garage or workshop. Having done this, any repairs should always be done under the cover of a roof.

Wherever possible, any dismantling should be done on a clean, flat workbench or table at a suitable working height.

Any workbench needs a vice: one with a jaw opening of 4 in (100 mm) is suitable for most jobs. As mentioned previously, some clean dry storage space is also required for tools, as well as for lubricants, cleaning fluids, touch-up paints and so on, which become necessary.

Another item which may be required, and which has a much more general usage, is an electric drill with a chuck capacity of at least $5/16$ in (8 mm). This, together with a good range of twist drills, is virtually

essential for fitting accessories such as mirrors and reversing lights.

Last, but not least, always keep a supply of old newspapers and clean, lint-free rags available, and try to keep any working area as clean as possible.

Spanner jaw gap comparison table

Jaw gap (in)	Spanner size
0.250	$1/4$ in AF
0.276	7 mm
0.313	$5/16$ in AF
0.315	8 mm
0.344	$11/32$ in AF; $1/8$ in Whitworth
0.354	9 mm
0.375	$3/8$ in AF
0.394	10 mm
0.433	11 mm
0.438	$7/16$ in AF
0.445	$3/16$ in Whitworth; $1/4$ in BSF
0.472	12 mm
0.500	$1/2$ in AF
0.512	13 mm
0.525	$1/4$ in Whitworth; $5/16$ in BSF
0.551	14 mm
0.563	$9/16$ in AF
0.591	15 mm
0.600	$5/16$ in Whitworth; $3/8$ in BSF
0.625	$5/8$ in AF
0.630	16 mm
0.669	17 mm
0.686	$11/16$ in AF
0.709	18 mm
0.710	$3/8$ in Whitworth; $7/16$ in BSF
0.748	19 mm
0.750	$3/4$ in AF
0.813	$13/16$ in AF
0.820	$7/16$ in Whitworth; $1/2$ in BSF
0.866	22 mm
0.875	$7/8$ in AF
0.920	$1/2$ in Whitworth; $9/16$ in BSF
0.938	$15/16$ in AF
0.945	24 mm
1.000	1 in AF
1.010	$9/16$ in Whitworth; $5/8$ in BSF
1.024	26 mm
1.063	$11/16$ in AF; 27 mm
1.100	$5/8$ in Whitworth; $11/16$ in BSF
1.125	$11/8$ in AF
1.181	30 mm
1.200	$11/16$ in Whitworth; $3/4$ in BSF
1.250	$11/4$ in AF
1.260	32 mm
1.300	$3/4$ in Whitworth; $7/8$ in BSF
1.313	$15/16$ in AF
1.390	$13/16$ in Whitworth; $15/16$ in BSF
1.417	36 mm
1.438	$17/16$ in AF
1.480	$7/8$ in Whitworth; 1 in BSF
1.500	$11/2$ in AF
1.575	40 mm; $15/16$ in Whitworth
1.614	41 mm
1.625	$15/8$ in AF
1.670	1 in Whitworth; $11/8$ in BSF
1.688	$111/16$ in AF
1.811	46 mm
1.813	$113/16$ in AF
1.860	$11/8$ in Whitworth; $11/4$ in BSF
1.875	$17/8$ in AF
1.969	50 mm
2.000	2 in AF
2.050	$11/4$ in Whitworth; $13/8$ in BSF
2.165	55 mm
2.362	60 mm

Conversion factors

Length (distance)
Inches (in)	X	25.4	= Millimetres (mm)	X 0.0394	= Inches (in)
Feet (ft)	X	0.305	= Metres (m)	X 3.281	= Feet (ft)
Miles	X	1.609	= Kilometres (km)	X 0.621	= Miles

Volume (capacity)
Cubic inches (cu in; in³)	X	16.387	= Cubic centimetres (cc; cm³)	X 0.061	= Cubic inches (cu in; in³)
Imperial pints (Imp pt)	X	0.568	= Litres (l)	X 1.76	= Imperial pints (Imp pt)
Imperial quarts (Imp qt)	X	1.137	= Litres (l)	X 0.88	= Imperial quarts (Imp qt)
Imperial quarts (Imp qt)	X	1.201	= US quarts (US qt)	X 0.833	= Imperial quarts (Imp qt)
US quarts (US qt)	X	0.946	= Litres (l)	X 1.057	= US quarts (US qt)
Imperial gallons (Imp gal)	X	4.546	= Litres (l)	X 0.22	= Imperial gallons (Imp gal)
Imperial gallons (Imp gal)	X	1.201	= US gallons (US gal)	X 0.833	= Imperial gallons (Imp gal)
US gallons (US gal)	X	3.785	= Litres (l)	X 0.264	= US gallons (US gal)

Mass (weight)
Ounces (oz)	X	28.35	= Grams (g)	X 0.035	= Ounces (oz)
Pounds (lb)	X	0.454	= Kilograms (kg)	X 2.205	= Pounds (lb)

Force
Ounces-force (ozf; oz)	X	0.278	= Newtons (N)	X 3.6	= Ounces-force (ozf; oz)
Pounds-force (lbf; lb)	X	4.448	= Newtons (N)	X 0.225	= Pounds-force (lbf; lb)
Newtons (N)	X	0.1	= Kilograms-force (kgf; kg)	X 9.81	= Newtons (N)

Pressure
Pounds-force per square inch (psi; lbf/in²; lb/in²)	X	0.070	= Kilograms-force per square centimetre (kgf/cm²; kg/cm²)	X 14.223	= Pounds-force per square inch (psi; lbf/in²; lb/in²)
Pounds-force per square inch (psi; lbf/in²; lb/in²)	X	0.068	= Atmospheres (atm)	X 14.696	= Pounds-force per square inch (psi; lbf/in²; lb/in²)
Pounds-force per square inch (psi; lbf/in²; lb/in²)	X	0.069	= Bars	X 14.5	= Pounds-force per square inch (psi; lbf/in²; lb/in²)
Pounds-force per square inch (psi; lbf/in²; lb/in²)	X	6.895	= Kilopascals (kPa)	X 0.145	= Pounds-force per square inch (psi; lbf/in²; lb/in²)
Kilopascals (kPa)	X	0.01	= Kilograms-force per square centimetre (kgf/cm²; kg/cm²)	X 98.1	= Kilopascals (kPa)
Millibar (mbar)	X	100	= Pascals (Pa)	X 0.01	= Millibar (mbar)
Millibar (mbar)	X	0.0145	= Pounds-force per square inch (psi; lbf/in²; lb/in²)	X 68.947	= Millibar (mbar)
Millibar (mbar)	X	0.75	= Millimetres of mercury (mmHg)	X 1.333	= Millibar (mbar)
Millibar (mbar)	X	0.401	= Inches of water (inH₂O)	X 2.491	= Millibar (mbar)
Millimetres of mercury (mmHg)	X	0.535	= Inches of water (inH₂O)	X 1.868	= Millimetres of mercury (mmHg)
Inches of water (inH₂O)	X	0.036	= Pounds-force per square inch (psi; lbf/in²; lb/in²)	X 27.68	= Inches of water (inH₂O)

Torque (moment of force)
Pounds-force inches (lbf in; lb in)	X	1.152	= Kilograms-force centimetre (kgf cm; kg cm)	X 0.868	= Pounds-force inches (lbf in; lb in)
Pounds-force inches (lbf in; lb in)	X	0.113	= Newton metres (Nm)	X 8.85	= Pounds-force inches (lbf in; lb in)
Pounds-force inches (lbf in; lb in)	X	0.083	= Pounds-force feet (lbf ft; lb ft)	X 12	= Pounds-force inches (lbf in; lb in)
Pounds-force feet (lbf ft; lb ft)	X	0.138	= Kilograms-force metres (kgf m; kg m)	X 7.233	= Pounds-force feet (lbf ft; lb ft)
Pounds-force feet (lbf ft; lb ft)	X	1.356	= Newton metres (Nm)	X 0.738	= Pounds-force feet (lbf ft; lb ft)
Newton metres (Nm)	X	0.102	= Kilograms-force metres (kgf m; kg m)	X 9.804	= Newton metres (Nm)

Power
Horsepower (hp)	X	745.7	= Watts (W)	X 0.0013	= Horsepower (hp)

Velocity (speed)
Miles per hour (miles/hr; mph)	X	1.609	= Kilometres per hour (km/hr; kph)	X 0.621	= Miles per hour (miles/hr; mph)

Fuel consumption*
Miles per gallon, Imperial (mpg)	X	0.354	= Kilometres per litre (km/l)	X 2.825	= Miles per gallon, Imperial (mpg)
Miles per gallon, US (mpg)	X	0.425	= Kilometres per litre (km/l)	X 2.352	= Miles per gallon, US (mpg)

Temperature

Degrees Fahrenheit = (°C x 1.8) + 32

Degrees Celsius (Degrees Centigrade; °C) = (°F - 32) x 0.56

*It is common practice to convert from miles per gallon (mpg) to litres/100 kilometres (l/100km), where mpg (Imperial) x l/100 km = 282 and mpg (US) x l/100 km = 235

Safety first!

Professional motor mechanics are trained in safe working procedures. However enthusiastic you may be about getting on with the job in hand, do take the time to ensure that your safety is not put at risk. A moment's lack of attention can result in an accident, as can failure to observe certain elementary precautions.

There will always be new ways of having accidents, and the following points do not pretend to be a comprehensive list of all dangers; they are intended rather to make you aware of the risks and to encourage a safety-conscious approach to all work you carry out on your vehicle.

Essential DOs and DON'Ts

DON'T rely on a single jack when working underneath the vehicle. Always use reliable additional means of support, such as axle stands, securely placed under a part of the vehicle that you know will not give way.

DON'T attempt to loosen or tighten high-torque nuts (e.g. wheel hub nuts) while the vehicle is on a jack; it may be pulled off.

DON'T start the engine without first ascertaining that the transmission is in neutral (or 'Park' where applicable) and the parking brake applied.

DON'T suddenly remove the filler cap from a hot cooling system – cover it with a cloth and release the pressure gradually first, or you may get scalded by escaping coolant.

DON'T attempt to drain oil until you are sure it has cooled sufficiently to avoid scalding you.

DON'T grasp any part of the engine, exhaust or catalytic converter without first ascertaining that it is sufficiently cool to avoid burning you.

DON'T allow brake fluid or antifreeze to contact vehicle paintwork.

DON'T syphon toxic liquids such as fuel, brake fluid or antifreeze by mouth, or allow them to remain on your skin.

DON'T inhale dust – it may be injurious to health (see *Asbestos* below).

DON'T allow any spilt oil or grease to remain on the floor – wipe it up straight away, before someone slips on it.

DON'T use ill-fitting spanners or other tools which may slip and cause injury.

DON'T attempt to lift a heavy component which may be beyond your capability – get assistance.

DON'T rush to finish a job, or take unverified short cuts.

DON'T allow children or animals in or around an unattended vehicle.

DO wear eye protection when using power tools such as drill, sander, bench grinder etc, and when working under the vehicle.

DO use a barrier cream on your hands prior to undertaking dirty jobs – it will protect your skin from infection as well as making the dirt easier to remove afterwards; but make sure your hands aren't left slippery. Note that long-term contact with used engine oil can be a health hazard.

DO keep loose clothing (cuffs, tie etc) and long hair well out of the way of moving mechanical parts.

DO remove rings, wristwatch etc, before working on the vehicle – especially the electrical system.

DO ensure that any lifting tackle used has a safe working load rating adequate for the job.

DO keep your work area tidy – it is only too easy to fall over articles left lying around.

DO get someone to check periodically that all is well, when working alone on the vehicle.

DO carry out work in a logical sequence and check that everything is correctly assembled and tightened afterwards.

DO remember that your vehicle's safety affects that of yourself and others. If in doubt on any point, get specialist advice.

IF, in spite of following these precautions, you are unfortunate enough to injure yourself, seek medical attention as soon as possible.

Asbestos

Certain friction, insulating, sealing, and other products – such as brake linings, brake bands, clutch linings, torque converters, gaskets, etc – contain asbestos. *Extreme care must be taken to avoid inhalation of dust from such products since it is hazardous to health.* If in doubt, assume that they *do* contain asbestos.

Fire

Remember at all times that petrol (gasoline) is highly flammable. Never smoke, or have any kind of naked flame around, when working on the vehicle. But the risk does not end there – a spark caused by an electrical short-circuit, by two metal surfaces contacting each other, by careless use of tools, or even by static electricity built up in your body under certain conditions, can ignite petrol vapour, which in a confined space is highly explosive.

Always disconnect the battery earth (ground) terminal before working on any part of the fuel or electrical system, and never risk spilling fuel on to a hot engine or exhaust.

It is recommended that a fire extinguisher of a type suitable for fuel and electrical fires is kept handy in the garage or workplace at all times. Never try to extinguish a fuel or electrical fire with water.

Note: *Any reference to a 'torch' appearing in this manual should always be taken to mean a hand-held battery-operated electric lamp or flashlight. It does NOT mean a welding/gas torch or blowlamp.*

Fumes

Certain fumes are highly toxic and can quickly cause unconsciousness and even death if inhaled to any extent. Petrol (gasoline) vapour comes into this category, as do the vapours from certain solvents such as trichloroethylene. Any draining or pouring of such volatile fluids should be done in a well ventilated area.

When using cleaning fluids and solvents, read the instructions carefully. Never use materials from unmarked containers – they may give off poisonous vapours.

Never run the engine of a motor vehicle in an enclosed space such as a garage. Exhaust fumes contain carbon monoxide which is extremely poisonous; if you need to run the engine, always do so in the open air or at least have the rear of the vehicle outside the workplace.

If you are fortunate enough to have the use of an inspection pit, never drain or pour petrol, and never run the engine, while the vehicle is standing over it; the fumes, being heavier than air, will concentrate in the pit with possibly lethal results.

The battery

Never cause a spark, or allow a naked light, near the vehicle's battery. It will normally be giving off a certain amount of hydrogen gas, which is highly explosive.

Always disconnect the battery earth (ground) terminal before working on the fuel or electrical systems.

If possible, loosen the filler plugs or cover when charging the battery from an external source. Do not charge at an excessive rate or the battery may burst.

Take care when topping up and when carrying the battery. The acid electrolyte, even when diluted, is very corrosive and should not be allowed to contact the eyes or skin.

If you ever need to prepare electrolyte yourself, always add the acid slowly to the water, and never the other way round. Protect against splashes by wearing rubber gloves and goggles.

When jump starting a car using a booster battery, for negative earth (ground) vehicles, connect the jump leads in the following sequence: First connect one jump lead between the positive (+) terminals of the two batteries. Then connect the other jump lead first to the negative (–) terminal of the booster battery, and then to a good earthing (ground) point on the vehicle to be started, at least 18 in (45 cm) from the battery if possible. Ensure that hands and jump leads are clear of any moving parts, and that the two vehicles do not touch. Disconnect the leads in the reverse order.

Mains electricity and electrical equipment

When using an electric power tool, inspection light etc, always ensure that the appliance is correctly connected to its plug and that, where necessary, it is properly earthed (grounded). Do not use such appliances in damp conditions and, again, beware of creating a spark or applying excessive heat in the vicinity of fuel or fuel vapour. Also ensure that the appliances meet the relevant national safety standards.

Ignition HT voltage

A severe electric shock can result from touching certain parts of the ignition system, such as the HT leads, when the engine is running or being cranked, particularly if components are damp or the insulation is defective. Where an electronic ignition system is fitted, the HT voltage is much higher and could prove fatal.

Routine maintenance

Maintenance is essential for ensuring safety, and desirable for the purpose of getting the best in terms of performance and economy from your car. Over the years the need for periodic lubrication – oiling, greasing and so on – has been drastically reduced, if not totally eliminated. This has unfortunately tended to lead some owners to think that because no such action is required, components either no longer exist, or will last forever. This is a serious delusion. It follows therefore that the largest initial element of maintenance is visual examination and a general sense of awareness. This may lead to repairs or renewals, but should help to avoid roadside breakdowns.

Models up to July 1984

Every 250 miles (400 km) or weekly – whichever comes first

Engine (Chapter 1)
Check the engine oil level using the dipstick. The oil level must be maintained between the high and low markings at all times. Top up when necessary, but do not overfill

Cooling system (Chapter 2)
Check the coolant level, and top up if necessary
Check for signs of leakage, and hose security

Fuel system (Chapter 3)
Check for signs of leakage, and hose security

Clutch and brake hydraulic system (Chapters 5 and 9)
Check the hydraulic fluid level, and top up if necessary

Transmission (Chapter 6)
Check for oil or fluid leaks

Suspension and steering (Chapter 10)
Check the tyre pressures and examine tyre condition
Check the power steering fluid level (if applicable), and top up if necessary

Electrical system (Chapter 12)
Check the windscreen (and if applicable, tailgate) washer reservoir fluid levels, and top up if necessary, adding a screen wash such as Turtle Wax High Tech Screen Wash
Check that all lights are clean, and functioning correctly
Check the battery electrolyte level (except on low-maintenance or maintenance-free batteries), and top up if necessary

Every 5000 miles (8000 km) or 6 months – whichever comes first

Engine (Chapter 1)
Renew engine oil and filter

Cooling system (Chapter 2)
Check the coolant hoses for damage
Check drivebelt condition and tension

Ignition system (Chapter 4)
Clean and adjust the contact breaker points (if applicable)

Clutch and brake hydraulic system (Chapters 5 and 9)
Check clutch and brake hydraulic circuits for leaks and condition

Transmission (Chapter 6)
Check manual gearbox oil level, and top up if necessary
Check automatic transmission fluid level, and top up if necessary

Rear axle/final drive (Chapter 8)
Check rear axle/final drive unit oil level, and top up if necessary

Steering (Chapter 10)
Check power steering pump drivebelt condition and tension (if applicable)

Every 15 000 miles (24 000 km) or 18 months – whichever comes first

Engine (Chapter 1)
Adjust the valve clearances

Fuel system (Chapter 3)
Check and adjust the accelerator cable
Renew the fuel pre-filter (fuel injection engines)

Ignition system (Chapter 4)
Check and adjust ignition timing
Renew spark plugs

Rear axle/final drive (Chapter 8)
Check the driveshaft rubber bellows (Saloon)

Braking system (Chapter 9)
Check the operation of the handbrake

Every 20 000 miles (32 000 km) or 2 years – whichever comes first

Cooling system (Chapter 2)
Renew the antifreeze mixture

Fuel system (Chapter 3)
Check the oil bath type air filter

Clutch and brake hydraulic system (Chapters 5 and 9)
Renew the hydraulic fluid

Propeller shaft (Chapter 7)
Grease the propeller shaft centre bearing
Grease the torque tube front bearing (Estate)

Every 30 000 miles (48 000 km) or 3 years – whichever comes first

Fuel system (Chapter 3)
Renew the air filter element
Renew the main fuel filter (fuel injection engines)

Transmission (Chapter 6)
Renew the manual gearbox oil
Renew the automatic transmission fluid

Rear axle/final drive (Chapter 8)
Renew the rear axle/final drive unit oil

Suspension and steering (Chapter 10)
Check front hub bearing adjustment
Check suspension rubber bushes
Check shock absorbers
Check suspension and steering balljoints

Every 40 000 miles (64 000 km) or 4 years – whichever comes first

Engine (Chapter 1)
Renew the rocker shaft oil filter (overhead camshaft engines)
Renew the timing belt (overhead camshaft engines)

Models from July 1984 on

Every 250 miles (400 km) or weekly – whichever comes first

Engine (Chapter 1)
Check the engine oil level using the dipstick. The oil level must be maintained between the high and low markings at all times. Top up when necessary, but do not overfill

Cooling system (Chapter 2)
Check the coolant level, and top up if necessary
Check for signs of leakage, and hose security

Fuel system (Chapter 3)
Check for signs of leakage, and hose security

Clutch and brake hydraulic system (Chapters 5 and 9)
Check the hydraulic fluid level, and top up if necessary

Transmission (Chapter 6)
Check for oil or fluid leaks

Suspension and steering (Chapter 10)
Check the tyre pressures, and examine tyre condition
Check the power steering fluid level (if applicable), and top up if necessary

Electrical system (Chapter 12)
Check the windscreen (and if applicable, tailgate) washer revervoir fluid levels, and top up if necessary, adding a screen wash such as Turtle Wax High Tech Screen Wash
Check that all lights are clean, and functioning correctly
Check the battery electrolyte level (except on low-maintenance or maintenance-free batteries), and top up if necessary

Every 6000 miles (9500 km) or 6 months – whichever comes first

Engine (Chapter 1)
Renew engine oil and filter

Cooling system (Chapter 2)
Check the coolant hoses for damage
Check drivebelt condition and tension

Ignition system (Chapter 4)
Clean and adjust the contact breaker points (if applicable)

Clutch and brake hydraulic system (Chapters 5 and 9)
Check clutch and brake hydraulic circuits for leaks and condition

Transmission (Chapter 6)
Check manual gearbox oil level, and top up if necessary
Check automatic transmission fluid level and top up if necessary

Rear axle/final drive (Chapter 8)
Check rear axle/final drive unit oil level, and top up if necessary

Steering (Chapter 10)
Check power steering pump drivebelt condition and tension (if applicable)

Every 12 000 miles (19 000 km) or 12 months – whichever comes first

Engine (Chapter 1)
Adjust the valve clearances

Fuel system (Chapter 3)
Check and adjust the accelerator cable
Renew the fuel pre-filter on fuel injection engines

Ignition system (Chapter 4)
Check and adjust ignition timing
Renew spark plugs

Rear axle/final drive (Chapter 8)
Check the driveshaft rubber bellows (Saloon)

Braking system (Chapter 9)
Check the operation of the handbrake

Every 18 000 miles (29 000 km) or 18 months – whichever comes first

Fuel system (Chapter 3)
Clean the oil bath type air filter

Propeller shaft (Chapter 7)
Grease the propeller shaft centre bearing
Grease the torque tube front bearing (Estate)

Every 24 000 miles (38 000 km) or 2 years – whichever comes first

Cooling system (Chapter 2)
Renew the antifreeze mixture

Fuel system (Chapter 3)
Renew the air filter element

Clutch and brake hydraulic system (Chapters 5 and 9)
Renew the hydraulic fluid

Transmission (Chapter 6)
Renew the manual gearbox oil
Renew the automatic transmission fluid

Rear axle/final drive (Chapter 8)
Renew the rear axle/final drive unit oil

Suspension and steering (Chapter 10)
Check front hub bearing adjustment
Check suspension rubber bushes
Check shock absorbers
Check suspension and steering balljoints

Every 36 000 miles (58 000 km) or 3 years – whichever comes first

Engine (Chapter 1)
Renew the rocker shaft oil filter (overhead camshaft engines)
Renew the timing belt (overhead camshaft engines)

Fuel system (Chapter 3)
Renew the main fuel filter (fuel injection engines)

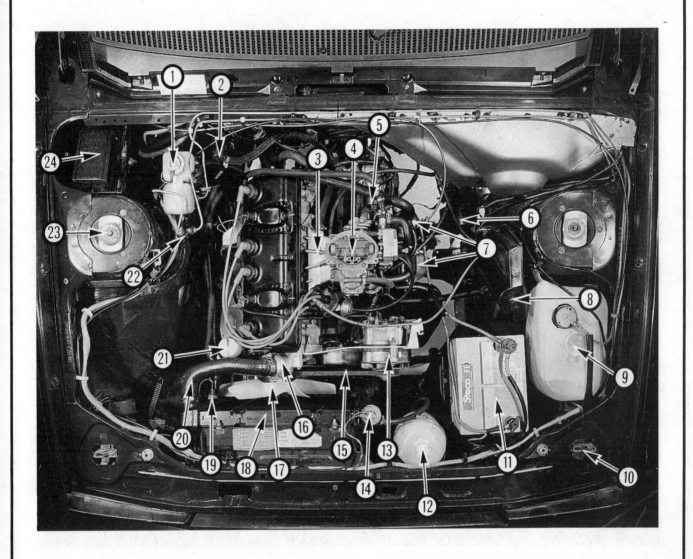

Under-bonnet view (XN1 engine) – air cleaner removed for clarity

1 Brake fluid reservoir
2 Brake vacuum servo unit
3 Inlet manifold
4 Carburettor
5 Starter motor
6 Heater control vacuum reservoir
7 Engine oil dipstick and filler tube
8 Ignition coil and module cover
9 Washer fluid reservoir

10 Bonnet lock
11 Battery
12 Cooling system expansion tank
13 Alternator
14 Coolant level switch
15 Drivebelt
16 Thermostat housing and water pump
17 Self-disengaging fan unit

18 Radiator
19 Fan temperature switch
20 Top hose
21 Power-assisted steering fluid reservoir
22 Brake master cylinder
23 Front suspension top mounting
24 Fusebox

View of front underside of Saloon (XN1 engine)

1 Power-assisted steering pump
2 Towing hook
3 Power-assisted steering pump drivebelt
4 Front jacking point
5 Crossmember
6 Engine oil drain plug
7 Front anti-roll bar
8 Front radius arm
9 Front brake caliper
10 Steering track rod
11 Clutch slave cylinder
12 Gearchange rod
13 Gearbox drain plugs
14 Steering gear
15 Exhaust downpipe
16 Front coil spring

View of rear underside of Saloon (XN1 engine)

- 1 Rear jacking point
- 2 Rear anti-roll bar link mounting
- 3 Handbrake cable
- 4 Rear shock absorber
- 5 Rear suspension trailing arm
- 6 Fuel tank
- 7 Rear anti-roll bar
- 8 Spare wheel
- 9 Spare wheel carrier
- 10 Exhaust rear silencer
- 11 Driveshaft
- 12 Rear brake flexible hose
- 13 Final drive unit
- 14 Propeller shaft link tube
- 15 Rear suspension crossmember
- 16 Rear brake compensator

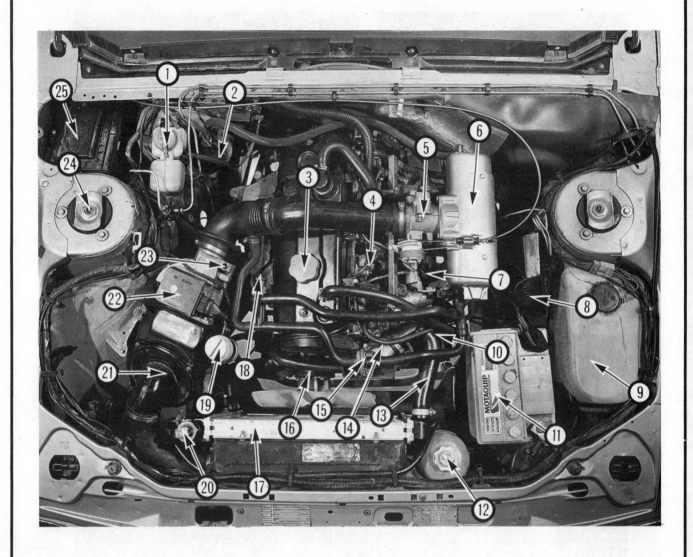

Under-bonnet view (ZDJ engine)

1   Brake fluid reservoir
2   Brake vacuum servo unit
3   Engine oil filler cap
4   Fuel injector
5   Throttle housing
6   Inlet manifold and air box
7   Distributor
8   Ignition coil and module cover
9   Washer fluid reservoir
10 Engine oil level dipstick
11 Battery
12 Cooling system expansion tank
13 Top hose
14 Thermostat housing
15 Supplementary air device
16 Self-disengaging fan unit
17 Radiator
18 Idle air adjustment screw
19 Power-assisted steering fluid reservoir
20 Coolant level switch
21 Air cleaner
22 Airflow sensor
23 Mixture adjustment screw
24 Front suspension top mounting
25 Fusebox

View of front underside of Estate (ZDJ engine)

1 Power-assisted steering pump
2 Crossmember
3 Front jacking point
4 Engine oil drain plug
5 Alternator
6 Front radius arm
7 Front anti-roll bar
8 Steering track rod
9 Clutch slave cylinder
10 Gearchange rod
11 Gearbox drain plugs
12 Steering gear
13 Exhaust downpipe
14 Front brake caliper

View of middle underside of Estate (ZDJ engine)

1 Hydraulic brake lines	5 Rear brake compensator	8 Exhaust system mounting
2 Fuel feed and return lines	6 Torque tube	9 Intermediate exhaust pipe
3 Electric fuel pump	7 Torque tube stay bar	and silencers
4 Main fuel filter		

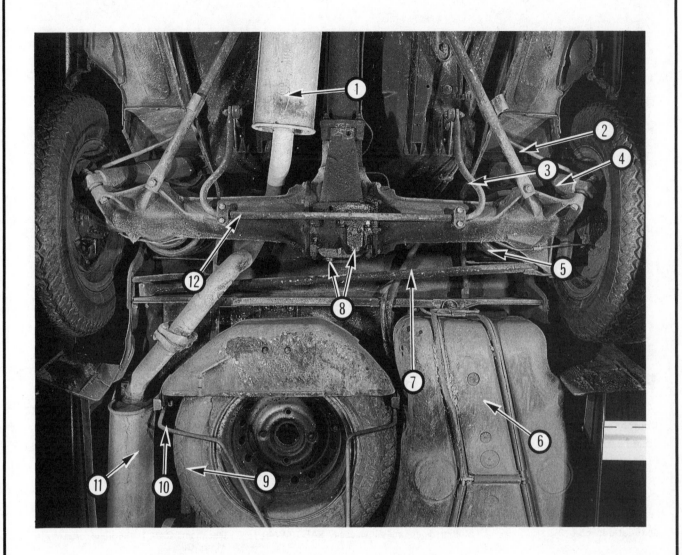

View of rear underside of Estate (ZDJ engine)

1 Torque tube
2 Handbrake cable
3 Rear anti-roll bar
4 Rear shock absorber
5 Rear coil spring

6 Fuel tank
7 Panhard rod
8 Rear axle filler and drain
plugs

9 Spare wheel
10 Spare wheel carrier
11 Rear exhaust pipe and
silencer
12 Rear axle

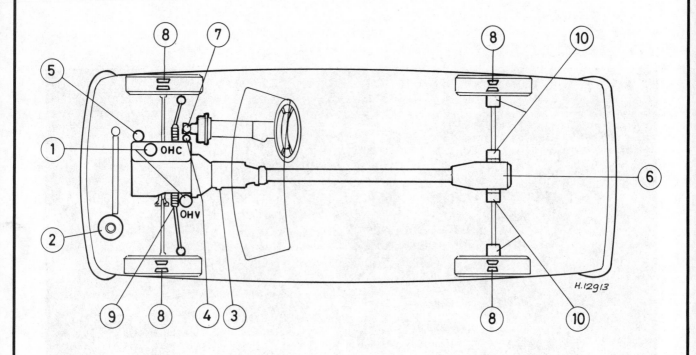

Recommended lubricants and fluids

Component or system	Lubricant type/specification	Duckhams recommendation
Engine (1)	Multigrade engine oil, viscosity SAE 10W/40	Duckhams QXR, Hypergrade, or 10W/40 Motor Oil
Cooling system (2)	Ethylene glycol based antifreeze	Duckhams Universal Antifreeze and Summer Coolant
Manual gearbox (3)	Multigrade engine oil, viscosity SAE 10W/40	Duckhams QXR, Hypergrade, or 10W/40 Motor Oil
Automatic transmission (4)	Dexron II ATF	Duckhams D-Matic
Power steering reservoir (5)	Dexron II ATF	Duckhams D-Matic
Rear axle/final drive unit (6):		
Except limited-slip differential	Gear oil, viscosity SAE 80W/90	Duckhams Hypoid 80S
Limited-slip differential	Gear oil, viscosity SAE 90	Duckhams Hypoid 90DL
Brake/clutch fluid reservoir (7)	Hydraulic fluid to SAE J1703 or DOT 3	Duckhams Universal Brake and Clutch Fluid
Hub bearings (8) and general greasing	Multi-purpose lithium-based grease	Duckhams LB 10
Steering rack (9)	Lithium-based molybdenum disulphide grease	Duckhams LBM 10
Driveshaft CV joints (10)	Special lubricant supplied in repair kit	

Fault diagnosis

Introduction

The vehicle owner who does his or her own maintenance according to the recommended schedules should not have to use this section of the manual very often. Modern component reliability is such that, provided those items subject to wear or deterioration are inspected or renewed at the specified intervals, sudden failure is comparatively rare. Faults do not usually just happen as a result of sudden failure, but develop over a period of time. Major mechanical failures in particular are usually preceded by characteristic symptoms over hundreds or even thousands of miles. Those components which do occasionally fail without warning are often small and easily carried in the vehicle.

With any fault finding, the first step is to decide where to begin investigations. Sometimes this is obvious, but on other occasions a little detective work will be necessary. The owner who makes half a dozen haphazard adjustments or replacements may be successful in curing a fault (or its symptoms), but he will be none the wiser if the fault recurs and he may well have spent more time and money than was necessary. A calm and logical approach will be found to be more satisfactory in the long run. Always take into account any warning signs or abnormalities that may have been noticed in the period preceding the fault – power loss, high or low gauge readings, unusual noises or smells, etc – and remember that failure of components such as fuses or spark plugs may only be pointers to some underlying fault.

The pages which follow here are intended to help in cases of failure to start or breakdown on the road. There is also a Fault Diagnosis Section at the end of each Chapter which should be consulted if the preliminary checks prove unfruitful. Whatever the fault, certain basic principles apply. These are as follows:

Verify the fault. This is simply a matter of being sure that you know what the symptoms are before starting work. This is particularly important if you are investigating a fault for someone else who may not have described it very accurately.

Don't overlook the obvious. For example, if the vehicle won't start, is there petrol in the tank? (Don't take anyone else's word on this particular point, and don't trust the fuel gauge either!) If an electrical fault is indicated, look for loose or broken wires before digging out the test gear.

Cure the disease, not the symptom. Substituting a flat battery with a fully charged one will get you off the hard shoulder, but if the underlying cause is not attended to, the new battery will go the same way. Similarly, changing oil-fouled spark plugs for a new set will get you moving again, but remember that the reason for the fouling (if it wasn't simply an incorrect grade of plug) will have to be established and corrected.

Don't take anything for granted. Particularly, don't forget that a 'new' component may itself be defective (especially if it's been rattling round in the boot for months), and don't leave components out of a fault diagnosis sequence just because they are new or recently fitted. When you do finally diagnose a difficult fault, you'll probably realise that all the evidence was there from the start.

Carrying a few spares may save a long walk!

Electrical faults

Electrical faults can be more puzzling than straightforward mechanical failures, but they are no less susceptible to logical analysis if the basic principles of operation are understood. Vehicle electrical wiring exists in extremely unfavourable conditions – heat, vibration and chemical attack – and the first things to look for are loose or corroded connections and broken or chafed wires, especially where the wires pass through holes in the bodywork or are subject to vibration.

All metal-bodied vehicles in current production have one pole of the battery 'earthed', ie connected to the vehicle bodywork, and in nearly all modern vehicles it is the negative (–) terminal. The various electrical components – motors, bulb holders etc – are also connected to earth, either by means of a lead or directly by their mountings. Electric current flows through the component and then back to the battery via the bodywork. If the component mounting is loose or corroded, or if a good path back to the battery is not available, the circuit will be incomplete and malfunction will result. The engine and/or gearbox are also earthed by means of flexible metal straps to the body or subframe; if these straps are loose or missing, starter motor, generator and ignition trouble may result.

Assuming the earth return to be satisfactory, electrical faults will be due either to component malfunction or to defects in the current supply. Individual components are dealt with in Chapter 12. If supply wires are broken or cracked internally this results in an open-circuit, and the easiest way to check for this is to bypass the suspect wire temporarily with a length of wire having a crocodile clip or suitable connector at each end. Alternatively, a 12V test lamp can be used to verify the presence of supply voltage at various points along the wire and the break can be thus isolated.

If a bare portion of a live wire touches the bodywork or other earthed metal part, the electricity will take the low-resistance path thus formed back to the battery: this is known as a short-circuit. Hopefully a short-circuit will blow a fuse, but otherwise it may cause burning of the insulation (and possibly further short-circuits) or even a fire. This is why it is inadvisable to bypass persistently blowing fuses with silver foil or wire.

Spares and tool kit

Most vehicles are supplied only with sufficient tools for wheel changing; the *Maintenance and minor repair* tool kit detailed in *Tools and working facilities*, with the addition of a hammer, is probably sufficient for those repairs that most motorists would consider attempting at the roadside. In addition a few items which can be fitted without too much trouble in the event of a breakdown should be carried. Experience and available space will modify the list below, but the following may save having to call on professional assistance:

> *Spark plugs, clean and correctly gapped*
> *HT lead and plug cap – long enough to reach the plug furthest from the distributor*
> *Distributor rotor, condenser and contact breaker points (as applicable)*
> *Drivebelt(s) – emergency type may suffice*
> *Spare fuses*
> *Set of principal light bulbs*
> *Tin of radiator sealer and hose bandage*
> *Exhaust bandage*
> *Roll of insulating tape*
> *Length of soft iron wire*
> *Length of electrical flex*
> *Torch or inspection lamp (can double as test lamp)*
> *Battery jump leads*
> *Tow-rope*
> *Ignition water dispersant aerosol*
> *Litre of engine oil*
> *Sealed can of hydraulic fluid*
> *Emergency windscreen*
> *Worm drive clips*

If spare fuel is carried, a can designed for the purpose should be used to minimise risks of leakage and collision damage. A first aid kit and a warning triangle, whilst not at present compulsory in the UK, are obviously sensible items to carry in addition to the above.

When touring abroad it may be advisable to carry additional spares

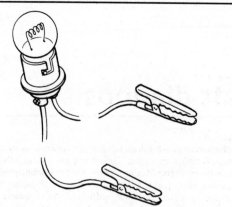

A simple test lamp is useful for tracing electrical faults

Do not use on fuel injection system circuits

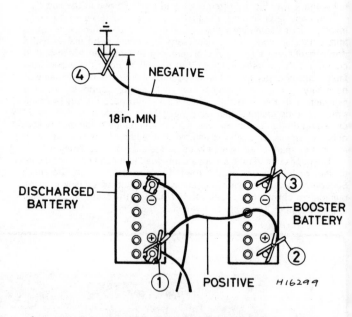

Jump start lead connections for negative earth vehicles – connect leads in order shown

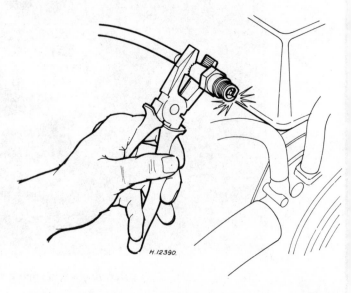

Crank engine and check for spark. Note use of insulated tool to hold plug lead

which, even if you cannot fit them yourself, could save having to wait while parts are obtained. The items below may be worth considering:

Choke and throttle cables (as applicable)
Cylinder head gasket
Alternator brushes
Fuel pump repair kit (if applicable)
Tyre valve core

One of the motoring organisations will be able to advise on availability of fuel etc in foreign countries.

Engine will not start

Engine fails to turn when starter operated
Flat battery (recharge, use jump leads, or push start)
Battery terminals loose or corroded
Battery earth to body defective
Engine earth strap loose or broken
Starter motor (or solenoid) wiring loose or broken
Automatic transmission selector in wrong position, or inhibitor switch faulty
Ignition/starter switch faulty
Major mechanical failure (seizure)
Starter or solenoid internal fault (see Chapter 12)

Starter motor turns engine slowly
Partially discharged battery (recharge, use jump leads, or push start)
Battery terminals loose or corroded
Battery earth to body defective
Engine earth strap loose
Starter motor (or solenoid) wiring loose
Starter motor internal fault (see Chapter 12)

Starter motor spins without turning engine
Flat battery
Starter motor pinion sticking on sleeve
Flywheel gear teeth damaged or worn
Starter motor mounting bolts loose

Engine turns normally but fails to start
Damp or dirty HT leads and distributor cap (crank engine and check for spark) – try moisture dispersant such as Holts Wet Start
Dirty or incorrectly gapped distributor points (if applicable)
No fuel in tank (check for delivery at carburettor)
Excessive choke (hot engine) or insufficient choke (cold engine)
Fouled or incorrectly gapped spark plugs (remove, clean and regap)
Other ignition system fault (see Chapter 4)
Other fuel system fault (see Chapter 3)
Poor compression (see Chapter 1)
Major mechanical failure (eg camshaft drive)

Engine fires but will not run
Insufficient choke (cold engine)
Air leaks at carburettor or inlet manifold
Fuel starvation (see Chapter 3)
Ballast resistor defective, or other ignition fault (see Chapter 4)

Engine cuts out and will not restart

Engine cuts out suddenly – ignition fault
Loose or disconnected LT wires
Wet HT leads or distributor cap (after traversing water splash)
Coil or condenser failure (check for spark)
Other ignition fault (see Chapter 4)

Engine misfires before cutting out – fuel fault
Fuel tank empty
Fuel pump defective or filter blocked (check for delivery)
Fuel tank filler vent blocked (suction will be evident on releasing cap)
Carburettor jets blocked (fuel contaminated)
Other fuel system fault (see Chapter 3)

Engine cuts out – other causes
Serious overheating
Major mechanical failure (eg camshaft drive)

Engine overheats

Ignition (no-charge) warning light illuminated
Slack or broken drivebelt – retension or renew (Chapter 2)

Ignition warning light not illuminated
Coolant loss due to internal or external leakage (see Chapter 2)
Thermostat defective
Low oil level
Brakes binding
Radiator clogged externally or internally
Self-disengaging cooling fan not operating correctly
Engine waterways clogged
Ignition timing incorrect or automatic advance malfunctioning
Mixture too weak

Note: *Do not add cold water to an overheated engine or damage may result*

Low engine oil pressure

Gauge reads low or warning light illuminated with engine running
Oil level low or incorrect grade
Defective gauge or sender unit
Wire to sender unit earthed
Engine overheating
Oil filter clogged or bypass valve defective
Oil pressure relief valve defective
Oil pick-up strainer clogged
Oil pump worn or mountings loose
Worn main or big-end bearings

Note: *Low oil pressure in a high-mileage engine at tickover is not necessarily a cause for concern. Sudden pressure loss at speed is far more significant. In any event, check the gauge or warning light sender before condemning the engine.*

Engine noises

Pre-ignition (pinking) on acceleration
Incorrect grade of fuel
Ignition timing incorrect
Distributor faulty or worn
Worn or maladjusted carburettor or airflow sensor
Excessive carbon build-up in engine

Whistling or wheezing noises
Leaking vacuum hose
Leaking carburettor or manifold gasket
Blowing head gasket

Tapping or rattling
Incorrect valve clearances
Worn valve gear
Worn timing chain or belt
Broken piston ring (ticking noise)

Knocking or thumping
Unintentional mechanical contact (eg fan blades)
Worn drivebelt
Peripheral component fault (alternator, water pump etc)
Worn big-end bearings (regular heavy knocking, perhaps less under load)
Worn main bearings (rumbling and knocking, perhaps worsening under load)
Piston slap (most noticeable when cold)

Chapter 1 Engine

Contents

Specifications

Overhead valve engines (XM7 and XN1)

Type	Four-cylinder, overhead valve, wet liners, alloy cylinder head, cast iron block

General
Code and displacement:	
XM7A	1796 cc
XN1/A	1971 cc
Bore:	
1796 cc	84.0 mm
1971 cc	88.0 mm
Stroke	81.0 mm
Compression ratio	8.8 : 1
Firing order	1-3-4-2 (No 1 at flywheel end)

Cylinder head
Nominal height	92.5 ± 0.15 mm
Maximum distortion	0.10 mm
Minimum height	92.1 mm

Valves
Valve seat combined angle:	
Inlet	120°
Exhaust	90°
Valve spring free length:	
Inner	39.6 mm
Outer	44.0 mm
Valve clearances (cold):	
Inlet	0.10 mm (0.004 in)
Exhaust	0.25 mm (0.010 in)

Camshaft
Endfloat	0.05 to 0.14 mm
Maximum run-out	0.02 mm

Cylinder liners

Protrusion (fitted) above block:	
Models with hexagon-head cylinder head bolts	0.07 to 0.14 mm
Models with Torx type cylinder head bolts	0.03 to 0.10 mm
Maximum height difference between adjacent liners	0.04 mm
Maximum ovality and taper	0.03 mm

Piston-to-liner matching:

Liner notches	Piston reference
1	A
2	B
3	C
4	D

Pistons and rings

Material	Aluminium and silicon
Ring gaps:	
Top compression	0.20 to 0.50 mm
Oil scraper (middle)	0.40 to 0.55 mm
Oil control (bottom)	0.25 to 0.40 mm

Crankshaft

Endfloat	0.08 to 0.20 mm

Lubrication system

Oil pump type	Two-gear type, driven from camshaft
Oil pressure:	
At 850 rpm	2.7 ± 0.8 bar (39.2 ± 11.6 lbf/in²)
At 2000 rpm	3.3 ± 0.7 bar (47.9 ± 10.2 lbf/in²)
At 4000 rpm	3.8 ± 0.8 bar (55.1 ± 11.6 lbf/in²)
Oil type/specification	Multigrade engine oil, viscosity SAE 10W/40 (Duckhams QXR, Hypergrade, or 10W/40 Motor Oil)
Sump capacity	4 litres (7 pints)
Oil filter:	
1971 cc (1979 to 1983)	Champion G201
1971 cc (1983 to 1990)	Champion F104

Torque wrench settings

	Nm	lbf ft
Cylinder head bolts – hexagon-head type:		
Stage 1	50	37
Stage 2: Loosen in sequence, then	20	15
Further tighten:		
M12 bolts	Angle-tighten 90°	
M11 bolts	Angle-tighten 180°	
Stage 3	Warm up engine to normal operating temperature	
Stage 4 (up to VIN 1 845 001)	Let engine cool for six hours, then repeat stage 2	
Stage 4 (VIN 1 845 001 on)	Angle-tighten 35°	
Cylinder head bolts – Torx type:		
Stage 1	60	44
Stage 2: Loosen in sequence then	20 + 300°	15 + 300°
No further tightening necessary		
Rocker arm assembly nuts	15	11
Front engine plate	10	7
Camshaft thrust plate	17	13
Camshaft sprocket	23	17
Oil filter housing	13	10
Oil pressure switch	40	30
Crankshaft main bearing bolts	75	55
Big-end cap nuts	40	30
Flywheel/driveplate bolts	68	50
Crankshaft pulley nut	170	125
Oil pump	10	7
Sump	10	7
Crankshaft balance weight	68	50
Timing cover	10	7
Engine mounting to crossmember	35	26

Overhead camshaft engines (ZEJ and ZDJ)

Type	Four-cylinder overhead camshaft, wet liners, alloy cylinder head and block

General

Code and displacement:	
ZEJK	1995 cc
ZDJL	2165 cc
Bore	88.0 mm
Stroke:	
1995 cc	82.0 mm
2165 cc	89.0 mm

Compression ratio:
    1995 cc .... 9.2 : 1
    2165 cc .... 9.8 : 1
Firing order .... 1-3-4-2 (No 1 at flywheel end)

Cylinder head
Nominal height .... 111.6 mm
Maximum distortion .... 0.05 mm

Valves
Valve seat combined angle:
    Inlet .... 120°
    Exhaust .... 90°
Valve spring free length .... 46.0 mm
Valve clearances (cold):
    Inlet .... 0.10 mm (0.004 in)
    Exhaust .... 0.25 mm (0.010 in)
Valve timing (0.35 mm clearance):
    Inlet valve opens .... 20° BTDC
    Inlet valve closes .... 60° ABDC
    Exhaust valve opens .... 60° BBDC
    Exhaust valve closes .... 20° ATDC

Camshaft
Endfloat .... 0.05 to 0.13 mm

Cylinder liners
Protrusion (fitted) above the block .... 0.08 to 0.15 mm
Maximum height difference between adjacent liners .... 0.04 mm
Maximum ovality and taper .... 0.03 mm
Piston-to-liner matching:

Liner notches	Piston identification
1	Green
2	Blue
3	Red

Pistons
Material .... Aluminium and silicon
Ring gaps:
    Top compression .... 0.20 to 0.35 mm
    Oil scraper (middle) .... 0.40 to 0.55 mm
    Oil control (bottom) .... 0.25 to 0.40 mm

Crankshaft
Endfloat:
    ZEJ engine .... 0.05 to 0.25 mm
    ZDJ engine .... 0.05 to 0.30 mm
Thrustwasher thicknesses available .... 2.80, 2.85, 2.90 and 2.95 mm

Lubrication system
Oil pump type .... Two-gear type, driven from intermediate shaft
Oil pump clearances:
    Gear teeth-to-body .... 0.05 to 0.12 mm
    Gear endfloat .... 0.02 to 0.10 mm
Oil pressure (minimum):

	ZEJ	ZDJ
At 900 rpm	1.0 bar (14.5 lbf/in²)	1.5 bar (21.8 lbf/in²)
At 3000 rpm	3.0 bar (43.5 lbf/in²)	3.5 bar (50.8 lbf/in²)

Oil type/specification .... Multigrade engine oil, viscosity SAE 10W/40 (Duckhams QXR, Hypergrade, or 10W/40 Motor Oil)
Sump capacity .... 5 litres (8.8 pints)
Oil filter:
    ZEJ (1979 to 1983) .... Champion C106
    ZDJ (1983 to 1990) .... Champion F104

Torque wrench settings

	Nm	lbf ft
Cylinder head bolts:		
Stage 1	50	37
Stage 2: Loosen a quarter-turn in sequence, then	95	70
Stage 3	Warm up engine to normal operating temperature, then allow to cool for two hours	
Stage 4: Loosen a quarter-turn in sequence, then	95	70
Timing gear sprockets	50	37
Intermediate shaft housing	13	10
Timing belt tensioner	25	18
Crankshaft pulley bolt:		
ZEJ	80	59
ZDJ	130	96

Torque wrench settings (cont)

	Nm	lbf ft
Flywheel/driveplate	65	48
Oil pump	45	33
Main bearing caps	95	70
Big-end caps:		
ZEJ	48	35
ZDJ	65	48
Rocker shaft filter bolt	20	15

PART A : GENERAL

◼ General description

Overhead valve engines (XM7 and XN1)

The XM7 and XN1 engines are of the same basic design, but of different capacities, the increased capacity of the XN1 being achieved by a larger bore size. The engine is mounted longitudinally at the front of the vehicle, and is fitted with a carburettor. It is canted to the right, to lower the bonnet line, and because of this, the sump has an irregular shape.

The three-bearing camshaft is located high in the left-hand side of the cast iron cylinder block, and is driven by a timing chain from the front of the crankshaft. A hydraulic chain tensioner is employed. The crankshaft incorporates five main bearings.

The light alloy cylinder head is of crossflow design, with inlet valves on the left-hand side, and exhaust valves on the right. The rocker arm assembly is secured to the top of the cylinder head by the cylinder head bolts, and also by nuts on studs. The valves are opened and closed by pushrods located in tappets on the camshaft.

The lubrication system consists of a two-gear type oil pump, driven by the camshaft and located in the sump, and a canister-type oil filter, located on the left-hand side of the engine. An externally-mounted lubrication pipe supplies oil to the rocker arm assembly from the oil gallery in the cylinder block.

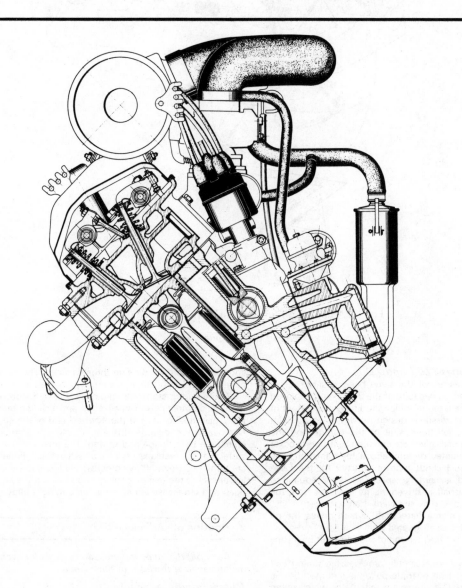

Fig. 1.1 Cross-section of the overhead valve engine (Sec 1)

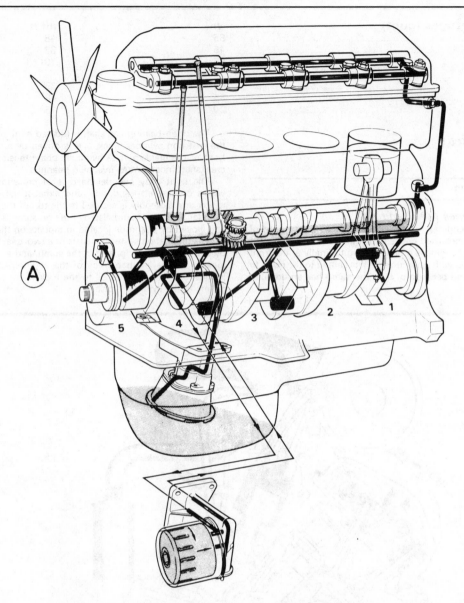

Fig. 1.2A Engine oil lubrication diagram (Sec 1)

Overhead valve engine

Overhead camshaft engines (ZEJ and ZDJ)

The ZEJ and ZDJ engines are of the same basic design, but of different capacities, the increased capacity of the ZDJ being achieved by a longer stroke. The engine is mounted longitudinally at the front of the vehicle. It incorporates a crossflow design head, having the inlet valves and manifold on the left-hand side of the engine and the exhaust on the right. The inclined valves are operated by a single rocker shaft assembly, which is mounted directly above the camshaft. The rocker arms have a stud-and-locknut type of adjuster for the valve clearances, providing easy adjustment. No special tools are required to set the clearances. The camshaft is driven via its sprocket from the timing belt, which in turn is driven by the crankshaft sprocket.

This belt also drives an intermediate shaft, which drives the oil pump by means of a short driveshaft geared to it.

The distributor is driven from the rear end of the camshaft by means of an offset dog.

A spring-loaded jockey wheel assembly provides the timing belt tension adjustment. A single, twin or triple pulley is mounted on the front of the crankshaft, and this drives the alternator/water pump drivebelt, the power steering pump drivebelt, and the air conditioning compressor drivebelt, as applicable. The crankshaft runs in the main bearings, which are shell-type aluminium/tin material. The crankshaft endfloat is taken up by side thrustwashers. The connecting rods also have aluminium/tin shell bearing type big-ends.

Aluminium pistons are employed, the gudgeon pins being a press fit in the connecting rod small-ends, and a sliding fit in the pistons. The No 1 piston is located at the flywheel end of the engine (at the rear). Removable wet cylinder liners are employed, each being sealed in the crankcase by a flange and O-ring. The liner protrusion above the top surface of the crankcase is crucial; when the cylinder head and gasket are tightened down, they compress the liners to provide the upper and lower seal of the engine coolant circuit within the engine. The cylinder head and crankcase are manufactured in light alloy.

2   Routine maintenance

Carry out the following procedures at the intervals given in Routine maintenance *at the front of this manual*

Check engine oil level

1   Remove the oil level dipstick from the left-hand side of the engine (photo). Wipe it clean with a cloth, then re-insert it and withdraw it again.

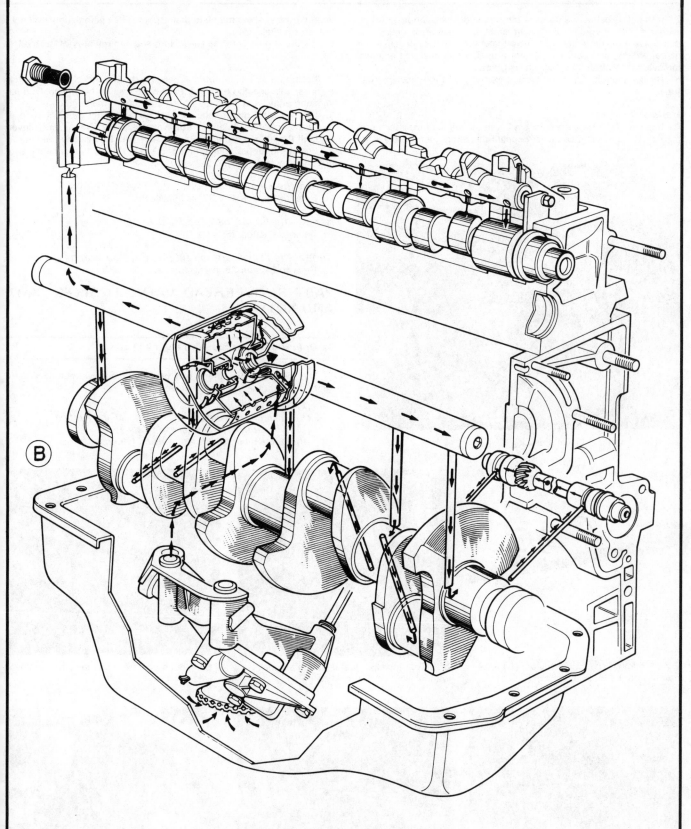

(B)

Fig. 1.2B Engine oil lubrication diagram (Sec 1)

Overhead cam engine

2   If the oil is below the upper notch on the dipstick (photo), top up with the correct grade of oil. On carburettor engines, unclip the crankcase ventilation filter from the oil filter tube on the left-hand side of the engine, and pour oil into the tube. On fuel injection engines, remove the cap from the valve cover (photo).

3   On completion, refit the filter or cap, and insert the dipstick in its tube.

Renew the engine oil

4   It is best to change the engine oil with the engine hot, after a run.

5   Position a suitable container beneath the sump, then unscrew the drain plug and allow the oil to drain (photo). On completion, refit and tighten the drain plug.

6   Fill the engine with the specified grade and quantity of fresh oil.

Renew the oil filter

7   Position a suitable container beneath the oil filter. On carburettor engines, it is located on the front left-hand side of the engine. On fuel injection engines, it is on the right-hand side of the engine.

8   Unscrew and discard the oil filter, using a filter removal strap if necessary (photos). If one is not available, drive a large screwdriver through the filter canister, and use it as a lever to unscrew the filter.

9   Smear the rubber sealing ring of the new filter with engine oil, and tighten it by hand only.

Adjust the valve clearances

10 Refer to Section 4 or 22, as applicable.

Renew the timing belt (ZEJ/ZDJ engines)

11 Refer to Section 23.

Renew the rocker arm oil filter (ZEJ/ZDJ engines)

12 Refer to Section 25, paragraph 22.

PART B: OVERHEAD VALVE ENGINES (XM7 AND XN1)

---

3   Operations possible with engine in car

The following operations can be carried out without having to remove the engine from the vehicle:

(a) Valve clearances – adjustment
(b) Timing chain and sprockets – removal and refitting
(c) Cylinder head – removal and refitting
(d) Engine mountings – removal and refitting

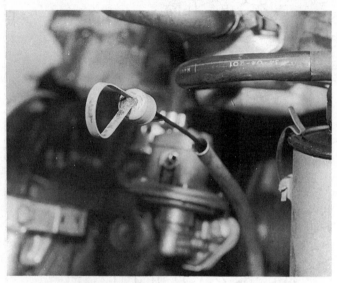

2.1 Removing the oil level dipstick

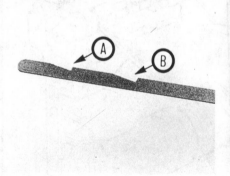

2.2A Minimum (A) and maximum (B) level notches on the oil level dipstick

2.2B Topping-up a fuel injection engine with oil

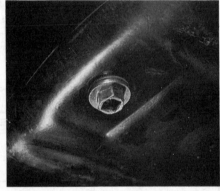

2.5 Oil drain plug on a fuel injection engine

2.8A Removing the oil filter with a removal strap

2.8B Removing the oil filter on a fuel injection engine

2.8C Removing the oil filter on a carburettor engine

4 Valve clearances – adjustment

1 The valve clearances must be adjusted with the engine cold. First remove the air cleaner (Chapter 3).
2 Disconnect the HT leads and extensions from the spark plugs. Unscrew and remove the spark plugs.
3 Unscrew the valve cover retaining bolts, noting the location of the diagnostic socket bracket and HT lead holder.
4 Lift off the valve cover.
5 Turn the engine with a spanner on the crankshaft pulley nut, until exhaust valve No 1 (right-hand rear) is fully open.
6 Using feeler blades, check that the clearance between the end of the valve stem and the rocker arm is as given in the Specifications, for inlet valve 3 and exhaust valve 4. Note that the inlet and exhaust valve clearances are different.
7 If adjustment is necessary, loosen the locknut on the rocker arm, reposition the ball stud, and retighten the locknut (photo). The feeler

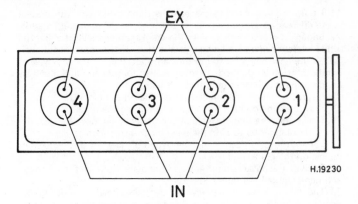

Fig. 1.3 Cylinder head valve positions (Sec 4)

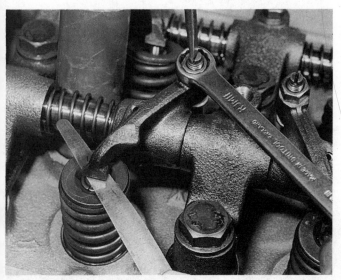

4.7 Adjusting the valve clearances

blade should be a firm sliding fit after completing the adjustment.
8 Turn the engine half a turn clockwise, so that No 3 exhaust valve is now fully open. The clearances of inlet valve 4 and exhaust valve 2 may now be checked and adjusted.
9 Using the following table, check and adjust the remaining valve clearances:

Exhaust valve open	Adjust inlet valve	Adjust exhaust valve
1	3	4
3	4	2
4	2	1
2	1	3

10 On completion, refit the valve cover, spark plugs, HT leads, and air cleaner.

5 Timing chain and sprockets – removal and refitting

1 Remove the air cleaner (Chapter 3).
2 Disconnect the battery negative lead.
3 Remove the radiator, drivebelt and fan (Chapter 2), and the spark plugs (Chapter 4).
4 Remove the power steering and air conditioning compressor drivebelts (Chapters 10 and 11) as applicable.
5 Pivot the alternator away from the engine.
6 Position the crankshaft with No 1 piston (rearmost) at TDC on the compression stroke.

7 Release the wiring harness from the clips on the timing cover.
8 The crankshaft must now be locked, in order to unscrew the crankshaft pulley nut. If the engine is in the vehicle, remove the gearbox front cover, and use a wide-bladed screwdriver to lock the starter ring gear. If the engine is removed, the starter ring gear may be locked using a bolt and bent piece of metal (photo). If the sump is removed, use a block of wood to jam the crankshaft.
9 Unscrew the crankshaft pulley nut, and slide the pulley from the nose of the crankshaft (photos).
10 Unscrew the nuts and bolts, and remove the timing cover and gasket (photos).
11 Remove the oil thrower from the crankshaft (photo).
12 Push the timing chain tensioner plunger fully into the body, then lock it by inserting a small screwdriver in the hole, and turning the pawl anti-clockwise (photo).
13 Unbolt and remove the timing chain tensioner, and extract the tensioner oil filter from the block (photos).
14 Flatten the lockwasher and unscrew the bolts securing the camshaft sprocket to the camshaft (photo).
15 Remove the camshaft sprocket, and release the timing chain from both sprockets (photo).
16 Slide the crankshaft sprocket off, and remove the Woodruff key (photos).
17 Clean the components, and check them for wear and damage. Wear in the timing chain is indicated if it is deeply bowed when held horizontally. Wear of the sprocket teeth is indicated if they are deeply undercut.
18 Commence refitting by pressing the Woodruff key squarely into the crankshaft nose (photo).
19 Slide the sprocket fully onto the crankshaft and over the key.
20 Check that the crankshaft and camshaft are aligned as shown in Fig. 1.5. Both the crankshaft sprocket mark and the camshaft bolt hole indicated must be on the centre-line (photo). Reposition the camshaft and crankshaft if necessary.

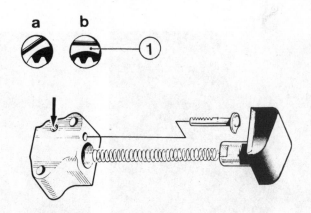

Fig. 1.4 Exploded view of the timing chain tensioner (Sec 5)

1 *Locking pawl – (a) locked, (b) released*

21 Fit the timing chain to the camshaft sprocket, with the double white reference marks either side of the mark on the sprocket (photo).
22 Engage the timing chain with the crankshaft sprocket, so that the white reference mark is aligned with the mark on the sprocket (photo).
23 Fit the camshaft sprocket to the camshaft, then fit the lockwasher and bolts. Tighten the bolts to the specified torque, and lock them by bending the lockwasher onto the bolt flats (photos).
24 Insert the timing chain tensioner oil filter in the block.
25 Refit the timing chain tensioner, and tighten the bolts.
26 Check that the reference marks are correctly aligned. Release the tensioner plunger by turning the pawl clockwise (photo).
27 Locate the oil thrower, and the Woodruff key for the crankshaft pulley, on the crankshaft.
28 Position the gasket on the engine front plate. Refit the timing cover, and hand-tighten the nuts and bolts.
29 The timing cover must now be centralised before refitting the crankshaft pulley. Peugeot garages use a special tool for this purpose, but the pulley may be used by wrapping adhesive tape around it (photo). If the cover is not centralised correctly, oil may leak past the pulley, or the pulley may emit noise.
30 Slide the pulley (taped) onto the crankshaft (engaging the Woodruff key) and into the timing cover, so that it holds the cover firmly.
31 Tighten the timing cover nuts and bolts to the specified torque (photo).
32 Remove the pulley, peel off the tape, then refit it, taking care to engage the Woodruff key in the pulley slot.
33 Fit the crankshaft pulley nut, and tighten to the specified torque with the crankshaft locked as described in paragraph 8 (photo).
34 Clip the wiring harness to the timing cover.
35 Refit the power steering and air conditioning compressor drivebelts (Chapters 10 and 11).
36 Refit the spark plugs (Chapter 4), and the drivebelt, fan, and radiator (Chapter 2).
37 Reconnect the battery negative lead.
38 Refit the air cleaner (Chapter 3).

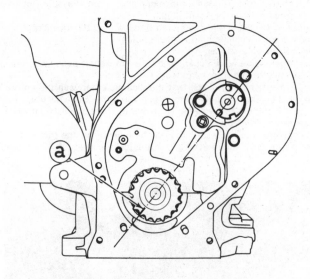

Fig. 1.5 Alignment of the camshaft and crankshaft sprocket prior to fitting the timing chain (Sec 5)

a   Mark on sprocket

5.8 One method of locking the starter ring gear

5.9A Unscrew the crankshaft pulley nut ...

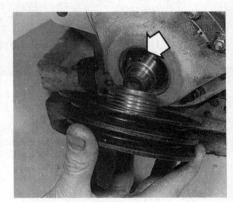

5.9B ... and withdraw the pulley – note Woodruff key (arrowed)

5.10A Timing cover retaining nuts

5.10B Timing cover retaining nut and bolt (arrowed)

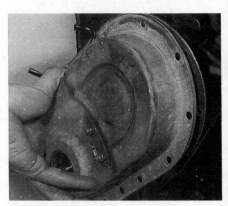

5.10C Removing the timing cover ...

5.10D ... and gasket

5.11 Removing the oil thrower

5.12 Timing chain tensioner locked in the compressed position

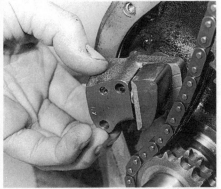

5.13A Removing the timing chain tensioner

5.13B Timing chain tensioner oil filter (arrowed)

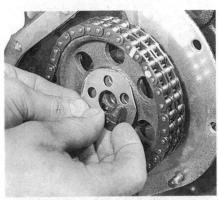

5.14 Removing the camshaft sprocket bolts and lockwasher

5.15 Removing the camshaft sprocket and timing chain

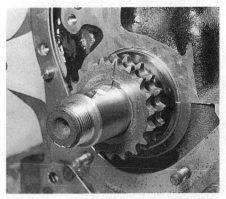

5.16A Withdraw the crankshaft sprocket ...

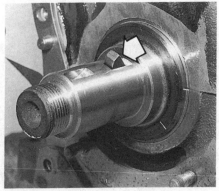

5.16B ... and Woodruff key (arrowed)

5.18 Woodruff key fitted to crankshaft nose

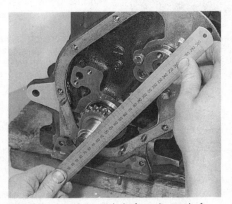

5.20 Aligning the crankshaft and camshaft for timing chain fitment

5.21 Timing chain and camshaft sprocket alignment marks (arrowed)

5.22 Timing chain and crankshaft sprocket alignment marks (arrowed)

5.23A Tighten the camshaft sprocket bolts ...

5.23B ... and bend the lockwasher onto the bolt flats

5.26 Releasing the timing chain tensioner

5.29 Adhesive tape wrapped around the crankshaft pulley for centralising the timing cover

5.31 Centralised timing cover

5.33 Tightening the crankshaft pulley nut

6 Cylinder head – removal and refitting

Note: *Special tools may be necessary to carry out certain operations. Read through the entire Section before proceeding*

1   Drain the cooling system as described in Chapter 2.
2   Temporarily jack up the front of the vehicle, support it on axle stands, and detach the exhaust downpipe from the manifold and two front mounting brackets.
3   Disconnect the battery negative lead.
4   Disconnect the wiring harness from the cylinder head, noting the location of individual wires.
5   Remove the air cleaner and carburettor (Chapter 3).
6   Remove the drivebelt, fan, and radiator top hose, with reference to Chapter 2.
7   Disconnect the HT leads and unclip the distributor cap. Remove the spark plug extensions.
8   Disconnect the heater and bypass hoses.
9   Disconnect the heater, econostat and brake servo vacuum hoses from the inlet manifold.
10 Unbolt the power-assisted steering fluid reservoir from the cylinder head.
11 Disconnect the crankcase ventilation hose from the inlet manifold, and unclip the oil separator from the oil filler tube (photos).
12 Unclip the diagnostic socket from its bracket on the valve cover (photo).
13 If the engine is out of the vehicle, remove the inlet and exhaust manifolds at this stage.
14 Unscrew the valve cover retaining bolts, noting the location of the diagnostic socket bracket and HT lead holder (photos).
15 Lift off the valve cover, and remove the rubber seals from the bolts (photos).
16 Remove the valve cover gasket (photo).
17 Remove the rubber seals and seatings from the spark plug tubes (photos).
18 Unscrew and remove the spark plugs.
19 Unscrew the union bolts, and remove the rocker arm lubrication pipe from the rear of the cylinder head and block (photo). Recover the copper washers.
20 Progressively unscrew the cylinder head bolts, using a reversal of the tightening sequence shown in Fig. 1.8. Recover the washers if fitted.
21 Remove the rocker arm assembly from the cylinder head, after

6.11A Disconnecting the crankcase ventilation hose from the inlet manifold

6.11B Removing the oil separator from the oil filler tube

6.12 Diagnostic socket and bracket

6.14A Valve cover retaining bolt with diagnostic socket bracket and earth cable

6.14B Unscrew the bolts ...

6.15A ... and remove the valve cover

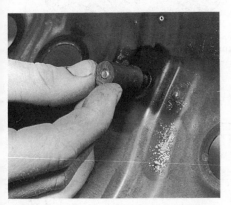

6.15B Removing the rubber seals from the valve cover bolts

6.16 Valve cover gasket removal

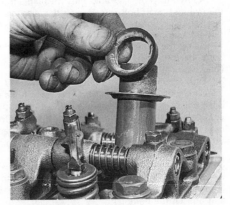

6.17A Removing the spark plug tube rubber seals ...

6.17B ... and seatings

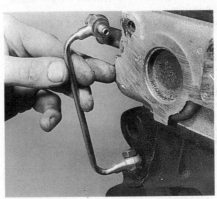

6.19 Rocker arm lubrication pipe removal

removing the retaining nuts (photo).

22 Make some holes in a piece of cardboard, corresponding to the pushrod positions in the cylinder head, then remove the pushrods and place them in the cardboard to ensure correct refitting. Note that the exhaust pushrods are longer than the inlet pushrods (photos).

23 Rock the cylinder head to release it from the gasket. The Peugeot tool for doing this is shown in Figs. 1.6 and 1.7, and consists of the two right-angled levers.

24 If the cylinder head retaining bolts are of the hexagon-headed type, remove the cylinder head by sliding it sideways across the gasket (photo). This is necessary to prevent the cylinder liners from being disturbed, and possibly breaking the lower seals. If the head bolts are of the Torx-head type, positioning dowels are used to locate the cylinder head on the block and it will therefore not be possible to slide it sideways. However, provided that the cylinder head to gasket seal has been released as described in paragraph 23, it should now be possible to lift off the head. Remove the gasket from the block (photo). If further work is to be carried out on the engine, such as cleaning the pistons, the liners must be clamped in position using clamps made from metal plate and suitable bolts (photos). Do not turn the engine without having the clamps fitted.

25 Before commencing reassembly obtain a new cylinder head gasket. Note that different gaskets are used according to the type of cylinder head bolts used and the two gasket types are not interchangeable. If Torx type retaining bolts are used, measure their overall length and renew them as a complete set if any are found to be longer than 189.0 mm (7.44 in).

26 Thoroughly clean the mating faces of the cylinder head and block, then commence reassembly by removing the liner clamps.

27 Locate the new cylinder head gasket on the block with the word 'DESSUS' uppermost. If working on engines without locating dowels on the cylinder block, obtain the special Peugeot head centralising bolts (if available) and insert them in the right-hand corner holes. Alternatively, use suitable long studs.

28 Lower the cylinder head onto the gasket.

29 Refit the pushrods and rocker arm assembly.

30 Apply Molykote G-Rapid Plus (available from Peugeot dealers) to the cylinder head bolt threads and the washers (if fitted), then insert the bolts and lightly tighten them (photos). Remove the guide studs (where applicable) and fit the corner bolts.

31 Using the sequence shown in Fig. 1.8, tighten the cylinder head bolts to the Stage 1 torque, given in the Specifications Section (photo).

32 Tighten the rocker arm nuts to the specified torque (photo).

33 Carry out Stage 2 on all cylinder head bolts in sequence.

34 Note that Stage 2 involves three operations on each bolt – complete all three operations on each bolt before proceeding to the next one. Use an angle indicator to ensure correct tightening (photo).

35 Refit the rocker arm lubrication pipe, together with new copper washers, and tighten the union bolts.

36 Fit the seatings and rubber seals to the spark plug tubes.

37 Adjust the valve clearances with reference to Section 4.

38 Refit the valve cover together with a new gasket and rubber seals, and tighten the bolts.

39 Refit the inlet and exhaust manifolds, if removed (Chapter 3).

40 Clip the diagnostic socket to its bracket.

41 Refit the separator to the oil filler tube, and connect the crankcase ventilation hose to the inlet manifold.

42 Refit the power-assisted steering fluid reservoir, and tighten the bolt.

43 Refit the vacuum and coolant hoses.

44 Refit the spark plugs and their extensions, and the HT leads.

45 Refit the radiator top hose, fan, and drivebelt, with reference to Chapter 2.

46 Refit the carburettor and air cleaner (Chapter 3).

47 Refit the wiring harness.

48 Reconnect the exhaust downpipe.

49 Reconnect the battery negative lead.

50 Refill the cooling system (Chapter 2).

51 Run the engine at 2000 rpm for approximately twelve minutes, or until the self-disengaging fan cuts in, then run it at 1200 rpm for five minutes.

52 On vehicles up to VIN 1 845 001, switch off the engine, and allow it to cool for six hours.

53 Depressurize the cooling system by temporarily removing the pressure cap from the expansion tank. Where appropriate, take

precautions against scalding by placing a pad of cloth over the cap as it is unscrewed.

54 On cylinder heads secured with hexagon-headed retaining bolts, remove the valve cover and carry out the Stage 4 tightening on all cylinder head bolts in sequence, using an angle indicator to ensure correct tightening where necessary.

55 On all engines, adjust the valve clearances as described in Section 4, then refit the valve cover.

56 On vehicles up to and including VIN 1 620 021, the cylinder head bolts should be retightened, and the valve clearances adjusted, after 1000 to 1500 miles (1600 to 2400 km).

57 On vehicles with a VIN later than 1 620 021, and all engines with Torx type cylinder head bolts, only the valve clearances need be adjusted after the mileage given above. The cylinder head bolts do not require retightening.

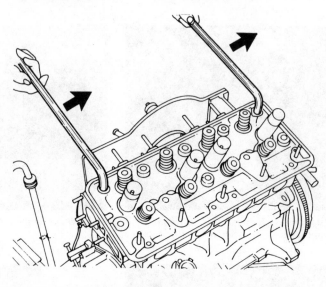

Fig. 1.6 Using the special tools to free the cylinder head (Sec 6)

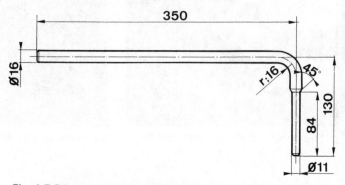

Fig. 1.7 Dimensions (in mm) of the cylinder head removal special tools (Sec 6)

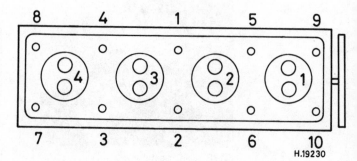

Fig. 1.8 Cylinder head bolt tightening sequence (Sec 6)

6.21 Rocker arm assembly removal

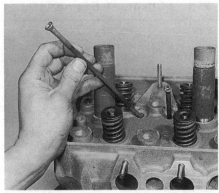
6.22A Removing the pushrods

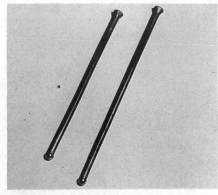
6.22B Inlet pushrods (left) and exhaust pushrod (right)

6.24A Removing the cylinder head

6.24B Removing the cylinder head gasket

6.24C Liner clamps fitted to the block

6.24D Liner clamps

6.27 Cylinder head gasket top marking

6.30A Applying grease to the cylinder head bolts ...

6.30B ... and washers

6.31 Tightening the cylinder head bolts

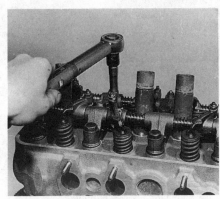
6.32 Tightening the rocker arm nuts

6.34 Angle-tightening the cylinder head bolts

7 Engine mountings – removal and refitting

1 Remove the air cleaner (Chapter 3).
2 Unscrew and remove the bolts securing the mountings to the front crossmember.
3 Support the weight of the engine with a hoist.
4 Unscrew and remove the nut(s), and remove the mounting pillar from the bracket. Recover the shield (photos).
5 Unbolt the bracket from the cylinder block (photo).
6 Refitting is a reversal of removal, but tighten the nuts and bolts to the specified torque.

8 Engine – removal

1 Remove the bonnet, as described in Chapter 11.
2 Remove the battery, as described in Chapter 12.
3 Remove the air cleaner assembly, as described in Chapter 3.
4 Remove the radiator and fan, as described in Chapter 2.

5 Disconnect the radiator top and bottom hoses from the engine (photos).
6 Disconnect the heater hoses from the water pump and cylinder head. Also disconnect the bypass hose (photos).
7 Disconnect the fuel feed and return hoses from the fuel pump and carburettor.
8 Disconnect the heater econostat and brake servo vacuum hoses from the inlet manifold (photos).
9 Disconnect the accelerator cable from the carburettor.
10 The engine wiring harness may be left on the engine if desired by disconnecting the multi-plugs beneath the coil location. If it is decided to remove it at this stage, disconnect it from the temperature sensor, oil level switch, reversing lamp switch, alternator, oil pressure switch, and starter motor (photos).
11 Disconnect the coil HT lead.
12 Remove the starter motor as described in Chapter 12.
13 Apply the handbrake, then jack up the front of the vehicle and support on axle stands.
14 Unbolt and remove the gearbox front cover and the TDC sensor cover, without disturbing the setting of the sensor (photos).
15 On automatic transmission models, mark the torque converter in relation to the driveplate, then unscrew the four bolts. The engine will need to be turned to gain access to each bolt.
16 Unscrew the nut and disconnect the engine-to-body earth cable. Unbolt the battery negative lead from the cylinder block (photos).
17 Position a container beneath the engine sump, then unscrew the drain plug and drain the engine oil (photo). On completion, refit and tighten the drain plug.
18 Unscrew the exhaust downpipe-to-manifold nuts, and tie the downpipe to one side.
19 On models fitted with air conditioning, remove the compressor from the engine, and support it on one side **without** disconnecting the pipes. Similarly remove the condenser.
20 On models fitted with power-assisted steering, remove the pump, and support it on one side without disconnecting the pipes.
21 Unscrew and remove the bolts securing the engine mounting brackets to the crossmember (photo).
22 Connect a hoist to the engine, and raise it until the gearbox touches the body. Support the gearbox in this position with a trolley jack.
23 Using a 10 mm Allen key, unscrew the gearbox-to-engine bolts (photo).
24 Pull the engine forwards, and disconnect it from the gearbox and clutch. On automatic transmission models, make sure that the torque converter remains fully engaged with the transmission (refer to Chapter 6 if necessary).
25 Lift the engine from the engine compartment, taking care not to damage the surrounding components (photo).

7.4A Left-hand engine mounting

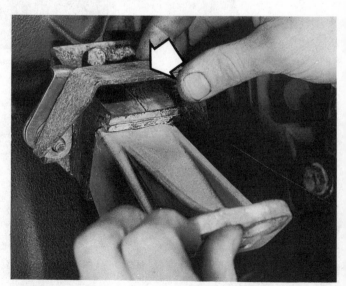

7.4B Removing the right-hand engine mounting shield (arrowed)

7.5 Removing the right-hand engine mounting bracket

8.5A Disconnecting the top hose from the engine

8.5B Disconnecting the bottom hose from the water pump

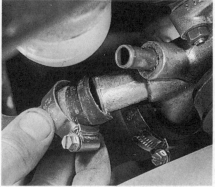
8.6A Disconnecting the heater hose from the water pump

8.6B Disconnecting the heater hose from the cylinder head

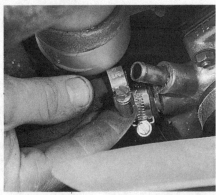
8.6C Disconnecting the bypass hose from the water pump ...

8.6D ... and carburettor

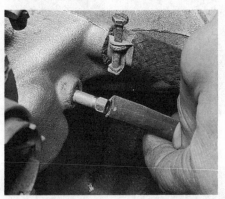
8.8A Disconnect the heater vacuum hose ...

8.8B ... and brake servo vacuum hose from the inlet manifold

8.10A Engine wiring harness multi-plugs

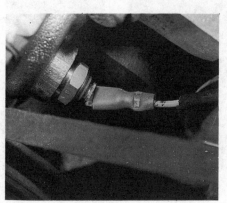
8.10B Coolant temperature sensor and wiring

8.10C Oil level warning switch (arrowed) and wiring

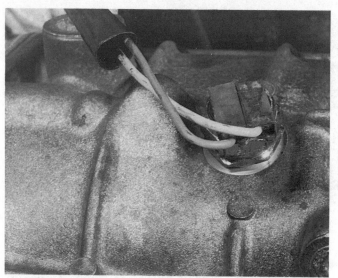

8.10D Reversing lamp switch and wiring

8.10E Coolant temperature switch and wiring

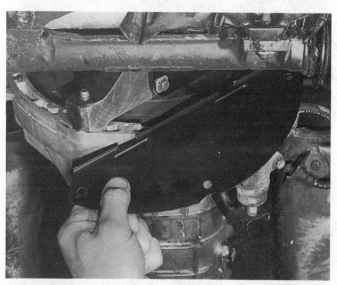

8.14A Removing the gearbox front cover

8.14B Removing the TDC sensor cover

8.16A Engine-to-body earth cable (arrowed)

8.16B Battery negative lead-to-engine securing bolt (arrowed)

8.17 Unscrewing the engine oil drain plug

8.21 Engine mounting bracket-to-crossmember bolt (arrowed)

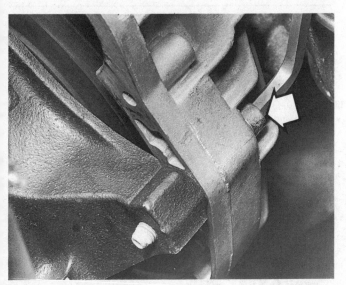

8.23 Unscrewing a gearbox-to-engine bolt (arrowed)

8.24 Lifting the engine from the engine compartment

9 Engine dismantling – general

1   Stand the engine on a strong bench so as to be at a comfortable working height. Failing this, it can be stripped down on the floor, but at least stand it on a sheet of hardboard.
2   During the dismantling process, the greatest care should be taken to keep the exposed parts free from dirt. As the engine is stripped, clean each part in a bath of paraffin.
3   Never immerse parts with internal oilways in paraffin – to clean, wipe down carefully with a paraffin-dampened rag. Oilways can be cleaned out with a piece of wire. If an air line is available, all parts can be blown dry and the oilways blown through as an added precaution.
4   Re-use of old gaskets is false economy, and can give rise to oil and water leaks, if nothing worse. To avoid the possibility of trouble after the engine has been reassembled, always use new gaskets throughout.
5   Do not throw the old gaskets away, as it sometimes happens that an immediate replacement cannot be found, and the old gasket is then very useful as a template. Hang up the gaskets on a suitable nail or hook as they are removed.
6   To strip the engine, it is best to work from the top downwards. The engine oil sump is an irregular shape, and it will be necessary to use wooden blocks to support the engine in an upright position on the bench. When the stage is reached where the sump and pistons are to be removed, turn the engine on its side. Turn the block upside-down to remove the crankshaft.
7   Wherever possible temporarily refit nuts, bolts and washers finger-tight from wherever they were removed. This helps avoid later loss and muddle. If they cannot be refitted, then lay them out in such a fashion that is clear where they came from.

10 Engine ancillary components – removal

Before complete engine dismantling begins, remove the following items:

Inlet and exhaust manifolds (Chapter 3)
Alternator (Chapter 12)
Clutch (Chapter 5)
Engine mounting brackets (Section 7)
Oil filter (Section 2)
Distributor (Chapter 4)
Water pump (Chapter 2)
Fuel pump (Chapter 3)

11 Engine – complete dismantling

1   Remove the timing chain and sprockets as described in Section 5.
2   Unbolt the oil filler housing from the block. Remove the gasket (photo).
3   Remove the oil level dipstick.
4   Unbolt the oil filter housing from the block, and remove the gasket (photo).
5   Remove the cylinder head as described in Section 6.
6   Remove the tappets from the block, keeping them identified for position (photos).
7   Unscrew the bolt and withdraw the distributor bracket (photo).
8   Using a hooked instrument, remove the oil pump driveshaft (photo).
9   Unscrew the bolts securing the sump to the block (photo). Where an alloy sump is fitted, unbolt the steel plate for access to the four concealed bolts.
10 Remove the sump and gasket (photos).
11 Unscrew the bolts and remove the oil pump (photos).
12 Recover the O-ring seal from the oil pump base, and remove the location dowels from the block (photos).
13 Unscrew the bolts and remove the front plate from the dowels on the cylinder block. Remove the gasket (photos).
14 Unscrew the bolt and slide out the camshaft thrustplate (photo).
15 Remove the camshaft from the block, being careful not to damage the bearing surfaces (photos).
16 Mark the big-end caps and connecting rods in relation to each other, so that they may be refitted in the correct positions. Number them from the flywheel end.
17 Turn the crankshaft so that No 1 piston is at the bottom of its stroke. Unscrew the big-end nuts and remove the cap (photo). Using the handle of a hammer, push the No 1 connecting rod and piston from its liner. If the bearing shells are to be used again, keep them taped to the cap or connecting rod.
18 Remove the remaining pistons using the procedure described in paragraph 17.
19 Lock the camshaft by placing a block of wood inside the crankcase, then unscrew the flywheel/driveplate bolts and remove the flywheel/driveplate.
20 Check that the main bearing caps are identified for position. The No 1 cap (rear) is identified by its seal slots. No 2 cap should have a dab of red paint on it, No 3 (centre) is marked with green paint, No 4 with white paint, and No 5 (front) with blue paint. If necessary, mark the caps with a centre-punch.
21 Before removing the main bearing bolts, check the crankshaft endfloat, using a feeler blade between the rear crankshaft web and the thrustwasher on the rear main bearing cap (photo).
22 Unscrew the main bearing bolts, and remove the caps. Remove the seals and thrustwashers from the rear cap (photo).
23 Lift the crankshaft from the crankcase, and recover the thrustwashers (photo).
24 Remove the main bearing shells, keeping them identified for position.
25 Remove each liner from the cylinder block, using a wooden mallet to tap them free if necessary (photo). Mark the liners for position, using a spirit marker pen, or by scratching the liners on their outer surfaces.
26 Remove the base shims from the liners.

12 Crankcase ventilation system – description

1   The crankcase ventilation system is designed to extract oil fumes and blow-by gases from within the crankcase, and to feed them into the combustion chambers, where they are burnt.
2   The system consists of a wire-mesh oil separator, located on the top of the oil filler tube, and two hoses to the inlet manifold and air cleaner.
3   On high-mileage engines, the hoses and separator may become blocked with sludge, and the system should therefore be periodically checked and cleaned.

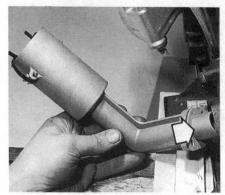

11.2 Removing the oil filler housing and gasket (arrowed)

11.4 Removing the oil filter housing and gasket

11.6 Removing a tappet

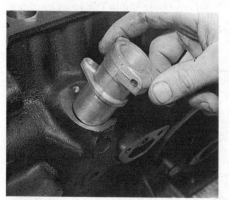

11.7 Removing the distributor bracket

11.8 Oil pump drive shaft removal

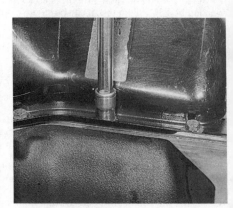

11.9 Unscrewing the sump bolts

11.10A Removing the sump ...

11.10B ... and gasket

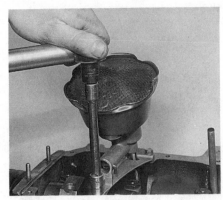

11.11A Unscrew the bolts ...

11.11B ... and remove the oil pump

11.12A Removing the oil pump O-ring seal ...

11.12B ... and the location dowels

11.13A Unscrew the bolts ...

11.13B ... and remove the front plate ...

11.13C ... and gasket

11.14 Removing the camshaft thrustplate

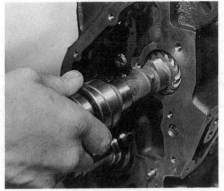

11.15A Removing the camshaft

11.15B Camshaft removed from the engine

11.17 Removing a big-end cap

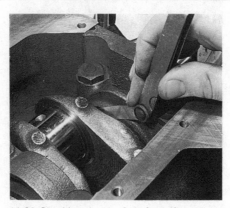

11.21 Checking the crankshaft endfloat with a feeler blade

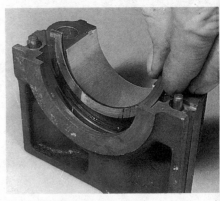

11.22 Thrustwasher removal from the rear main bearing cap

11.23 Lifting the crankshaft from the crankcase

11.25 Removing a liner from the cylinder block

13 Engine components – examination and renovation (general)

1   With the engine dismantled, all components must be thoroughly cleaned and examined for wear, as described in the following Sections.
2   If a high mileage has been covered, either from new or since the last engine rebuild, and general wear is evident, consideration should be given to replacing the engine with a reconditioned one.
3   If a single component has malfunctioned, and the rest of the engine is in good condition, endeavour to find out the cause of its failure if it is not readily apparent. For example, if a bearing has failed, check that the adjoining oilways are clear; the new bearing will not last long if it is not being lubricated.
4   If uncertain about the condition of any components, seek a second opinion from a Peugeot garage.
5   Check on the availability of replacement parts before discarding the old ones. Check the new part against the old, to ensure that you have the correct replacement.
6   Some of the measurements necessary will require the use of feeler blades, a micrometer or vernier gauge, and a dial test indicator. However, in many instances wear will be visually evident, as the old component can be compared with a new one.

14 Cylinder head – dismantling, decarbonising and reassembly

1   Using a valve spring compressor, compress the first valve spring and remove the split collets (photos).
2   Gently release the compressor and remove it.
3   Take off the spring retainer, the springs and the spring seat (photos).
4   Remove all the other valves in a similar way, keeping them in their original fitted sequence, together with their associated components (photo). Remove and discard the valve stem oil seals.

5   Bearing in mind that the cylinder head is of light alloy construction and is easily damaged, use a blunt scraper or rotary wire brush to clean all traces of carbon deposits from the combustion spaces and the ports. The valves and valve guides should also be freed from any carbon deposits. Wash the combustion spaces and ports down with paraffin, and scrape the cylinder head surface free of any foreign matter with the side of a steel rule, or a similar article.
6   If the engine is installed in the car, clean the pistons and the top of the cylinder bores. If the pistons are still in the block, then it is essential that great care is taken to ensure that no carbon gets into the cylinder bores, as this could scratch the cylinder walls or cause damage to the piston and rings. To ensure this does not happen, first turn the crankshaft so that two of the pistons are at the top of their bores. Stuff rag into the other two bores, or seal them off with paper and masking tape. The waterways should also be covered with small pieces of masking tape, to prevent particles of carbon entering the cooling system and damaging the coolant pump.
7   Press a little grease into the gap between the cylinder walls and the two pistons which are to be worked on. With a blunt scraper, carefully scrape away the carbon from the piston crown, taking great care not to scratch the aluminium. Also scrape away the carbon from the surrounding lip of the cylinder wall. When all carbon has been removed, scrape away the grease, which will be contaminated with carbon particles, taking care not to press any into the bores. To assist prevention of carbon build up, the piston crown can be polished with a metal polish. Remove the rags or masking tape from the other two cylinders, and turn the crankshaft so that the two pistons which were at the bottom are now at the top. Place rag in the cylinders which have been decarbonised, and proceed as just described.
8   Examine the head of the valves for pitting and burning, especially the heads of the exhaust valves. The valve seats should be examined at the same time. If the pitting on the valve and seat is very slight, the marks can be removed by grinding the seats and valves together with coarse, and then fine, valve grinding paste.
9   Where bad pitting has occurred to the valve seats, it will be necessary to recut them and fit new valves. This latter job should be entrusted to the local agent or engineering works. In practice, it is very

seldom that the seats are so badly worn. Normally, it is the valve that is too badly worn for refitting, and the owner can easily purchase a new set of valves and match them to the seats by valve grinding.

10 Valve grinding is carried out as follows. Smear a trace of coarse carborundum paste on the seat face, and apply a suction grinder tool to the valve head. With a semi-rotary motion, grind the valve head to its seat, lifting the valve occasionally to redistribute the grinding paste (photo). When a dull matt even surface is produced on both the valve seat and the valve, wipe off the paste and repeat the process with fine carborundum paste, lifting and turning the valve to redistribute the paste as before. A light spring placed under the valve head will greatly ease this operation. When a smooth unbroken ring of light grey matt finish is produced, on both valve and valve seat faces, the grinding operation is complete. Carefully clean away every trace of grinding compound, take great care to leave none in the valve guides. Clean the valves and valve seats with a paraffin-soaked rag, then with a clean rag. Finally, if an air line is available, blow the valve, valve guides and valve ports clean.

11 Check that all valve springs are intact. If any one is broken, all should be renewed. Check the free height of the springs against new ones. If some springs are not within specifications, replace them all.

Springs suffer from fatigue, and it is a good idea to renew them even if they look serviceable.

12 The cylinder head can be checked for warping either by placing it on a piece of plate glass, or using a straight-edge and feeler blades (photo). If there is any doubt about its condition or if its block face is corroded, have it re-faced by your dealer or motor engineering works.

13 Test the valves in their guides for side-to-side play. If this is any more than almost-imperceptible, new guides must be fitted, again a job for your dealer.

14 Commence reassembly by pressing the new valve stem oil seals into position, using a suitable size socket to press them on (photo).

15 Oil the stem of the first valve, and push it into its guide.

16 Fit the spring seat, inner and outer springs, and spring retainer (photo).

17 Compress the valve spring, and using a little grease, locate the split cotters in the valve stem cut-out.

18 Gently release the compressor, checking to see that the collets are not displaced.

19 Fit the remaining valves in the same way.

20 Tap the end of each valve stem with a plastic or copper-faced hammer to settle the components.

14.1A Compress the valve spring with the tool ...

14.1B ... and remove the split collets (arrowed)

14.3A Remove the spring retainer ...

14.3B ... outer spring ...

14.3C ... inner spring ...

14.3D ... and spring seat

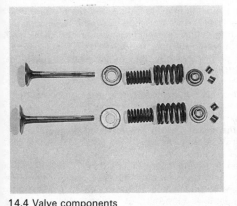

14.4 Valve components

14.10 Grinding-in the valves

14.12 Checking for cylinder head distortion

14.14 Fitting the new valve stem oil seals

14.16 Valve spring refitted

15 Examination and renovation of dismantled components

1   With the engine stripped down, and all parts thoroughly clean, it is now time to examine everything for wear. The following items should be checked, and where necessary renewed or renovated, as described in the following sub-Sections.

Cylinder block and crankcase
2   Clean away all old gasket material, and then examine the casting for cracks, particularly around bolt holes. If they are found, specialist welding or cold repair will be required.
3   Clean out the oilways and galleries with compressed air or wire.
4   If the cylinder bores are worn, this will be evident by the emission of exhaust smoke and general deterioration in engine performance, together with increased oil consumption. A good way to test the condition of the engine when it is still in the car is to test the compression. Have the engine at normal operating temperature with the spark plugs removed, Screw a compression tester (available from most accessory stores) into the first plug hole. Hold the accelerator pedal fully depressed, and crank the engine on the starter motor for several revolutions. Record the reading. Zero the tester, and check the remaining cylinders in the same way. All four compression figures should be approximately equal, and a minimum of 10.3 bar (150 lbf/in²). If they are all low, suspect piston ring or cylinder bore wear. If only one reading is down, suspect a valve not seating, or a broken piston ring.
5   The cylinder bores must be checked for taper, ovality, scoring and scratching. Start by examining the top of the cylinder bores. If they are at all worn, a ridge will be felt on the thrust side. This ridge marks the limit of piston ring travel.
6   An internal micrometer or dial gauge can be used to check bore wear and taper, but this is a pointless operation if the engine is obviously worn, as indicated by excessive oil consumption.
7   The engine is fitted with renewable 'wet' cylinder liners, and these are supplied complete with piston, rings and gudgeon pin.

Pistons and connecting rods
8   The pistons may be separated from the connecting rods by extracting a circlip and pushing out the gudgeon pin (photos). Make sure that the components are identified for location, if they are to be re-used.
9   When reassembling the pistons, make sure that the arrow on the piston crown points in the direction shown in Fig. 1.9, in relation to the oil spray hole in the connecting rod (photo). With new components, it may be necessary to immerse the piston in boiling water, to expand it prior to pressing in the gudgeon pin.
10   Remove the piston rings from the top of the piston (photo). To avoid breaking a ring, either during removal or refitting, slide two or three old feeler blades at equidistant points behind the top ring, and

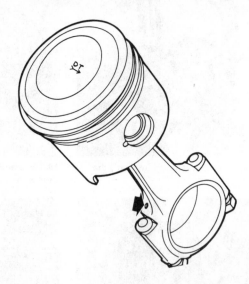

Fig. 1.9 Relationship of connecting rod oil spray hole to the arrow on the piston crown (Sec 15)

slide it up them. Remove the other rings in a similar way.
11   Clean carbon from the ring grooves; a segment of old piston ring is useful for this purpose.
12   Clean out the oil return holes in the piston ring grooves, and fit the new piston rings.
13   If proprietary rings are being fitted to old pistons, the top ring will be supplied stepped, so that it does not impinge on the wear ridge.
14   Insert each piston ring in turn squarely into its bore, and check the ring end gap. If it is not within the specified tolerance, carefully grind the end face of the ring. This does not apply to new rings supplied as part of Peugeot piston/liner sets, which are pre-gapped, and must not be altered.
15   Now check the fit of each compression ring in its groove with a feeler gauge. If it is tight, the ring may be ground on a sheet of wet-and-dry paper, laid flat on a piece of plate glass.
16   Fit the rings to the piston, using the feeler blade method as described for removal. Work from the top of the piston, fitting the oil control ring first.
17   Lubricate the piston rings, and locate the compression ring gaps at 120° intervals from the join in the oil control ring expander. Position the oil control ring rail gaps approximately 20 to 50 mm (0.8 to 2.0 in) each side of the expander join (photo).

Crankshaft

18 Examine the crankpin and main journal surfaces for signs of scoring or scratches, and check the ovality and taper of the crankpins and main journals. If the bearing surfaces are excessively scored or worn oval, the crankpins and/or main journals will have to be reground.

19 Big-end and crankpin wear is accompanied by a distinct metallic knocking, particularly noticeable when the engine is pulling from low revs, and some loss of oil pressure. .

20 Main bearing and main journal wear is accompanied by severe engine vibration rumble – getting progressively worse as engine revs increase – and again by loss of oil pressure.

21 If the crankshaft requires regrinding, take it to an engine reconditioning specialist, who will machine it for you and supply the correct undersize bearing shells. The balance weights must be removed before regrinding the crankshaft, but the reconditioning specialist will do this, and mark them so that they are refitted in their original positions.

22 Check the spigot bearing in the rear of the crankshaft, together with the oil seal. If necessary, prise out the oil seal, and use an extractor to remove the bearing bush (photo). If an extractor is not available, fill the bush with grease, then drive a close-fitting metal dowel through the bush. The hydraulic action should force out the bush. Drive in the new bush, followed by the oil seal, and lightly grease it (photo).

Big-end and main bearing shells

23 Inspect the big-end and main bearing shells for signs of general wear, scoring, pitting and scratches. The bearings should be matt grey in colour. With lead-indium bearings, should a trace of copper colour be noticed, the bearings are badly worn, as the lead material has been worn away to expose the indium underlay. Renew the bearings if they are in this condition, or if there are any signs of scoring or pitting. **You are strongly advised to renew the bearings – regardless of their condition at time of major overhaul. Refitting used bearings is a false economy.**

24 The undersizes available are designed to correspond with crankshaft regrind sizes. The bearings are, in fact, slightly more than the stated undersize as running clearances have been allowed for during their manufacture.

25 Main and big-end bearing shells can be identified as to size by the marking on the back of the shell (photos). Standard size shell bearings are marked STD or .00, undersize shells are marked with the undersize such as 0.020 u/s. This marking method applies only to replacement bearing shells, and not to those used during production.

Flywheel/drivebelt and starter ring gear

26 If the starter ring gear teeth on the flywheel (manual transmission) or torque converter driveplate (automatic transmission) are excessively worn, it will be necessary to obtain complete new assemblies. It is not possible to obtain separate ring gears.

27 On manual transmission models, examine the clutch mating surface of the flywheel, and renew the flywheel if scoring or cracks are evident.

28 On automatic transmission models, the driveplate face should be checked for run-out, using a dial gauge. The maximum permissible run-out is 0.3 mm (0.012 in). Renew the plate if this figure is exceeded.

29 The flywheel/driveplate retaining bolts must be renewed on assembly.

Camshaft

30 Inspect the camshaft journals and lobes – scoring or general wear will indicate the need for new parts.

31 The camshaft sprocket teeth should not be chipped or badly worn.

32 The camshaft thrustplate should not be badly scored, otherwise camshaft endfloat will be excessive.

33 Also check the oil pump/distributor driveshaft gear for wear and damage.

Timing chain

34 Refer to Section 5.

Cylinder head

35 Refer to Section 14.

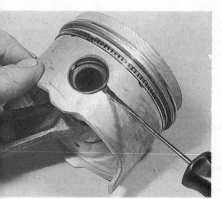

5.8A Extract one of the circlips ...

15.8B ... and press out the gudgeon pin to remove the connecting rod

15.9 Oil spray hole (arrowed) in the connecting rod

5.10 Removing the piston rings

15.17 Correct positioning of the oil control ring rails and expander

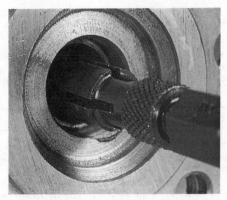

15.22A Using an extractor to remove the spigot bearing bush from the crankshaft

15.22B Driving in the new oil seal

15.25A Main bearing shell marking

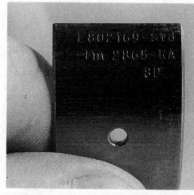

15.25B Big-end bearing shell marking

15.37A Unscrew the end bolt ...

15.37B ... and dismantle the rocker arm assembly

15.38 Rocker arm showing bush (arrowed)

36 If the cylinder head is machined, its depth must not be reduced to less than 92.1 mm (3.63 in). On XN1A engines, it is also necessary to fit a special 1.6 mm (0.063 in) thick head gasket. On later engines, modifications have been carried out to the cylinder head and head gasket. These later components are identifiable by the Torx type cylinder head retaining bolts which replace the hexagon-headed type used on earlier engines. The later type cylinder head may be fitted to an earlier engine provided that the modified gasket and Torx-headed bolts are used as well. The earlier type cylinder head must not be fitted to an engine originally fitted with Torx type retaining bolts.

Rocker arm assembly
37 If necessary, the assembly may be dismantled by unscrewing the end bolts from the shafts (photos). Keep each component on the bench in the order of removal, to ensure correct reassembly.
38 Check the rocker arm bushes for excessive wear (photo). Also check the ball-studs, and the hardened surface on the ends of the arms.
39 Clean all the components, in particular internal oilways, then reassemble in reverse order.

Oil pump
40 The oil pump may be dismantled by unbolting the bottom filter and cover, and removing the two gears.
41 The gears can be removed as a set, and this is recommended if the engine has covered a high mileage, even if wear appears to be minimal.
42 After reassembling the oil pump, prime it with engine oil.

16 Engine – reassembly (general)

1 To ensure maximum life with minimum trouble from a rebuilt engine, not only must everything be correctly assembled, but must also be spotlessly clean, all the oilways must be clear, locking washers and spring washers must always be fitted where indicated, and all bearing and other working surfaces must be thoroughly lubricated during assembly.

2 Before assembly begins, renew any bolts or studs if the threads are in any way damaged, and whenever possible use new spring washers.
3 Apart from your normal tools, a supply of clean rags, an oil can filled with engine oil (an empty plastic detergent bottle, thoroughly cleaned and washed out, will do just as well), a new supply of assorted spring washers, a set of new gaskets, and a torque wrench, should be collected together.

17 Engine – complete reassembly

Crankshaft and main bearings
1 Place the cylinder block upside-down on the bench.
2 Press the new main bearing shells into their locations in the crankcase (photo). Note that if the crankshaft has sediment chambers (Fig. 1.10), Nos 1, 3, and 5 shells are grooved, and Nos 2 and 4 shells are plain. Where the crankshaft does not have sediment chambers, the shells are grooved in the block, and plain in the caps. Make sure that the shell tabs engage the cut-outs.

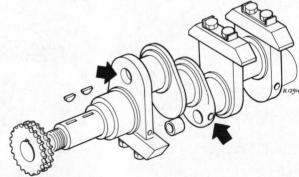

Fig. 1.10 Crankshaft with sediment chambers – arrowed (Sec 17)

3 Oil the bearing shells, then lower the crankshaft into the crankcase (photos).

4 Insert the thrustwashers without location tabs each side of No 1 journal, with the lubrication grooves towards the crankshaft (ie away from the bearing) (photo).

5 Press the new bearing shells into the main bearing caps, and oil the shells (photos).

6 Apply a little grease to the plain sides of the thrustwashers (with location tabs), then stick them to the No 1 main bearing cap, with the lubrication grooves facing outwards.

7 Fit Nos 2 to 5 main bearing caps, insert the bolts and tighten to the specified torque. **Note:** *The casting marks must be on the flywheel side; caps 2 and 3 have two marks, and caps 4 and 5 have one mark (photo).*

8 Fit the special rubber seals to the grooves in No 1 main bearing cap, and lightly grease their outer edges (photo).

9 Cut some thin strips of celluloid to prevent the rubber seals stretching when refitting the cap. Grease the strips, then press them against the seals, and carefully lower the No 1 cap into position (photo).

10 Insert and tighten the main bearing cap bolts to the specified torque (photo).

11 Using a pair of pliers, pull out the strips of celluloid (photo).

12 Trim the ends of the rubber seals to 2.0 mm (0.08 in) above the face of the block, using two feeler blades as a guide (photo).

13 Using a dial test indicator or feeler blades, check that the crankshaft endfloat is as given in the Specifications (photo).

Flywheel or driveplate (automatic transmission)

14 Locate the flywheel/driveplate on the crankshaft flange. Fit the locking plate and insert the bolts. If there is no locking plate, apply locking fluid to the threads of the bolts (photo).

15 Lock the crankshaft using a block of wood in the crankcase, and tighten the bolts to the specified torque (photo). Bend the locking plate tabs to lock the bolts where applicable.

Cylinder liners/pistons and connecting rods

16 Support the engine upright, then fit the liners without their seals in the previously-noted positions. Make sure that the flats are adjacent to each other and evenly spaced (photo).

17 The liner protrusion above the face of the cylinder block must now be measured in order to calculate the correct shims to fit on the base of each liner. Using a dial test indicator and magnetic stand, zero the indicator on the face of the cylinder block (photo).

18 Record the protrusion of each liner at the four points indicated in Fig. 1.11 (photo). The maximum difference between the four measurements on one liner must not exceed 0.07 mm (0.003 in). If all the liners are new, they may be repositioned and checked again in order to obtain the correct measurements.

19 Note the highest protrusion of each liner, and select a seal thickness to give the specified protrusion, preferably as near to the upper limit as possible. Only one seal is permitted to be fitted to each liner. On engines manufactured before April 1981, the seals are of synthetic-fibre paper, but since this date, they are of aluminium-coated steel. Select the correct thickness seals by referring to Fig. 1.12 or 1.13 (photo).

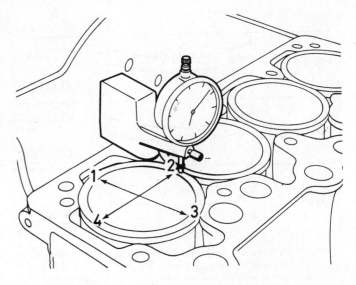

Fig. 1.11 Four points for checking the cylinder liner protrusion (Sec 17)

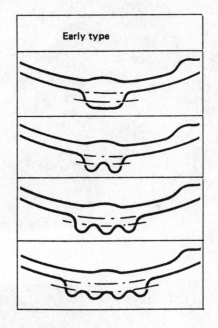

Early type

Liner seal (made from white synthetic fibre paper)

HIGHEST POINT ON LINER, WITHOUT SEAL	LINER SEAL TO BE FITTED		
	IDENTIFICATION		THICKNESS
from + 0.039 to + 0.045 mm			0.070 to 0.105 mm
from + 0.019 to + 0.038 mm			0.085 to 0.120 mm
from − 0.006 to + 0.018 mm			0.105 to 0.140 mm
from − 0.095 to − 0.007 mm			0.130 to 0.165 mm

Fig. 1.12 Cylinder liner seal selection chart for pre-1981 models with fibre seals (Sec 17)

	x		A
0,10			+0,021 +0,010
0,12			−0,009 +0,020
0,15			−0 080 −0,010

Fig. 1.13 Cylinder liner seal selection chart for 1981-on
models with aluminium seals – sizes in mm (Sec 17)
A   Liner protrusion without seal   x   Seal to be fitted

17.2 Fitting a main bearing shell in the crankcase

17.3A Oiling the main bearing shells

17.3B Crankshaft located in the crankcase

17.4 Fitting the crankshaft upper thrustwashers

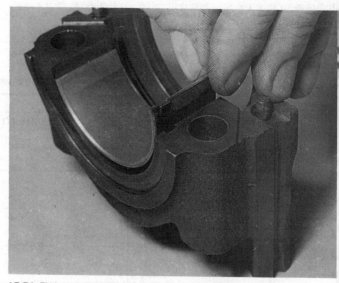

17.5A Fitting a main bearing shell to the rear cap

17.5B Oiling the main bearing shells

17.7 Casting marks on the main bearing caps (arrowed)

17.8 Fitting the rubber seals to No 1 main bearing cap

17.9 Fitting No 1 main bearing cap

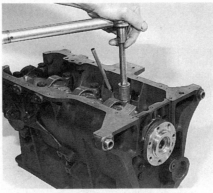
17.10 Tightening the main bearing cap bolts

17.11 Removing the strips of celluloid from No 1 main bearing cap

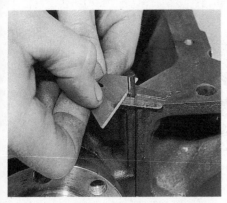
17.12 Trimming the rubber seals on No 1 main bearing cap

17.13 Checking the crankshaft endfloat with a dial test indicator

17.14 Applying locking fluid to the flywheel bolts

17.15 Tightening the flywheel bolts

17.16 The liner flats must be adjacent to each other, and evenly spaced

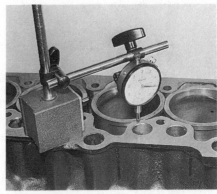
17.17 Zero the dial test indicator on the cylinder block

20 Fit the seals to the base of each liner (photo). On pre-April 1981 engines, fold the scalloped sections into the grooves, and locate the tabs at right-angles to the liner flats, as shown in Fig. 1.14. On later engines, position the seal tongues at right-angles to the liner flats, as shown in Fig. 1.12.

21 Refit the liners in the block. The liners must now be compressed, and their protrusions rechecked. A tool for doing this may be constructed as shown in the photo, using blocks of wood and cylinder head bolts. Old valve springs may be used to compress the liner.

22 Record the maximum protrusion of each liner (photo). If the difference between two adjacent liners exceeds the specified allowable amount, reduce the thickness of the seal on the liner with the most protrusion.

23 With the correct liner seals fitted, clamp the liners, using the clamps described in Section 6.

24 Press the big-end bearing shells into the big-end caps and connecting rods, with the locating tabs engaged with the cut-outs (photo). Oil the shells.

25 Check that the piston rings are correctly positioned as described in Section 15, then compress them with a piston ring clamp.

26 Turn the crankshaft so that No 1 big-end journal is at its lowest point. Oil the bore of the liner, then insert the piston so that the arrow on its crown is pointing towards the front of the engine (photos).

27 Using the handle of a hammer, tap the piston into the bore, while guiding the connecting rod onto the big-end journal.

28 Fit the big-end cap, and tighten the nuts to the specified torque (photo). Check that the crankshaft rotates freely.

29 Refit the remaining pistons, using the procedure described in paragraphs 25 to 28.

Camshaft and timing chain

30 Oil the camshaft bearing journals, then insert the camshaft in the block.

31 Engage the thrustplate in the groove. Insert and tighten the bolt to the specified torque (photo).

32 Locate the gasket on the front of the cylinder block, then fit the front plate and tighten the bolts to the specified torque.

33 Refit the timing chain and sprockets, with reference to Section 5.

Oil pump and distributor driveshaft

34 Turn the engine so that No 4 piston (front) is at the top of its stroke, with the camshaft lobe high points pointing upwards (ie valves rocking).

35 Using a dial test indicator, set the piston to its TDC position (photo).

36 Check that the timing mark on the crankshaft pulley is aligned with the TDC notch on the timing plate. If not, loosen the nuts and reposition the plate, then tighten the nuts, and apply a dab of paint on them to seal them. Remove the dial test indicator on completion.

37 Insert the oil pump/distributor driveshaft with the slot parallel to the crankshaft. As it engages the camshaft gear, it will turn anti-clockwise to the position shown in Fig. 1.15. Make sure that the smaller segment on the driveshaft is towards the block (photos).

38 Fit the distributor bracket, and tighten the bolt.

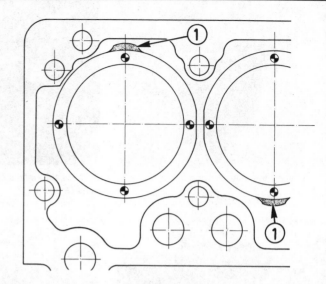

Fig. 1.14 Correct locations of the cylinder liner seal tabs (1) (Sec 17)

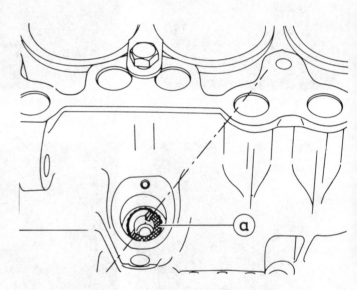

Fig. 1.15 TDC position of the oil pump/distributor driveshaft (Sec 17)

a   Larger segment

17.18 Checking the liner protrusion

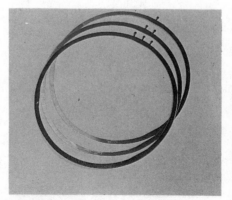

17.19 The aluminium-coated seals are available in three different thicknesses

17.20 Fitting a seal to a liner

17.22 Measuring the maximum protrusion of the liners

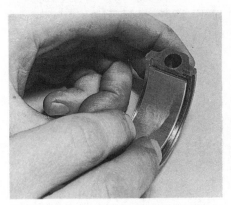

17.24 Fitting a big-end bearing shell to its cap

17.26A Inserting the piston (fitted with clamp) into the cylinder liner

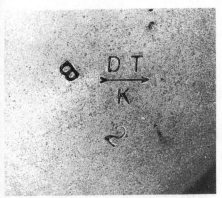

17.26B Arrow and markings on piston crown

17.28 Tightening the big-end cap nuts

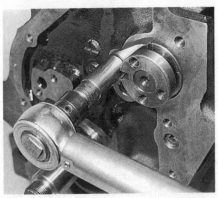

17.31 Tightening the camshaft thrust plate bolt

17.35 Determining the TDC position of No 4 piston

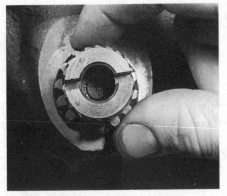

17.37A Initial fitting position of the oil pump/distributor driveshaft

17.37B Final fitted position of the oil pump/distributor driveshaft

39 Press the oil pump location dowels in the block.
40 Smear a little grease on the O-ring seal, and locate it in the oil pump body recess.
41 Engage the oil pump with the driveshaft, then insert and tighten the bolts to the specified torque.

Sump
42 Clean the mating faces of the sump and block.
43 Apply a bead of silicone jointing compound to the join between the timing cover and block (photo).
44 Locate the gasket on the block, then refit the sump and tighten the bolts progressively to the specified torque. Where an alloy sump is fitted, apply locking fluid to the threads of the four concealed bolts before inserting them. Also fit the steel plate wih a new gasket.

45 If removed, refit the oil level switch to the sump and tighten it (photos).

Tappets and cylinder head
46 Oil the tappets, and insert them in their original locations.
47 Fit the cylinder head, with reference to Section 6.

Oil filter and filler housings and dipstick
48 Locate a new oil filter housing gasket on the block. If applicable, trim off the corner of the gasket not required (photo).
49 Refit the filter housing. Apply locking fluid to the bolt threads, then insert them and tighten to the specified torque (photo).
50 Insert the oil level dipstick in its tube.
51 Refit the oil filler housing, together with a new gasket, and tighten the bolts.

17.43 Applying jointing compound to the timing cover join

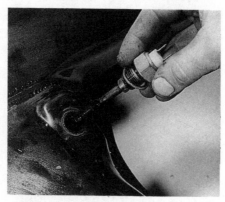

17.45A Inserting the oil level switch in the sump ...

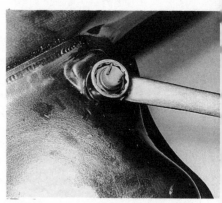

17.45B ... and tightening it

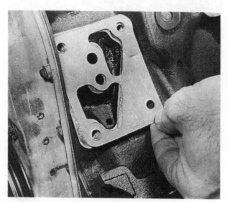

17.48 The right-hand lower corner of the oil filter housing gasket may be trimmed off

17.49 Applying locking fluid to the oil filter housing bolts

19.0 Filling the engine with oil

18 Engine ancillary components – refitting

Refer to Section 10, and refit the components with reference to the appropriate Chapter or Section.

19 Engine – refitting

Refitting is a reversal of the removal procedure given in Section 8. Pay particular attention to the following points:

(a) On automatic transmission models, apply grease to the spigot hole in the driveplate, and also apply locking fluid to the torque converter-to-driveplate bolt threads
(b) On manual gearbox models, apply a little high melting-point grease to the splines of the gearbox input shaft, and to the front of the shaft which enters the spigot bearing
(c) Adjust the TDC sensor, with reference to Chapter 4
(d) Fill the engine with oil (photo)
(e) Refill the cooling system, with reference to Chapter 2

20 Initial start-up after major overhaul

1   Before starting the engine, check that all hoses, controls and electrical leads have been connected.
2   Make sure that tools and rags have been removed from the engine compartment.
3   Starting may take a little longer than usual, as the fuel pump and carburettor must first fill with fuel.
4   Have the throttle speed screw turned in an extra turn to increase the engine idle speed. This will help to offset the stiffness of the new engine components.
5   If the majority of internal components have been renewed, treat the

engine as a new one, and restrict speed for the first 1000 km (600 miles).
6   It is recommended that the engine oil is renewed at the end of the first 1000 km (600 miles). Also the tension of the drivebelts should be checked, and the idle speed and mixture adjusted if necessary.
7   Refer to Section 6, paragraphs 51 to 57 for details of retightening the cylinder head bolts.

PART C : OVERHEAD CAMSHAFT ENGINES (ZEJ AND ZDJ)

21 Operations possible with engine in car

The following operations can be carried out without having to remove the engine from the vehicle.

(a) Valve clearances – adjustment
(b) Timing belt – removal and refitting
(c) Camshaft – removal and refitting
(d) Cylinder head – removal and refitting
(e) Engine mountings – removal and refitting

22 Valve clearances – adjustment

1   The valve clearances must be adjusted with the engine cold. First remove the inlet air ducting from over the rocker cover.
2   Disconnect the crankcase ventilation hoses from the rocker cover.
3   Remove the diagnostic socket.
4   On the ZEJ engine, remove the injectors and cold start valve, and position the fuel pipes on the right-hand inner wing.
5   Unscrew the nuts and remove the rocker cover.
6   Remove the spark plugs.

7 Turn the engine with a socket on the crankshaft pulley bolt, until the exhaust valve of No 1 cylinder is fully open. The clearances for No 3 cylinder inlet valve and No 4 cylinder exhaust valve can now be checked and adjusted using a feeler blade. Remember No 1 cylinder is at the flywheel end of the engine, and of course the inlet and exhaust valves are on the side adjacent to their respective manifolds.

8 If the clearance requires adjustment, loosen the locknut, and with the feeler in position, turn the adjuster screw until the feeler blade is nipped and will not move. Now unscrew the adjuster until the feeler blade is a stiff sliding fit. Tighten the locknut and recheck the clearance. Refer to the Specifications for the correct clearances (photo).

9 Repeat the adjustment procedure using the following sequence:

Exhaust valve open	Adjust inlet valve	Adjust exhaust valve
1	3	4
3	4	2
4	2	1
2	1	3

10 Refit the rocker cover, together with a new gasket, and tighten the nuts.

11 Refit the remaining components removed, using a reversal of the removal procedure.

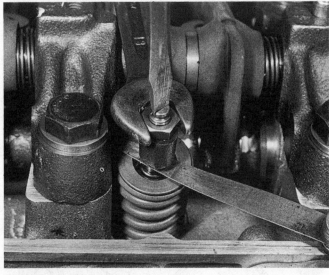
22.8 Adjusting the valve clearances

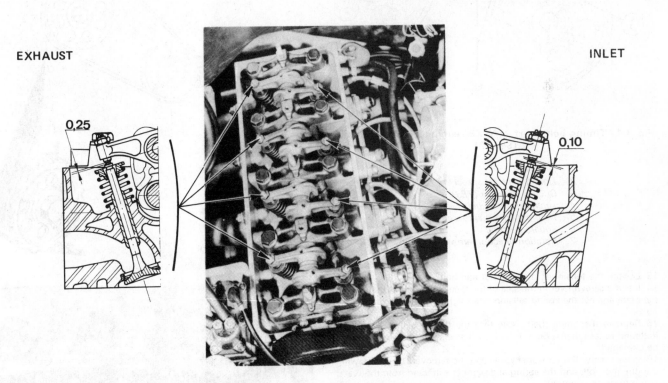

Fig. 1.16 Valve clearance adjustment – clearances in mm (Sec 22)

EXHAUST   0,25   0,10   INLET

23 Timing belt – removal and refitting

1 Remove the radiator, drivebelt and fan, with reference to Chapter 2.

2 On models fitted with power steering, remove the pump drivebelt (Chapter 10).

3 On models fitted with air conditioning, remove the compressor drivebelt (Chapter 11).

4 Disconnect the battery negative lead.

5 Remove the spark plugs (Chapter 4).

6 Remove the thermostat housing and the additional air valve (Chapters 2 and 3).

7 Remove the alternator (Chapter 12).

8 On manual gearbox models, have an assistant engage top gear and depress the brake pedal. Unscrew and remove the crankshaft pulley bolt.

9 On automatic transmission models, remove the TDC sensor plate on the front of the transmission, and have an assistant lock the starter ring gear with a wide-bladed screwdriver. Unscrew and remove the crankshaft pulley bolt.

10 Remove the pulley from the front of the crankshaft sprocket (photo).

11 Remove the timing belt cover(s) (photo).

12 Refit the pulley bolt, then turn the engine clockwise until the timing mark on the camshaft sprocket is between the 10 and 11 o'clock position (ie 45° from horizontal position). This is not in fact the No 1 TDC position, although No 1 piston is half way up its compression stroke. Where the camshaft sprocket has a square hole in it, check its position with reference to Fig. 1.17.

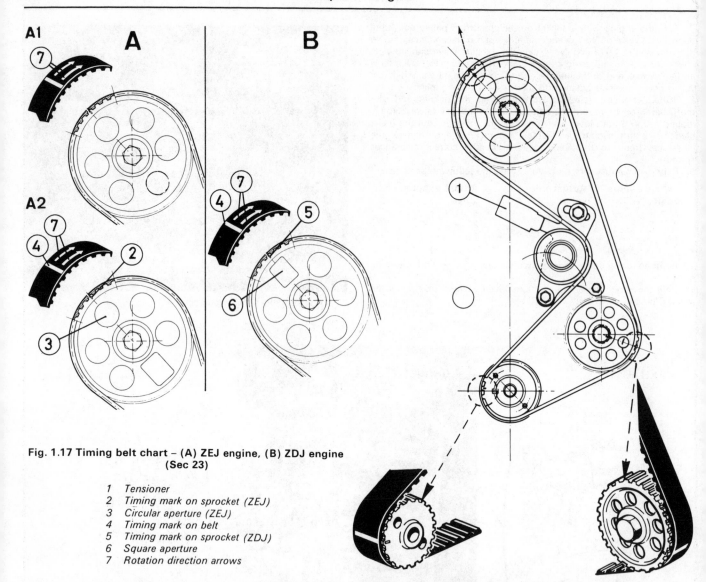

**Fig. 1.17 Timing belt chart – (A) ZEJ engine, (B) ZDJ engine
(Sec 23)**

    1   Tensioner
    2   Timing mark on sprocket (ZEJ)
    3   Circular aperture (ZEJ)
    4   Timing mark on belt
    5   Timing mark on sprocket (ZDJ)
    6   Square aperture
    7   Rotation direction arrows

13 Loosen the tensioner retaining nut and bolt.

14 Insert a screwdriver in the side of the tensioner support plate, lever the plate against the spring tension, then tighten the nut to retain the plate.

15 Remove the timing belt. Note that the timing belt must not be flattened to less than a 60 mm (2.4 in) diameter arc, otherwise it may be damaged.

16 If necessary, the tensioner roller may be removed by unscrewing the nut and bolt, and the spring and plunger extracted from the water pump housing (photos).

17 Commence reassembly by refitting the tensioner roller, together with its spring and plunger. Lock the support plate in its retracted position (photo).

18 Using a feeler blade, check that the clearance between the support plate and the intermediate sprocket housing bolt is between 0.1 and 0.15 mm (0.004 and 0.006 in). If necessary, loosen the nut, remove the bolt, apply locking fluid to its threads, then refit and adjust. Tighten the locking nut.

19 Offer the timing belt to the sprockets, with the directional arrows pointing clockwise. Besides the arrows, there should be three marks on the timing belt, which should align with the timing marks on the camshaft, intermediate shaft, and crankshaft sprockets when the belt is fitted. If the belt has no such marks, make some by referring to Fig. 1.20.

20 Centralise the belt on the sprockets, and recheck that the timing marks are aligned.

21 Loosen the tensioner nut, and allow the spring to tension the timing belt. Tighten the tensioner retaining nut and bolt (photo).

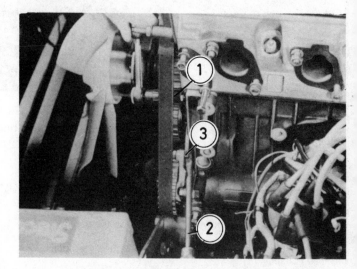

Fig. 1.18 Retracting the tensioner support plate (Sec 23)

    1   Nut
    2   Screwdriver
    3   Support plate

Fig. 1.19 Checking the support plate clearance (Sec 23)

1 Support plate
2 Adjustment screw and locknut

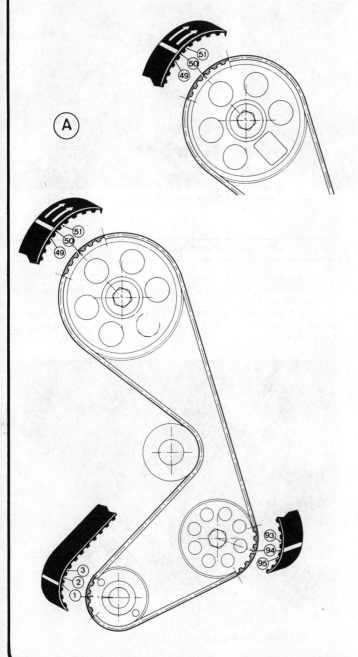

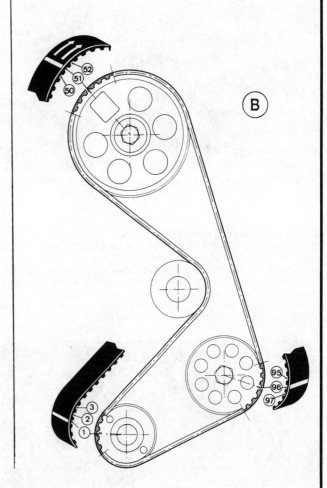

Fig. 1.20 Timing belt marking diagram (Sec 23)

A ZEJ engine (116 teeth, white markings)
B ZDJ engine (118 teeth, yellow markings)

23.10 Removing the crankshaft pulley

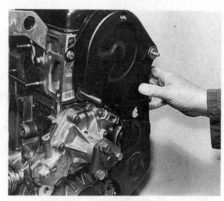

23.11 Removing the timing belt cover

23.16A Removing the timing belt tensioner roller ...

23.16B ... followed by the spring and plunger

23.17 Tensioner roller locked in its retracted position

23.21 Tightening the tensioner nut and bolt

22 Refit the timing belt cover(s).
23 Check that the locating pins are fitted (photo), then fit the crankshaft pulley against the sprocket.
24 Clean the threads of the crankshaft pulley bolt, then apply a little locking fluid, insert the bolt, and tighten it to the specified torque (photo). Lock the crankshaft with reference to paragraphs 8 or 9.
25 Refit all the removed components with reference to the appropriate Chapters, and reconnect the battery negative lead.

24 Camshaft – removal and refitting

1 Remove the timing belt as described in Section 23.
2 Remove the rocker cover after disconnecting the inlet air ducting. Recover the stud seals (photos).
3 Hold the camshaft sprocket stationary by inserting a lever through one of its holes. Rest the lever on a piece of wood to prevent damage to the cylinder head.

23.23 Crankshaft pulley locating pins (arrowed)

23.24 Tightening the crankshaft pulley bolt

4 Note the camshaft sprocket position in relation to the camshaft, as this varies according to engine type, and it is possible to fit the sprocket 180° out.

5 Unscrew the retaining bolt, and remove the sprocket (photo). Take great care, as the sprocket is manufactured in sintered metal, and is therefore relatively fragile. Extract the Woodruff key.

6 Unbolt the timing belt rear cover (photo).

7 If desired, make up a special tool as shown in Fig. 1.21 for depressing the valves, in order to free the rocker arms from the camshaft. Make the tool out of channel-section metal, and tighten down on the rocker cover studs. Alternatively, the rocker arm adjusters should be fully loosened.

8 Unbolt the camshaft thrustplate from the front rocker arm pedestal.

9 To remove the front oil seal, refer to Fig. 1.22. Locate the sprocket the wrong way round on the camshaft, against two strips of metal or wood on the cylinder head. Insert and tighten the bolt, to pull out the camshaft and force out the oil seal (photo).

10 The camshaft can now be withdrawn carefully through the seal aperture in the front of the cylinder head (photo). Take care during its removal not to snag any of the lobe corners on the bearings as they are passed through the cylinder head.

11 When refitting, first check that the respective camshaft location bearings in the cylinder head are perfectly clean, and lubricate with some engine oil. Similarly lubricate the camshaft journals and lobes.

12 Insert the camshaft carefully into the cylinder head, guiding the cam sections through the bearing apertures so as not to score the bearing surfaces.

13 With the camshaft in position, the front oil seal can be carefully drifted into position. Lubricate the seal lips with oil, and drive into its location using a suitable tube drift.

14 Locate the thrust plate in the camshaft groove, then insert and tighten the bolts.

15 Refit the timing belt rear cover, and tighten the bolts.

16 Refit the camshaft sprocket with Woodruff key, and tighten the retaining bolt to the specified torque (photos). Note that the offset 'a' in Fig. 1.23 faces towards the cylinder head. Make sure that the sprocket is fitted the correct way round, according to the engine type (refer to Section 23 if necessary).

17 Remove the special tool, if used.

18 Refit the timing belt with reference to Section 23.

19 Adjust the valve clearances (Section 22).

20 Refit the rocker cover.

Fig. 1.21 Using the valve depressing tool (1) for camshaft removal without removing cylinder head (Sec 24)

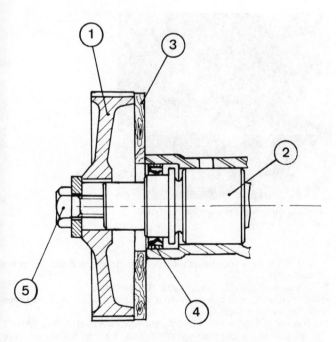

Fig. 1.22 Method of removing camshaft front oil seal (Sec 24)

1 Sprocket
2 Camshaft
3 Strips of metal or wood
4 Oil seal
5 Bolt

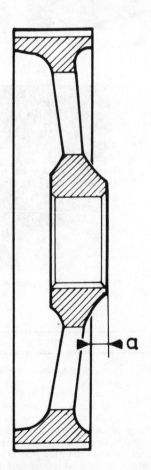

Fig. 1.23 Camshaft sprocket (Sec 24)

a Offset towards cylinder head

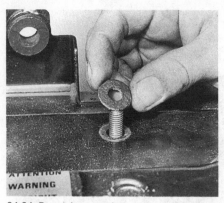
24.2A Removing a rocker cover stud seal

24.2B Rocker cover removal

24.5 Camshaft sprocket and bolt

24.6 Unbolting the timing belt rear cover

24.9 Camshaft front oil seal removal

24.10 Removing the camshaft

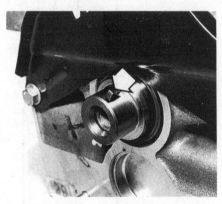
24.16A Camshaft sprocket Woodruff key (arrowed)

24.16B Tightening the camshaft sprocket bolt

25 Cylinder head – removal and refitting

Note: *Special tools may be required to release the cylinder head from its gasket. Refer to paragraph 19*

1   Remove the timing belt as described in Section 23.
2   Remove the air cleaner (Chapter 3).
3   On the ZEJ engine, remove the mixture regulator, pipes and injectors, cold start injector, and control pressure regulator.
4   On the ZDJ engine, remove the airflow sensor and air ducting.
5   Unscrew the exhaust downpipe-to-manifold nuts, and tie the downpipe to one side.
6   Disconnect the heater hoses from the cylinder head, and unbolt the pipe leading to the water pump (photo).

7   On automatic transmission models, disconnect the kickdown cable (Chapter 3).
8   Disconnect the accelerator cable (Chapter 3).
9   Disconnect the heater, econostat and brake servo vacuum hoses from the inlet manifold.
10 Disconnect the wiring from the thermal time switch, supplementary air device, temperature switch and sender, and the oil pressure switch.
11 Unclip the HT leads from their holders.
12 Unclip and remove the diagnostic socket, and unbolt the wiring retaining clip.
13 Disconnect the crankcase ventilation pipe.
14 Remove the inlet and exhaust manifolds (Chapter 3).
15 Unbolt the thermostat support casing. On certain models, it is also necessary to remove the alternator and bracket.

16 Unbolt the rocker cover, and remove the gasket.

17 Progressively unscrew the cylinder head bolts, using a reversal of the tightening sequence shown in Fig. 1.24.

18 Remove the rocker shaft assembly (photo).

19 Rock the cylinder head to release it from the gasket. The Peugeot tool for doing this is shown in Figs. 1.6 and 1.7, and is easily fabricated.

20 Remove the cylinder head from the block by sliding it across the gasket (photo). This is necessary to prevent the cylinder liners from being disturbed, and possibly breaking their lower seals. If further work is to be carried out on the engine, such as cleaning the pistons, the liners must be clamped in position, using clamps made from metal plate and suitable bolts – refer to Section 6. Do not turn the engine without having the clamps fitted.

21 Before refitting the cylinder head, check that all the mating surfaces are perfectly clean. Loosen the rocker arm adjuster screws fully back. Also ensure that the cylinder head bolt holes in the crankcase are clean and free of oil. Syringe or soak up any oil left in the bolt holes, and in the oil feed hole on the rear left-hand corner of the block. This is most important, in order that the correct bolt tightening torque can be applied.

22 Where fitted, unbolt and clean the oil filter from the rear of the cylinder head, then refit and tighten it.

23 If the crankshaft has been moved, reposition it with the timing mark on the sprocket at 9 o'clock. Check that the location dowel is in position at the front right-hand corner of the block.

24 Remove the liner clamps.

25 Fit the cylinder head gasket onto the cylinder block upper face, and ensure that it is exactly located (photo). If possible, screw a couple of guide studs into position. They must be long enough to pass through the cylinder head so that they can be removed when it is in position.

26 Lower the cylinder head into position, engaging with the dowel, and then locate the rocker assembly. Make sure that all the locating dowels are in position, and as the assembly is lowered into position, locate the thrust plate in the camshaft groove.

27 Lubricate the cylinder head bolt threads and washers with engine oil, then screw them into position. Tighten them progressively in the sequence shown in Fig. 1.24. Tighten all bolts to the Stage 1 torque specified, then in sequence, loosen each bolt a quarter-turn, and tighten to the specified Stage 2 torque (photo).

28 Refit the timing belt, with reference to Section 23.

29 Adjust the valve clearances (Section 22).

30 Refit the rocker cover and gasket.

31 Refit all the removed components, with reference to the appropriate Chapters where necessary.

32 Run the engine at 2000 rpm for approximately twelve minutes, or until the self-disengaging fan cuts in.

33 Switch off the ignition, and allow the engine to cool down for two hours.

34 Depressurize the cooling system by temporarily removing the pressure cap from the expansion tank. Take precautions against scalding.

35 Remove the rocker cover, then in the correct sequence, loosen each bolt a quarter-turn, and immediately retighten to the specified Stage 4 torque.

36 Check, and if necessary adjust, the valve clearances (Section 22).

37 Refit the rocker cover.

38 Where the timing cover can be removed without removing the crankshaft pulley, remove it, and re-tension the timing belt by loosening the tensioner nut and bolt, then retightening them. On completion, refit the timing cover.

26 Engine mountings – removal and refitting

1 Apply the handbrake, then jack up the front of the vehicle and support on axle stands.

2 Using a hoist or a trolley jack, support the weight of the engine.

3 Unbolt the engine mountings from the crossmember and engine brackets. If necessary, also unbolt the brackets.

4 Refitting is a reversal of removal.

25.6 Water pump return pipe

25.18 Rocker shaft assembly removal

25.20 Cylinder head removal

25.25 Locating the cylinder head gasket on the block

25.27 Tightening the cylinder head bolts

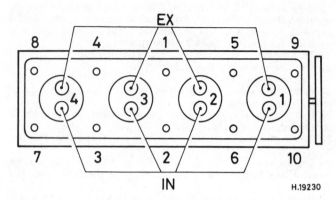

Fig. 1.24 Cylinder head valve positions and bolt tightening sequence (Sec 25)

Fig. 1.25 Left-hand engine mounting bolts (1) and nut (2) (Sec 26)

27 Engine – removal

1   Remove the bonnet (Chapter 11).
2   Remove the battery (Chapter 12).
3   Remove the air cleaner (Chapter 3).
4   Remove the radiator (Chapter 2).
5   On the ZEJ engine, remove the mixture regulator, together with the pipes and injectors, with reference to Chapter 3. Also disconnect the cold start pipe and the remaining air ducting.
6   On the ZDJ engine, remove the airflow sensor assembly and remaining air ducting with reference to Chapter 3.
7   Disconnect the accelerator cable (Chapter 3).
8   The engine wiring harness can remain on the engine if desired by disconnecting the multi-plugs, or it may be removed by disconnecting from the various electrical components, and identifying each wire for location.
9   On models fitted with power steering, remove the power steering pump (Chapter 10).
10 On models fitted with air conditioning, remove the compressor from the engine, and support it on one side, **without** disconnecting the pipes. Similarly remove the condenser.
11 Remove the starter motor (Chapter 12).
12 Apply the handbrake, then jack up the front of the vehicle and support on axle stands.
13 For additional working room it is recommended that the front crossmember is lowered by 50 mm (2.0 in). To do this, disconnect the steering column from the steering gear, replace two of the crossmember bolts with longer ones, remove the remaining two bolts, and lower the crossmember.
14 Unbolt and remove the gearbox front cover, and the TDC sensor cover, without disturbing the setting of the sensor.
15 On automatic transmission models, mark the torque converter in relation to the driveplate, then unscrew the four bolts. The engine will need to be turned to gain access to each bolt.
16 Position a container beneath the engine sump, then unscrew the drain plug and drain the engine oil. On completion, refit and tighten the drain plug.
17 Unscrew the exhaust downpipe-to-manifold nuts, and tie the downpipe to one side.
18 Disconnect the radiator top and bottom hoses from the engine.
19 Disconnect the fuel feed and return hoses.
20 On automatic transmission models, disconnect the kickdown cable.
21 Disconnect the heater, econostat and brake servo vacuum hoses from the inlet manifold.
22 Disconnect the coil HT lead.
23 Disconnect the heater hoses from the cylinder head, and the pipe leading to the water pump.
24 Unscrew and remove the bolts securing the engine mounting brackets to the crossmember.
25 Connect a hoist to the engine, and take its weight.
26 Unscrew the upper bolts securing the gearbox to the engine.
27 Raise the engine until the gearbox touches the body. Support the

gearbox in this position with a trolley jack.
28 Unbolt and remove the engine mountings.
29 Pull the engine forwards, and disconnect it from the gearbox and clutch. On automatic transmission models, make sure that the torque converter remains fully engaged with the transmission (refer to Chapter 6 if necessary).
30 Lift the engine from the engine compartment, taking care not to damage the surrounding components.

Fig. 1.26 Removing the engine (Sec 27)

28 Engine dismantling – general

Refer to Section 9.

29 Engine ancillary components – removal

Before complete engine dismantling begins, remove the following items:

Distributor (Chapter 4)
Clutch (Chapter 5)
Oil filter (Section 2)
Water pump (Chapter 2) and coolant return pipe

30 Engine – complete dismantling

1 Remove the cylinder head as described in Section 25.
2 Unbolt the timing belt tensioner, and remove it.
3 Hold the starter ring gear stationary using a wide-bladed screwdriver.
4 Unscrew the bolts and remove the flywheel (or driveplate – automatic transmission). The flywheel bolt holes are offset, so it can only be fitted one way. Renew the flywheel bolts when refitting.
5 Unscrew the intermediate shaft sprocket bolt (photo), passing a screwdriver shaft or rod through one of the holes in the sprocket, to lock against the front of the block, and retain the sprocket in position whilst it is being unscrewed.
6 Withdraw the sprocket (photo), and remove the Woodruff key from the shaft.
7 Unbolt and remove the intermediate shaft housing cover, and the forked lockplate (photos).
8 The oil seal can now be extracted. Prise it free with a screwdriver, but take care not to damage the housing.
9 Before the intermediate shaft can be withdrawn, extract the distributor drive pinion and oil pump driveshaft. Withdraw the intermediate shaft from the front of the block.
10 Turn the engine on its side, then unscrew the securing screws and remove the sump pan. If it is stuck tight, tap it gently with a mallet. Remove the gasket.
11 Unbolt and remove the oil pump. The pump flange is located on dowels so pull it straight off.
12 Identify each big-end cap and rod to enable refitting in the correct position.
13 The main and big-end bearing caps are numbered from 1 to 4, from the flywheel end of the block. The main bearing cap numbers are read from the oil filter side of the crankcase (photo).
14 The big-end bearing caps and their connecting rods are not very clearly marked, so it is best to centre-punch them at adjacent points, and on the oil filter side, so that there is no doubt as to their position and orientation in the block.

15 The big-end caps will not pass out through the cylinder liners, so each liner/piston/connecting rod must be removed as an assembly out of the top of the cylinder block. Before doing this however, centre-punch each liner rim and adjacent surface on the top of the cylinder block, so that they will be refitted in their original position and orientation, if, of course, they are not being renewed completely.
16 Unbolt the big-end bearing caps, keeping the bearing shells taped to their original cap or connecting rod if they are to be used again, although this is **not** to be recommended.
17 Withdraw the cylinder liner/piston/rod assemblies.
18 Unbolt and remove the main bearing caps, again keeping their bearing shells with their respective caps if they are to be refitted, again **not** to be recommended.
19 Note that the front and rear main bearing caps are located on dowels, so if they are tight, tap them straight off, **not** in a sideways direction.
20 Withdraw the crankshaft, noting the two semi-circular thrust washers located in the crankcase. Remove the bearing shells, and identify them by marking with numbered tape if they are to be used again.
21 Using two screwdrivers inserted at opposite points, lever off the crankshaft sprocket. Extract the Woodruff key, and remove the belt guide.
22 Remove the crankshaft front and rear oil seals, and discard them.
23 The flywheel mounting flange on the rear of the crankshaft incorporates a sealed spigot bearing. This may be extracted if worn by filling it full of grease, and then driving in a close-fitting rod. The hydraulic pressure created will force out the bearing.

31 Crankcase ventilation system – description

1 Refer to Section 12.
2 The system consists of hose connections from the rocker cover to the inlet air ducting and inlet manifold.

30.5 Unscrew the bolt ...

30.6 ... and remove the intermediate shaft sprocket

30.7A Unscrew the bolts ...

30.7B ... and remove the intermediate shaft housing cover

30.7C Unscrew the bolt (arrowed) ...

30.7D ... and remove the forked lockplate

32 Engine components – examination and renovation (general)

Refer to Section 13.

33 Cylinder head – dismantling, decarbonising and reassembly

1   Remove the camshaft, with reference to Section 24.
2   Refer to Section 14 for valve removal and refitting, and decarbonising procedures. Single valve springs are fitted (photos).
3   Examine the camshaft for wear or scoring of the journals or cam lobes. Any wear or scoring in the camshaft bearings will mean renewal of the cylinder head, as the bearings are line-bored, and cannot be replaced independently. It may be possible to have worn cam lobes reprofiled by a specialist firm.
4   Refit the camshaft, together with a new oil seal, with reference to Section 24.
5   Note that it is not permitted to re-face the cylinder head, so if the warpage exceeds the specified amount, the head will have to be renewed.

30.13 Main bearing cap number

33.2A Compressing the valve spring to remove the split collets

33.2B Removing the retainer ...

33.2C ... valve spring ...

33.2D ... spring seat ...

33.2E ... and valve

34 Examination and renovation of dismantled components

1   Refer to Section 15, noting the differences given in the following sub-Sections.

Pistons and connecting rods
2   The gudgeon pin is an interference fit in the connecting rod small end, and removal or refitting and changing a piston is a job best left to your dealer or engine specialist. This is owing to the need for a press and jig, and careful heating of the connecting rod.

Crankshaft
3   The crankshaft is not fitted with removable balance weights.
4   Renewal of the ball-bearing type spigot bearing is covered in Sections 30 and 36.

Camshaft
5   Check the bearings in the cylinder head. If worn, a new head will be required.
6   Inspect the camshaft journals and lobes – scoring or general wear will indicate the need for new parts.
7   The camshaft sprocket teeth should not be chipped or badly worn.

8 The camshaft thrust plate should not be badly scored, otherwise camshaft endfloat will be excessive.

Intermediate shaft

9 Check the journals and gear teeth for wear, chipping or scoring.
10 The sprocket teeth should be free from wear and damage.
11 The forked thrustplate should be unworn, otherwise excessive shaft endfloat will occur.
12 Wear in the shaft bearings can only be rectified by the purchase of a new crankcase.

Timing belt and tensioner

13 The belt should be without any sign of fraying, cuts or splits, and there should be no deformation of the teeth.
14 Even if the timing belt appears to be in good condition, it is recommended that it is renewed at the specified intervals.
15 Check the belt tensioner pulley. It should spin freely, without noise. If it does not, renew it.

Rocker gear

16 Slight wear in the heels of the rocker arms can be removed using an oilstone, but ensure that the contour is maintained.
17 Scoring or wear in the components can only be rectified by dismantling and renewing the defective components.
18 Unscrew the end plug from the shaft, and extract the plug and filter. This filter must be renewed at the specified intervals, or whenever it is removed.
19 Number the rocker arms and pedestals/bearings. Note that bearing No 5 has two threaded holes to retain the thrustplate which controls the camshaft endfloat, and a hole for the roll pin, which locates the shaft and pedestal. Renew the roll pin if it is not the solid type.
20 Keep the respective parts in order as they are removed from the shaft, and note their respective locations. Note also that the machined flat sections on top of pedestals 1 to 4 all face towards the camshaft sprocket.
21 Lubricate each component as it is assembled with engine oil. Lay the pedestals, spacers, springs and rockers out in order.
22 Support the rocker shaft in a soft-jawed vice, and insert the new filter into the end of it, fit the retaining bolt and tighten it to the specified torque.
23 Assemble the respective pedestals, rocker arms, springs and spacers onto the shaft. When the shaft assembly is complete, compress the last pedestal to align the retaining pin hole in the shaft and pedestal. Drive a new pin into position to secure it. Early models fitted with a hollow type roll pin should have the later solid type pin fitted on reassembly.

Oil pump

24 It is essential that all parts of the pump are in good condition for the pump to work effectively.

34.26 Extracting a gear from the oil pump

25 To dismantle the pump, remove the cover retaining bolts and detach the cover (photo).
26 Extract the gears and clean the respective components (photo).
27 Inspect for any signs of damage or excessive wear. Use a feeler gauge to check the clearance between the rotor (gear) teeth and the inner housing.
28 Also, check the gear endfloat using a straight-edge rule laid across the body of the pump and feeler gauge inserted between the rule and gears.
29 Compare the clearances with the allowable tolerances given in the Specifications at the start of this Chapter and, if necessary, renew any defective parts, or possibly the pump unit.
30 Do not overlook the relief valve assembly. To extract it, remove the split pin and withdraw the cup, spring, guide and piston. Again, look for signs of excessive wear or damage and renew as applicable.
31 Check the pump driveshaft for signs of wear or distortion, and renew if necessary.

35 Engine – reassembly (general)

Refer to Section 16.

34.25 Oil pump with cover removed

36 Engine – complete reassembly

Crankshaft and main bearings

1 Invert the block, and locate the main bearing upper shells into position, engaging the lock tabs into the cut-outs in the bearing recesses. Note that all of the upper shells are grooved (photo).
2 Lubricate the shells with clean engine oil, fit the thrust washers to No 2 main bearing so that the oil grooves are visible, and lower the crankshaft into position (photos).
3 Locate the shells in the main bearing caps in a similar manner to that of the block, and lubricate. Note that on the ZEJ engine, the shells are all grooved, whereas on the ZDJ engine they are all plain.
4 Fit the bearing caps into position, then insert and tighten the bolts (photos). Do not fit any side seals to caps 1 and 5 at this stage.
5 Now check the crankshaft endfloat, using a dial gauge or feeler blade (photo). If necessary, select new thrust washers, and fit them to No 2 main bearing.
6 Using twist drills, measure the gap between the block and the bottom of the groove in Nos 1 and 5 main bearing caps (Fig. 1.27). If less than 5.0 mm (0.197 in), fit a 5.15 mm (0.203 in) thick side seal (no reference mark). If more than 5.0 mm (0.197 in), fit a 5.4 mm (0.213 in) thick side seal (white reference mark). Note that seals must also be fitted where the caps were previously sealed by injecting silicone sealant, but first clean away all traces of the silicone.

7 Remove Nos 1 and 5 main bearing caps, and fit the side seals so that they protrude 0.2 mm (0.008 in) towards the block face. Smear the seals with oil.

8 Refit the caps, and tighten the bolts. To prevent the seals stretching, it is recommended that strips of celluloid are temporarily placed against the seals as the caps are inserted. Pull out the strips after tightening the bolts. Trim the visible ends of the seals so that they protrude 0.7 mm (0.028 in).

9 Lubricate the new front and rear crankshaft oil seals, and carefully locate them into their apertures, tapping them fully into position using a tubular drift of a suitable diameter. Ensure that the seals face the correct way round, with the cavity/spring side towards the engine. Should the seal lip accidentally become damaged during fitting, remove and discard it, and fit another new seal (photos).

10 If a new clutch spigot bearing is being fitted, now is the time to do it. Drive it home using a suitable diameter tubular drift. **Note:** *When fitting this bearing to the crankshaft, smear the outer bearing surface with a suitable thread-locking compound.* To the crankshaft front end, fit the belt guide, the Woodruff key and sprocket (roll pins visible) (photos).

Flywheel or driveplate (automatic transmission)

11 Locate the flywheel or driveplate on the crankshaft mounting flange. The bolt holes are offset, so it will only go on one way (photo).

12 Use new fixing bolts, and having cleaned their threads, apply thread-locking fluid to them. Insert and tighten the bolts (photos).

Cylinder liners/pistons/connecting rods

Note: *A piston ring compressor will be required for this operation*

13 Before fitting the piston and connecting rod assemblies into the liners, the liners must be checked in the crankcase for depth of fitting. This is carried out as follows.

14 Although the cylinder liners fit directly onto the crankcase inner flange, O-ring seals are fitted between the chamfered flanges as shown in Fig. 1.28. New O-rings must always be used once the cylinders have been disturbed from the crankcase.

15 First, insert a liner into the crankcase *without its O-ring*, and measure how far it protrudes from the top face of the crankcase. Lay a straight-edge rule across its top face, and measure the gap to the top face of the cylinder block with feeler gauges. It should be as given in the Specifications.

16 Now check the height on the other cylinders in the same way, and note each reading. Check that the variation in protrusion on adjoining liners does not exceed the amount specified.

17 New liners can be interchanged for position to achieve this if necessary, and when in position, should be marked accordingly 1 to 4 from the flywheel end. The protrusion dimensions should become progressively smaller from No 1 cylinder to No 4 cylinder.

18 Remove each liner in turn, and position an O-ring seal onto its lower section so that it butts into the chamfered section, taking care not to twist or distort it.

19 Wipe the liners and pistons clean, and smear with clean engine oil, prior to their respective fitting.

20 Refit the pistons to the liners, using a piston ring compressor tightened around well-oiled rings to install the piston into the lower end of the cylinder liners. Fit the liners/pistons into the cylinder block. Fit the big-end caps with shells (photos).

21 Observe the following important points:

(a) *The arrows on top of the pistons must point towards the flywheel (photo)*

(b) *The big-end shells with oil holes must be fitted to the connecting rods, and the shells without oil holes to the caps (photo)*

(c) *The connecting rod and cap bolts must be tightened to the specified torque, with the numbered markings in alignment (photo)*

(d) *When assembled, reclamp the liners and rotate the crankshaft to ensure it rotates smoothly*

Oil pump

22 Lubricate the respective parts of the oil pump, and reassemble.

23 Insert the rotors and refit the cover. No gasket is fitted on this face.

24 Tighten the retaining bolts to secure the cover.

25 Insert the oil pressure relief valve assembly, fitting the piston into the spring, and the cup over the spring at the opposite end. Compress

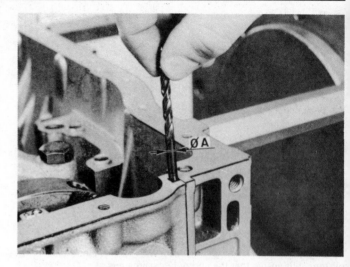

Fig. 1.27 Measuring the side seal grooves of Nos 1 and 5 main bearing caps – for A, see text (Sec 36)

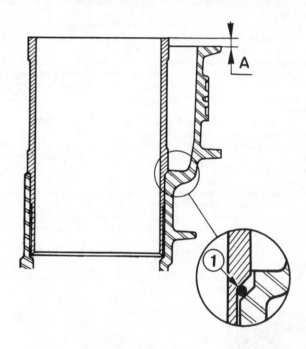

Fig. 1.28 Cylinder liner O-ring seal (1) and protrusion (A) (Sec 36)

into the cylinder, and insert a new split pin to retain the valve assembly in place.

26 Fit the assembled pump into position on the locating dowels. Tighten the retaining bolts (photos).

Intermediate shaft and timing belt tensioner

27 Lubricate the shaft, and insert it through the front of the crankcase (photo).

28 Slide the lockplate fork into the protruding shaft location groove, and secure the plate with the bolt and washer. Check that the shaft is free to rotate on completion.

29 Fit the new oil seal into the intermediate shaft front cover, and lubricate its lips.

30 Fit the front cover, together with a new gasket, and tighten the nut and bolts.

31 Fit the Woodruff key into its groove in the shaft, and carefully locate the intermediate shaft drive sprocket into position, with its large

36.1 Fitting the main bearing upper shells

36.2A Oiling main bearing shells

36.2B Fitting thrust washers to No 2 main bearing

36.2C Crankshaft located in crankcase

36.4A Fitting the main bearing caps – note the location dowel (arrowed)

36.4B Tightening the main bearing cap bolts

36.5 Checking the crankshaft endfloat with feeler blades

36.9A Fitting crankshaft front oil seal

36.9B Fitting crankshaft rear oil seal

36.10A Clutch spigot bearing in crankshaft rear flange

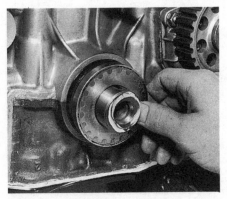
36.10B Timing belt spacer/guide

36.10C Fitting crankshaft sprocket Woodruff key

36.10D Fitting crankshaft sprocket

36.11 Fitting the flywheel

36.12A Apply locking fluid ...

36.12B ... then insert and tighten the flywheel bolts

36.20A Fitting a piston and connecting rod into the cylinder liner

36.20B Fitting the liners/pistons in the block

36.20C Fitting a big-end cap

36.21A Arrow mark on the top of the piston

36.21B Tightening a big-end cap bolt

36.26A Fit the oil pump ...

36.26B ... and tighten the retaining bolts

36.27 Fitting the intermediate shaft

offset inner face towards the crankcase. Use a suitable diameter drift to tap the sprocket into position over the key.
32 Prevent the sprocket from rotating by inserting a screwdriver blade or similar through a sprocket hole, and tighten the retaining nut (complete with flat washer) to the specified torque.
33 Refit the water pump, with reference to Chapter 2.
34 Refit the timing belt tensioner, spring and plunger. Lever the support plate against the spring tension, and tighten the nut and bolt to hold the tensioner in its retracted position.
35 Grease the end of the oil pump driveshaft, then insert it through the distributor aperture and into the oil pump (photo). Make sure that the limiting circlip is in position on the driveshaft, and temporarily stick some tape over the hole to prevent it falling out.

Sump pan
36 Locate a new gasket on the sump or crankcase.
37 Locate the sump pan, then insert and tighten the securing screws.

Cylinder head and timing belt
38 Refer to Section 25.

Distributor drive pinion
39 Set the engine at TDC on No 1 cylinder. The mark on the camshaft sprocket should be aligned with the tongue in the timing belt cover aperture.

40 Engage the distributor drive pinion initially with the oil pump driveshaft, then turn the pinion so that its groove is parallel with the crankshaft, with the smaller segment facing outwards (photo).
41 Press the drive pinion fully into mesh with the intermediate shaft gear, and check that its final position is as shown in Fig. 1.29.

37 Engine ancillary components – refitting

Refer to Section 29, and refit the components with reference to the appropriate Chapter or Section. Note that the water pump has already been refitted.

38 Engine – refitting

Refitting is a reversal of the removal procedure given in Section 27, with particular attention to the points given in Section 19.

39 Initial start-up after major overhaul

Refer to Section 20, ignoring the reference to Section 6.

36.35 Inserting the oil pump driveshaft

36.40 Fitting the distributor/oil pump drive pinion

Fig. 1.29 TDC position of the distributor drive pinion (Sec 36)

PART D : FAULT DIAGNOSIS

40 Fault diagnosis – engine

Symptom	Reason(s)
Engine will not crank, or cranks very slowly	Discharged battery Poor battery connections Starter motor fault
Engine cranks, but will not start	No fuel reaching engine Ignition circuit fault Fuel system fault Leak in crankcase vent system hoses Leak in intake manifold
Engine stalls, or rough idle	Leak in crankcase vent system hoses Leak in intake manifold Very weak mixture Incorrect valve clearances
Hesitation or poor acceleration	Incorrectly adjusted mixture Clogged air cleaner Incorrect valve clearances
Excessive oil consumption	Worn piston rings or cylinder bores Worn oil seals or leaking gaskets
Excessive mechanical noise from engine	Incorrect valve clearances General internal wear
Pinking on acceleration	Fuel octane too low Overheating Carbon build-up in engine Excessive oil vapour being drawn into crankcase breather system Upper cylinder lubricant being used Weak mixture

Chapter 2 Cooling system

Contents

Specifications

Type .... Pressurised with expansion bottle, front-mounted radiator with belt-driven fan; water pump and thermostat

Coolant

Antifreeze type/specification .... Ethylene glycol based antifreeze (Duckhams Universal Antifreeze and Summer Coolant)

Antifreeze mixture:
    Protection to −15°C (5°F) .... 27% antifreeze
    Protection to −35°C (−31°F) .... 50% antifreeze
System capacity:
    Carburettor models (manual gearbox) .... 8.4 litres (14.8 pints)
    Carburettor models (automatic transmission) .... 7.3 litres (12.8 pints)
    Fuel injection models .... 7.5 litres (13.2 pints)

Pressure cap setting .... 0.8 bar (11.6 lbf/in²), or 1.0 bar (14.5 lbf/in²), depending on model

Thermostat

Starts to open:
    Carburettor models .... 75 or 82°C (167 or 180°F)
    ZEJ engine models .... 83°C (181°F)
    ZDJ engine models .... 87°C (189°F)
Fully open (7.5 mm/0.3 in):
    Except GTI models .... 95°C (203°F)
    GTI models .... 94°C (201°F)

Fan/warning lamp operating temperatures

Radiator fan cut-in temperature .... 88°C (190°F)
Radiator fan cut-out temperature .... 79°C (174°F)
Temperature warning lamp cut-in temperature:
    Early (blue) .... 105°C (221°F)
    Later (white) .... 110°C (230°F)

Torque wrench settings

	Nm	lbf ft
Water pump	15	11
Thermostat housing cover	15	11

1 General description

The cooling system is of pressurised type, incorporating an expansion bottle, front-mounted crossflow radiator with belt-driven fan, water pump, and thermostat. The cooling fan is temperature-controlled, and is only driven when it is really needed, with a consequent reduction in noise and power consumption. The viscous-type fan employs a fluid drive and temperature-controlled valve. The self-disengaging fan employs an electro-magnetic drive, which is energised by a thermoswitch in the radiator.

The cooling system functions in the following way. After a cold start, the thermostat valve is shut, and coolant circulation is restricted to the engine and heater matrix. When the coolant reaches the normal engine operating temperature, the thermostat starts to open, allowing the coolant to also circulate through the radiator. The coolant is cooled by the action of the airflow through the radiator, enhanced when necessary by the fan.

The radiator incorporates a low coolant level indicator warning switch.

2 Routine maintenance

Carry out the following procedures at the intervals given in Routine maintenance *at the front of this manual.*

Check coolant level
1 Position the vehicle on level ground.
2 With the engine cold, check that the coolant level in the expansion bottle is up to the 'MAXI' mark (photo).
3 If necessary, unscrew the pressure cap and top up with the correct antifreeze mixture (photo). Refit the cap on completion.

Check coolant hoses
4 Examine all coolant hoses for leaks, and tighten the securing clips where necessary. At the same time, check the radiator and water pump for signs of leakage.

Check the drivebelt
5 Check the full length of the drivebelt for signs of fraying, glazing and cracking.
6 If the drivebelt needs tensioning or renewal, refer to Section 7.

Renew antifreeze mixture
7 Drain the cooling system, and refill with new antifreeze mixture, with reference to Section 3.

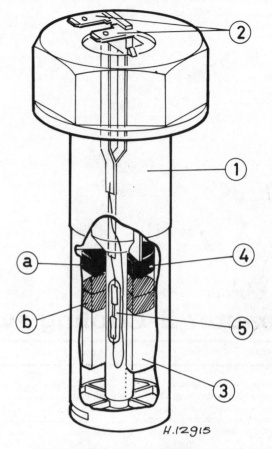

H.12915

Fig. 2.1 Cutaway view of the low coolant level indicator warning switch (Sec 1)

1 *Body*
2 *Terminals*
3 *Float*
4 *Magnet*
5 *Encapsulated reed contact*
a *Switch in 'off' position*
b *Switch in 'on' position*

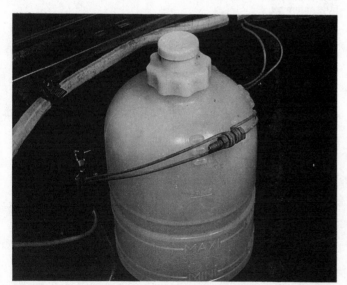

2.2 Cooling system expansion bottle

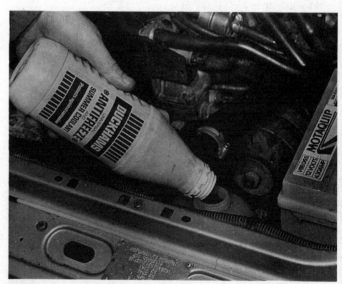

2.3 Topping-up the cooling system

3 Cooling system – draining, flushing and refilling

1 Position the heater temperature control on full heat.

2 Unclip the expansion bottle, and pour its contents into a container.

3 Suspend the expansion bottle from a convenient point on the bonnet, as high as the connecting hose will allow.

4 Place a suitable container beneath the left-hand side of the radiator, then unscrew the drain plug and drain the coolant (photo).

5 Drain the cylinder block by removing the plug located on the right-hand rear (carburettor engines), or left-hand front (fuel injection engines), of the block.

6 Disconnect the wiring from the coolant level sender on the radiator. Unscrew the cap, and withdraw the sender from the radiator (photos).

7 Provided that the coolant has been renewed at the specified intervals, flushing the system should not be necessary. If, however, maintenance has been neglected, and the coolant when drained contains excessive amounts of sediment, the system should be flushed as follows. Remove the thermostat as described in Section 5, then refit the housing cover and the hose. Turn the heater control to the full heat setting. Disconnect the top hose at the radiator, refit the radiator drain plug, and remove the cylinder block drain plug. Flush the cylinder block using water from a garden hose, fed in through the top of the radiator, until the water emerging from the block drain plug is clear. Now refit the block drain plug and the thermostat, remove the radiator drain plug, and flush the radiator through the top hose inlet.

8 If after a reasonable period the water still does not run clear the radiator can be flushed with a good proprietary cleaning agent such as Holts Radflush or Holts Speedflush. It is important that the manufacturer's instructions are followed carefully.

9 In severe cases of contamination the system should be reverse flushed. To do this, remove the radiator, invert it and insert a garden hose in the outlet. This involves feeding water through the bottom hose port. Continue flushing until clear water runs out of the top hose.

10 When flushing is complete, ensure that all water has been drained from the block and radiator, then refit the hoses and plugs as necessary.

11 To refill the system, first loosen the bleed screw (if fitted). This will be located either on the uppermost coolant hose on carburettor engines (photo), or on the throttle housing on later fuel injection engines. On carburettor engines without a bleed screw, disconnect the coolant hose from the carburettor automatic choke housing.

12 Fill the radiator with fresh coolant (photo), and tighten the bleed screw, or refit the hose, when the coolant emerges in a continuous stream, free of bubbles.

13 Pour coolant into the expansion bottle until the radiator overflows, then immediately refit the level sender and tighten the cap. Reconnect the wiring.

14 Fill the expansion bottle to 25 mm (1.0 in) above the 'MAXI' level mark, then fit and tighten the cap.

15 Temporarily loosen the bleed screw or heater hose to release any trapped air.

16 Run the engine at a fast idle speed until it reaches its normal operating temperature, indicated by the fan engaging, then allow the engine to idle.

17 Accelerate the engine briefly several times to assist the bleeding process, then switch it off.

18 Refit the expansion bottle, beside the radiator.

19 Allow the engine to cool completely.

20 Check that the coolant is up to the 'MAXI' level mark, and top up if necessary.

Fig. 2.2 Cylinder block drain plug location on carburettor engines (Sec 3)

Fig. 2.3 Cylinder block drain plug location on the fuel injection engines (Sec 3)

Fig. 2.5 Refilling the cooling system through the expansion bottle (1) (Sec 3)

Fig. 2.4 Coolant bleed screw on the throttle housing of later fuel injection engines (Sec 3)

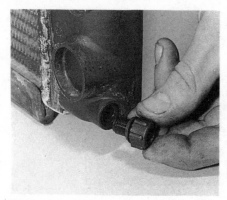

3.4 Removing the radiator drain plug

3.6A Disconnect the level sender wiring ...

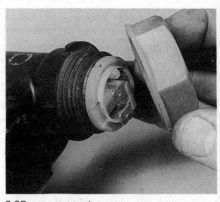

3.6B ... unscrew the cap ...

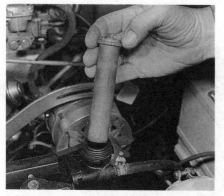

3.6C ... and withdraw the sender

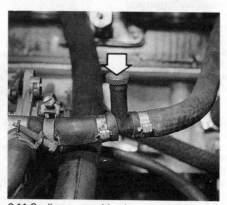

3.11 Cooling system bleed screw (arrowed) on carburettor engines

3.12 Filling the radiator with coolant

4 Antifreeze mixture – general

1   Plain water should never be used in the cooling system. Apart from giving protection against freezing, an antifreeze mixture protects the engine internal surfaces and components against corrosion.

2   Ideally, a 50% mixture of antifreeze and soft or demineralised water should be used, to maintain maximum protection against freezing and corrosion. **On no account** use less than 25% antifreeze.

3   The coolant must be renewed at the specified intervals, as the corrosion inhibitors contained in the antifreeze gradually lose their effectiveness if maintenance is neglected.

5 Thermostat – removal, testing and refitting

1   The thermostat housing on carburettor engines is integral with the water pump, located on the front of the cylinder head. On fuel injection engines, it is separate to the water pump, on the front left-hand side of the cylinder head.

2   Drain the cooling system as described in Section 3.

3   Disconnect the radiator top hose from the thermostat housing.

4   Unscrew and remove the two thermostat housing cover bolts, and remove the cover (photos). This may need to be tapped lightly with a wooden or plastic-faced mallet to free it.

5   Remove the thermostat (photo). If it is stuck, use a sharp knife to cut free the rubber seal from the housing.

6   Ease the rubber seal from the edge of the thermostat.

7   If the thermostat is suspected of being faulty, suspend it in a container of water which is being heated. Using a thermometer, check that the temperatures at which the thermostat starts to open, and at which it is fully open, are as specified.

8   Remove the thermostat from the water, and allow it to cool. Check that the thermostat closes fully.

9   If the unit fails to operate as described, or is stuck open or shut, renew it with one of identical temperature rating (photo).

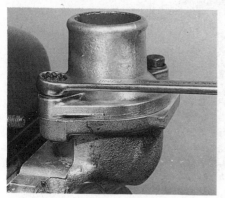

5.4A Unscrew the bolts ...

5.4B ... and remove the thermostat housing cover (carburettor engine)

5.5 Removing the thermostat (carburettor engine)

10 Fit the rubber seal on the thermostat flange, noting that the tab locates in the seal extension on carburettor engines (photo).
11 Locate the thermostat in the housing.
12 Clean the mating surfaces, then fit the cover and tighten the bolts.
13 Reconnect the radiator top hose, and refill the system as described in Section 3.

6 Radiator – removal, repair and refitting

1 Drain the cooling system as described in Section 3.
2 Disconnect the top and bottom hoses from the radiator. On automatic transmission models, also disconnect the fluid cooler pipes.
3 Disconnect the expansion bottle hose from the left-hand side of the radiator (photo).
4 Disconnect the wiring from the thermoswitch for the self-disengaging cooling fan, where fitted (photo).
5 Unscrew and remove the upper mounting bolts, and lift the radiator from the bottom mounting brackets (photos). Take care not to damage the radiator matrix.
6 If necessary, remove the rubber mounting pads and unscrew the thermoswitch (photos).
7 In an emergency minor leaks from the radiator can be cured by using a radiator sealant such as Holts Radweld with the radiator *in situ*. If the leak is more serious then it is recommended that the radiator is exchanged/renewed or the repairs left to a specialist.
8 Clean any debris from the matrix with water from a hose.
9 Refitting is a reversal of removal. Refill the cooling system with reference to Section 3.

7 Drivebelt – removal, refitting and adjustment

1 Loosen the alternator adjustment and pivot bolts, and swivel the alternator towards the engine.
2 Slip the drivebelt from the alternator, water pump, and crankshaft pulleys, and remove it over the fan (photo).
3 Refitting the drivebelt is a reversal of removal, but adjust the belt tension as follows. Pivot the alternator so that the belt deflection, under firm thumb pressure at a point midway between the pulleys, is approximately 12.5 mm (0.5 in). Do not over-tension, as this may damage the alternator bearings. Tighten the alternator adjustment and pivot bolts on completion. After a nominal mileage has been covered, check the tension of the drivebelt again.

8 Water pump – removal and refitting

1 Disconnect the battery negative lead.
2 Drain the cooling system as described in Section 3, and remove the radiator as described in Section 6.
3 Remove the drivebelt as described in Section 7.
4 Disconnect the heater, and where applicable, the automatic choke return hoses.
5 Disconnect the radiator bottom hose, and on carburettor models, the top hose from the water pump.
6 Disconnect the wire from the self-disengaging fan brush holder, where fitted (photo).
7 Disconnect the wire from the coolant temperature sender.
8 Unscrew the nuts and remove the fan (photos).
9 Where a viscous coupling is fitted, unscrew the centre nut to remove it, then unbolt the pulley.
10 Unscrew the mounting nuts and bolts, noting the location of the different length bolts, then withdraw the water pump from the engine (photos). On fuel injection engines, press the water pump towards the timing belt when removing it, and after removing it, extract the tensioner spring and plunger from the water pump.
11 Remove the gasket (photo).
12 Clean the water pump and gasket surfaces (photo).
13 Where necessary, unscrew and remove the temperature sender (photo), then release the spring clip and withdraw the self-disengaging fan brush holder.

5.9 The temperature rating is stamped on the thermostat

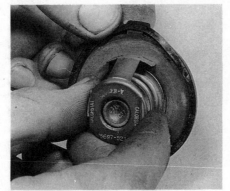

5.10 Fitting the rubber seal (carburettor engine)

6.3 Disconnecting the expansion bottle hose from the radiator

6.4 Self-disengaging cooling fan thermoswitch (arrowed)

6.5A Unscrewing the radiator upper mounting bolts

6.5B A radiator bottom mounting bracket

6.6A Removing a radiator rubber mounting pad

6.6B Cooling fan thermoswitch (arrowed)

7.2 Removing the drivebelt (fan removed for clarity)

14 To remove the self-disengaging fan hub and pulley, unscrew the centre nut, then slide the hub and pulley from the impeller shaft (photos).

15 If the water pump is worn or leaking, it must be renewed. If only the bearing in the self-disengaging fan hub is worn, it may be renewed separately. Extract the circlip (photo) and use a soft-metal drift to drive out the bearing. Press or drive the new bearing into the hub, using a metal tube on the outer track. Refit the circlip.

16 After reassembling the self-disengaging fan hub, check that the gap between the hub and pulley is 0.3 mm (0.012 in) using a feeler gauge. If necessary, adjust the three screws on the hub (photos).

17 Refitting is a reversal of removal. Tension the drivebelt as described

in Section 7. Refill the cooling system as described in Section 3.

9 Self-disengaging fan thermoswitch – removal and refitting

1 Drain the cooling system as described in Section 3.

2 Disconnect the two wires, then unscrew the thermoswitch from the radiator side tank.

3 Refitting is a reversal of removal. Refill the cooling system as described in Section 3.

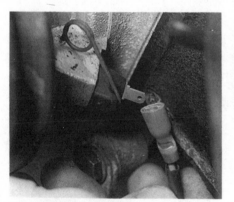

8.6 Disconnecting wire from self-disengaging fan brush holder

8.8A Unscrew the nuts (arrowed) ...

8.8B ... and remove the fan

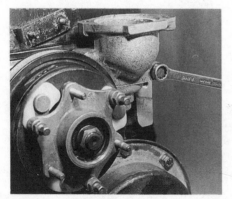

8.10A Unscrew the mounting bolt ...

8.10B ... and nuts ...

8.10C ... and remove the water pump (carburettor engine)

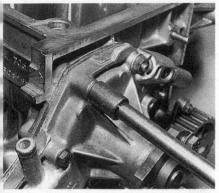

8.10D Unscrew the mounting nuts and bolts ...

8.10E ... and remove the water pump (fuel injection engine)

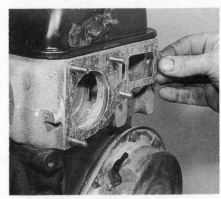

8.11 Removing the water pump gasket (carburettor engine)

8.12 Rear view of water pump (fuel injection engine)

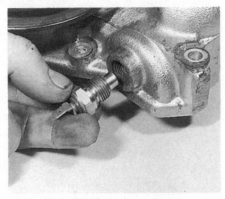

8.13 Removing the temperature sender (carburettor engine)

8.14A Unscrew the nut ...

8.14B ... and remove the self-disengaging fan hub ...

8.14C ... and pulley (carburettor engine)

8.14D Basic water pump (carburettor engine)

8.15 Removing the circlip from the self-disengaging fan hub

8.16A Reassembled self-disengaging fan unit

8.16B Adjusting the gap on the self-disengaging fan unit

10 Fault diagnosis – cooling system

Symptom	Reason(s)
Overheating	Insufficient coolant in system
	Loose drivebelt
	Faulty self-disengaging fan or thermoswitch
	Radiator blocked either internally or externally
	Thermostat not opening
Overcooling	Faulty, incorrect or missing thermostat
Loss of coolant	Damaged hoses or loose clips
	Radiator leaking
	Expansion tank pressure cap defective

Chapter 3 Fuel and exhaust systems

Contents

Specifications

General
Fuel tank capacity

Pre-1984 models	52 litres (11.4 gallons)
1984-on models	70 litres (15.4 gallons)

Carburettor engines
System type .... Rear-mounted fuel tank, mechanical fuel pump, single, fixed jet, downdraught carburettor

Air cleaner element
1971 cc (1979 to 1990) .... Champion W165

Fuel filter
1971 cc (1983 to 1990) .... Champion L101

Carburettor calibrations and settings

Zenith 35-40 INAT:

	Primary	Secondary
Venturi diameter	22 mm	28 mm
Main jet	X 112.5	X130
Progression jet	–	50
Constant CO calibrator	50	–
Air compensator	150	90
Emulsion tube	9R	4N
Vent and idle jet	120/45	–
Pump injector tube	0.5 + 0.03	0.5 + 0.03
Enrichener valve	40	–
Fast idle speed	2800 rpm	
Idle speed	900 rpm	
CO% at idle	2 ± 0.5	

Carburettor calibrations and settings (cont)

Solex 32-35 TMIMA:	Primary	Secondary
Venturi diameter	24 mm	27 mm
Main jet:		
Code 211/1	120	160
Except code 211/1	122.5	160
Air correction jet:		
Code 211/1	155	180
Except code 211/1	165	130
Idle fuel jet:		
Code 211/1	42	40
Except code 211/1	46	40
Idle air jet	160	4.3 mm diameter
Constant CO jet	30	–
Accelerator pump jet	40	50
Needle valve	1.7	1.7
Econostat fuel jet	–	80
Enrichener fuel jet	60	–
Fast idle speed:		
Code 211/1	3200 ± 50 rpm	
Except code 211/1	3800 ± 50 rpm	
Idle speed	900 rpm	
CO% at idle	2 ± 0.5	

Solex 32-35 MIMSA:	Primary	Secondary
Venturi diameter	24 mm	27 mm
Main jet:		
Code 231/1/2	122.5	140
Code 232/1/2	120	140
Air correction jet:		
Code 232/2	160	140
Except code 232/2	165	130
Idle fuel jet:		
Code 231/1/2	46	40
Code 232/1/2	42	40
Idle air jet	160	150
Constant CO jet	30	–
Accelerator pump injector	40	50
Needle valve	1.7	1.7
Econostat fuel jet:		
Code 231/232/1	–	80
Code 231/232/2	–	70
Idle speed	900 rpm	
CO% at idle	2 ± 0.5	

Solex 34 BICSA 3:	
Venturi diameter	27 mm
Main jet:	
Code 299	140
Code 300	137.5
Code 342	137
Air correction jet:	
Code 299	220
Code 300	200
Code 342	180
Idle jet:	
Code 299	47
Code 300	45
Code 342	43
Constant CO jet	35
Accelerator pump injector	45
Needle valve	1.5
Econostat fuel jet:	
Codes 299 and 300	60
Code 342	50
Idle speed	900 rpm
CO% at idle	2 ± 0.5

Solex 34-34 Z1:	Primary	Secondary
Venturi diameter	25 mm	27 mm
Main jet	117	130
Air correction jet	140	130
Emulsion tube	28	ZC
Idling fuel jet	41	50
Idling air jet	140	80
Enrichener fuel jet	50	–
Needle valve	1.8	1.8

Carburettor calibrations and settings (cont)	Primary	Secondary
Solex 34-34 Z1 (cont):		
Accelerator pump injector	40	55
Fast idle speed	3400 ± 50 rpm	
Idle speed	900 rpm	
CO% at idle	1.5 ± 0.5	
Solex 32-34 CISAC:	**Primary**	**Secondary**
Venturi diameter	24 mm	26 mm
Main jet	117	127
Air correction jet:		
Code 388	180	150
Code 388-1	155	155
Emulsion tube	27	18
Idle fuel jet	43	70
Idle air jet	180	150
Enrichener fuel jet	50	–
Needle valve	1.8	1.8
Accelerator pump injector	35	40
Fast idle speed	3400 ± 50 rpm	
Idle speed	900 rpm	
CO% at idle	1.5 ± 0.5	
Solex 34-34 CISAC:	**Primary**	**Secondary**
Venturi diameter	25 mm	27 mm
Main jet	117	130
Air correction jet:		
Code 394	140	130
Code 396	140	80
Emulsion tube	28	ZC
Idling fuel jet	41	50
Idling air jet	140	80
Enrichener fuel jet	50	–
Needle valve	1.8	1.8
Accelerator pump injector	40	55
Fast idle speed	3400 ± 50 rpm	
Idle speed	900 rpm	
CO% at idle	1.5 ± 0.5	

Torque wrench settings	Nm	lbf ft
Carburettor mounting nuts	18	13

Fuel injection engines

System type .... Rear-mounted fuel tank, Bosch K-Jetronic or LE2-Jetronic fuel injection system, electric fuel pump

Air filter
Champion V407

Fuel filter
1995 cc (ZEJ engine only) .... Champion L204

K-Jetronic fuel injection system
Idle speed:
- Manual gearbox models with ZDJ engine .... 750 to 800 rpm
- All other models .... 900 to 950 rpm

CO% at idle .... 1.5 to 2.5

Fuel feed pressure:
- ZEJ engine .... 4.5 to 5.2 bar (65 to 75 lbf/in²)
- ZDJ engine .... 4.7 to 5.4 bar (68 to 78 lbf/in²)

Fuel pump delivery rate .... 750 cc/30 seconds (minimum)

Thermal time switch cut-off temperature .... 30 to 40°C (86 to 104°F)

Fuel control pressure (hot):
- ZEJ engine .... 3.4 to 3.8 bar (49 to 55 lbf/in²)
- ZDJ engine (no vacuum) .... 2.5 to 2.9 bar (36 to 42 lbf/in²)

LE2-Jetronic fuel injection system
Idle speed:
- Manual gearbox models .... 750 to 800 rpm
- Automatic transmission models .... 900 to 950 rpm

CO% at idle .... 0.5 to 1.5

Fuel pressure .... 2.3 to 2.7 bar (33 to 39 lbf/in²)

Fuel pump delivery rate .... 540 cc/15 seconds (minimum)

Torque wrench settings	Nm	lbf ft
Main fuel filter union bolts	35	26

PART A : GENERAL

1 General description and use of unleaded fuel

Description

The fuel system comprises a rear-mounted fuel tank, single downdraught carburettor on overhead valve engines, and a Bosch K-Jetronic or LE2-Jetronic fuel injection system on overhead camshaft engines.

On carburettor engines, the fuel pump is mounted on the cylinder block, and driven by a plunger from an eccentric on the camshaft. On fuel injection engines, the electric fuel pump is located by the fuel tank beneath the rear of the vehicle.

Unleaded fuel

Unleaded high-octane (95 RON) fuel can be used successfully on certain models – refer to the list below. Where an ignition timing adjustment is required, refer to the procedures given in Chapter 4. Note that, for example, retarding the ignition by 2° on a car normally timed at 10° BTDC gives a new setting of 8° BTDC. Although the details given here are correct at the time of writing, be sure to refer to a Peugeot dealer for the latest information.

*XM7A, XN1, and XN1A engine models, 1986 model year on :
Unleaded fuel may be used without modification
All ZEJK and ZDJL engine models : Unleaded fuel may be used,
but retard the ignition timing by 2°
All other models : Unleaded fuel must not be used*

2 Routine maintenance

Carry out the following procedures at the intervals given in Routine maintenance *at the front of this manual.*

Clean oil bath type air cleaner

1 Some very early fuel injection models may be fitted with an oil bath type air cleaner. To clean it, remove the base and pour away the old oil. Clean the element in paraffin, then add 0.26 litres (0.46 pints) of engine oil and reassemble.

Check and adjust the accelerator cable

2 Check the accelerator cable for smooth operation, and for signs of fraying.
3 Adjust the cable if necessary, with reference to Section 17 or 36, as applicable.

Renew the air cleaner element

4 Refer to Section 3 or 21, as applicable.

Renew the fuel pre-filter (fuel injection engines)

5 Refer to Section 26.

Renew the main fuel filter (fuel injection engines)

6 Refer to Section 26.

PART B : CARBURETTOR ENGINES

3 Air cleaner element – renewal

1 The air cleaner element is removed from the rear of the assembly, and therefore it is necessary to remove the air cleaner completely .
2 Loosen the clip and disconnect the hot air hose (photo).
3 Loosen the clip and disconnect the air inlet ducting from the carburettor (photos).
4 Unscrew the mounting nuts, withdraw the assembly, and disconnect the crankcase ventilation hose (photos).
5 Loosen the end cover screw(s), remove the cover and extract the element (photos).
6 Wipe clean the inside of the main body and end cover.
7 Fit the new element using a reversal of the removal procedure.

3.2 Disconnecting the hot air hose

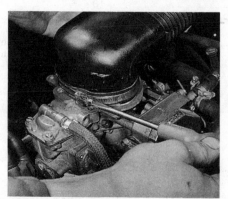
3.3A Loosen the clip ...

3.3B ... and disconnect the air inlet ducting

3.4A Unscrew the mounting nuts ...

3.4B ... and withdraw the air cleaner assembly

3.5A Loosen the screws ...

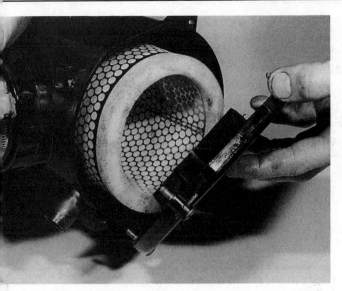

3.5B ... remove the cover ...

3.5C ... and extract the air cleaner element

4 Fuel pump – cleaning

Note: *The fuel pump may be one of several types, and may differ from the one described in this Section.*

1 Disconnect the outlet hose.
2 Remove the two screws and lift off the cover and gasket (photo).
3 Extract the gauze filter from the pump body (photo).
4 Using a small brush, clean the pump body and filter with fuel. If necessary, mop out the fuel from the body and wipe away any sediment.
5 Check and if necessary renew the gasket.
6 Refit the gauze filter and cover, and tighten the screws.
7 Reconnect the outlet hose.

5 Fuel pump – removal and refitting

1 Disconnect the inlet and outlet hoses (photos). Plug the inlet hose.
2 Unscrew the pump mounting bolts, and lift the pump away from the block (photos).
3 Remove the gasket, and if necessary extract the pushrod (photos).
4 Although it may be possible to dismantle the fuel pump, it is not possible to obtain genuine Peugeot spare parts, so if the pump is defective, it is recommended that it is renewed.
5 Refitting is a reversal of removal, but fit a new gasket. If crimp type clips are fitted, it may be possible to re-use them and tighten them with pincers (photo), but if they are broken or bent, replace them with screw type clips.

4.2 Removing the fuel pump cover

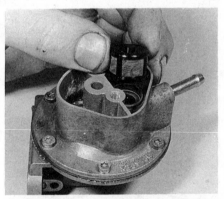

4.3 Gauze filter removal from the fuel pump

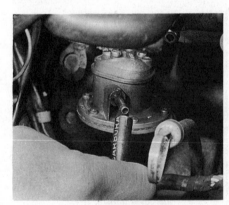

5.1A Disconnect the fuel pump inlet ...

5.1B ... and outlet hoses

5.2A Unscrew the fuel pump mounting bolts

5.2B Fuel pump removed

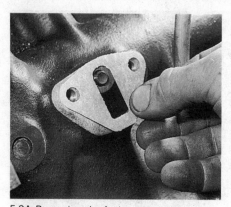

5.3A Removing the fuel pump gasket ...

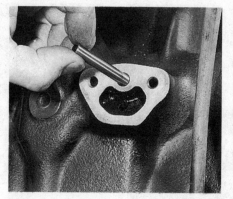

5.3B ... and pushrod

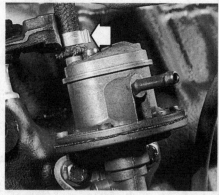

5.5 Tightening the fuel pump outlet hose clip (arrowed)

6 Fuel level transmitter – removal and refitting

1 Disconnect the battery negative lead.
2 Remove the floor covering from the luggage compartment.
3 Prise out the plastic cover to expose the fuel level transmitter (photo).
4 Disconnect the wiring plug.
5 Using two screwdrivers, crossed in a scissor-like arrangement, unscrew the retaining ring.
6 Withdraw the transmitter unit, taking care not to damage the float as it passes through the hole in the tank. Remove the gasket.
7 Refitting is a reversal of removal, but fit a new gasket.

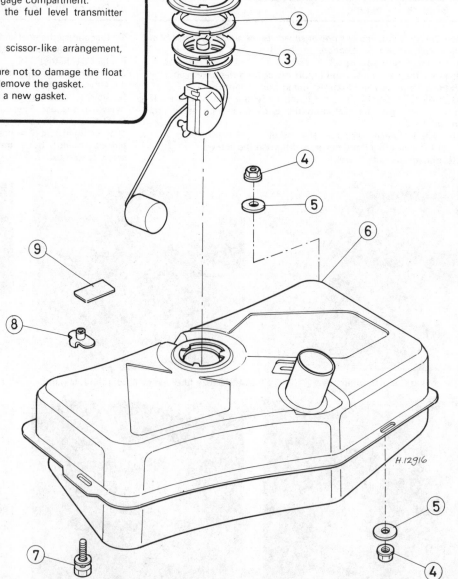

Fig. 3.1 Fuel tank and fuel level transmitter on early models (Sec 6)

1   Retaining ring
2   Spacer
3   Fuel level transmitter
4   Nut
5   Washer
6   Fuel tank
7   Bolt
8   Bolt plate
9   Rubber buffer

H.12916

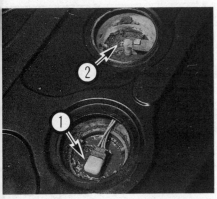

6.3 Fuel level transmitter (1) and filter (2)

7.7 Fuel tank filler hose connection – clip arrowed

7.8 Fuel tank mounting bolt (arrowed)

7 Fuel tank – removal, repair and refitting

1   Chock the front wheels, then jack up the rear of the vehicle and support on axle stands.
2   Remove the spare wheel.
3   Disconnect the battery negative lead.
4   Remove the floor covering from the luggage compartment.
5   Prise out the plastic covers. Disconnect the wiring plug from the level transmitter and the hose(s) from the filter.
6   If the fuel tank has more than a small amount of fuel in it, syphon out the fuel. The filler neck may however be fitted with wire gauze to prevent unscrupulous syphoning, in which case proceed to the next paragraph.
7   Loosen the clip and disconnect the filler hose (photo).
8   Support the weight of the tank, then unscrew the mounting bolt(s) and unhook the support cage at the rear (photo), where fitted.
9   Lower the fuel tank, and at the same time disconnect the vent and fuel return hoses as applicable.
10 If the tank is leaking or is badly rusted, leave any repair to a specialist. **On no account** attempt to solder or weld a fuel tank, as it requires a great deal of purging before every trace of explosive vapour is removed.
11 If the tank is suspected of containing sediment, pour in some fuel and shake the tank vigorously, repeating as necessary until all traces of sediment are removed.
12 Refitting the tank is a reversal of removal.

8 Carburettor – general

A single carburettor is fitted, of Zenith or Solex manufacture and of downdraught type. According to model, the carburettor is either single or twin choke, and may have either a manual or automatic choke for cold starting.

9 Carburettor – idle speed and mixture adjustment

Note: *The following adjustments must be made with the ignition timing correctly adjusted, the air cleaner and filter element fitted, and the engine at normal operating temperature. On automatic transmission models, select 'P'.*

1   Turn the idle speed screw until the engine idles at the specified speed (photo).
2   If available, use an exhaust gas analyser to check that the CO content is as specified. If necessary, turn the mixture screw as required then re-adjust the idle speed screw to set the engine speed to that specified. Note that the mixture screw may be fitted with a tamperproof cap (photo).
3   To adjust the mixture without an analyser, remove the tamperproof cap if fitted, and turn the mixture screw to obtain the highest engine speed. Screw in the idle speed screw to obtain 950 rpm, then screw in the mixture screw to obtain the specified speed.

Fig. 3.2 Idle speed (1) and mixture (2) screws on the Zenith 35-40 INAT carburettor (Sec 9)

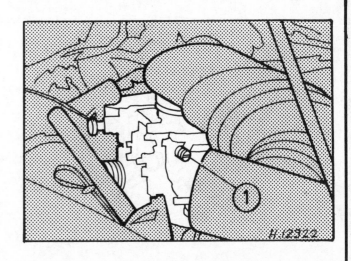

Fig. 3.3 Idle speed screw (1) on the Solex 32-35 TMIMA carburettor (Sec 9)

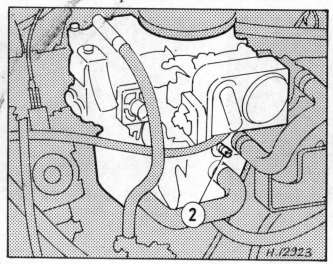

Fig. 3.4 Idle mixture screw (2) on the Solex 32-35 TMIMA carburettor (Sec 9)

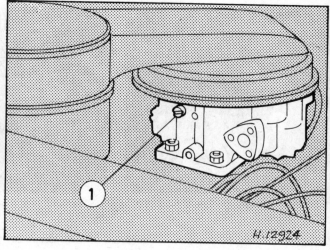

Fig. 3.5 Idle speed screw (1) on the Solex 32-35 MIMSA carburettor (Sec 9)

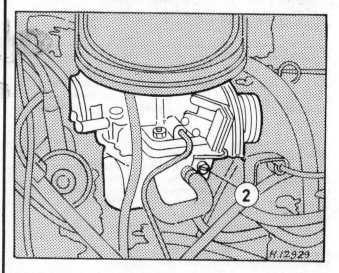

Fig. 3.6 Idle mixture screw (2) on the Solex 32-35 MIMSA carburettor (Sec 9)

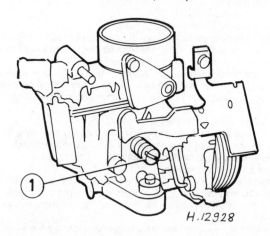

Fig. 3.7 Idle speed screw (1) on the Solex 34 BICSA 3 carburettor (Sec 9)

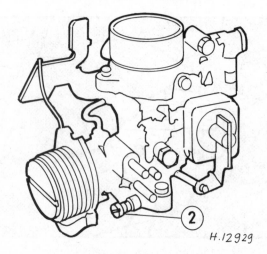

Fig. 3.8 Idle mixture screw (2) on the Solex 34 BICSA 3 carburettor (Sec 9)

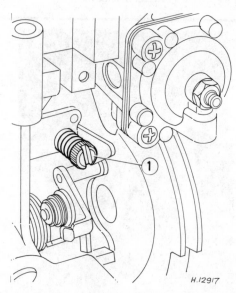

Fig. 3.9 Idle speed screw (1) on the Solex CISAC carburettor (Sec 9)

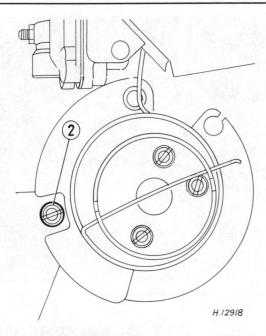

Fig. 3.10 Idle mixture screw (2) on the Solex CISAC
carburettor (Sec 9)

9.1 Idle speed screw (arrowed) – Solex 32-35 TMIMA

10.2 Disconnecting the coolant hose for the automatic choke

9.2 Tamperproof cap fitted to the mixture adjustment screw
(arrowed) – Solex 32-35 TMIMA

10 Carburettor – removal and refitting

1   Remove the air cleaner as described in Section 3.
2   Where a coolant-operated automatic choke is fitted, drain the
cooling system (Chapter 2), then disconnect the coolant hoses from
the carburettor (photo).
3   Disconnect the distributor vacuum hose.
4   Disconnect the fuel inlet hose.
5   Unhook the accelerator inner cable from the throttle lever, and
remove the outer cable from the bracket (photos).
6   As applicable, disconnect the choke cable or automatic choke
wiring.
7   Unscrew the mounting nuts and lift the carburettor from the inlet
manifold. Remove the gaskets (photos).
8   Refitting is a reversal of removal, but fit new gaskets. Adjust the
accelerator and choke cables with reference to Sections 17 and 18,
and fill the cooling system with reference to Chapter 2.

10.5A Unhooking the accelerator inner cable (arrowed)

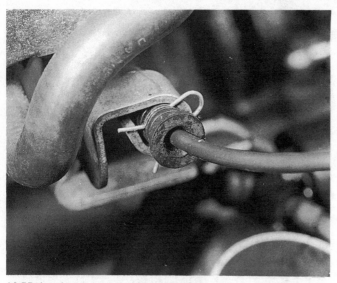

10.5B Accelerator outer cable and bracket

10.7A Unscrew the mounting nuts ...

10.7B ... and remove the carburettor ...

10.7C ... and gaskets

11 Carburettor (Zenith 35-40 INAT) – dismantling, reassembly and adjustment

1   Dismantle the carburettor with reference to Figs. 3.11 to 3.13, keeping each part identified for location.
2   Clean all the components in fuel, and obtain a repair kit of gaskets and washers.
3   Reassembly is a reversal of dismantling, but carry out the procedures given in the following paragraphs.
4   Apply locking fluid to the diffusion nozzle screws before inserting and tightening them.
5   When refitting the second barrel operating capsule, press it against the internal spring before tightening the mounting screws.
6   Adjust the accelerator pump jets with reference to Fig. 3.14.
7   The secondary throttle idling position is set at the factory, and should not normally be tampered with. If a new throttle valve has been fitted, proceed as follows. Open the throttle, open the choke, then release the throttle. Adjust the secondary throttle stop screw so that it is just possible to see light between the valve and carburettor barrel. This should represent a gap of approximately 0.05 mm (0.002 in) at the extremity of the valve. Do not use feeler blades to check the gap, as the width of the blade will mean that the gap at the extremity of the valve is excessive.

8   To adjust the automatic choke, hold the throttle lever open and turn the automatic choke operating lever anti-clockwise. Using a feeler blade, check that there is a gap of 0.15 mm (0.006 in) between the operating lever and the modulated spool without compressing the spring. If necessary, adjust the connection at the top of the choke operating rod.
9   Open the throttle lever, close the choke valve, then release the throttle lever. Refer to Fig. 3.15 and check that the stop screw is positioned as shown. If not, bend the intermediate lever.
10 The operation of the electric choke flap can be checked as follows. Open the throttle lever, close the choke flap, then release the lever. Apply battery voltage to the automatic choke. At an ambient temperature of 18 to 20°C (64 to 68°F) the choke flap should open in four minutes.
11 To adjust the idle speed and mixture screws to their initial settings, first screw them right in. Unscrew the idle speed screw three turns, and the mixture screw four turns.
12 With the carburettor refitted to the engine, the fast idle adjustment can be checked as follows. Run the engine to normal operating temperature, then switch off. Open the throttle lever, close the choke valve, then release the lever. Start the engine, and check that it is idling at the specified fast idle speed. If necessary, insert a screwdriver through the bottom of the automatic choke housing, and turn the adjusting screw as required.

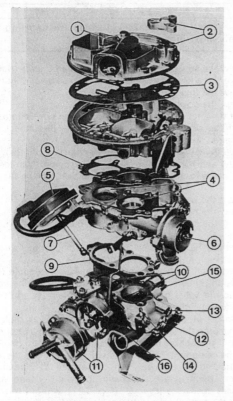

Fig. 3.11 Exploded view of the Zenith 35-40 INAT carburettor (Sec 11)

1	Choke flap	9	Insulating pad
2	Vacuum capsule and enrichener valve	10	Throttle valves
		11	Automatic choke
3	Gasket	12	Constant CO circuit adjusting screw
4	Venturis/diffusion nozzles		
5	Secondary throttle operating capsule	13	Mixture screw
		14	Idle speed screw
6	Control quadrant shaft	15	Distributor vacuum take-off
7	Control spring	16	Accelerator cable bracket
8	Gasket		

Fig. 3.13 Cover components of the Zenith 35-40 INAT carburettor (Sec 11)

1	Primary air compensator	12	Primary main jet
2	Secondary air compensator	13	Secondary main jet
3	Idle jet	14	Progressive transfer jet
4	Primary accelerator pump	15	Accelerator pump suction valves
5	Secondary accelerator pump		
6	Enrichening valve	16	Pressure valves
7	Fuel inlet union	17	Needle valve
8	Pump piston control levers	18	Float
9	Jet arms	19	Constant CO calibrator
10	Additional air jet	20	Full-load enrichener calibrator
11	Accelerator pump injectors		

Fig. 3.12 Automatic choke components of the Zenith 35-40 INAT carburettor (Sec 11)

1a	Anti-flooding intermediate lever	2b	Choke opening 'modulated' spool
1b	Anti-flooding lever	2c	Choke opening control capsule
2a	Choke opening intermediate lever		

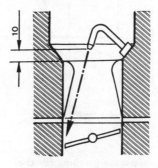

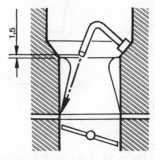

1st Barrel   2nd Barrel

Fig. 3.14 Accelerator pump jet adjustment in the Zenith 35-40 INAT carburettor – dimensions in mm (Sec 11)

12 Carburettor (Solex 32-35 TMIMA) – dismantling, reassembly and adjustment

1   Unscrew the studs from the base of the carburettor (photo).

2   Remove the automatic choke cover (two screws) (photos).

3   Unscrew the fuel supply tube (photo).

4   Unscrew the cover screws (photo).

5   Extract the circlip from the choke operating arm (photo).

6   Lift off the cover, and at the same time, disconnect the choke operating arm (photos).

7   Remove the cover gasket and the O-ring seal (photos).

8   Unscrew and remove the various jets, keeping them identified for location. Access to the main jets is gained by removing the side plugs (photos).

9   Push out the pivot pin and remove the float (photo).

10   Unscrew the needle valve (photo).

11   Clean all the components in fuel, and obtain a repair kit of gaskets and washers.

12   Reassembly is a reversal of dismantling, but carry out the procedures given in the following paragraphs.

13   To check the float level adjustment, make a cardboard template to the dimensions shown in Fig. 3.16. Lightly press on the float arm so that the needle valve ball is compressed, then use the template to check the float height without the gasket fitted (photo).

14   Adjustment of the float level is by progressively tightening the needle valve onto the special washer. Do not exceed a torque of 25 Nm (18 lbf ft). If the float is below the required level, fit a new washer.

15   With the carburettor refitted to the engine, the fast idle adjustment can be checked as follows. Run the engine to normal operating temperature. Remove the automatic choke cover, and remove the spring. Push down the lever '2' (Fig. 3.17) without forcing it, and check that the fast idle speed is now as specified. If necessary, adjust the screw. Refit the spring and cover on completion.

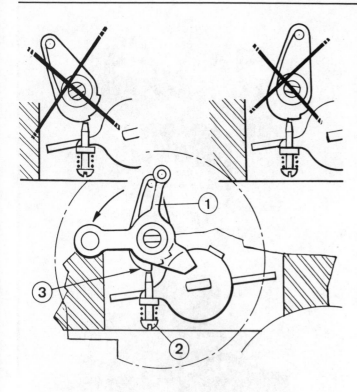

Fig. 3.15 Automatic choke adjustment on the Zenith 35-40 INAT carburettor (Sec 11)

1   Operating lever   3   Cam
2   Fast idle screw

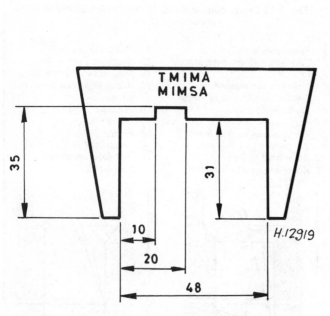

Fig. 3.16 Float level template dimensions (in mm) for the Solex 32-35 TMIMA (and MIMSA) (Sec 12)

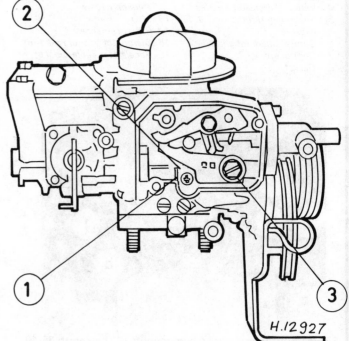

Fig. 3.17 Fast idle adjustment on the Solex 32-35 TMIMA carburettor (Sec 12)

1   Spring   3   Stop screw
2   Lever

12.1 Removing the carburettor base studs

12.2A Removing the automatic choke cover

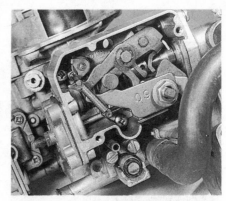
12.2B View of automatic choke with cover removed

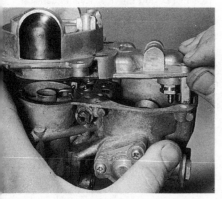
12.3 Fuel supply tube removal

12.4 Removing carburettor cover screws

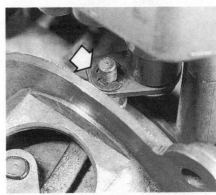
12.5 Circlip (arrowed) on the choke operating arm

12.6A Lift off the carburettor cover ...

12.6B ... and disconnect the choke operating arm (arrowed)

12.7A Removing the cover gasket

12.7B O-ring seal (arrowed) in the cover

12.8A Removing an idle fuel jet

12.8B Accelerator pump jet removal

12.8C Remove the side plugs ...

12.8D ... for access to the primary main jet (arrowed) ...

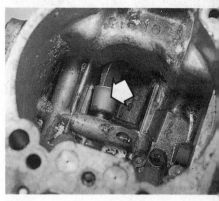

12.8E ... and secondary main jet (arrowed)

12.9 Removing the float pivot pin (arrowed)

12.10 Removing the needle valve

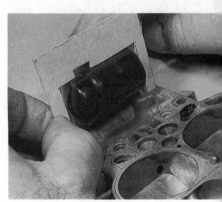

12.13 Checking the float level dimension with a cardboard template

13 Carburettor (Solex 32-35 MIMSA) – dismantling, reassembly and adjustment

1   The dismantling procedure is very similar to that described for the TMIMA carburettor in Section 12.
2   After cleaning the components, obtain a repair kit of gaskets and washers.
3   Reassemble using a reversal of the dismantling procedure, but carry out the procedures given in the following paragraphs.
4   Check the float level adjustment as described in Section 12, paragraphs 13 and 14.
5   To check the choke opening after starting (COAS) setting, press down the choke operating link, and check that the gap between the choke valve and barrel is 2.0 mm (0.08 in) using a twist drill. If adjustment is necessary, loosen the locknut, turn the screw as required, then tighten the locknut.

14 Carburettor (Solex 34 BICSA 3) – dismantling, reassembly and adjustment

1   Disconnect the fast idle rod from the choke lever.
2   Remove the screws, and separate the cover from the main body. Remove the gasket.
3   Unscrew and remove the various jets, keeping them identified for location.
4   Clean all the components, and obtain a repair kit of gaskets and washers.
5   Reassembly is a reversal of dismantling, but carry out the procedures given in the following paragraphs.
6   To check the float level adjustment, make a cardboard template to the dimensions shown in Fig. 3.20. With the gasket fitted, and the

needle valve ball compressed, use the template to check the float height. If necessary, bend the float arm to adjust.
7   To adjust the accelerator pump stroke, allow the throttle valve to close onto a 4.0 mm (0.16 in) twist drill. Back off the adjustment nut until clear of the pump lever, then screw it in until it just touches the lever.

15 Carburettor (Solex 34-34 Z1) – dismantling, reassembly and adjustment

1   The procedures are similar to those described in Section 14. It is not possible to adjust the choke opening after starting (COAS) system, due to the need for special equipment.

16 Carburettor (Solex 32-34 and 34-34 CISAC) – dismantling, reassembly and adjustment

1   The dismantling and reassembly procedures are similar to those described for the TMIMA carburettor in Section 12, but carry out the procedures given in the following paragraphs.
2   To check the float level adjustment, make a cardboard template to the dimensions shown in Fig. 3.21. With the gasket fitted and the needle valve ball compressed, use the template to check the height of the floats. If necessary, bend the float tongue or arms.
3   To check the choke opening after starting (COAS) setting, close the choke flap, then push the COAS rod against its stop. Check that the gap between the choke flap and barrel is 2.3 mm (0.09 in) using a twist drill. If necessary, adjust the position of the stop screw.
4   To check the fast idle adjustment, refer to Section 12, paragraph 15.

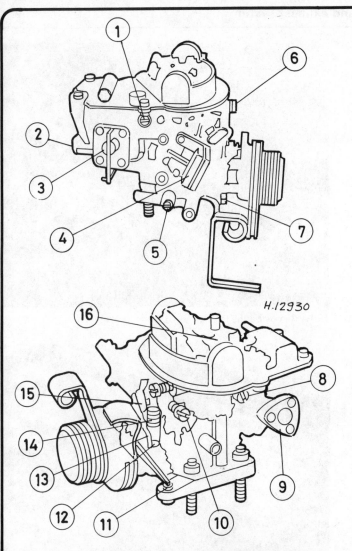

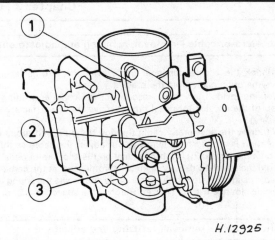

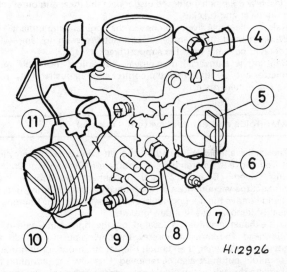

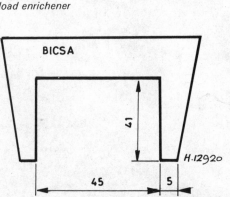

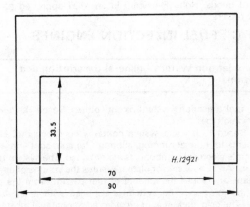

H.12930

H.12925

H.12926

Fig. 3.18 Solex 32-35 MIMSA carburettor components (Sec 13)

Fig. 3.19 Solex 34 BICSA 3 carburettor components (Sec 14)

1	Primary idle jet	10	Constant CO screw
2	Plugs	11	Secondary throttle stop screw
3	Accelerator pump	12	Fast idle screw
4	Pneumatic choke opener	13	Lever
5	Mixture screw	14	Return spring
6	Choke control	15	Quadrant
7	Primary throttle stop screw	16	Econostat
8	Secondary idle jet		
9	Full-load enrichener		

1	Choke lever	7	Pump adjusting nut
2	Throttle stop screw	8	Main jet plug
3	Constant CO screw	9	Mixture screw
4	Fuel filter plug	10	Idling jet
5	Accelerator pump	11	Fast idle link
6	Pump valve and filter		

Fig. 3.20 Float level template dimensions (in mm) for the Solex 34 BICSA 3 carburettor (Sec 14)

Fig. 3.21 Float level template dimensions for the Solex CISAC carburettor (Sec 16)

17 Accelerator cable – removal, refitting and adjustment

1   Unhook the accelerator inner cable from the throttle lever, and remove the outer cable from the bracket.
2   Working inside the vehicle, disconnect the cable end fitting from the top of the accelerator pedal arm (remove the lower facia panel if necessary).
3   Withdraw the accelerator cable through the bulkhead grommet.
4   Refitting is a reversal of removal, but adjust the cable as follows. Position a 5.0 mm (0.20 in) thick spacer on the accelerator pedal stop, and hold the pedal on it. Fully open the throttle lever at the carburettor, then apply slight tension to the outer cable and locate the spring clip in the ferrule slot nearest the bracket. Remove the spacer on completion.

18 Choke cable – removal, refitting and adjustment

1   Remove the carburettor air inlet ducting.
2   Unscrew the pinch-bolts and disconnect the inner and outer cables from the lever and bracket.
3   Release the cable from the clips in the engine compartment.
4   Working inside the vehicle, disconnect the warning lamp wiring and detach the cable from the support bracket.
5   Refitting is a reversal of removal, but adjust the cable at the carburettor end, so that when the control knob is pushed fully in, the choke flap is fully open.

19 Manifolds and exhaust system – general

1   The inlet manifold is located on the left-hand side of the cylinder head. To remove it, first remove the carburettor (Section 10). Drain the cooling system (Chapter 2) and disconnect the coolant hoses. Disconnect the vacuum hose(s), then unscrew the mounting nuts and bolts and remove the inlet manifold and gasket (photos). Refitting is a reversal of removal, but fit a new gasket.
2   The exhaust manifold is located on the right-hand side of the cylinder head. To remove it, unscrew the downpipe-to-manifold nuts. Remove the air cleaner, then unbolt the hot air shroud, noting that the rear manifold nut must also be removed. Unscrew the mounting nuts and remove the exhaust manifold and gaskets (photos). Refitting is a reversal of removal, but fit new gaskets. Check that the gaskets are fitted the correct way round on the head.
3   The exhaust system is in four sections: the downpipe, front silencer, intermediate pipe, and rear pipe and silencers (photos). It is suspended on flexible rubber mountings. To remove the complete system, the intermediate pipe must be separated from the tailpipe. When fitting the exhaust system, locate it loosely in position, then connect the downpipe to the exhaust manifold, together with a new gasket, and tighten the nuts. Tighten the joint clamps and mountings to complete.
4   Holts Flexiwrap and Holts Gun Gum exhaust repair systems can be used for effective repairs to exhaust pipes and silencer boxes, including ends and bends. Holts Flexiwrap is an MOT-approved permanent exhaust repair.

PART C : FUEL INJECTION ENGINES

20 Fuel injection system – general description and precautions

The fuel injection system is of either Bosch K-Jetronic or LE2-Jetronic type.
The Bosch K-Jetronic system contains no specialised electronic components for normal running, although for cold start and warm-up, some simple electrical components are provided. The system functions as follows. An airflow sensor plate measures the volume of air entering the engine, and varies the amount of fuel passing from the metering unit to the injectors. The system is supplied with a regulated fuel pressure. The cold start injector provides additional fuel for starting the engine, and the mixture is automatically adjusted during the warm-up period by the pressure regulator.
The Bosch LE2-Jetronic system incorporates an electronic control unit (ECU), located behind the glovebox (photo), which is continually

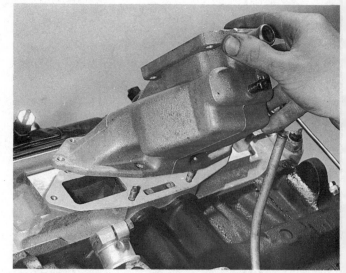
19.1A Removing the inlet manifold ...

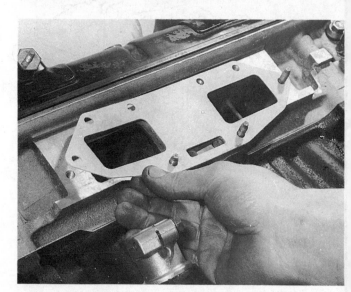
19.1B ... and gasket

19.2A Unscrew the bolts ...

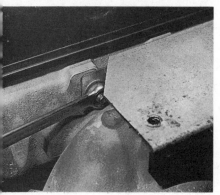
19.2B ... and nut ...

19.2C ... and remove the hot air shroud

19.2D Unscrew the nuts ...

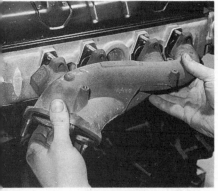
19.2E ... and remove the exhaust manifold ...

19.2F ... and gaskets

19.3A Exhaust system front mounting ...

19.3B ... downpipe-to-front silencer connection ...

19.3C ... intermediate pipe-to-rear pipe connection ...

19.3D ... intermediate mounting ...

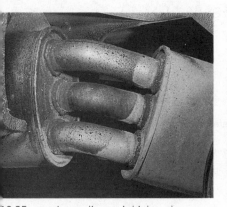
19.3E ... and rear silencer bridging pipes

20.1 Bosch LE2-Jetronic electronic control unit

20.2 Bosch LE2-Jetronic fuel cut-off relay

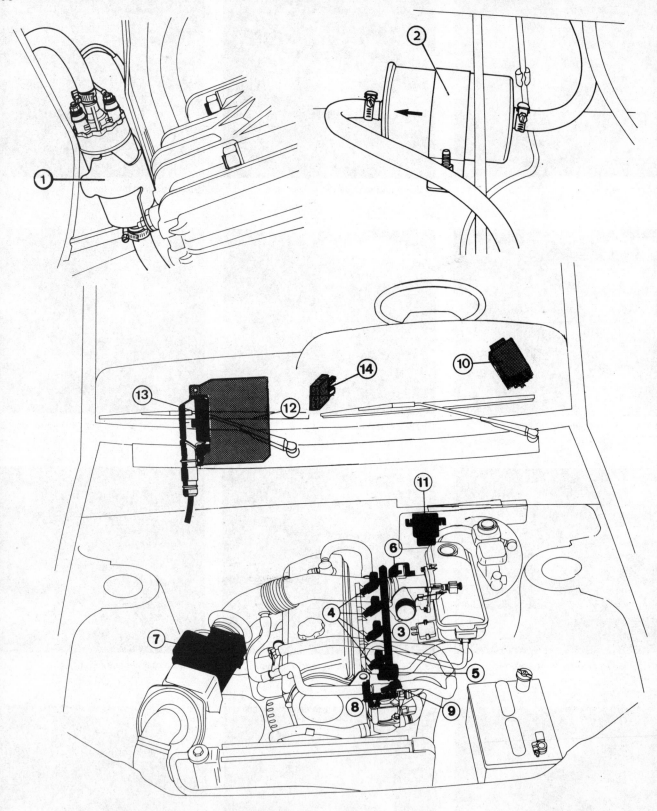

Fig. 3.22 Bosch LE2-Jetronic fuel injection system components – LHD shown, RHD similar (Sec 20)

1 Fuel pump	4 Injectors	8 Supplementary air device	12 Electronic control unit
2 Fuel filter	5 Fuel pressure regulator	9 Temperature sensor	(ECU)
3 Distribution and	6 Throttle switch	10 Tachymetric relay	13 Wiring connector
accumulator pipe	7 Airflow sensor	11 Fuel cut-off relay	14 System fuse

supplied with information from the airflow sensor, throttle switch, engine temperature sensor, and ignition coil. From this information, the ECU determines the injection period of the injectors, and activates them accordingly. The system does not include a cold start injector or thermal time switch for cold starting, as is the case on the K-Jetronic system, since this junction is incorporated in the ECU. The throttle switch incorporates an idle contact switch and a full-load contact switch. The idle switch cuts the fuel supply on overrun if the engine speed is above 1300 rpm, and works in conjunction with the fuel cut-off relay (photo). The full-load contact switch enrichens the mixture for full power.

The following Sections describe procedures which can be carried out by the home mechanic. Work involving the use of pressure gauges is not included.

In order to prevent damage to the electrical components of the LE2-Jetronic system, the following precautions should be noted:

(a) *The battery must not be disconnected with the engine running*
(b) *The ECU must not be disconnected with the ignition on*
(c) *A test lamp should not be used for checking the circuits or components in situ*

21.2A Unscrew the nuts ...

21 Air cleaner element – renewal

1 Disconnect the air duct from the front of the air cleaner.
2 Unscrew the nuts and remove the end cover (photos).
3 Extract the element (photo).
4 Discard the element, and wipe the casing interior and cover clean.
5 Insert the new element, then refit the end cover and air duct.

22 Air cleaner – removal and refitting

Refer to Section 21 and remove the air cleaner element. Thereafter, the procedure is the same as that described for the airflow sensor in Section 31, paragraph 2 onwards.

23 K-Jetronic system – idle speed and mixture adjustment

1 Run the engine to normal operating temperature.
2 Connect a tachometer to the engine, and check that the idle speed is as given in the Specifications Section.
3 If adjustment is necessary, turn the air adjustment screw on the left-hand side of the by-pass casing.
4 If available, use an exhaust gas analyser to check that the CO

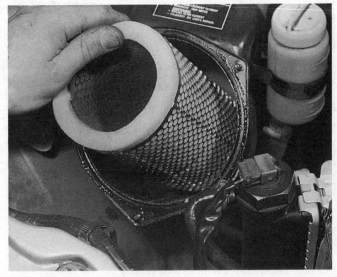

21.2B ... and remove the end cover

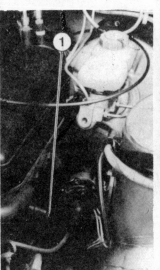
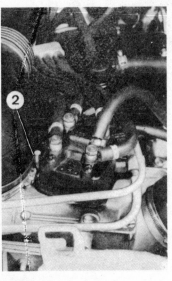

Fig. 3.23 K-Jetronic idle air adustment screw (1) and mixture screw (2) (Sec 23)

21.3 Air cleaner element removal

content is as specified. If necessary, remove the tamperproof plug on the metering/distribution unit, and use an Allen key to adjust the mixture screw. Adjustment is very sensitive, and it is only necessary to turn the mixture screw a few degrees either way. Turn the screw in to richen the mixture, and out to weaken the mixture.

5   After making an adjustment, remove the Allen key, then increase the engine speed several times and reset the idle speed.

6   To adjust the mixture without using an exhaust gas analyser, turn the air adjustment screw to obtain an idle speed 50 rpm above the specified speed. Turn the mixture screw to obtain the maximum engine speed, then re-adjust the air screw to obtain the original speed. Now **unscrew** the mixture screw to obtain the specified idle speed.

7   Remove the tachometer, and if applicable, the exhaust gas analyser.

24 K-Jetronic system – throttle butterfly initial setting

Note: *A vacuum gauge is necessary for this procedure*

ZEJ engines

1   Run the engine to normal operating temperature. The following procedure must be carried out with the cooling fan disengaged (ie after cutting out).

2   Loosen the locknut on the throttle housing, and unscrew the stop screw until clear of the stop.

3   Turn the stop screw until it just contacts the stop, then screw it in a further quarter-turn.

4   Connect a vacuum gauge to the distributor advance take-off point on the throttle housing.

5   With the engine idling, screw in the air adjustment screw (on the left-hand side of the bypass casing) as far as it will go.

6   Adjust the idle speed to between 700 and 750 rpm by turning the stop screw on the throttle housing.

7   Check that the vacuum gauge reads less than 55 mm Hg (2.2 in Hg), then tighten the locknut and apply a dab of paint to it.

8   Remove the vacuum gauge and connect the advance hose.

9   Adjust the idle speed and mixture as described in Section 23.

ZDJ engines

10   Run the engine to normal operating temperature. The following procedure must be carried out with the cooling fan disengaged.

11   Connect a vacuum gauge to the distributor advance take-off point on the throttle housing. With the engine idling, check that the vacuum

gauge reads less then 55 mm Hg (2.2 in Hg). If more, proceed as follows.

12   Remove the butterfly stop screw by screwing it right through the housing. When removed, clean the locking fluid from its threads.

13   Apply fresh locking fluid to the threads, then refit the stop screw and turn it until it just contacts the lever. Screw it in a further 1¼ turns.

14   With the engine idling, check that the vacuum gauge reads less than 55 mm Hg (2.2 in Hg).

15   Remove the vacuum gauge and connect the advance hose.

16   Adjust the idle speed and mixture as described in Section 23.

25 K-Jetronic system components – checking

1   Air leaks in the inlet ducting after the metering/distributor unit will weaken the mixture entering the combustion chambers. Before checking the system components, check the areas arrowed on Fig. 3.24 for possible air leaks.

Sensor plate

2   Using a 0.10 mm (0.004 in) feeler blade, check that the sensor plate is centralised. If necessary, loosen the bolt, reposition the plate, then tighten the bolt. Note that the plate has five punch marks, or the word 'TOP', on its upper face.

3   Check that with the sensor plate at rest, its upper edge is aligned as shown in Fig. 3.26. Bend the spring if necessary.

Mixture regulator

4   Run the fuel pump for ten seconds by switching on the ignition, then switch off.

5   Gently lift the sensor plate, and check that its resistance is even. Release the plate, and check that it returns to its original position.

Cold start injector

6   Disconnect the wiring from the control pressure regulator and additional air device.

7   Remove the cold start injector, then operate the fuel pump by switching on the ignition, and check that the injector is fuel-tight. A maximum of one drop per minute is allowable, otherwise renew the injector.

8   Point the injector into a suitable container then operate the starter (engine cold). The fuel spray angle should be approximately 80°, and the spraying time between six and ten seconds.

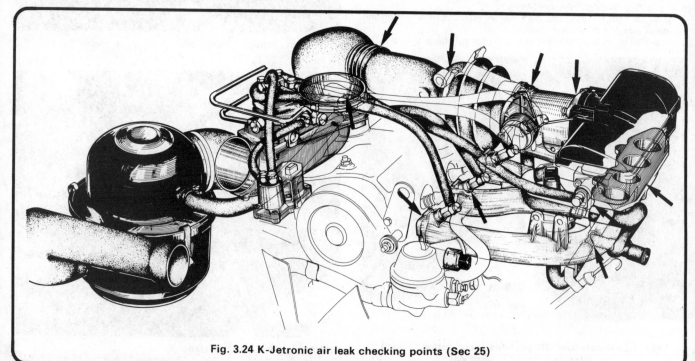

Fig. 3.24 K-Jetronic air leak checking points (Sec 25)

Thermal time switch

9   Remove the thermal switch, immerse the probe end in water, and connect it to a battery and test lamp as shown in Fig. 3.28.

10 With the water temperature below 30°C (86°F) the test lamp should light.

11 Slowly heat the water, and check that the test lamp is extinguished between 30 and 40°C (86 and 104°F).

Additional air device

12 Disconnect the wiring from the control pressure regulator, and disconnect the outlet hose from the additional air device.

13 At an ambient temperature of 20°C (68°F), the hole should be visible in the device valve.

14 Operate the fuel pump by switching on the ignition, and check that the valve closes after approximately five minutes.

Fuel injectors

15 For accurate checking of the fuel injector opening pressures, they should be removed and taken to a Peugeot dealer.

16 The operation of the injectors may be checked by removing them and pointing them into a suitable container with the fuel pipes connected. Operate the fuel pump by switching on the ignition, then lift the sensor plate, and check that the fuel spray angle from each injector is approximately 35°.

26 Fuel filters – renewal

1   Chock the front wheels, then jack up the rear of the car and support on axle stands.

2   Fit hose clamps to the outlet hoses from the fuel tank and main fuel filter.

3   Loosen the clips and disconnect the hoses from the pre-filter. Fit the new pre-filter with the flow arrow pointing away from the fuel tank. Tighten the clips.

4   Unscrew the union bolts and disconnect the inlet and outlet hoses from the main filter. Recover the copper washers.

5   Unscrew the clamp bolt and remove the main filter. Refitting is a reversal of removal, but fit new copper washers, and make sure that the flow arrow points away from the fuel tank.

6   Remove the hose clamps and lower the vehicle to the ground.

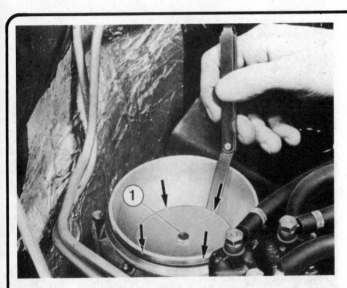

Fig. 3.25 K-Jetronic sensor plate centralisation (Sec 25)

1   Mounting bolt

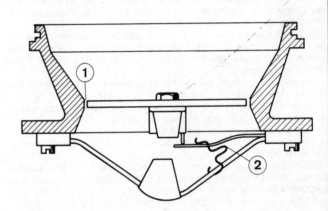

Fig. 3.26 K-Jetronic sensor plate alignment (Sec 25)

1   Lip of cone   2   Spring

Fig. 3.27 Checking the cold start injector on the K-Jetronic system (Sec 25)

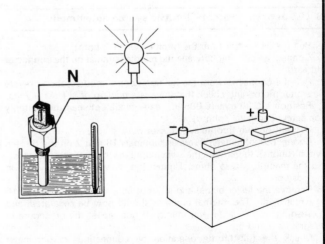

Fig. 3.28 Checking the thermal time switch on the K-Jetronic system (Sec 25)

27 LE2-Jetronic system – idle speed and mixture adjustment

1 Run the engine to normal operating temperature, then run it at 3000 rpm, and wait until the cooling fan has cut in and out twice.
2 Connect a tachometer to the engine, and check that the engine idle speed is as given in the Specifications Section.
3 If adjustment is necessary, turn the air adjustment screw on the bypass hose near the airflow sensor (photo).
4 Adjustment of the idle mixture is only possible using an exhaust gas analyser. The mixture adjustment screw is located in the airflow sensor and may be covered with a tamperproof plug, which must be drilled and prised out.
5 Check that the CO content is as specified. If necessary, insert an Allen key and turn the mixture screw clockwise to richen, and anti-clockwise to weaken (photo).
6 After making an adjustment, remove the Allen key, then increase the engine speed several times and finally reset the idle speed.
7 Remove the tachometer and exhaust gas analyser.

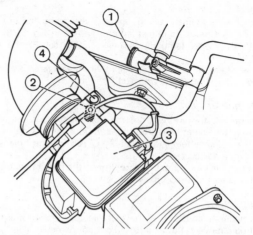

Fig. 3.29 LE2-Jetronic idle speed and mixture adjustment screws (Sec 27)

1 Air adjustment screw (idle speed)	3 Airflow sensor
2 Mixture adjustment screw	4 Tamperproof plug

28 LE2-Jetronic system – throttle butterfly initial setting

Note: A vacuum gauge is necessary for this procedure.

1 Run the engine to normal operating temperature. The following procedure must be carried out with the cooling fan disengaged (ie after cutting out).
2 Connect the vacuum gauge to the distributor advance take-off point on the throttle housing. With the engine idling, check that the vacuum gauge reads less than 75 mm Hg (3.0 in Hg). If it is more, proceed as follows.
3 Remove the butterfly stop screw by screwing it right through the housing. When removed, clean the locking fluid from its threads.
4 Apply fresh locking fluid to the threads, then refit the stop screw, and turn it until it just starts to open the throttle.
5 Turn the air adjustment screw fully in.
6 Using an Allen key, turn the mixture screw in from its normal position by six full turns.
7 Start the engine, and adjust the mixture screw until the idle speed is 600 rpm. With an exhaust gas analyser, check that the CO reading is as specified. Adjust the screw if necessary.
8 Check that vacuum reading is less than 75 mm Hg (3.0 in Hg). If not, adjust the butterfly stop screw as necessary.
9 Remove the vacuum gauge and connect the advance hose. Remove the exhaust gas analyser and tachometer.
10 Adjust the throttle switch (Section 29).
11 Adjust the idle speed and mixture (Section 27).

27.3 Adjusting the idle speed with the air adjustment screw (arrowed)

29 LE2-Jetronic system – throttle switch adjustment

1 Pull the connector from the throttle switch (photo).
2 Connect a voltmeter between the middle terminal on the connector and earth.
3 Pull the connector from the ignition control module, then operate the starter motor, and check that there is a reading of at least 9 volts.
4 Position a 0.20 mm (0.008 in) feeler blade between the butterfly stop screw and lever (photo).
5 Loosen the two throttle switch screws.
6 Connect an ohmmeter between terminals 18 and 2 on the throttle switch (photo), then rotate the switch until the internal contacts close, and the reading is zero ohms. Tighten the screws with the switch in this position.
7 Remove the feeler blade, and insert in its place a 0.40 mm (0.016 in) feeler blade. The internal contacts should now be separated, and the reading on the ohmmeter infinity. If not, repeat the procedure in paragraphs 5 and 6.
8 Check the full-throttle operation by connecting an ohmmeter between terminals 18 and 3. The reading should change from infinity to zero when the throttle lever is 4.0 mm (0.16 in) from the fully-open stop (photo).
9 If the switch does not operate correctly, it should be renewed.

27.5 Adjusting the mixture screw

29.1 Pulling the connector from the throttle switch

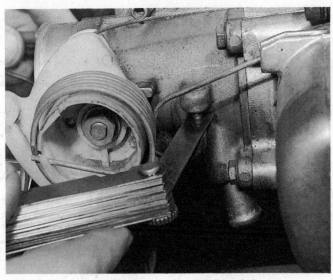

29.4 Feeler blade position for adjusting throttle switch

29.6 Using an ohmmeter to adjust the throttle switch

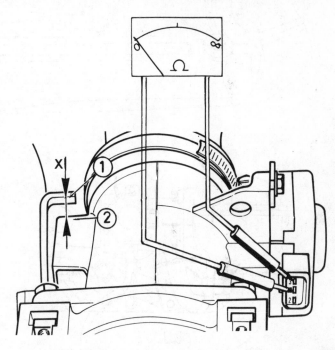

Fig. 3.30 Checking the full-throttle operation of the throttle switch on the LE2-Jetronic system (Sec 29)

1   Throttle lever   X   = 4.0 mm
2   Fully-open stop   (0.16 in)

30 LE2-Jetronic system components – checking

1   Air leaks in the inlet ducting and hoses will weaken the mixture entering the combustion chambers. Before checking the system components, examine the air ducting and hoses for condition and security, with reference to Fig. 3.31.

Airflow sensor

2   Pull the connector from the airflow sensor (photo), and connect a voltmeter between wire 18A and earth.
3   Disconnect the ignition control unit, then operate the starter motor, and check that a minimum of 9 volts is obtained.

29.8 Throttle lever (A) and fully-open stop (B)

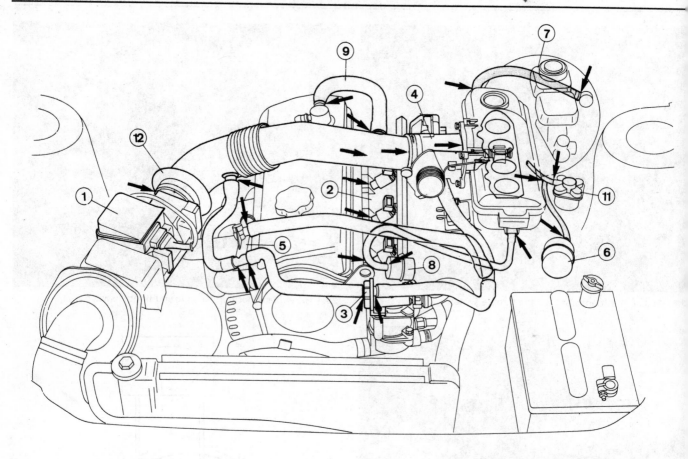

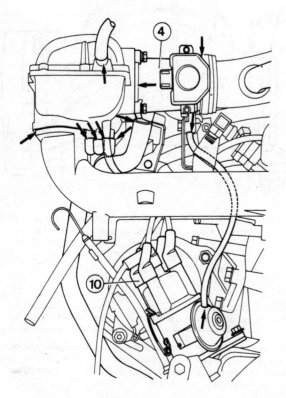

Fig. 3.31 LE2-Jetronic air leak checking points – LHD shown, RHD similar (Sec 30)

1 Airflow sensor
2 Cylinder head
3 Supplementary air device
4 Throttle housing
5 Idle speed adjustment
    housing
6 Vacuum reservoir for heater
    controls

7   Brake servo
8   Fuel pressure regulator
9   Crankcase ventilation hose
10 Distributor
11 Econoscope vacuum
     pick-up
12 Air intake pipe

4 Disconnect the battery negative lead.

5 Connect an ohmmeter between wire M18 and earth, and check that the reading is less than 1 ohm.

6 Remove the air cleaner element (Section 21).

7 Using a screwdriver, open and close the sensor flap to check its action, which should be smooth and easy. Clean the interior of the sensor if necessary.

8 Connect an ohmmeter between terminals 5 and 8 on the airflow sensor, and check that a reading of 340 to 450 ohms is obtained.

9 Connect the ohmmeter between terminals 9 and 8, and check that the reading is now between 160 and 300 ohms.

10 Connect the ohmmeter between terminals 5 and 7, then move the flap with a screwdriver. The resistance should vary between 60 and 1000 ohms.

Engine temperature sensor

11 Disconnect the wiring plug from the engine temperature sensor (photo), and connect the ohmmeter between wire M49 and earth. The reading should be less than 1 ohm.

12 Connect the ohmmeter across the two terminals of the sensor. If the reading is infinity, renew the sensor.

Supplementary air device

13 Connect a voltmeter between wire 48 on the supplementary air device wiring plug and earth (photo).

14 Disconnect the ignition control unit, then operate the starter motor, and check that the reading is at least 9 volts.

15 With the battery disconnected, connect an ohmmeter between wire M34 on the connector and earth. The reading should be less than 1 ohm.

16 Disconnect both hoses from the device, and check that, at an ambient temperature of 20°C (68°F), the opening in the diaphragm is visible through the end of the unit (photo).

17 Connect an ohmmeter across the terminals of the unit, and check that a reading of 35 to 45 ohms is obtained at an ambient temperature of 20°C (68°F).

18 Connect a 12 volt supply to the terminals of the unit. After five minutes, the diaphragm must be completely shut.

31 LE2-Jetronic system – airflow sensor removal and refitting

1 Remove the air cleaner element (Section 21).

2 Disconnect the inlet air ducting.

3 Disconnect the wiring plug.

4 Unbolt the power-assisted steering reservoir, and support to one side (photo).

5 Unscrew the mounting nut and lift the assembly from the rubber mounting(s) (photos).

6 Flatten the locktabs and unbolt the air cleaner from the airflow sensor (photo).

7 Refitting is a reversal of removal. After tightening the air cleaner bolts, lock them by bending the locktabs onto the bolt heads.

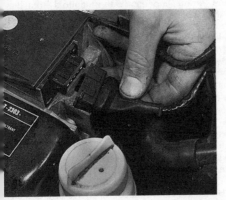

30.2 Pulling the connector from the airflow sensor

30.11 Engine temperature sensor location (arrowed)

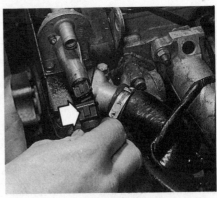

30.13 Supplementary air device wiring plug (arrowed)

30.16 Diaphragm opening (arrowed) visible through the supplementary air device

31.4 Unbolting the power-assisted steering reservoir from the airflow sensor

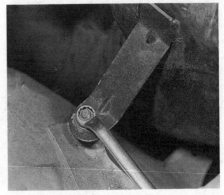

31.5A Air cleaner mounting nut ...

31.5B ... and rubber mounting

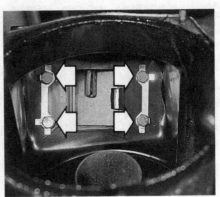

31.6 Air cleaner-to-airflow sensor bolts (arrowed)

32 LE2-Jetronic system – fuel injector removal and refitting

1   Disconnect the air inlet ducting from the throttle housing. If necessary, also disconnect the ducting above the engine rocker cover and from the crankcase ventilation port (photos).
2   Unscrew the union nut holding the fuel supply hose to the distribution pipe (photo).
3   Disconnect the hoses from the fuel pressure regulator (photos).
4   Disconnect the wiring plugs from the injectors (photo).
5   Unbolt the distribution pipe from the inlet manifold (photo).
6   The distribution pipe may now be removed together with the injectors, or the clips can be removed and the pipe and injectors removed separately (photos).
7   Remove the injector seals, and fit new ones.
8   Refitting is a reversal of removal, but smear a little petroleum jelly on the seals to assist reassembly.

33 Fuel pump – removal and refitting

1   Chock the front wheels, then jack up the rear of the car and support on axle stands.
2   Fit hose clamps to the pump inlet and outlet hoses (photo).
3   Where necessary, remove the main fuel filter, with reference to Section 26.
4   Disconnect the wiring.
5   Disconnect the inlet and outlet hoses.
6   Unscrew the mounting nuts and remove the fuel pump.
7   Refitting is a reversal of removal.

34 Fuel level transmitter – removal and refitting

Refer to Section 6.

35 Fuel tank – removal, repair and refitting

Refer to Section 7.

36 Accelerator cable – removal and refitting

The procedure is similar to that described in Section 17, but the adjustment ferrule is located on the inlet air box (photos).

37 Manifolds and exhaust system – general

1   The inlet manifold is located on the left-hand side of the cylinder head (photo). To remove it, disconnect the air inlet ducting and accelerator cable, then remove the injectors and fuel distribution pipe (Sections 32 and 36). Drain the cooling system (Chapter 2). Disconnect all hoses and wiring, and unbolt the manifold from the cylinder head. Remove the gaskets. Refitting is a reversal of removal, but fit new gaskets.
2   The exhaust manifold is located on the right-hand side of the cylinder head (photo). To remove it, remove the air cleaner and airflow sensor. Unscrew the downpipe-to-manifold nuts. Unbolt the hot air shroud, then unbolt the exhaust manifold from the cylinder head. Remove the gasket. Refitting is a reversal of removal, but fit new manifold and downpipe gaskets.
3   The exhaust system is in four sections: the downpipe, front silencer, intermediate pipe, and rear pipe and silencers (photos). It is suspended on flexible straps. To remove the complete system, all four sections should first be separated. Connect the sections loosely together initially when fitting, and fit a new gasket between the downpipe and exhaust manifold. Tighten all connections and mountings securely to complete.
4   Holts Flexiwrap and Holts Gun Gum exhaust repair systems can be used for effective repairs to exhaust pipes and silencer boxes, including ends and bends. Holts Flexiwrap is an MOT-approved permanent exhaust repair.

32.1A Disconnecting the air inlet ducting from the throttle housing

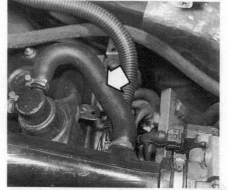
32.1B Crankcase ventilation hose (arrowed)

32.1C Air ducting connection above rocker cover

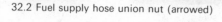
32.2 Fuel supply hose union nut (arrowed)

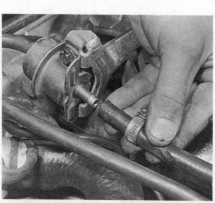
32.3A Disconnecting the fuel return hose from the fuel pressure regulator

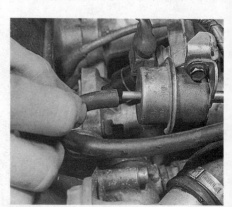
32.3B Disconnecting the vacuum hose from the fuel pressure regulator

32.4 Injector wiring plug removal

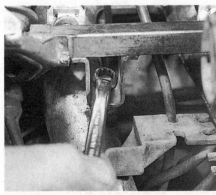

32.5 Unbolting the distribution pipe

32.6A Injector connection to distribution pipe (arrowed)

32.6B Remove the clips ...

32.6C ... and pull off the distribution pipe

32.6D Injector removed separately

32.6E Distribution pipe removal together with injectors

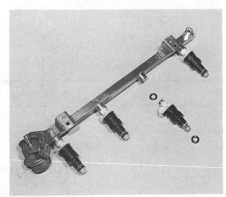

32.6F Distribution pipe, injectors, and seals

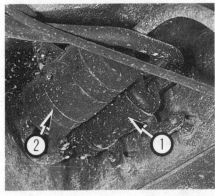

33.2 Fuel pump (1) and main filter (2)

36.1A Accelerator cable adjustment ferrule (arrowed)

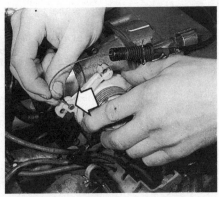

36.1B Disconnecting the accelerator inner cable (arrowed)

37.1 Inlet manifold and air box

37.2 Exhaust manifold and hot air shroud

37.3A Exhaust system front mounting ...

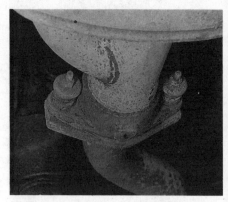

37.3B ... downpipe-to-front silencer connection ...

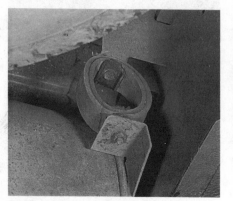

37.3C ... front intermediate silencer mounting ...

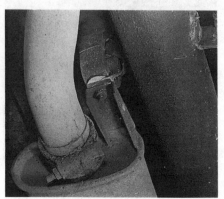

37.3D ... rear intermediate silencer mounting and connection ...

37.3E ... and intermediate pipe-to-rear pipe connection

PART D: FAULT DIAGNOSIS

38 Fault diagnosis – fuel and exhaust systems

Symptom	Reason(s)
Difficult starting from cold	Choke faulty (carburettor) Fuel pump fault Blocked fuel line or filter Supplementary air device faulty (fuel injection) Cold start injector faulty (fuel injection) Temperature sensor faulty (fuel injection)
Difficult starting when hot	Choked air cleaner element Fuel pump fault Choke sticking on (carburettor)
Excessive fuel consumption	Mixture too rich Excessive fuel pressure (fuel injection) Temperature sensor faulty (fuel injection) Metering unit or airflow sensor faulty (fuel injection)
Uneven idling	Mixture setting incorrect Air leak in intake system Throttle switch out of adjustment (fuel injection) Loose electronic control unit connector (fuel injection)

Chapter 4 Ignition system

Contents

Specifications

Type .... Conventional (contact breaker), or transistorised

Distributor
Rotor rotation .... Clockwise
Firing order .... 1-3-4-2 (No 1 at flywheel end)
Contact breaker points gap (conventional) .... 0.40 mm (0.016 in)
Dwell angle (conventional) .... 57 ± 2°
Dwell percentage (conventional) .... 63 ± 2%
Pick-up coil resistance (transistorised):
    Magneti-Marelli .... 815 ± 55 ohms
    Bosch (pre-January 1986) .... 1100 ± 110 ohms
    Bosch (January 1986 on) .... 320 ± 30 ohms
    Ducellier (pre-January 1986) .... 1100 ± 110 ohms
    Ducellier (January 1986 on) .... 190 ± 30 ohms

Ignition timing (vacuum hose disconnected)
XM7A engine .... 10° BTDC at idle
XN1 engine:
    Single choke carburettor .... 10° BTDC at idle
    Twin choke carburettor .... 8° BTDC at idle
XN1A engine .... 10° BTDC at idle
ZEJ engine .... 8° BTDC at idle
ZDJ engine .... 10° BTDC at idle

Spark plugs
Type:
    XM7A and XN1/A engines .... Champion N9YCC or N9YC
    ZEJ and ZDJ engines .... Champion S7YCC or S7YC
Electrode gap:
    N9YCC and S7YCC plugs .... 0.8 mm (0.032 in)
    S9YC and S7YC plugs .... 0.6 mm (0.024 in)

HT leads
ZEJ (1979 to 1983) .... Champion CLS 2, boxed set
ZDJ (1983 to 1990) .... Champion CLS 7, boxed set

Ignition coil

	Conventional	Transistorised
Primary resistance	3.1 ohms	0.7 ohms
Secondary resistance	6000 ohms	3850 ohms

Torque wrench settings

	Nm	lbf ft
Spark plug – with sealing washer	22	16
Spark plug – taper-seat	15 to 20	11 to 15

1 General description

The ignition system is of either conventional (contact breaker) type or transistorised type, employing an ignition coil and distributor.

In order that the engine may run correctly, it is necessary for an electrical spark to ignite the fuel/air mixture in the combustion chamber at exactly the right moment in relation to engine speed and load.

Basically, the ignition system functions as follows. Low tension voltage from the battery is fed to the ignition coil, where it is converted into high tension voltage. The high tension voltage is powerful enough to jump the spark plug gap in the cylinder many times a second under high compression pressure, providing that the ignition system is in good working order.

The ignition system consists of two individual circuits, known as the low tension (LT) circuit and high tension (HT) circuit.

The low tension circuit (sometimes known as the primary circuit) comprises the ignition switch, primary ignition coil windings, and the contact breaker or control module. The high tension circuit (sometimes known as the secondary circuit) comprises the secondary ignition coil windings, distributor cap, rotor arm, spark plugs and HT leads.

The primary circuit is initially switched on by the contact breaker or control module, and a magnetic field is formed within the ignition coil. At the precise point of ignition, the primary circuit is switched off, and high tension voltage is then induced in the secondary circuit and fed to the spark plug via the distributor cap and rotor arm.

The ignition is advanced and retarded automatically by centrifugal weights and a vacuum capsule, to ensure that the spark occurs at the correct instant in relation to engine speed and load.

Note: *When working on the transistorised ignition system, remember that the high tension voltage can be considerably higher than on the conventional system, and in certain circumstances could prove fatal.*

2 Routine maintenance

Carry out the following procedures at the intervals given in Routine maintenance *at the front of this manual.*

Renew the spark plugs
1 Remove the old spark plugs and fit new ones with reference to Section 15.

Check the ignition timing
2 Check and if necessary adjust the ignition timing, as described in Section 11.

Clean and adjust the contact breaker points
3 Remove, clean and refit the contact breaker points as described in Sections 3 to 6, as appropriate.
4 Always check the ignition timing after cleaning the contact breaker points.

3 Contact breaker points (standard) – adjustment

1 Release the two clips and lift away the distributor cap. Clean the inside and outside of the cap with a dry cloth and, if the four segments are slightly burned, scrape the deposit away with a screwdriver. Should the segments be badly burned, the cap must be renewed.
2 Check that the carbon brush is free to move in the cap, and that it protrudes by at least 6 mm (0.25 in).
3 Prise the contact breaker points apart and examine the two faces. If they are rough, pitted, or dirty they must be removed for resurfacing or renewal as described in Section 4. Note that the contour of the fixed contact must be retained for the system to operate successfully.

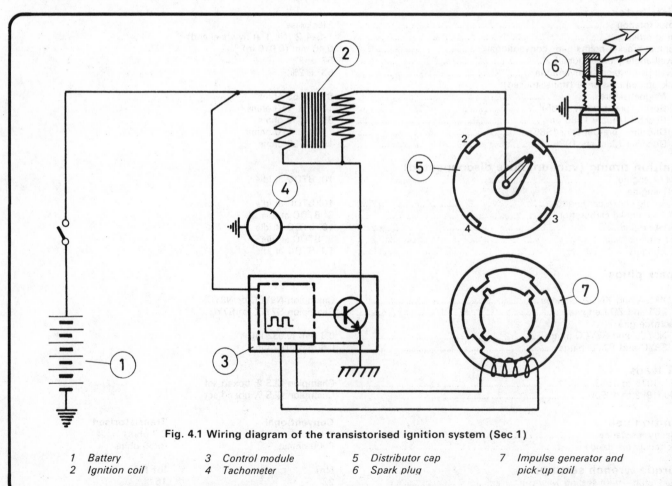

Fig. 4.1 Wiring diagram of the transistorised ignition system (Sec 1)

1 *Battery*	3 *Control module*	5 *Distributor cap*	7 *Impulse generator and*
2 *Ignition coil*	4 *Tachometer*	6 *Spark plug*	*pick-up coil*

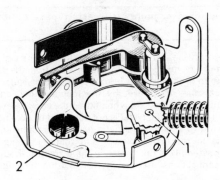

Fig. 4.2 Contact breaker points assembly – standard type (Sec 3)

1   Adjuster for vacuum control   2   Fixed contact locking screw

4   To adjust the contact breaker points accurately, a dwell meter will be required, but to obtain an initial setting, first rotate the engine until the heel of the contact breaker arm is on the peak of one of the four cam lobes.

5   Loosen the fixed contact locking screw, and position the fixed contact so that a feeler gauge of the specified size just fits between the two points. Tighten the locking screw and recheck the adjustment.

6   Connect a dwell meter and tachometer to the engine, then run the engine at 2000 rpm (vacuum pipe disconnected). The dwell angle must be as specified. If this is not the case, stop the engine and reduce the points gap to increase the dwell angle, and *vice-versa*. Note that a hole is provided in the baseplate for fitting an eccentric contact point adjuster, but this tool is not an essential requirement.

7   The operation of the vacuum advance unit alters the ignition timing by repositioning the moving contact point. This action produces a variation of the dwell angle, which will cause uneven timing unless set correctly. If the serrated cam or eccentric adjuster on the distributor baseplate have been disturbed, they must be readjusted by a suitably-equipped garage. To make a quick check on the adjustment, move the vacuum control rod through its entire stroke, and make sure that the moving contact operates over the central portion of the fixed contact.

8   After adjusting the contact breaker points, refit the distributor cap.

4   Contact breaker points (standard type) – removal and refitting

1   If the contact breaker points are burned, pitted or badly worn, they should be removed and either replaced or their faces must be filed smooth.

2   To remove the points, first detach the distributor cap and rotor arm.

3   Unscrew and lift away the fixed plate locking screw and washer, taking care not to drop them into the body of the distributor.

4   Unclip and lift away the hairpin shaped clip.

5   Slacken the LT cables securing nuts, but do not completely remove them. Slide the contact breaker points cable terminal connector up from the terminal. Note it is located between the terminal bolt head and the insulator.

6   Lift off the moving point pivot washer, and then very carefully remove the points assembly. Make a note of the location of the insulation washers.

7   Refitting the contact breaker points is the reverse sequence to removal. Reset the points gap as described in Section 3.

5   Contact breaker points (cassette type) – adjustment

1   The condition of the contact breaker points within the cassette can be determined by measuring the voltage drop across them with the gap closed. If the voltage reading obtained exceeds 0.2 volts, then suspect a fault. Apart from points in bad condition, faults may include the low tension wire between the HT coil and distributor being defective, a defective earth between the distributor body and the engine, or an internal fault in the distributor.

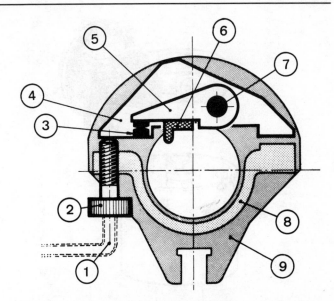

Fig. 4.3 Contact breaker points assembly – cassette type (Sec 5)

1 Allen key	*6 Heel or cam follower*
2 Adjusting screw	*7 Arm and support pivot pin*
3 Contact points	*8 Metal quadrant*
4 Fixed contact	*9 Contact breaker plate*
5 Contact breaker arm	

2   There are two methods of checking and adjusting the gap between the contact breaker points. The most accurate method is by using a dwellmeter to determine the dwell angle, which is the angle through which the distributor cam turns between the instance of closure and opening of the contact breaker points during one ignition cycle. A reduction of the points gap will increase the dwell angle, and *vice-versa*.

3   With the dwellmeter attached to the ignition system in accordance with the equipment manufacturer's instructions, measure the dwell angle. This angle must be as specified. If the correct type of meter is available, then measure the dwell percentage, which must also be as specified. If necessary, use a 3 mm Allen key on the special adjusting screw with the engine idling. Turn the key clockwise to increase dwell, or anti-clockwise to decrease dwell.

4   The second method of adjustment requires the manufacture of a special tool, that is a length of metal bar with a diameter of 17.0 mm (0.67 in). Insert this tool into the centre of the cassette in place of the drive spindle, and then adjust the points gap to 0.40 mm (0.016 in) by using a feeler gauge.

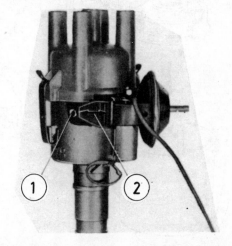

Fig. 4.4 Access to cassette points adjustment (Sec 5)

1   Adjustment aperture   2   Sliding cover

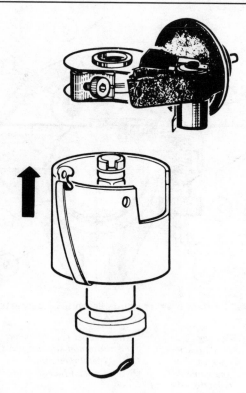

6 Contact breaker points (cassette type) – removal and refitting

1   The contact breaker points form an integral part of the cassette. Figs. 4.5 and 4.6 show removal of the cassette from the distributor, and disconnection of the cassette from the vacuum capsule.

2   New cassettes are preset by the manufacturer, and require no further adjustment. Take care when fitting the cassette over the cam, to make sure that the contact heel is not damaged by coming into contact with the apex of a cam. When refitting the rotor arm, ensure that it is fully home in the drive spindle, and that the complete cassette/condenser assembly is fully home in the distributor body. Recheck all electrical connections after assembly. Reset the initial ignition timing.

Fig. 4.5 Withdrawing the cassette from the distributor body (Sec 6)

Fig. 4.6 Disconnecting the cassette wiring (Sec 6)

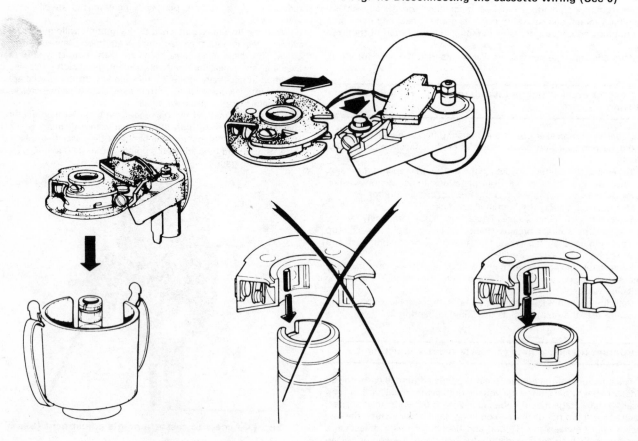

Fig. 4.7 Refitting the cassette on the SEV-Marchal distributor (Sec 6)

7 Condenser – removal, testing and refitting

1 The purpose of the condenser (sometimes known as a capacitor) is to ensure that when the contact breaker points open there is no sparking across them, which would waste voltage and cause wear.
2 The condenser is fitted in parallel with the contact breaker points. If it develops a short circuit, it will cause ignition failure, as the points will be prevented from interrupting the low tension circuit.
3 If the engine becomes very difficult to start, or begins to misfire after several miles running, and the breaker points show signs of excessive burning, then the condition of the condenser must be suspect. A further test can be made by separating the points manually (using an insulated screwdriver) with the ignition switched on. If this is accompanied by a flash, it is indicative that the condenser has failed.
4 Without special test equipment, the only sure way to diagnose condenser trouble is to replace a suspected unit with a new one, and noting if there is any improvement.
5 To remove the condenser from the distributor, first detach the condenser lead from the LT terminal post on the side of the distributor body.
6 Undo and remove the one securing screw, spring and shakeproof washer, noting the locations of the washers. Lift away the condenser.
7 Refitting of the condenser is simply a reversal of the removal procedure.

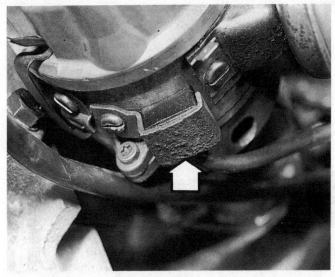
8.3 Distributor wiring clamp (arrowed)

8 Distributor – removal and refitting

1 On fuel injection models, remove the battery to provide additional working room.
2 Disconnect the HT leads from the plugs and coil.
3 Disconnect the wiring from the distributor. On some models, the wiring plug is secured by a metal clamp retained by a screw (photo).
4 Disconnect the vacuum advance pipe (photo).
5 Mark the distributor body and mounting in relation to each other to ensure the correct ignition timing on refitment.
6 Unscrew the pinch-bolt (carburettor engine) or mounting nuts (fuel injection engine), and withdraw the distributor from the cylinder block (photos).
7 Check the condition of the O-ring seal on the base of the distributor, and renew it if necessary.
8 Refitting is a reversal of removal, but remove the distributor cap and turn the rotor arm as required to align the driving dog with the offset slot in the drivegear. If the old distributor is being refitted, align the previously-made marks before tightening the pinch-bolt or mounting nuts. If a new distributor is being fitted, transfer the mark from the old unit for an approximate setting.
9 Finally adjust the ignition timing as described in Section 11.

8.4 Disconnecting the vacuum advance pipe

Fig. 4.8 O-ring seal (1) on the base of the distributor fitted to fuel injection engines (Sec 8)

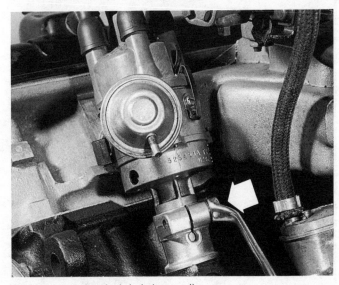
8.6A Unscrew the pinch-bolt (arrowed) ...

8.6B ... and withdraw the distributor

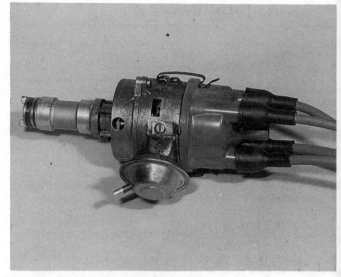

8.6C The complete distributor (Ducellier type)

9 Distributor – dismantling and reassembly

Note: *This Section describes the dismantling and reassembly procedures for a distributor fitted to a 1971 cc carburettor engine. Exploded views of other distributors are shown in Figs. 4.10 and 4.11, and the procedures for these are similar*

1   Release the clips and remove the distributor cap.
2   Remove the carbon brush from inside the cap (photo).
3   Pull off the rotor arm and remove the plastic cover (photos).

4   Mark the upper and lower housings in relation to each other. Unscrew the cross-head screws and separate the housings (photos).
5   Invert the upper housing and mark the plastic ring in relation to the housing. Prise out the ring (photo).
6   Remove the pick-up coil (photo).
7   Using circlip pliers, extract the circlip (photo).
8   Remove the washer. Note where the vacuum advance capsule arm is fitted, then remove the stator. The stator should be marked on its underside at the hole where the arm fits (photos).
9   Remove the screws and withdraw the vacuum advance capsule from the upper housing (photos).

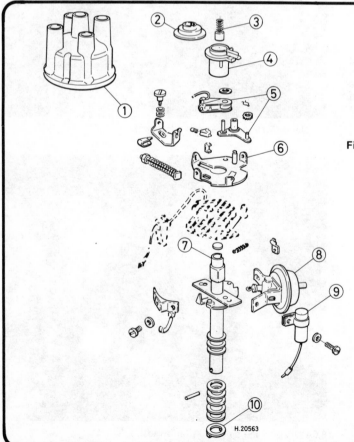
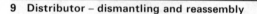

Fig. 4.9 Exploded view of the conventional Ducellier distributor (Sec 9)

1   Distributor cap
2   Cover
3   Carbon brush
4   Rotor arm
5   Contact breaker points
6   Baseplate
7   Cam and driveshaft
8   Vacuum advance capsule
9   Condenser
10 Drive dog

H.20563

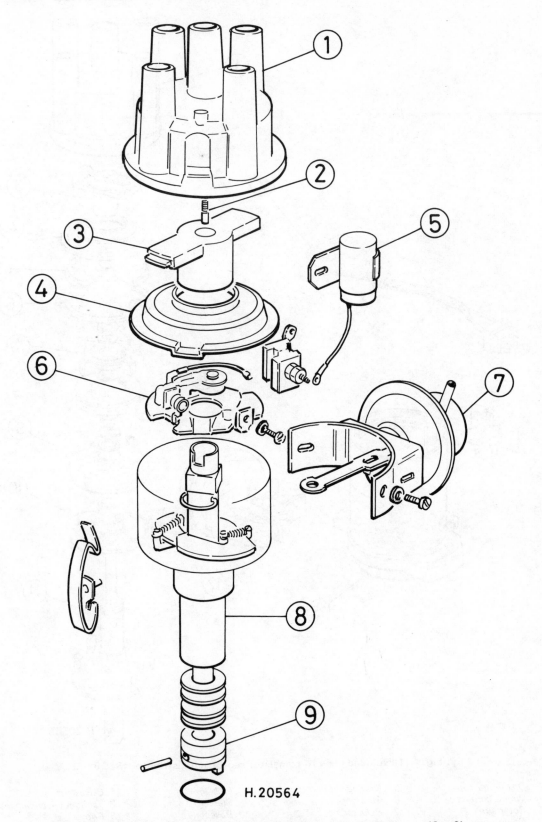

H.20564

Fig. 4.10 Exploded view of conventional Paris-Rhône distributor (Sec 9)

1 Distributor cap
2 Carbon brush
3 Rotor arm

4 Cover
5 Condenser

6 Baseplate and contact
   points

7 Vacuum advance capsule
8 Body
9 Drive dog

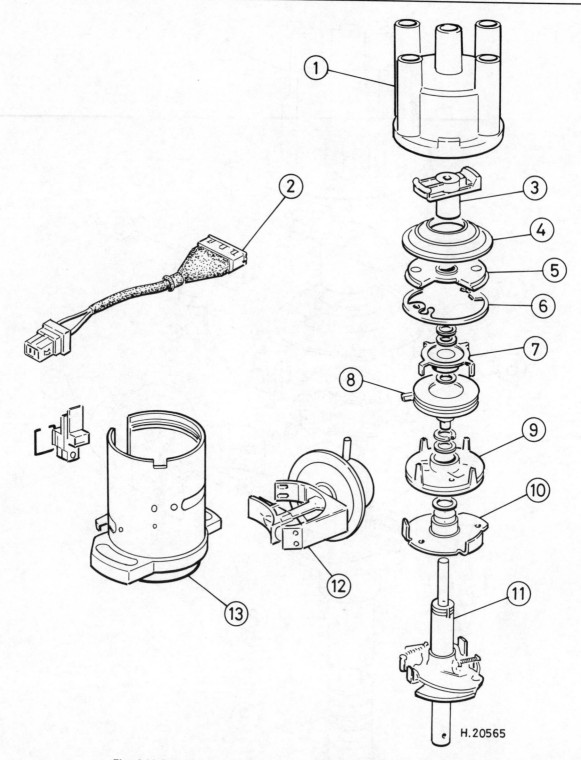

Fig. 4.11 Exploded view of transistorised Bosch distributor (Sec 9)

H.20565

1	Distributor cap	5	Bearing support	8	Pick-up coil	11	Driveshaft
2	Wiring harness	6	Stop ring	9	Stator	12	Vacuum advance capsule
3	Rotor arm	7	Reluctor	10	Baseplate	13	Body
4	Cover						

10 Working on the lower housing, mark the reluctor in relation to the centrifugal weight base.

11 Extract the circlip, disconnect the centrifugal weight springs, and remove the reluctor from the shaft (photos).

12 The centrifugal weights cannot be removed from the lower housing (photo). Lightly oil the pivots, and apply two or three drops of oil beneath them to lubricate the shaft bearing.

13 Reassembly is a reversal of dismantling. When refitting the carbon brush in the distributor cap, check that it moves freely and protrudes by at least 6 mm (0.25 in).

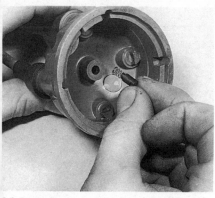

9.2 Removing the carbon brush from the distributor cap

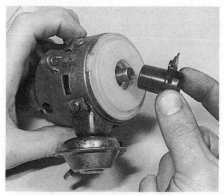

9.3A Removing the rotor arm ...

9.3B ... and plastic cover

9.4A Remove the screws ...

9.4B ... and separate the housings (Ducellier type)

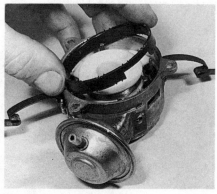

9.5 Removing the plastic ring

9.6 Pick-up coil removal

9.7 Extract the circlip ...

9.8A ... remove the washer ...

9.8B ... and lift off the stator

9.8C Mark (arrowed) indicates vacuum capsule arm location

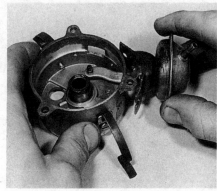

9.9A Vacuum advance capsule removal

9.9B The dismantled upper housing

9.11A Extract the circlip (arrowed) ...

9.11B ... disconnect the springs (arrowed) ...

9.11C ... and remove the reluctor

9.12 Centrifugal weights in the lower housing

10 Ignition module – removal and refitting

1   Slide the plastic cover off the ignition coil and module (photo).
2   Disconnect the battery negative lead.
3   Disconnect the wiring plug from the module (photo).
4   Unbolt the module from the alloy plate.
5   Refitting is a reversal of removal, but to ensure adequate cooling, clean the alloy plate and apply a little heat-conductive grease to the base of the module.

10.1 Sliding the plastic cover from the ignition coil and module

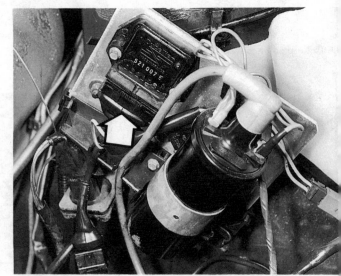

10.3 Wiring plug (arrowed) on the ignition module

11 Ignition timing – checking and adjustment

Note: *The ignition timing may be checked and adjusted using the engine diagnostic socket, but the special Peugeot instrument necessary will not normally be available to the home mechanic*

Initial setting (for starting engine after reassembly)

1 Remove the spark plug from No 1 cylinder (flywheel end of engine).
2 Disconnect the battery negative lead.
3 Turn the engine in its normal direction of rotation using a spanner on the crankshaft pulley bolt, and stop when air is forced out of No 1 cylinder through the spark plug hole.
4 Slowly turn the engine in the same direction until the ignition timing mark on the crankshaft pulley is aligned with the timing mark on the timing plate (photo). Note that there are two timing marks on the pulley, at 180° from each other, but only the mark identified by white paint must be used for timing No 1 cylinder. The other mark is used by the factory when setting the timing plate.
5 Remove the distributor cap, and check that the rotor arm is pointing to the No 1 HT lead segment position. If not, reposition the distributor body.
6 On conventional ignition models, check that the contact breaker points are just separating. To do this, connect a 12 volt test lamp between the coil-to-distributor wire and earth. Temporarily reconnect the battery and switch on the ignition, then move the distributor body until the test lamp just lights, indicating that the contact points have separated. Tighten the mounting bolt or nuts.
7 On transistorised ignition models, check that the reluctor and stator arms are in line with each other. Where the reluctor is completely enclosed, this will not be possible, but the rotor arm should be pointing towards the mark etched on the rim of the distributor body.
8 Refit the distributor cap and No 1 spark plug, then reconnect the battery negative lead.

Final setting

9 Run the engine to normal operating temperature and allow it to idle.
10 Disconnect the vacuum pipe from the vacuum capsule on the distributor and plug it.
11 With the engine stopped, connect a stroboscopic timing light to No 1 HT lead (flywheel end of the engine) in accordance with the equipment maker's instructions.
12 Check that all leads are clear of moving parts, then start the engine.
13 With the engine idling, point the timing light at the timing marks on the front of the engine and crankshaft pulley. The marks will appear stationary and, if the timing is correct, in alignment. The correct ignition timing is usually indicated on one of the HT leads (photo).
14 If the marks are not aligned, loosen the distributor pinch-bolt or mounting nuts, and move the distributor body slightly to bring them in line. Tighten the bolt or nuts, and recheck.
15 The centrifugal weight advance mechanism may be checked by increasing the engine speed, and noting that the timing mark on the crankshaft pulley moves in an anti-clockwise direction. On the ZDJ engine fitted with LE2-Jetronic injection, an additional mark is provided on the timing plate showing the correct timing at 4000 rpm (24° BTDC).
16 When adjustment is complete, switch off the engine, remove the timing light and reconnect the vacuum pipe.

12 Timing plate (fuel injection engines) – setting

1 The timing plate is located on the front of the timing cover and is set during production. If the plate has been moved or the timing cover renewed, carry out the following procedure.
2 Remove the crankcase plug next to the distributor.
3 Switch off the ignition.
4 Using a spanner on the crankshaft pulley bolt, turn the engine in its normal direction of rotation until the timing mark on the camshaft gear just enters the aperture in the timing cover.
5 If available, insert the special Peugeot tool 80133 in the crankcase plug hole, then slowly turn the crankshaft until the tool is felt to drop into the cut-out in the counterbalance weight of the crankshaft. If the

11.4 Ignition timing marks

11.13 Ignition timing indicated on one of the HT leads

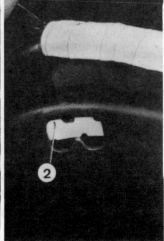
Fig. 4.12 Setting the timing plate (Sec 12)

1 Crankcase plug
2 TDC timing mark on camshaft gear

special tool is not available, use an 8.0 mm (0.31 in) diameter, 100 mm (3.9 in) long, rod instead.
6   Loosen the timing plate nuts, and align the 0° (TDC) mark with the mark on the pulley.
7   Tighten the nuts, and apply a dab of paint on them to safeguard the setting.
8   Remove the special tool, and refit the crankcase plug.

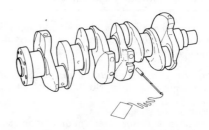

Fig. 4.13 Method of using the special timing tool (Sec 12)

13 Ignition coil – removal, testing and refitting

1   Slide the plastic cover off the ignition coil and module.
2   Disconnect the low tension wiring, noting its location.
3   Disconnect the high tension (HT) lead from the coil tower (photo).
4   Unbolt the coil from the mounting plate.
5   Using an ohmmeter, check the resistance of the primary and secondary windings. Connect the ohmmeter between the low tension terminals to check the primary windings, and between the 15(+) terminal and the HT terminal to check the secondary windings. Refer to the Specifications Section for the values.
6   Refitting is a reversal of removal.

14 TDC sensor – removal and refitting

1   The TDC sensor is for use with the diagnostic socket, and is located on the front cover of the gearbox or automatic transmission. As a special instrument and adaptor are required to make use of it, it will normally be used only by a Peugeot garage.
2   To remove the sensor, unscrew the mounting screw.
3   The sensor forms part of the diagnostic socket assembly so, if it is to be completely removed, the socket must be unclipped from its bracket, and the remaining wiring and earth leads disconnected.
4   Refitting is a reversal of removal, but the adjustment procedure for new and used sensors differs. New sensors have three extensions on the inner face, and the unit should be inserted through the mounting until the extensions just touch the flywheel. The clamp screw is then tightened, and clearance is provided as the flywheel rotates and wears the ends of the extensions. This method should not be used when refitting a used sensor. In this case, cut off the extensions completely, then insert the sensor until it touches the flywheel, move it out 1.7 mm (0.07 in), and clamp it in this position.

15 Spark plugs, HT leads and distributor cap – general

1   The correct functioning of the spark plugs is vital for the correct running and efficiency of the engine. It is essential that the plugs fitted are appropriate for the engine, and the suitable type is specified at the beginning of this chapter. If this type is used and the engine is in good condition, the spark plugs should not need attention between scheduled replacement intervals. Spark plug cleaning is rarely necessary and should not be attempted unless specialised equipment is available as damage can easily be caused to the firing ends.
2   To remove the plugs, first open the bonnet and disconnect the HT leads, noting their positions (photos).
3   On carburettor engines, remove the rubber tubes from the valve cover (photo), and from the air cleaner.
4   Unscrew and remove the spark plugs from the cylinder head. On carburettor engines, the plugs are deeply recessed, and a long plug spanner will be necessary to remove them (photos).
5   Unscrew the plug extension rods on carburettor engines (photo).
6   Examination of the spark plugs will give a good indication of the condition of the engine.
7   If the insulator nose of the spark plug is clean and white, with no deposits, this is indicative of a weak mixture, or too hot a plug (a hot plug transfers heat away from the electrode slowly, a cold plug transfers heat away quickly).
8   If the tip and insulator nose are covered with hard black-looking deposits, then this is indicative that the mixture is too rich. Should the plug be black and oily, then it is likely that the engine is fairly worn, as well as the mixture being too rich.
9   If the insulator nose is covered with light tan to greyish-brown deposits, then the mixture is correct, and it is likely that the engine is in good condition.

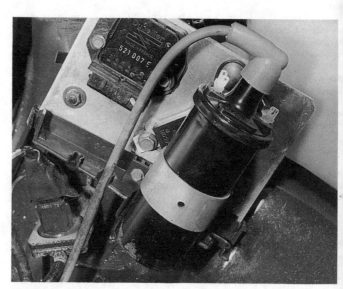

13.3 Ignition coil and HT lead

10   The spark plug gap is of considerable importance, as, if it is too large or too small, the size of the spark and its efficiency will be seriously impaired. For the best results, the spark plug gap should be set in accordance with the Specifications Section at the beginning of this Chapter.
11   To set it, measure the gap with a feeler gauge and then bend the outer electrode until the correct gap is achieved. The centre electrode should never be bent, as this may crack the insulation and cause plug failure, if nothing worse.
12   Special spark plug electrode gap adjusting tools are available from most motor accessory stores.
13   Before fitting new spark plugs apply a smear of grease to the plug threads.
14   Screw each plug in by hand. This will ensure that there is no chance of cross-threading.
15   Tighten to the specified torque. If a torque wrench is not available, just **lightly** tighten each plug. It is better to undertighten than strip the threads from the light alloy cylinder head. Also where the taper-seat type plugs are used (no sealing washers) overtightening can make them very difficult to unscrew.
16   When connecting the spark plug leads, make sure that they are connected in their correct order.

Are your plugs trying to tell you something?

Normal.
Grey-brown deposits, lightly coated core nose. Plugs ideally suited to engine, and engine in good condition.

Heavy Deposits.
A build up of crusty deposits, light-grey sandy colour in appearance.
Fault: Often caused by worn valve guides, excessive use of upper cylinder lubricant, or idling for long periods.

Lead Glazing.
Plug insulator firing tip appears yellow or green/yellow and shiny in appearance.
Fault: Often caused by incorrect carburation, excessive idling followed by sharp acceleration. Also check ignition timing.

Carbon fouling.
Dry, black, sooty deposits.
Fault: over-rich fuel mixture.
Check: carburettor mixture settings, float level, choke operation, air filter.

Oil fouling.
Wet, oily deposits. Fault: worn bores/piston rings or valve guides; sometimes occurs (temporarily) during running-in period.

Overheating.
Electrodes have glazed appearance, core nose very white – few deposits. Fault: plug overheating. Check: plug value, ignition timing, fuel octane rating (too low) and fuel mixture (too weak).

Electrode damage.
Electrodes burned away; core nose has burned, glazed appearance. Fault: pre-ignition. Check: for correct heat range and as for 'overheating'.

Split core nose.
(May appear initially as a crack). Fault: detonation or wrong gap-setting technique. Check: ignition timing, cooling system, fuel mixture (too weak).

WHY DOUBLE COPPER IS BETTER FOR YOUR ENGINE.

Unique Trapezoidal Copper Cored Earth Electrode — 50% Larger Spark Area

Copper Cored Centre Electrode

Champion Double Copper plugs are the first in the world to have copper core in both centre <u>and</u> earth electrode. This innovative design means that they run cooler by up to 100°C – giving greater efficiency and longer life. These double copper cores transfer heat away from the tip of the plug faster and more efficiently. Therefore, Double Copper runs at cooler temperatures than conventional plugs giving improved acceleration response and high speed performance with no fear of pre-ignition.

TRAPEZOIDAL COPPER CORED EARTH ELECTRODE
NEW TRAPEZOIDAL COPPER CORED EARTH ELECTRODE / CONVENTIONAL SOLID NICKEL ALLOY EARTH ELECTRODE
50% INCREASE IN SPARK AREA

EARTH ELECTRODE TEMPERATURE VS ENGINE SPEED
SOLID NICKEL EARTH ELECTRODE
COPPER CORED EARTH ELECTRODE
TEMPERATURE / ENGINE SPEED

Champion Double Copper plugs also feature a unique trapezoidal earth electrode giving a 50% increase in spark area. This, together with the double copper cores, offers greatly reduced electrode wear, so the spark stays stronger for longer.

 FASTER COLD STARTING

 FOR UNLEADED OR LEADED FUEL

 ELECTRODES UP TO 100°C COOLER

 BETTER ACCELERATION RESPONSE

 LOWER EMISSIONS

 50% BIGGER SPARK AREA

 THE LONGER LIFE PLUG

Plug Tips/Hot and Cold.
Spark plugs must operate within well-defined temperature limits to avoid cold fouling at one extreme and overheating at the other.
Champion and the car manufacturers work out the best plugs for an engine to give optimum performance under all conditions, from freezing cold starts to sustained high speed motorway cruising.
Plugs are often referred to as hot or cold. With Champion, the higher the number on its body, the hotter the plug, and the lower the number the cooler the plug. For the correct plug for your car refer to the specifications at the beginning of this chapter.

Plug Cleaning
Modern plug design and materials mean that Champion no longer recommends periodic plug cleaning. Certainly don't clean your plugs with a wire brush as this can cause metal conductive paths across the nose of the insulator so impairing its performance and resulting in loss of acceleration and reduced m.p.g.
However, if plugs are removed, always carefully clean the area where the plug seats in the cylinder head as grit and dirt can sometimes cause gas leakage.
Also wipe any traces of oil or grease from plug leads as this may lead to arcing.

CHAMPION

DOUBLE COPPER

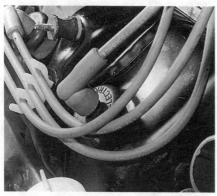

15.2A HT leads on the carburettor engine

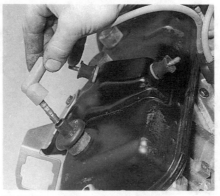

15.2B Disconnecting an HT lead

15.3 Removing a rubber tube on the carburettor engine

15.4A Using a long plug spanner on the carburettor engine

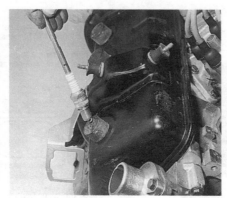

15.4B Removing a spark plug

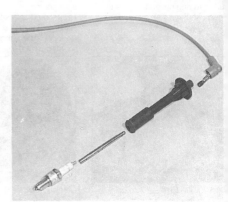

15.5 Spark plug and HT lead components (carburettor engine)

17 The spark plug leads require no routine attention other than being kept clean by wiping them regularly.

18 In order to minimise corrosion in the distributor cap lead sockets, smear the HT cable end fittings with a light coating of petroleum jelly.

19 Check the distributor cap whenever it is removed. If there are any very thin black lines running between the electrodes, this indicates tracking, and a new cap should be fitted. Check the rotor arm in a similar way. Check that the spring-tensioned carbon brush in the centre of the cap is free to move, and is not worn excessively.

16 Fault diagnosis – ignition system

1 If the engine fails to start, and yet was running normally when last used, first check that there is fuel in the fuel tank. If the engine turns over normally on the starter motor, and the battery is evidently well-charged, first check the HT (high tension) circuit.

2 If the engine fails to start due to either damp HT leads or damp distributor cap, a moisture dispersant, such as Holts Wet Start, can be very effective. To prevent the problem recurring Holts Damp Start can be used to provide a sealing coat, so excluding any further moisture from the ignition system. In extreme difficulty, Holts Cold Start will help to start a car when only a very poor spark occurs.

3 If the engine still fails to start, first disconnect an HT lead from any spark plug. Using a nail inserted into the end fitting if necessary, hold the lead approximately 5.0 mm (0.2 in) away fom the cylinder head with well-insulated pliers. While an assistant spins the engine on the starter motor, check that a regular blue spark occurs. If so, the spark plugs are probably the cause of non-starting, and they should therefore be removed, cleaned, and regapped.

4 If no spark occurs, disconnect the main feed HT lead from the distributor cap, and check for a spark as in paragraph 3. If sparks now occur, check the distributor cap, rotor arm, and HT leads as described in Section 15, and renew them as necessary.

5 Check the security of the wiring to the ignition coil, distributor and, where applicable, the electronic module.

6 On conventional ignition models, check the contact breaker points with reference to Sections 3 to 6, as applicable. If necessary, also check the condenser with reference to Section 7.

7 On transistorised ignition models, using an ohmmeter, check the resistance of the distributor pick-up coil and the ignition coil windings. Renew them if the readings are not as given in the Specifications Section. If necessary, dismantle the distributor, and check that the gaps between the reluctor arms and the stator ports are all equal.

8 Using a voltmeter, check that there is battery voltage at the ignition coil low tension 15 (+) terminal with the ignition switched on.

9 On transistorised ignition models, connect the voltmeter across the coil LT terminals, and check that the reading is zero with the ignition switched on. If it is not zero, the module may be defective, or the coil-to-module wire may be earthed.

Chapter 5 Clutch

Contents

Specifications

Type .... Diaphragm spring, single dry plate, hydraulic operation

General

Friction plate diameter .... 215.0 mm (8.47 in)
Maximum machining of flywheel from new .... 0.5 mm (0.02 in)
Clutch pedal free movement .... 5 to 10 mm (0.2 to 0.4 in)

Clutch fluid type/specification .... Hydraulic fluid to SAE J1703 or DOT 3 (Duckhams Universal Brake and Clutch Fluid)

Torque wrench settings

	Nm	lbf ft
Clutch cover	15	11

1 General description

The clutch is of diaphragm spring, single dry plate type, with hydraulic operation.

The clutch pedal pivots in a bracket mounted under the facia, and operates a pushrod on the master cylinder. The slave cylinder, mounted on the left-hand side of the gearbox, pushes the clutch release fork which pivots on a ball stud, and moves the release bearing against the centre of the diaphragm spring within the clutch cover. As the centre of the diaphragm spring is pushed in, its outer edge pivots out and moves the pressure plate away from the friction disc.

When the clutch pedal is released, the diaphragm spring forces the pressure plate into contact with the friction disc, which moves along the input shaft splines and contacts the flywheel. The friction disc is now firmly sandwiched between the pressure plate and flywheel, so the drive is taken up.

No adjustment is necessary to compensate for wear of the friction disc linings, as hydraulic fluid is allowed to bleed back to the reservoir when the clutch pedal is at rest. As wear occurs, the slave cylinder piston simply assumes a rest position which is further in the cylinder.

2 Routine maintenance

Carry out the following procedures at the intervals given in Routine maintenance *at the front of this manual*

Check the hydraulic circuit for leaks and condition

1 Apply the handbrake. Jack up the front of the vehicle and support on axle stands.
2 Check the hydraulic circuit flexible hoses and rigid line for leaks, damage and deterioration.
3 Check the slave cylinder for leakage of fluid from the rubber boot, indicating that the internal seal is worn.
4 Check the master cylinder for leaks, both in the engine compartment and from inside the vehicle.

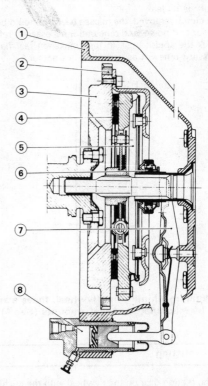

Fig. 5.1 Cross-section of the clutch components (Sec 1)

1	Clutch housing	5 Clutch cover and pressure
2	Starter ring gear	plate
3	Flywheel	6 Release bearing
4	Friction disc	7 Release fork
		8 Slave cylinder

3 Clutch – removal

1   Access to the clutch is by either removing the gearbox or engine. Unless work is also necessary on the gearbox, it is recommended that the engine is removed, as this involves less work. Because the propeller shaft is enclosed, removal of the gearbox involves moving the final drive or rear axle rearwards. Removal of the engine is described in Chapter 1, and removal of the gearbox in Chapter 6.
2   Mark the clutch cover in relation to the flywheel in case it is to be re-used.
3   Using an Allen key, progressively unscrew the cover retaining bolts. If the cover binds on the dowels, use a screwdriver to release it before removing the bolts.
4   Lift the clutch cover and friction disc from the flywheel.

4 Clutch – inspection and renovation

1   The clutch friction disc should be inspected for wear and for contamination by oil. Wear is gauged by the depth of the rivet heads below the surface of the friction material. If this is less than 0.6 mm (0.024 in), the linings are worn enough to justify renewal.
2   Examine the friction surfaces of the flywheel and clutch cover. These should be bright and smooth. If the linings have worn too much, it is possible that the metal surfaces may have been scored by the rivet heads. Dust and grit can also have the same effect. If the scoring is very severe, it could mean that even with a new friction disc, slip and juddering and other malfunctions may recur.
3   If the flywheel face is deeply scored, either renew the flywheel, or have it machined by a specialist. Note that if it is machined, the area on which the cover locates must be machined by the same amount (Fig. 5.2) in order to maintain the same diaphragm pressure.
4   Renew the cover if the pressure plate is scored excessively, or if it has a blue discolouration, indicating that it has been overheated by excessive slipping at some time.
5   If the friction disc is contaminated with oil, renew it and also rectify the source of the oil leak.
6   With the clutch removed, the release bearing should be checked for excessive wear and noise, and renewed if necessary – refer to Section 8. Also check the spigot bush in the crankshaft rear flange for wear and, if necessary, renew it as described in Chapter 1.

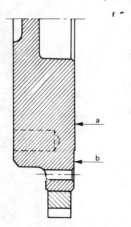

Fig. 5.2 When machining the flywheel, faces a and b must be machined by equal amounts (Sec 4)

5 Clutch – refitting

1   Locate the friction disc on the flywheel with the cushioning spring hub facing outwards (photo), then place the cover assembly over it, with the dowels and holes correctly aligned, and fit the bolts finger-tight.
2   It is now necessary to align the centre of the friction disc with that of the flywheel. To do this, use a special alignment tool located in the crankshaft spigot bush (photo), or alternatively, a suitable diameter bar

5.1 Locating the friction disc on the flywheel

5.2 Using an alignment tool to centre the friction disc

5.3 Tightening the clutch cover bolts

r wooden dowel can be used. If the gearbox has been dismantled, use
he input shaft, or even an old shaft from another gearbox.
With the friction disc centralized, the cover bolts should be
ightened diagonally and evenly to the specified torque (photo).
Remove the alignment tool.
Refit the engine (Chapter 1) or gearbox (Chapter 6) as applicable.

Master cylinder – removal, overhaul and refitting

Unscrew the filler cap from the brake fluid reservoir, and remove the
evel warning lamp switch.
Using a pipette or syringe, draw fluid from the reservoir until the
evel is below the clutch master cylinder supply hose port.
Position a container or rags beneath the master cylinder to catch
ny spilled fluid.
Loosen the clip and disconnect the supply hose from the reservoir.
Unscrew the union nut and disconnect the outlet pipe. Plug the
ipe end to prevent ingress of dirt.
Working inside the vehicle, remove the lower facia panel.
Extract the split pin, remove the washer, and disconnect the

pushrod from the clutch pedal (photo). Withdraw the pushrod from
the master cylinder.
8 Unscrew the two mounting nuts and withdraw the master cylinder
from the bulkhead (photo). Recover the gasket.
9 Clean the external surfaces of the master cylinder. Disconnect the
supply hose.
10 Extract the spring clip from the mouth of the cylinder, and remove
the piston, seals and return spring. Prise out the inlet pipe and
grommet.
11 Clean the components in methylated spirit or fresh hydraulic fluid,
then examine them for wear and damage. The seals should be renewed
as a matter of course. If a genuine Peugeot repair kit is obtained, it will
include a new piston and return spring in addition to the new seals.
Check the cylinder bore for signs of corrosion or excessive wear, and if
evident, renew the complete master cylinder.
12 Commence reassembly by inserting the return spring in the
cylinder, large diameter end first.
13 Dip the piston and seals in fresh hydraulic fluid, and insert them,
making sure that the seal lips face inwards.
14 Depress the piston with a screwdriver, then refit the spring clip in
its groove.
15 Refitting the master cylinder is a reversal of removal, but bleed the
system as described in Section 9.

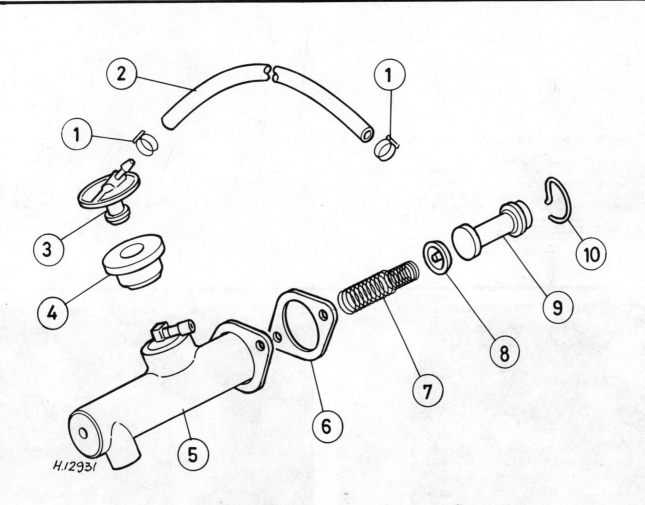

H.12931

Fig. 5.3 Clutch master cylinder components (Sec 6)

1 Chips	4 Grommet	7 Return spring	9 Piston
2 Supply hose from reservoir	5 Master cylinder body	8 Seal	10 Spring clip
3 Inlet pipe	6 Gasket		

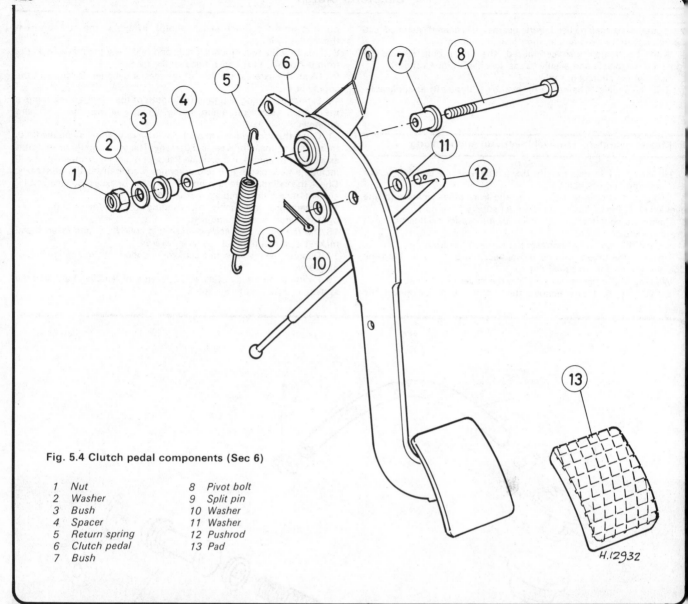

Fig. 5.4 Clutch pedal components (Sec 6)

1 Nut	8 Pivot bolt
2 Washer	9 Split pin
3 Bush	10 Washer
4 Spacer	11 Washer
5 Return spring	12 Pushrod
6 Clutch pedal	13 Pad
7 Bush	

H.12932

6.7 Clutch master cylinder pushrod (arrowed)

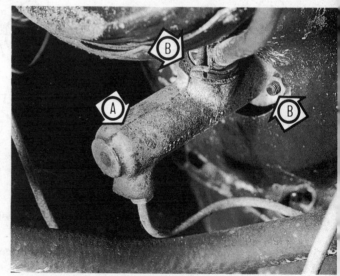

6.8 Clutch master cylinder (A) and mounting nuts (B)

7 Slave cylinder – removal, overhaul and refitting

1 Apply the handbrake. Jack up the front of the vehicle and support on axle stands.
2 Fit a hose clamp to the slave cylinder supply hose.
3 Loosen the hydraulic hose union at the slave cylinder.

Early carburettor models

4 The slave cylinder is retained by a circlip located in a groove near to the rubber boot end of the cylinder. This must be released using a screwdriver. Detach the front circlip from the gearbox.
5 Temporarily detach the steering rack and pinion from the front crossmember and column, leaving the track rods attached to the steering arms.
6 Draw the slave cylinder towards the front of the clutch bellhousing, noting that the pushrod will remain connected to the clutch release fork.
7 Unscrew the slave cylinder from the hose.

Except early carburettor models

8 Unbolt the slave cylinder from the gearbox, then unscrew it from the hose (photos).

All models

9 Prise off the rubber boot and remove the pushrod where fitted.
10 Extract the piston and seal, if necessary tapping the cylinder on a block of wood. On early carburettor models, also extract the return spring.
11 Clean the components in methylated spirit or fresh hydraulic fluid, then examine them for wear and damage. Renew the seal and rubber boot as a matter of course. The genuine Peugeot repair kit for early carburettor models includes a piston and return spring in addition to the seal and boot. Check the cylinder bore for signs of corrosion or excessive wear, and if evident, renew the complete slave cylinder.
12 Commence reassembly by inserting the return spring where fitted, large diameter end first.
13 Dip the seal in fresh hydraulic fluid, and fit it to the piston.
14 Insert the piston and seal in the slave cylinder. Fit the pushrod where applicable, followed by the rubber boot.
15 Refitting the slave cylinder is a reversal of removal, but bleed the system as described in Section 9.

8 Release bearing and fork assembly – removal and refitting

1 Remove the engine or the gearbox (refer to Section 3, paragraph 1).
2 Remove the release bearing by turning it anti-clockwise to disengage the clip (photo).
3 To remove the fork, initially pull it outwards to disconnect the spring clip from the pivot ball, then withdraw it from inside the bellhousing (photo).
4 Check the release bearing for wear by rotating it by hand. Any undue slackness, noise, or binding means the bearing should be renewed.
5 Check the fork, pivot ball, and rubber damper for wear, and if necessary renew them. The rubber damper may be prised from the groove in the pivot ball, and the pivot ball may be extracted from the gearbox housing, preferably after removing the housing.
6 Apply a little locking fluid to the shank of the pivot ball before pressing it into the gearbox housing. Fit the rubber damper in the groove.
7 Smear a little grease on the underside of the fork where it contacts the pivot ball.
8 Refit the fork by inserting it through the bellhousing hole from inside, then lifting the spring clip over the rubber damper and pushing the fork towards the guide sleeve. Note that the damper must be between the spring clip and fork (photo).
9 Smear a little grease on the guide sleeve, then refit the release bearing and turn it clockwise (photo).
10 Refit the engine or gearbox as applicable.

7.8A Clutch slave cylinder mounting bolts (arrowed)

7.8B Clutch slave cylinder removed

8.2 Removing the clutch release bearing

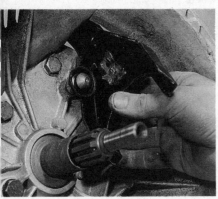
8.3 Removing the release fork

8.8 View of fork spring clip (A) and rubber damper (B) from outside the gearbox

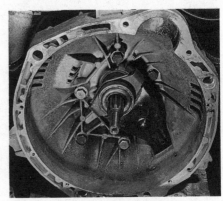
8.9 Fitted release bearing and fork

9 Clutch hydraulic system – bleeding

1   Bleeding the clutch hydraulic system using the method described for the braking system in Chapter 9 may not prove successful, because air bubbles will tend to be trapped in the vertical hydraulic lines. Reverse-bleeding is recommended, whereby fluid is forced through the slave cylinder bleed screw and air is forced back through the system.
2   Peugeot garages use a special hand pump, but if this cannot be obtained, the following method may be used.
3   Apply the handbrake. Jack up the front of the vehicle and support on axle stands.
4   Obtain a length of rubber or plastic tubing long enough to reach the left-hand brake caliper from the clutch slave cylinder. Fill the tubing with fresh hydraulic fluid, and connect it up to both bleed nipples.
5   Loosen both nipples by a quarter of a turn each, and have an assistant slowly depress the footbrake pedal. Remove the brake/clutch fluid reservoir cap, and continue to force fluid into the system until bubbles cease to surface; then tighten the nipples.
6   Top up the fluid in the reservoir if necessary, then check the operation of the clutch and brakes. If air has been drawn into the braking system, it will be necessary to bleed the system as described in Chapter 9. Remove the bleed tube from the nipples.
7   Lower the car to the ground.

10 Hydraulic flexible hose – removal and refitting

1   Apply the handbrake. Jack up the front of the vehicle and support on axle stands.
2   Position a container beneath the clutch slave cylinder to catch any spilled fluid.
3   To remove the upper (supply) flexible hose, use a pipette or syringe to draw fluid from the reservoir until the level is below the outlet port. Loosen the clips and remove the hose from the reservoir and master cylinder.
4   To remove the lower (pressure) flexible hose, first fit a hose clamp to the upper hose. Unscrew the rigid pipe union nut from the end fitting, then pull out the clip and disconnect the hose from the bracket (photos). Unscrew the hose from the slave cylinder.
5   Refitting is a reversal of removal, but bleed the hydraulic system as described in Section 9.

10.4A Inner view of clutch flexible hose bracket

10.4B Outer view of clutch flexible hose bracket

11 Fault diagnosis – clutch

Symptom	Reason(s)
Clutch pedal spongy	Air in hydraulic system Deteriorated master cylinder or slave cylinder seals
Judder when taking up drive	Loose engine/gearbox mountings Friction linings badly worn or contaminated with oil Worn spigot bush in crankshaft
Clutch slip	Worn friction linings Cover diaphragm spring weak or broken Friction linings contaminated with oil
Noise when depressing pedal	Dry, worn or damaged release bearing

Chapter 6 Manual gearbox and automatic transmission

Contents

Specifications

Manual gearbox

Type .... Four or five forward speeds, all with synchromesh, and one reverse

Ratios (typical)

BA7/4:	XN1 and ZEJ engines	XM7 engine
1st	0.2784	0.2700
2nd	0.4752	0.4608
3rd	0.7320	0.7098
4th	1.0000	1.0000
Reverse	0.2752	0.2669
BA7/5:	XN1 and ZDJ engines	
1st	0.2784	
2nd	0.4789	
3rd	0.7313	
4th	1.0000	
5th	1.2153	
Reverse	0.2752	
BA10/5:	ZEJ engine	XN1 engine
1st	0.2893	0.2589
2nd	0.4851	0.4580
3rd	0.7109	0.6922
4th	1.0000	1.0000
5th	1.2174	1.1854
Reverse	0.2863	0.2788

Lubrication

Oil type/specification .... Multigrade engine oil, viscosity SAE 10W/40 (Duckhams QXR, Hypergrade, or 10W/40 Motor Oil)

Capacity (drain/refill):
BA7/4 .... 1.15 litres (2.0 pints)
BA7/5 .... 1.45 litres (2.6 pints)
BA10/5 .... 1.60 litres (2.8 pints)

Torque wrench settings

	Nm	lbf ft
Mainshaft nut	55	41
Bearing retaining plate	10	7
Detent plug	12	9
Main casing bolts – 7 mm	10	7
Main casing bolts – 8 mm	15	11
Clutch housing (to main casing)	28	21
Rear housing	15	11
Reverse lock-out plunger (4-speed)	15	11
Drain and filler plugs	28	21
Reversing light switch	28	21
Intermediate housing (5-speed)	18	13
Reverse driving gear (BA10/4)	25	19
Clutch housing to engine	55	41

Automatic tranmission

Type
Pre-1986 models .... ZF 3 HP22 (3-speed)
1986-on models .... ZF 4 HP22 (4-speed)

Ratios
3 HP22:
1st 0.4033
2nd 0.6759
3rd 1.0000
Reverse 0.4794
4 HP22:
1st 0.4033
2nd 0.6759
3rd 1.0000
4th 1.3734
Reverse 0.4795

Lubrication
Fluid type/specification .... Dexron II ATF (Duckhams D-Matic)
Capacity (from dry):
3 HP22 .... 5.2 litres (9.2 pints)
4 HP22 .... 5.0 litres (8.8 pints)
Capacity (drain/refill):
3 HP22 .... 1.6 litres (2.8 pints)
4 HP22 .... 2.6 litres (4.6 pints)

Torque wrench settings

	Nm	lbf ft
Torque converter housing to engine	55	41
Torque converter to driveplate	30	22
Dipstick tube union	28	21

1 General description

The manual gearbox is of four- or five-speed type, with synchromesh on all forward speeds, and one reverse. It incorporates an input shaft, mainshaft, and laygear. On 5-speed versions, the laygear extension incorporates the 5th speed driving gear, which is in constant mesh with the driven gear on the mainshaft. The main casing is split into two halves, the left half being fitted with the selector rods and forks.

The automatic transmission is of either three- or four-speed type, incorporating hydraulic control of the epicyclic geartrain. The four-speed version is fitted with a torque converter with an integral lock-up device, which eliminates all slip in 4th gear when the vehicle is travelling above 53 mph, and the transmission fluid temperature is above 20°C. Under these conditions, a valve in the valve block reverses the flow of fluid within the torque converter, and an internal clutch is brought into play.

2 Routine maintenance

Carry out the following procedures at the intervals given in Routine maintenance *at the front of this manual*

Renew manual gearbox oil
1 Apply the handbrake. Jack up the front of the vehicle and support on axle stands.
2 Position a suitable container beneath the gearbox, then unscrew and remove the drain and filler plugs, and drain the oil.
3 Refit and tighten the drain plug.
4 Jack up the rear of the vehicle until it is level, then fill the gearbox with oil until level with the bottom of the filler plug aperture.
5 Refit and tighten the filler plug. Lower the vehicle to the ground.

Renew automatic transmission fluid
6 Refer to Section 27.

Check manual gearbox oil level

7 Jack up the front and rear of the vehicle, and support on axle stands.

8 Unscrew the filler plug and check that the oil level is up to the bottom of the filler plug aperture. Top up if necessary.

9 Refit and tighten the filler plug, then lower the vehicle to the ground.

Check automatic transmission fluid level

10 The engine and transmission must be at normal operating temperature, after driving for at least 3 miles.

11 Position the vehicle on a level surface, and apply the handbrake firmly.

12 With the engine idling, move the selector lever slowly through all the positions, then select 'P'.

13 Remove the dipstick and wipe it clean, then re-insert and remove again. The level should be within the 'Hot' ('Chaud') section.

14 If necessary, top up the level through the dipstick tube, using a funnel. Do not top up over the maximum level mark. The difference between the level marks represents 0.5 pints (0.3 litres).

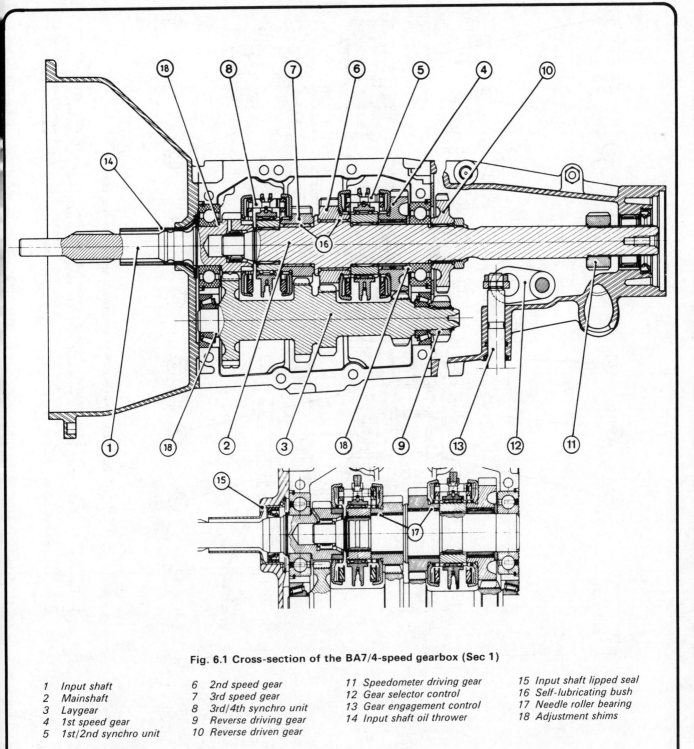

Fig. 6.1 Cross-section of the BA7/4-speed gearbox (Sec 1)

1 Input shaft	6 2nd speed gear	11 Speedometer driving gear	15 Input shaft lipped seal
2 Mainshaft	7 3rd speed gear	12 Gear selector control	16 Self-lubricating bush
3 Laygear	8 3rd/4th synchro unit	13 Gear engagement control	17 Needle roller bearing
4 1st speed gear	9 Reverse driving gear	14 Input shaft oil thrower	18 Adjustment shims
5 1st/2nd synchro unit	10 Reverse driven gear		

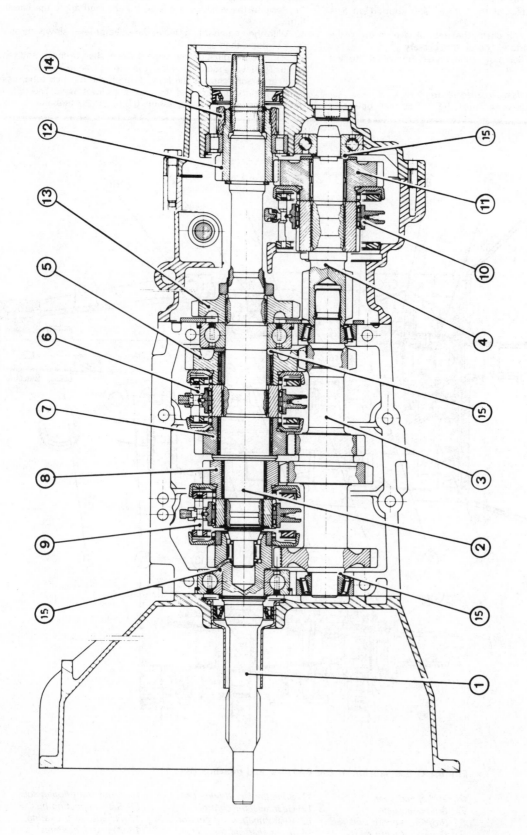

Fig. 6.2 Cross-section of the BA7/5-speed gearbox (Sec 1)

1 Input shaft
2 Mainshaft
3 Laygear
4 5th/reverse intermediate shaft
5 1st speed gear
6 1st/2nd synchro unit
7 2nd speed gear
8 3rd speed gear
9 3rd/4th synchro unit
10 5th/reverse synchro unit (no synchro on reverse)
11 5th speed driving gear
12 5th speed driven gear
13 Reverse driven gear
14 Speedometer driving gear
15 Adjustment shims

3 Manual gearbox (Saloon models) – removal and refitting

Note: *There are two methods of removing the gearbox. Method 1 involves removing the engine first and Method 2 involves moving the final drive unit rearwards*

Method 1

1   Remove the engine as described in Chapter 1.
2   Apply the handbrake. Jack up the front of the vehicle and support on axle stands.
3   Working inside the vehicle, remove the centre console with reference to Chapter 11.
4   Unscrew the gearstick knob.
5   Prise the rubber boot from the gearbox cover, and remove it from the gearstick (photo).
6   Remove the screws and lift off the gearbox cover (photos).
7   Disconnect the two gearchange rods from the gearbox levers (photos).
8   From inside the vehicle, disconnect the gearchange rod from the control lever (photo).
9   Unscrew the nut and slide the control lever from the gearbox stud (photos).
10 Remove the control lever from the rear mounting, and withdraw the lever from the vehicle (photo).
11 Using an Allen key or socket, unscrew the bolts securing the propeller shaft link tube to the gearbox (photo).
12 Unscrew the filler and drain plugs, and drain the gearbox oil into a suitable container (photos). Refit the plugs on completion.
13 Unscrew the nuts and detach the exhaust pipe bracket from the gearbox. Tie the exhaust pipe to one side.
14 Loosen the retaining bolt and withdraw the speedometer cable (photos).
15 Disconnect the reversing lamp switch wiring.
16 Remove the clutch slave cylinder (Chapter 5).
17 Support the front of the link tube with a trolley jack, then lift the gearbox forwards over the steering gear and crossmember. The steering gear may be temporarily unbolted from the crossmember if necessary, to provide additional clearance.
18 Refitting is a reversal of removal, with reference to Chapters 11 and 1. Fill the gearbox with oil, up to the bottom edge of the filler plug, then refit and tighten the plug.

Method 2

19 Jack up the front and rear of the vehicle, and support on axle stands. Disconnect the battery negative lead.
20 Unscrew the filler and drain plugs, and drain the gearbox oil into a suitable container. Refit the plugs on completion.
21 On carburettor engines, remove the air cleaner and air inlet duct.
22 On fuel injection engines, remove the air inlet duct, and unbolt the pressure regulator.

23 Unscrew the radiator top mounting bolts, and release the radiator from the lower supports. Position a piece of plywood or cardboard between the radiator matrix and fan blades.
24 Disconnect the exhaust downpipes from the manifold. Also disconnect all the exhaust system mountings except the rearmost one(s), and lower the exhaust to the ground.
25 Unbolt the exhaust heat shield and front seat stiffener.
26 Unbolt the link tube vibration damper and limiter, and remove the damper stud.
27 Disconnect the final drive unit mounting(s) (refer to Chapter 8). Lower the final drive unit so that the link tube rests on the rear crossmember.
28 Disconnect the steering column intermediate shaft lower coupling from the steering gear.
29 On manual steering models, unbolt the steering gear from the crossmember, and lower it without disconnecting the track rods.
30 On power steering models, remove the two front bolts from the crossmember, and in their place fit two long bolts which will allow the crossmember to be lowered by 50.0 mm (2.0 in). Remove the rear bolts and lower the crossmember.
31 Support the gearbox with a trolley jack.
32 Using an Allen key or socket, unscrew the bolts retaining the propeller shaft link tube to the gearbox.
33 Move the link tube rearwards by 20.0 mm (0.8 in). Refer to Chapter 7 and fit the propeller shaft support plate as described. Move the link tube rearwards until the propeller shaft is disengaged.
34 Unbolt the starter motor from the clutch housing.
35 Unbolt the TDC sensor and clutch housing cover.
36 Unscrew the nut and disconnect the gearchange control rod front mounting. If difficulty is experienced, remove the centre console and gearbox cover from inside the vehicle.
37 Disconnect the gearchange engagement and selection links.
38 Disconnect the reversing lamp switch wiring.
39 Unscrew the retaining bolt and withdraw the speedometer cable.
40 Remove the clutch slave cylinder (Chapter 5).
41 Lower the gearbox on the trolley jack to provide sufficient room to remove the gearbox. Slightly raise the front of the engine also, using a hoist or further trolley jack.
42 Unscrew the gearbox-to-engine bolts, then withdraw the gearbox direct from the engine and remove from under the vehicle.
43 Refitting is a reversal of removal, but note the following additional points:

(a)   Apply a little high melting-point grease to the splines of the gearbox input shaft, and to the front of the shaft which enters the spigot bearing
(b)   Check that the clutch release bearing and fork are correctly fitted
(c)   Refit the final drive unit with reference to Chapter 8
(d)   Fill the gearbox with oil, up to the bottom edge of the filler plug, then refit and tighten the plug

3.5 Removing the rubber boot from the gearbox cover

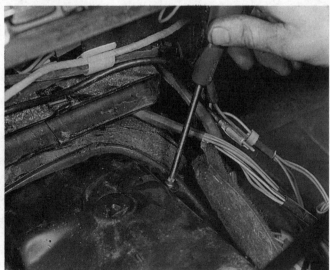

3.6A Remove the screws ...

3.6B ... and lift off the gearbox cover

3.7A Gate gearchange rod (arrowed)

3.7B Speed gearchange rod (arrowed)

3.8 Gate gearchange rod (arrowed) on the control lever

3.9A Unscrew the nut ...

3.9B ... and remove the control lever

3.10 Removing the control lever from the rear mounting

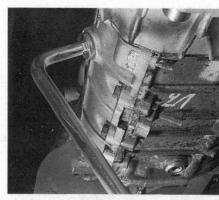
3.11 Unscrewing the link tube-to-gearbox bolts

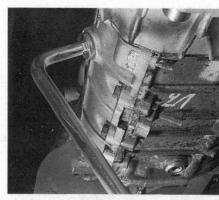
3.12A Removing the filler plug

3.12B Removing the drain plug

3.14A Loosen the retaining bolt (arrowed) ...

3.14B ... and withdraw the speedometer cable

4 Manual gearbox (Estate models) – removal and refitting

1 Jack up the front and rear of the vehicle, and support on axle stands.
2 Remove the centre console with reference to Chapter 11.
3 Unscrew the gearstick knob.
4 Prise the rubber boot from the gearbox cover and remove it from the gearstick.
5 Remove the screws and lift off the gearbox cover.
6 Prise out the plug in front of the gearstick, and unscrew the top bolt from the rear engine mounting frame.
7 Release the handbrake, then disconnect the inner cables from the equaliser.
8 Remove the bonnet (Chapter 11).
9 Disconnect the battery negative lead.
10 Unscrew the radiator top mounting bolts, and release the radiator from the lower supports. Position a piece of plywood or cardboard between the radiator matrix and fan blades.
11 Remove the starter motor (Chapter 12).
12 On carburettor engines, remove the air cleaner and air inlet duct.
13 On fuel injection engines, remove the air inlet duct, and unbolt the pressure regulator.
14 Disconnect the exhaust downpipes from the manifold and gearbox.
15 Unbolt the TDC sensor and clutch housing cover.
16 Remove the clutch slave cylinder (Chapter 5).
17 Disconnect the reversing lamp switch wiring.
18 Unscrew the retaining bolt and withdraw the speedometer cable.
19 Disconnect the steering column intermediate shaft lower coupling from the steering gear.
20 Unclip the hydraulic brake pipe from the torque tube.
21 Refer to Chapter 9 and remove the rear brake compensator, without disconnecting the pipes.
22 Unbolt the rear brake three-way union from the underbody.
23 Support the gearbox with a trolley jack.
24 Unbolt the engine rear mounting from the underbody and gearbox.
25 Unbolt the front seat reinforcement bar.
26 Unbolt the rear anti-roll bar from the underbody.
27 Support the rear axle on a trolley jack, then disconnect the shock absorber lower mountings.
28 Lower the rear axle sufficiently to allow the rear wheels to pass under the wing.
29 Lower the gearbox until the engine is almost touching the steering gear.
30 Unbolt the torque tube ball cover from the gearbox.
31 Move the rear axle rearwards, and disconnect it from the gearbox. Take care not to damage the hydraulic brake pipes. Support the torque tube on an axle stand.
32 Recover the engine rear mounting frame.
33 Remove the two front bolts from the front suspension crossmem-

ber, and in their place fit two long bolts which will allow the crossmember to be lowered by 50.0 mm (2.0 in). Remove the rear bolts and lower the crossmember, but do not allow the power steering pump pulley to contact the anti-roll bar.
34 Slightly raise the front of the engine, using a hoist or further trolley jack.
35 Unscrew the gearbox-to-engine bolts, then withdraw the gearbox direct from the engine and remove it from under the vehicle.
36 Refitting is a reversal of removal, but note the following additional points:

   (a) *Apply a little high melting-point grease to the splines of the gearbox input shaft, and to the front of the shaft which enters the spigot bearing*
   (b) *Check that the clutch release bearing and fork are correctly fitted*
   (c) *Make sure that the rear coil springs are correctly located in their seats*
   (d) *Fill the gearbox with oil, up to the bottom edge of the filler plug, then refit and tighten the plug*
   (e) *Grease the torque tube balljoint*

5 Manual gearbox (BA7) – dismantling into major assemblies

1 Clean the exterior of the gearbox.
2 Unscrew and remove the locking bolt and extract the speedometer pinion adaptor (photos).

4-speed gearbox

3 Move the selector lever to neutral.
4 Unscrew the bolts and withdraw the rear housing, using a wooden mallet if necessary to tap the housing carefully and release it (photo).

5-speed gearbox

5 Move the selector lever to neutral.
6 Using a square drive, unscrew the plastic plug from the rear housing (photo).
7 Unscrew the bolts securing the rear housing to the intermediate housing.
8 Remove the rear housing by carefully tapping it free with a wooden mallet, while at the same time using a block of wood through the plug hole to free the 5th/reverse intermediate shaft from its bearing (photos).
9 Extract the circlip from its groove in the mainshaft (photo).
10 Using a two-legged puller located under the 5th speed driven gear, draw the speedometer drivegear and 5th speed driven gear from the mainshaft (photos). Take care not to damage the gear teeth.
11 Using circlip pliers, extract the location circlip from the mainshaft (photos).

5.2A Remove the locking bolt ...

5.2B ... and extract the speedometer pinion adaptor

5.4 Removing the rear housing (4-speed gearbox)

5.6 Removing the plastic plug

5.8A Tapping the 5th/reverse intermediate shaft from its bearing

5.8B Removing the rear housing

5.9 Extract the circlip ...

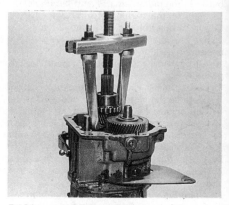

5.10A ... pull off the speedometer drivegear and 5th speed driven gear from the mainshaft ...

5.10B ... and remove the gear

5.11A Gear location circlip (arrowed) on mainshaft

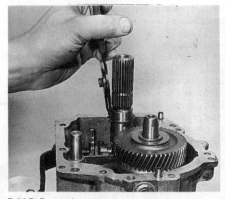

5.11B Removing the gear location circlip

12 Remove the shim and spacer from the end of the 5th/reverse intermediate shaft (photos).

13 Remove the 5th speed driving gear and needle roller bearing (photos).

14 Mark the 5th synchro unit hub and sleeve in relation to each other.

15 Select 5th gear position by raising the selector shaft and fork.

16 A tool must now be made to support the selector shaft while the fork retaining roll pin is driven out. This may be made out of 6 mm (0.25 in) thick steel plate, and should be bolted to the intermediate housing together with packing washers, to obtain the necessary height (photo) – refer also to Section 17, photos 17.20A and 17.20B. Remove the tool after driving out the roll pin.

17 Move the selector shaft to neutral, then withdraw the 5th synchro sleeve and fork, followed by the 5th synchro hub (photos).

18 Withdraw the 5th/reverse intermediate shaft (photos).

19 Disengage the selector finger from the selector dogs.

20 Unscrew the nuts and bolts securing the intermediate housing to the main casing halves, noting the location of the exhaust mounting bracket, then withdraw the housing (photos).

4- and 5-speed gearboxes

21 Remove the clutch release bearing and fork as in Chapter 5.

22 Unbolt and remove the clutch bellhousing.

23 Using an Allen key or socket, unscrew the bolts securing the bearing retaining plate to the main casing halves.

24 With the left-hand half of the main casing on the bench, unscrew the bolts and lift off the right-hand casing half (photos).

25 Lift the input shaft, mainshaft and layshaft together from the casing half (photo). Keep the laygear bearing outer tracks with their correct bearings, to ensure correct refitting.

26 Release the laygear from the bearing retainer.

27 Slide the 3rd/4th synchro sleeve to the 3rd gear position, then separate the input shaft from the mainshaft (photo).

28 Remove the needle roller bearing from the input shaft (photo).

5.12A Removing the shim ...

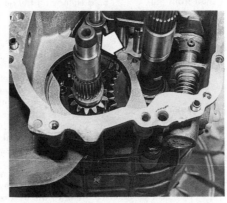

5.12B ... and spacer

5.13A Removing the 5th speed driving gear ...

5.13B ... and needle roller bearing

5.16 Using the special tool to support the selector shaft while removing the roll pin

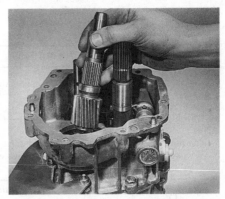

5.17A Removing the 5th synchro sleeve and fork ...

5.17B ... and 5th synchro hub

5.18A 5th/reverse intermediate shaft location (arrowed) ...

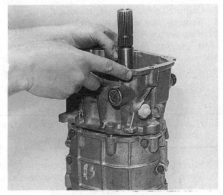

5.18B ... and removal

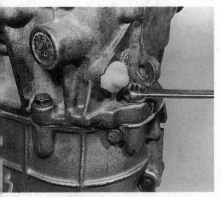

5.20A Unscrew the intermediate housing bolts

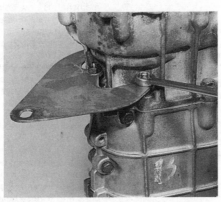

5.20B Removing the exhaust mounting bracket

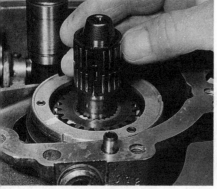

5.20C Removing the intermediate housing

5.24A Unscrew the bolts ...

5.24B ... and lift off the right-hand casing half

5.25 Gear shafts in the left-hand casing

5.27 Separating the input shaft from the mainshaft

5.28 Removing the needle roller bearing from the input shaft

6 Manual gearbox (BA7) – inspection

1 Clean all the components and examine them for general wear, distortion, and damage.
2 Examine the gears for excessive wear and chipping of the teeth.
3 Check all bearings for noisy operation and pitting of the balls or rollers.
4 Examine the selector forks, shafts and dogs for excessive wear.
5 Check the synchromesh units for excessive wear of the cone faces.

7 Manual gearbox input shaft (BA7) – dismantling and reassembly

1 Extract the circlip from the input shaft, followed by the special washer (photo).
2 Using a puller or press, remove the bearing.
3 Remove the oil thrower (if fitted) and the shims.
4 Reassemble in the reverse order to dismantling (photo). If the input shaft, 3rd/4th synchro unit, 3rd/4th selector fork and shaft, or the half-casings are renewed, fit the following shims:

0.35 mm (0.014 in) shim to input shaft with oil thrower
0.50 mm (0.020 in) shim to input shaft with oil seal

8 Manual gearbox mainshaft (BA7) – dismantling and reassembly

1 Mount the mainshaft in a vice, with the front end uppermost.
2 Mark the 3rd/4th synchro hub and sleeve in relation to each other, then remove the sleeve (photo).
3 Extract the circlip and special washer, then slide off the 3rd/4th synchro hub (photos). If it is tight, use a puller.

4 Slide off the 3rd speed gear, and remove the needle roller bearing (photos).
5 Invert the mainshaft in the vice, so that the rear end is uppermost.
6 On the 4-speed version, use a puller to remove the speedometer pinion drivegear (photo).
7 Unscrew the rear nut and remove it from the mainshaft (photo).
8 Using a puller located under the 2nd speed gear, draw the gear assembly from the mainshaft until the rear bearing is free. Alternatively, rest the 2nd speed gear on the jaws of the vice, and press or drive the mainshaft downwards.
9 Remove from the mainshaft the reverse gear, the bearing retaining plate, the bearing, the shim and the 1st speed gear (photos).
10 Remove the needle roller bearing and sleeve (photos).
11 Mark the 1st/2nd synchro hub and sleeve in relation to each other, then remove the unit complete (photos).
12 Remove the 2nd speed gear and the needle roller bearing. The mainshaft is now completely dismantled (photos).
13 Commence reassembly by refitting the needle roller bearing to the mainshaft rear section, followed by the 2nd speed gear (photo).
14 Refit the 1st/2nd synchro unit with the bar marks (photo) away from the 2nd speed gear.
15 Refit the sleeve and 1st speed gear needle roller bearing.
16 Refit the 1st speed gear and shim. Note that if the mainshaft, mainshaft gears and synchro unit, selector fork and shaft, or main casing halves are renewed, a 3.3 mm (0.130 in) thick shim should be fitted.
17 Position the bearing on the mainshaft, with the outer circlip facing rearwards.
18 Using a puller, draw the bearing fully onto the mainshaft. Note that the pressure should be applied to the bearing inner track only (photo). Alternatively, use a metal tube to drive on the bearing inner track.
19 If a new shim has been fitted, do not refit the bearing retaining plate and reverse gear at this stage, but refer to Sections 15 and 16.
20 If the original shim has been refitted, and the components mentioned in paragraph 16 have not been renewed, refit the bearing

7.1 Circlip (1) and special washer (2) on the input shaft

7.4 Reassembled input shaft

8.2 3rd/4th synchro hub removal

8.3A Remove the circlip ...

8.3B ... special washer ...

8.3C ... and 3rd/4th synchro hub

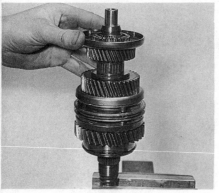

8.4A Removing the 3rd speed gear ...

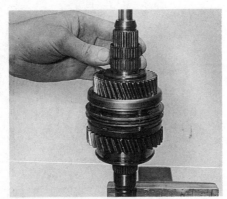

8.4B ... and needle roller bearing

8.6 Removing the speedometer pinion drivegear (4-speed gearbox)

8.7 Mainshaft rear nut removal

8.9A From the mainshaft, remove the reverse gear ...

8.9B ... the bearing retaining plate ...

8.9C ... the rear bearing ...

8.9D ... the shim ...

8.9E ... and the 1st speed gear

8.10A Removing the needle roller bearing ...

8.10B ... and sleeve

8.11A Mark the 1st/2nd synchro hub and sleeve in relation to each other (arrowed)

8.11B Removing the 1st/2nd synchro unit

8.12A Removing the 2nd speed gear ...

8.12B ... and needle roller bearing

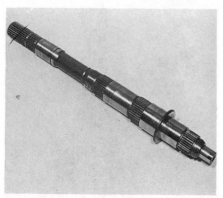
8.12C The dismantled mainshaft

8.13 Refitting the needle roller bearing

8.14 Bar marking (arrowed) on the 1st/2nd synchro unit

retaining plate, with the machined face against the bearing.

21 Refit the reverse gear, with the tooth chamfer facing rearwards.

22 Fit the mainshaft nut, and tighten it to the specified torque. Lock it by peening the shoulder into the mainshaft cut-out (photos).

23 On the 4-speed gearbox, use a metal tube to drive the speedometer pinion drivegear onto the mainshaft. If the gear has a spigot, as shown in Fig. 6.3, this must face rearwards.

24 Invert the mainshaft in the vice, so that the front end is uppermost.

25 Refit the needle roller bearing and 3rd speed gear.

26 Slide the 3rd/4th synchro hub on the mainshaft splines. Refit the special washer and circlip, and use a metal tube to tap the circlip fully in its groove (photo).

27 Refit the 3rd/4th synchro sleeve on the hub, making sure that the previously-made marks are aligned.

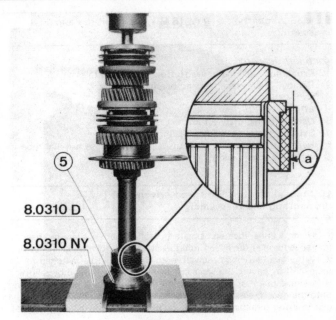

Fig. 6.3 Correct location of speedometer pinion drivegear (5) on the 4-speed gearbox (Sec 8)

a   Indicates spigot

8.0310 D

8.0310 NY

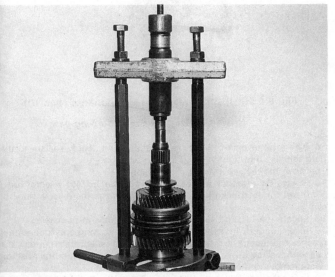

8.18 Using a puller to fit the mainshaft bearing

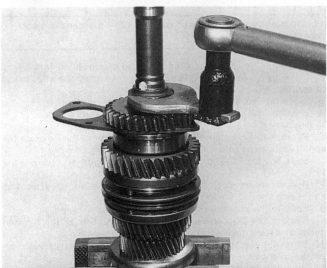

8.22A Tighten the mainshaft nut ...

8.22B ... then peen the shoulder into the cut-out (arrowed)

8.26 Refitting the circlip

9 Manual gearbox laygear (BA7) – dismantling and reassembly

4-speed gearbox
1   Extract the circlip and washer from the rear of the laygear.
2   Remove the reverse gear and bearing outer track.

4- and 5-speed gearboxes
3   Using a puller, draw off the rear bearing.
4   Similarly remove the front bearing and washer.
5   Reassembly is a reversal of dismantling, but use a metal tube or socket to drive the bearing inner tracks into position.

10 Manual gearbox 5th speed driven gear (BA7) – dismantling and reassembly

1   Using a puller located beneath the roller bearing, draw the bearing and speedometer drivegear from the 5th speed driven gear (photo).
2   If the gear is being renewed, note that it must be matched to the mainshaft by having the same colour mark – either green or yellow.
3   Using a puller or metal tubing on the inner track, drive the bearing onto the gear, then similarly drive the speedometer drivegear onto the gear, making sure that the spigot end is away from the bearing (photo).

11 Manual gearbox selector rods (BA7) – dismantling and reassembly

1   Move the 1st/2nd selector fork into 2nd gear position (photo).
2   Drive the roll pin from the 1st/2nd fork, then return the selector rod to neutral.
3   Move the 3rd/4th selector fork into 4th gear position.
4   Drive the roll pin from the 3rd/4th fork, then return the selector rod to neutral.
5   Remove the plug covering the 1st/2nd detent, then extract the spring and detent ball.
6   Slide out the 1st/2nd and 3rd/4th selector rods, and recover the forks.
7   Recover the interlock ball and plunger, and the 3rd/4th detent ball and spring.
8   Remove the interlock pin from the 3rd/4th selector rod.
9   Remove the plug covering the reverse (and 5th on the 5-speed gearbox) detent, then extract the spring and detent ball.
10 Slide out the reverse selector rod and fork, together with the reverse idler gear.
11 Drive the roll pin from the reverse idler shaft, then pull the shaft from the casing. Note that this roll pin is longer than the selector fork roll pins.
12 Commence reassembly by inserting the reverse idler shaft, aligning the holes, and driving in the roll pin.
13 Locate the reverse idler gear in the selector rod fork, then insert the rod and locate the gear on the shaft. Note that the groove in the gear must be away from the casing.

Fig. 6.4 5th speed driven gear components (Sec 10)

1 Bearing   2 Speedometer driving gear

14 Insert the reverse/5th detent ball and spring. Apply sealant to the plug threads, and tighten the plug into position.
15 Move the reverse selector rod to neutral.
16 Grease the interlock pin, and insert it in the 3rd/4th selector rod.
17 Insert the interlock plunger so that it contacts the reverse selector rod.
18 Locate the 1st/2nd and 3rd/4th selector forks in the casing.
19 Insert the 3rd/4th selector rod through the casing and fork, until it reaches the detent hole. Insert the spring and detent ball, depress the ball with a screwdriver, then push the selector rod into neutral position while removing the screwdriver.
20 Insert the interlock ball so that it contacts the 3rd/4th selector rod.
21 Insert the 1st/2nd selector rod through the casing and forks.
22 Insert the 1st/2nd detent ball and spring. Apply sealant to the plug threads, and tighten the plug into position.
23 Move the 1st/2nd selector rod to neutral.
24 Align the holes and drive the roll pins into the 1st/2nd and 3rd/4th selector forks.

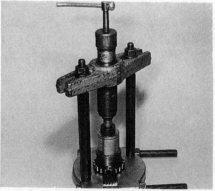

10.1 Using a puller to dismantle the 5th speed driven gear

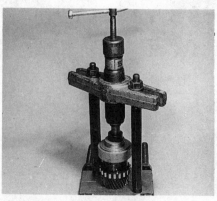

10.3 Reassembling the 5th speed driven gear using a puller

11.1 Selector rods inside the left-hand casing

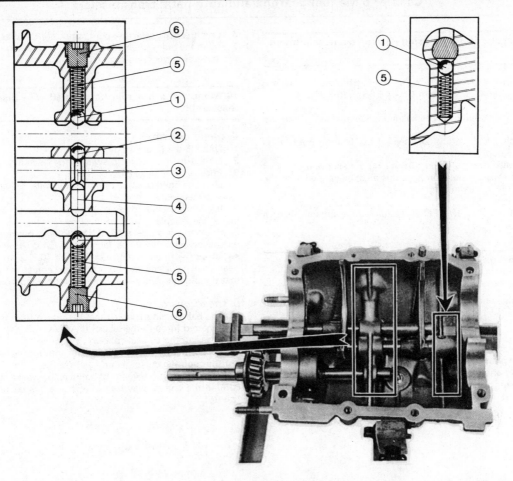

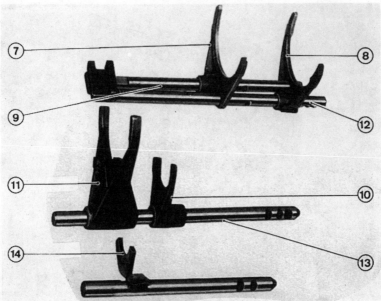

Fig. 6.5 Selector rod components (Sec 11)

1 Detent balls	6 Plugs	10 Reverse selector fork (5-speed gearbox)	13 5th/reverse selector rod (5-speed gearbox)
2 Interlock balls	7 1st/2nd selector fork		14 Reverse selector fork and rod (4-speed gearbox)
3 Interlock pin	8 3rd/4th selector fork	11 5th selector fork	
4 Interlock plunger	9 1st/2nd selector rod (5-speed gearbox)	12 3rd/4th selector rod	
5 Detent springs			

12 Manual gearbox clutch housing (BA7) – dismantling and reassembly

1   Using a dial test indicator, check that the gearbox contact face is not distorted by more than 0.10 mm (0.004 in) (photo). If it is, renew the housing.
2   Prise the oil seal from the release bearing guide tube in the housing (photo).
3   Extract the circlip, then drive out the release bearing guide tube with a block of wood (photos).
4   Refit the release bearing guide tube, using a mallet and block of wood. If the tube has a ventilation hole, this must be aligned with the corresponding hole in the housing (photos).
5   Refit the circlip.
6   Refit the oil seal (photo), and drive it into the tube squarely using a block of wood.

13 Manual gearbox intermediate housing (BA7/5) – dismantling and reassembly

1   Using a suitable punch, drive out the inner then outer roll pins from the selector finger.
2   Compress the selector spring, then extract the plastic half-shells (photos).
3   Withdraw the selector shaft, and recover the selector finger, spring, and O-ring seal (photos).
4   Oil the O-ring and shaft. Fit the O-ring and locate the end of the shaft in the housing (photo).
5   Insert the shaft, engaging the selector finger and spring (photo).

6   Compress the selector spring, and refit the plastic half-shells.
7   Align the holes, then drive in the outer and inner roll pins to secure the selector finger (photo).

14 Manual gearbox rear housing (BA7) – dismantling and reassembly

4-speed gearbox
1   Unhook the return spring.
2   Unbolt the reverse lamp switch, after marking its position.
3   Prise out the oil seal.
4   Note the fitted position of the needle roller bearing, then drive it out using a metal tube.
5   It is not possible to remove the selector mechanism, and if this is faulty, the complete housing must be renewed.
6   Reassembly is a reversal of dismantling, but note that the lettering on the bearing should be facing outwards. To set the reverse lamp switch position, place a spacer 8.2 mm (0.323 in) thick between the gear lever pivot and the housing, then adjust the switch position so that the plunger is just touching the rubber stop on the selector lever.

5-speed gearbox
7   The ball-bearing (photo) may be driven from the housing using a drift entered through the rear of the housing.
8   Prise out the oil seal (photo).
9   Extract the circlip, then drive out the bearing outer track, using a drift through the cut-outs provided (photo).
10   Reassembly is a reversal of removal, but make sure that the oil seal is fitted the correct way round, with the lips facing into the housing (photo).

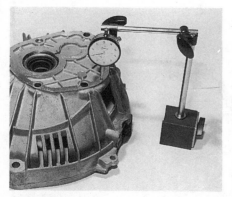

12.1 Checking the clutch housing face for distortion

12.2 Prising out the oil seal

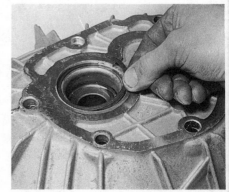

12.3A Extract the circlip ...

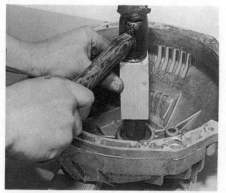

12.3B ... then drive out the release bearing guide tube

12.4A Entering the release bearing guide tube. Note the ventilation hole position (arrowed)

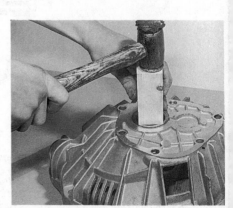

12.4B Final fitting of the release bearing guide tube

2.6 Refitting the oil seal

13.2A Fitted selector spring and half-shells

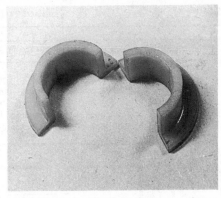

13.2B Plastic half-shells for selector spring

13.3A Withdrawing the selector shaft

13.3B Removing the O-ring seal

13.4 Refitting the selector shaft

13.5 Inserting the selector shaft through the selector finger and spring

13.7 Fitting the selector finger roll pins

14.7 Rear housing, showing the ball bearing (arrowed)

14.8 Removing the oil seal

14.9 Circlip (1) and bearing track removal cut-out (2)

14.10 Fitted oil seal

15 Manual gearbox synchro units (BA7) – centralisation

1   Assemble the input shaft and mainshaft together with the spigot bearing, and locate the assembly in the left-hand casing.
2   Fit the clutch housing and rear bearing retainer to the casing, as shown in Fig. 6.6, and check that the selector forks are in neutral.
3   Check that the synchro sleeves are centralised by checking the dimensions D1/D2 and D3/D4 in Fig. 6.6 using vernier calipers.
4   If adjustment is required for the 1st, 2nd and 3rd synchronisers, select a different shim for fitting under the rear bearing.
5   If adjustment is required for the 4th synchroniser, select different shims for fitting under the front bearing.
6   After making the adjustment, dismantle the clutch housing and rear bearing retainer, and separate the shafts. Proceed to check the laygear bearing preload as described in Section 16.

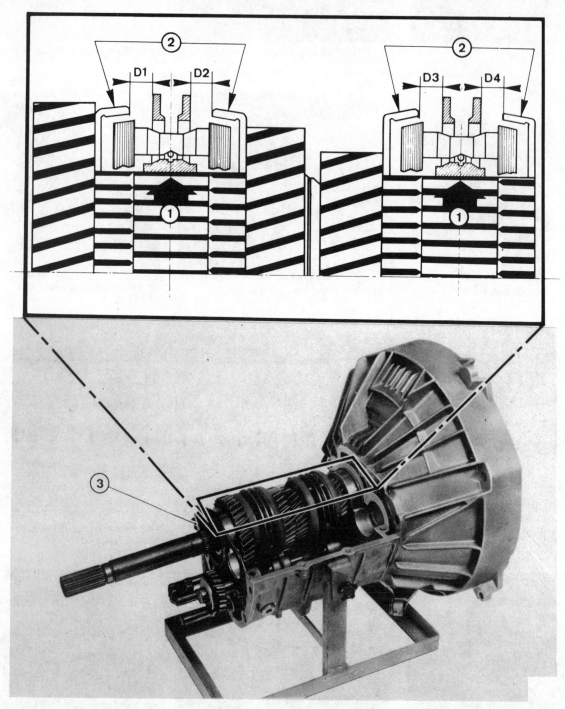

Fig. 6.6 Centralisation of the synchro units (Sec 15)

1   *Sliding sleeves*   3   *Bearing retaining plate*   D1 = D2
2   *Synchro cones*   D3 = D4

16 Manual gearbox laygear bearing (BA7) – preload adjustment

1 Lower the laygear in the left-hand casing, and fit the rear bearing retainer.
2 Fit the right-hand casing, and tighten the four corner bolts and bearing retainer bolts hand-tight.
3 Press on the front bearing outer track, while turning the laygear to seat the bearings.
4 On casing halves located by two roll pins, tighten the four casing bolts to 10 Nm (7 lbf ft), then tighten the bearing retainer bolts.
5 On casing halves located by one dowel, fit the clutch housing, using four bolts tightened to 10 Nm (7 lbf ft). Tighten the casing bolts, followed by the bearing retainer bolts, to the same torque, then remove the clutch housing. Check that the casing halves are not misaligned by more than 0.02 mm (0.0008 in). If they are, repeat the procedure again.
6 Using a dial test indicator, check that the run-out between casing face and the outer track is no more than 0.02 mm (0.0008 in). If it is, lightly tap the outer track to correct, but do not allow the laygear to bind.
7 Measure the difference between the outer track and casing face, then add 0.10 mm (0.004 in) to this for the thickness of the shim to be fitted under the laygear bearing.
8 After making the adjustment, dismantle the casing halves and remove the laygear. Reassemble the mainshaft as given in Section 8.

17 Manual gearbox (BA7) – reassembly

1 Fit the needle roller bearing to the input shaft, then assemble the mainshaft to the input shaft. Check that the synchro unit sleeves are in neutral.
2 Insert the laygear through the bearing retainer, and mesh it with the mainshaft and input shaft (photo). Make sure that the bearing outer tracks are located on the bearings.
3 Lower the gear shafts into the left-hand main casing, and engage the selector forks with the synchro sleeves.
4 Apply RTV sealant to the mating faces, then refit the right-hand casing (photo). Insert and tighten the four corner bolts to 5 Nm (3.5 lbf ft).
5 Smear RTV sealant on the mating face of the clutch housing. Fit the main casing to the clutch housing, and tighten the bolts progressively to 27.5 Nm (20 lbf ft) (photos).
6 Turn the input shaft to seat the laygear bearings.
7 Insert the bearing retaining plate bolts, and tighten them to 10 Nm (7 lbf ft) (photo).
8 Loosen the main casing corner bolts, then tap the casing halves with a wooden mallet while turning the input shaft. Retighten the bolts to 15 Nm (11 lbf ft) (photo).
9 On casing halves located by one dowel, check that the halves are not misaligned by more than 0.02 mm (0.0008 in). If they are, loosen the bolts and repeat the tightening procedure.

10 Insert the remaining casing bolts, and tighten them to the specified torque (photo).

4-speed gearbox
11 Smear RTV sealant on the casing rear face.
12 Refit the rear housing, at the same time engaging the selector finger with the selector dogs. Insert and tighten the bolts, noting that the studs for the exhaust bracket are located at the bottom.
13 Refit the speedometer pinion adaptor and O-ring. Insert and tighten the locking bolt/nut.

5-speed gearbox
14 Smear RTV sealant on the casing rear face (photo).
15 Refit the intermediate housing, at the same time engaging the selector finger with the selector dogs. Tighten the nuts and bolts.
16 Refit the 5th/reverse intermediate shaft.
17 Refit the 5th/reverse synchro hub (photo). If a new hub is being fitted, the grooved end must be towards the reverse gear.
18 Lift the 5th/reverse selector shaft to the 5th position.
19 Engage the 5th selector fork with the synchro sleeve, then lower them onto the selector shaft and synchro hub. Make sure that the previously-made marks on the synchro hub and sleeve are aligned (photo).
20 Fit the selector shaft support tool previously described in Section 5. Align the holes in the shaft and selector fork, then drive in the roll pin (photos). Remove the tool.
21 Select neutral, then refit the 5th speed needle roller bearing and driving gear.
22 Locate the spacer on the 5th speed driving gear.
23 If new components have been fitted, it is now necessary to calculate the thickness of the shim to fit on the 5th speed driving gear, in order to provide an endfloat of 0.05 mm (0.002 in). Temporarily refit the rear housing without the bearing, and measure the distance from the access hole to the spacer on the 5th speed driving gear. Now remove the housing, fit the bearing, and measure the distance from the access hole to the bottom face of the bearing inner track, using a flat metal disc under the bearing for a base point. From the difference, deduct the endfloat required, then obtain a shim of this thickness, and locate it on top of the 5th driving gear spacer.
24 Locate the circlip in the mainshaft groove.
25 Oil the machined portion of the mainshaft. Engage the 5th speed driven gear and speedometer drivegear splines with the mainshaft splines, then draw it fully onto the mainshaft using a long bolt, a nut, washer and metal tubing (photo). Do not allow the gear teeth to foul each other.
26 Fit the circlip to secure the speedometer drive gear (photo).
27 Check that the dowels are fitted to the rear housing. Smear RTV sealant on the mating faces, then locate the rear housing on the intermediate housing while engaging the selector fingers (photos).
28 Insert the bolts and progressively tighten them, occasionally striking the housing to assist seating of the bearing. Tighten the bolts to the specified torque (photo).
29 Fit the O-ring to the plastic plug, then tighten it into the rear housing.
30 Refit the speedometer pinion adaptor. Apply locking fluid to the locking bolt, align the holes, and tighten the bolt.

17.2 Meshing the laygear with the mainshaft and input shaft

17.4 Applying RTV sealant to the left-hand casing mating faces

17.5A Apply RTV sealant to the mating faces ...

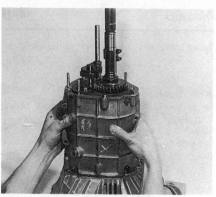
17.5B ... then lower the main casing on the clutch housing ...

17.5C ... and tighten the bolts

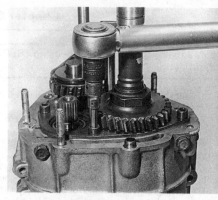
17.7 Tightening the bearing retaining plate bolts

17.8 Tightening the main casing corner bolts

17.10 Tightening the remaining main casing bolts

17.14 Applying RTV sealant to the main casing rear face

17.17 5th/reverse synchro hub (arrowed)

17.19 5th synchro unit alignment marks (arrowed)

17.20A Fit the special tool ...

17.20B ... and drive in the roll pin

17.25 Refitting the 5th speed driven gear and speedometer drivegear

17.26 Fitted circlip

17.27A Rear housing location dowel

17.27B Refitting the rear housing

17.28 Tighten the rear housing bolts progressively

18 Manual gearbox (BA7) – gearchange adjustment

1 Adjustment is only possible on the gate gearchange rod. The dimensions of the remaining gearchange components vary according to model, so it is important to obtain the correct part(s).
2 To adjust the gate gearchange rod, remove the rod then loosen the locknut and adjust the dimension between the socket centres to the following:

Saloon – BA7/4-speed: 111 mm (4.4 in)
Saloon – BA7/5-speed: 103.5 mm (4.1 in)
Estate – BA7/4-speed: 128 mm (5.0 in)
Estate – BA7/5 speed: 120 mm (4.7 in)

3 Tighten the locknut, then refit the rod.

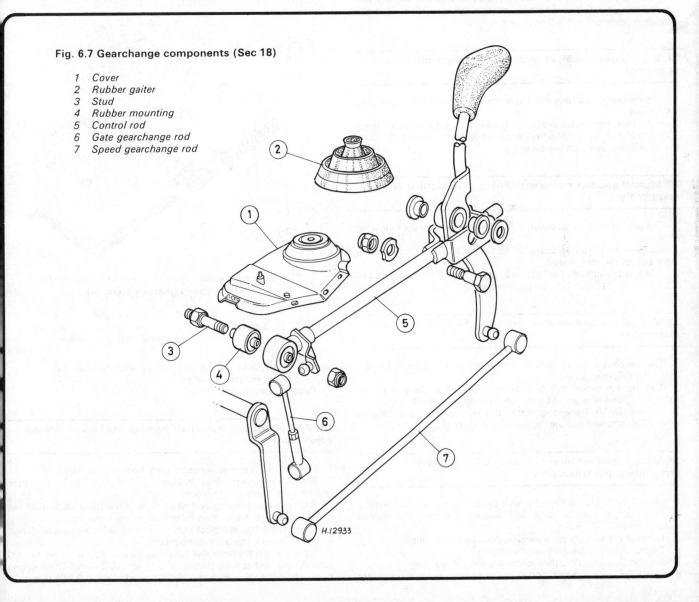

Fig. 6.7 Gearchange components (Sec 18)

1 Cover
2 Rubber gaiter
3 Stud
4 Rubber mounting
5 Control rod
6 Gate gearchange rod
7 Speed gearchange rod

H.12933

19 Manual gearbox (BA10) – overhaul (general)

1   Although components of the BA10 gearbox are not interchange-able with those of the BA7 gearbox, the basic design is the same, and the majority of overhaul procedures are similar.
2   Sections 20 to 26 inclusive describe the procedures which are different. The main areas of difference between the two gearbox types are as follows:

    (a) *Intermediate housing on the BA10/5 gearbox*
    (b) *Mainshaft rear taper roller bearings on early BA10/5 gearboxes*
    (c) *Speedometer drive taken from the 5th speed driving gear instead of the 5th speed driven gear on the BA10/5 gearbox*

20 Manual gearbox (BA10) – dismantling into major assemblies

1   The procedure is as described in Section 5, except for the following differences.
2   Instead of a plastic plug on the rear housing, a metal plate is fitted, with three securing bolts.
3   On the BA10/4-speed gearbox, it is not possible to withdraw the laygear through the rear bearing retaining plate, because the reverse driving gear is larger than the hole in the plate. Before separating the main casing halves, it is therefore necessary to unscrew the nut and remove the gear first. To do this, engage 4th gear, then lock the mainshaft while the nut is being undone.

21 Manual gearbox input shaft (BA10) – dismantling and reassembly

1   The procedure is as described in Section 7, except for the following differences.
2   If the parts mentioned in Section 7, paragraph 4 are renewed, use a 0.20 mm (0.008 in) shim on the input shaft with an oil seal, and just fit the oil thrower alone on the other type.

22 Manual gearbox mainshaft (BA10) – dismantling and reassembly

1   The procedure is as described in Section 8, except for the following differences.
2   On early BA10/5 gearboxes, an additional spacer is fitted on the inner side of the rear bearing.
3   If the parts mentioned in Section 8, paragraph 16 are renewed, use a 2.95 mm (0.116 in) shim next to the bearing.

23 Manual gearbox selector rods (BA10) – dismantling and reassembly

1   The procedure is as described in Section 11, except for the following differences.
2   The 3rd/4th detent ball and spring is located at the rear of the half-casing, and is retained by the rear bearing outer track.
3   On the BA10/4-speed gearbox, the reverse idler gear dog is retained by a detent ball and spring with a cover plug.

24 Manual gearbox intermediate housing (BA10/5) – dismantling and reassembly

1   Extract the circlip and washer from the end of the selector shaft.
2   Pull out the selector shaft, and disengage it from the splined selector finger.
3   Recover the spring cup, spring, bush and selector finger.
4   Extract the O-ring seals from the housing.
5   Dip the O-rings in oil, then locate them in the housing.
6   Insert the selector shaft, and at the same time locate the selector

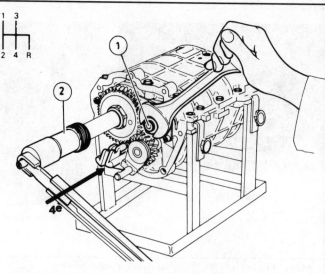

Fig. 6.8 Loosening the reverse driving gear retaining nut (Sec 20)

    1 Nut   *2 Adaptor*

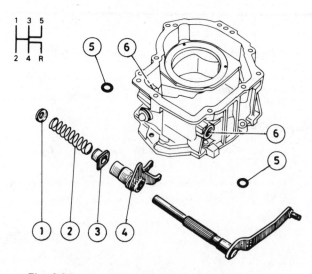

Fig. 6.9 Intermediate housing components on the BA10/5-speed gearbox (Sec 24)

1 Cup		*4 Selector finger*
2 Spring		*5 O-ring seals*
3 Bush		*6 Seal seating in housing*

finger on the splines, so that it is aligned with the shaft arm.
7   Refit the bush, spring and cup.
8   Refit the washer and circlip.

25 Manual gearbox mainshaft bearing (BA10/5) – preload adjustment

1   Remove the rear bearing outer track from the rear housing.
2   Remove any shims, then fit shims of 4.0 mm (0.158 in) thickness and refit the bearing outer track.
3   Refit the rear housing and hand-tighten the three bolts. Turn the mainshaft several times, then hand-tighten the bolts again.
4   Using feeler blades, check that the mating faces are parallel. If not, loosen or tighten the bolts as necessary.
5   Note the gap between the housings, then deduct this from the 4.0 mm (0.1 in), and add the preload of 0.10 mm (0.004 in). The resulting thickness is the shim thickness to fit instead of the 4.0 mm shim.

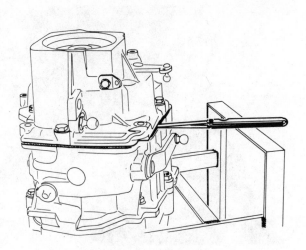

Fig. 6.10 Determining the mainshaft taper bearing preload on the BA10/5-speed gearbox (Sec 25)

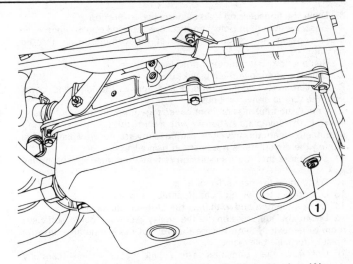

Fig. 6.11 Automatic transmission fluid drain plug (1) (Sec 27)

26 Manual gearbox (BA10) – gearchange adjustment

Refer to Section 18, but note the following dimension for the gate gearchange rod:

Saloon – BA 10/5-speed: 111 mm (4.4 in)

27 Automatic transmission fluid – draining and refilling

1 The engine and transmission must be at normal operating temperature, after driving for at least 3 miles.
2 Apply the handbrake. Jack up the front of the vehicle and support on axle stands.
3 Position a suitable container beneath the transmission.

4 Unscrew the drain plug, and allow the fluid to drain. As the fluid will be very hot, take precautions to prevent scalding.
5 Refit and tighten the drain plug.
6 Remove the dipstick, and refill the transmission with the correct grade and quantity of fresh fluid, using a funnel in the dipstick tube.
7 Run the engine for 4 or 5 minutes, then check that the level is within the 'Cold' ('Froid') section on the dipstick.

28 Automatic transmission – removal and refitting

1 On Saloon models, follow the procedure given in Section 3, paragraphs 19, and 21 to 33 inclusive.
2 On Estate models, follow the procedure given in Section 4, paragraph 1, then paragraphs 7 to 14 and 19 to 34.

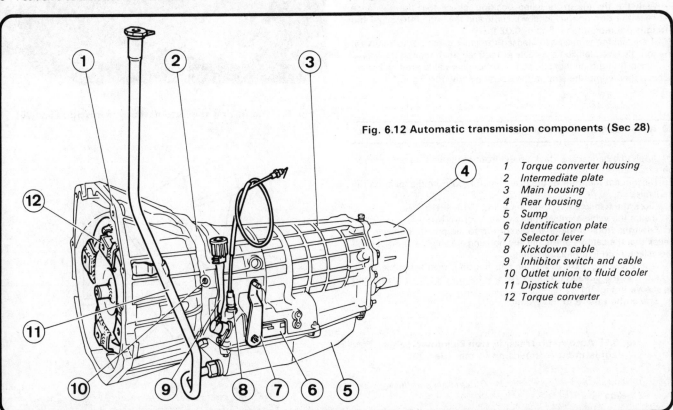

Fig. 6.12 Automatic transmission components (Sec 28)

1 Torque converter housing
2 Intermediate plate
3 Main housing
4 Rear housing
5 Sump
6 Identification plate
7 Selector lever
8 Kickdown cable
9 Inhibitor switch and cable
10 Outlet union to fluid cooler
11 Dipstick tube
12 Torque converter

3   Drain the transmission fluid as described in Section 27.
4   Unscrew the union bolts and disconnect the oil cooler pipes.
5   Disconnect the kickdown cable at the carburettor or throttle housing.
6   Remove the starter motor if not already done.
7   Unbolt and remove the dipstick tube.
8   On carburettor engines, unbolt and remove the left-hand cover from the torque converter housing.
9   Unbolt the transmission front cover, together with the TDC sensor.
10 Hold the driveplate stationary with a screwdriver in the starter ring gear teeth, then unscrew the torque converter-to-driveplate bolts, turning the driveplate as necessary to gain access.
11 Make sure that the transmission is firmly mounted on the trolley jack.
12 Disconnect the gear selector lever.
13 Disconnect the wiring from the inhibitor switch.
14 Loosen the bolt and withdraw the speedometer drive cable.
15 Lower the transmission on the trolley jack to provide sufficient room to remove it. Slightly raise the front of the engine also, using a hoist or further trolley jack.
16 Unscrew the transmission-to-engine bolts, then carefully withdraw the transmission, making sure that the torque converter remains fully engaged with the oil pump drive. As a precaution, a length of metal plate may be attached to the torque converter housing to keep the converter in place.
17 Refitting is a reversal of removal, but note the following additional points:

(a) Apply a little grease to the centre of the driveplate to assist location of the torque converter
(b) Apply locking fluid to the threads of the torque converter-to-driveplate bolts before inserting and tightening them
(c) Refill the transmission with fluid, with reference to Section 27
(d) Adjust the kickdown cable as described in Section 29
(e) Adjust the gear selector lever as described in Section 30

Fig. 6.13 Using a metal plate (1) to retain the torque converter (Sec 28)

29 Automatic transmission – kickdown cable adjustment

1   Run the engine to normal operating temperature, then switch it off.
2   With the throttle in its idling position, check that the clearance between the stop on the kickdown cable and the end of the cable end fitting is not more than 0.5 mm (0.02 in).
3   If adjustment is necessary, loosen the inner cable clamp screw on the throttle lever, tension the cable as required, then tighten the screw.
4   When fitting a new cable, pull out the inner cable until kickdown occurs, then crimp the stop in the position shown in Fig. 6.16.

Fig. 6.14 Removing the automatic transmission (Sec 28)

30 Automatic transmission gear selector lever – adjustment

1   Apply the handbrake. Jack up the front of the vehicle and support on axle stands.
2   Disconnect the front of the gear selector rod from the lever on the transmission.
3   Place the transmission lever in neutral ('N').
4   Inside the vehicle, move the selector lever to 'N'.
5   Offer the front of the gear selector rod to the pin on the lever, and check that the centres of the pin and housing are aligned. If not, adjust the selector rod length as required.
6   Apply a little grease to the pin and housing, then assemble them, noting that the vibration damper (where fitted) should be positioned as shown in Fig. 6.17.
7   Lower the vehicle to the ground.

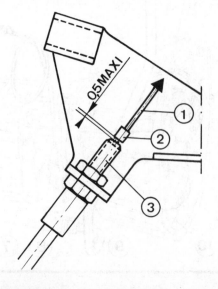

Fig. 6.15 Automatic transmission kickdown cable adjustment – dimension in mm (Sec 29)

1   Inner cable   3   Outer cable end fitting
2   Stop

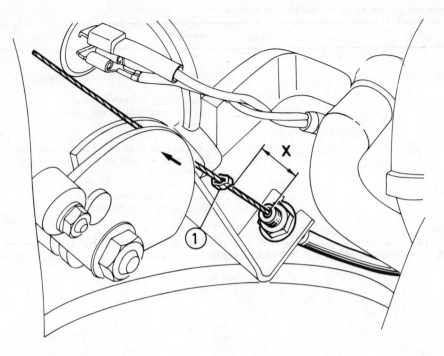

Fig. 6.16 Correct position of crimped stop (1) when kickdown occurs (Sec 29)

X = 39.0 mm (1.54 in)

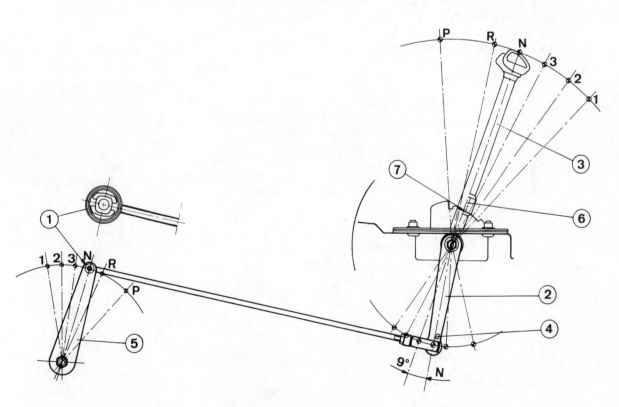

Fig. 6.17 Automatic transmission selector lever components (Sec 30)

1	Vibration damper	4	Identification mark	6	Locking finger
2	Lower lever	5	Transmission lever	7	Stop
3	Selector lever				

31 Fault diagnosis – manual gearbox and automatic transmission

Symptom	Reason(s)
Manual gearbox	
Weak or ineffective synchromesh	Synchromesh units worn or damaged
Jumps out of gear	Gearchange mechanism worn Synchromesh units badly worn Selector fork badly worn
Excessive noise	Incorrect grade of oil, or oil level too low Gear teeth excessively worn or damaged Worn bearings
Difficulty in engaging gears	Worn selector components Worn synchromesh units

Automatic transmission

Automatic transmission faults are almost always the result of low fluid level, or incorrect adjustment of the kickdown cable or selector lever. Apart from this, any fault is probably internal and should be diagnosed by a Peugeot dealer, who will have the special equipment necessary to pinpoint the problem.

Chapter 7 Propeller shaft

Contents

Specifications

Type

Saloon	Propeller shaft enclosed in link tube, attached to rear of gearbox and front of unsprung final drive unit
Estate	Propeller shaft enclosed in torque tube, attached to rear axle and pivoting on rear of gearbox

Torque wrench settings

	Nm	lbf ft
Saloon models		
Link tube mounting nuts/bolts	60	44
Vibration damper	35	26
Front seat reinforcement bar	18	13
Rear crossmember mounting nuts	35	26
Estate models		
Torque tube front ball cover halves	18	13
Torque tube to rear axle	55	41
Front ball cover to gearbox	43	32

General description

On Saloon models, the propeller shaft is enclosed in a link tube, which is bolted to the rear of the gearbox and the front of the final drive unit. The shaft incorporates internal splines at each end, which engage with the gearbox output shaft and final drive pinion shaft. A centre bearing supports the shaft within the link tube.

On Estate models, the propeller shaft is enclosed in a torque tube, which is bolted to the rear axle. The front end of the torque tube incorporates a spherical bearing, which allows the rear axle to move freely, so a universal joint is fitted between the gearbox output shaft and the propeller shaft. The rear of the propeller shaft has internal splines for engagement with the pinion shaft, whereas the front has external splines to engage the universal joint. As on Saloon models, a centre bearing supports the shaft within the torque tube.

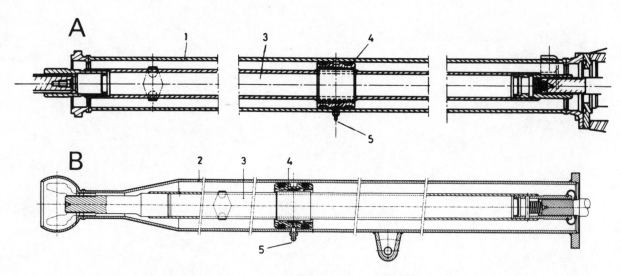

Fig. 7.1 Cross-section of the propeller shaft fitted to Saloon models (A) and Estate models (B) (Sec 1)

1 Link tube	3 Propeller shaft	5 Grease nipple
2 Torque tube	4 Centre bearing	

2 Routine maintenance

Carry out the following procedures at the intervals given in Routine maintenance *at the front of this manual*

Grease propeller shaft centre bearing

1 Chock the front wheels, then jack up the rear of the vehicle and support on axle stands. Locate the grease nipple in the middle of the link tube or torque tube.
2 Using a grease gun, force grease into the centre bearing.

Grease torque tube front bearing (Estate models only)

3 With the vehicle supported on axle stands, use a grease gun to force grease into the torque tube front ball, through the grease nipple on the ball cover halves.

3 Propeller shaft (Saloon models) – removal, inspection and refitting

1 Before commencing work, it is recommended that the special tool shown in Fig. 7.2 are obtained, or alternatively, fabricated. The guid pins (Peugeot tool 0906 ZZ) are necessary to support the re crossmember, but long bolts and washers may be used instead. Th plate is necessary to support the propeller shaft within the link tube and may be made from plywood about 20 mm (0.8 in) thick.
2 Chock the front wheels, then jack up the rear of the car and suppo on axle stands.
3 Refer to Chapter 3, and disconnect the exhaust system from th exhaust manifold and mounting rubbers. Tie the front end to th underbody, and rest the rear end on the rear crossmember.
4 As applicable, unbolt the exhaust heat shield and front sea reinforcement bar from the underbody.

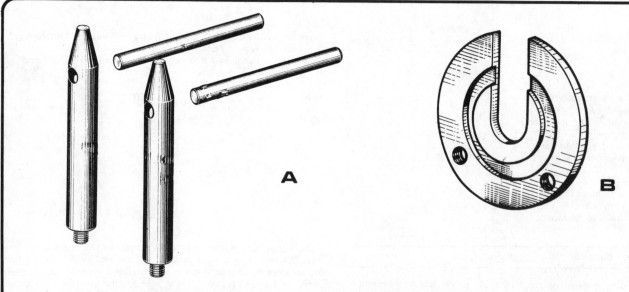

Fig. 7.2 Special tools required when removing the propeller shaft on Saloon models (Sec 3)

A Rear crossmember support guide pins   B Propeller shaft holding plate

5   Support the final drive unit, then either unbolt the side mountings or upper bracket (according to type), and lower the final drive unit so that the link tube rests on the rear crossmember.
6   Support the rear crossmember with a trolley jack.
7   Working inside the car, remove the rear seat to give access to the rear crossmember mounting nuts. Do not confuse these nuts with the rear suspension crossmember mounting nuts, which are not locked with tab washers.
8   Unscrew the front nut on each side, the lift the tab washers and remove the centre plug. Screw the guide pins or long bolts into the rear crossmember threaded holes. Leave the tommy bars in the guide pins, to support the rear crossmember.
9   Unscrew the rear nuts and remove the tab washers.
10 Lower the rear crossmember until the tommy bars or washers contact the floor.
11 Support the final drive unit with the trolley jack.
12 Unscrew the four nuts securing the final drive unit to the link tube, then withdraw the final drive unit rearwards, while guiding the propeller shaft from the splines on the pinion shaft. Extract the spring from inside the rear of the propeller shaft, and put it in a safe place.
13 Where applicable, unbolt the bump stop and bracket from the bottom of the link tube and crossmember.
14 Unscrew the four bolts securing the front of the link tube to the gearbox (photo), withdraw the link tube about 20 mm (0.81 in) and locate the support plate in the groove in the propeller shaft. Use two bolts to secure the plate to the bottom holes of the link tube.
15 Move the exhaust system to one side.
16 Release the propeller shaft from the gearbox output shaft splines, then lower the front of the link tube and withdraw the assembly forwards.
17 Clean the outer surface of the link tube.
18 Withdraw the propeller shaft from the link tube. Where fitted, unbolt the vibration damper from the link tube.
19 Examine the propeller shaft for wear and damage, especially at the splines, and at the centre, where it is supported in the needle bearing. Mount the shaft between centres, and use a dial test indicator to check the run-out on the centre bearing shoulder – it should not exceed 0.2 mm (0.008 in).
20 Similarly examine the link tube for wear and damage. With the tube mounted between centres, the run-out at the centre should not exceed 2.0 mm (0.079 in), and the run-out at each end should not exceed 0.05 mm (0.002 in).
21 Refitting is a reversal of removal, but note the following additional points:

(a) Lubricate the propeller shaft splines with a little grease
(b) Tighten all nuts and bolts to the specified torque
(c) Refer to Chapter 8 when refitting the final drive unit
(d) Refer to Chapter 3 when refitting the exhaust system

(e) Lock the rear crossmember mounting nuts by bending the tab washers
(f) Check, and if necessary top up, the gearbox oil level or automatic transmission fluid level
(g) Lubricate the propeller shaft centre bearing with grease through the nipple on the link tube
(h) Where a bump stop is fitted, the bracket must be centralised before tightening the bolts. With the circular bump stop rubber this is straightforward but with the elliptical rubber, refer to Figs. 7.6 and 7.7. A 5.0 mm (0.2 in) diameter twist drill should be used to set the clearance between the rear of the rubber and the bracket.

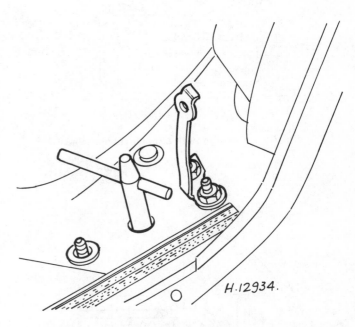

Fig. 7.3 Rear crossmember support guide pin and tommy bar in position (Sec 3)

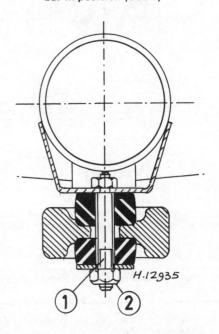

Fig. 7.4 Cross-section of the vibration damper (Sec 3)

1 Stud   2 Nut

3.14 Unscrewing the link tube-to-gearbox bolts

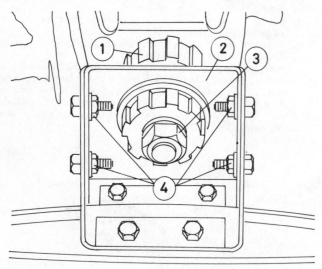

Fig. 7.5 Bump stop with circular rubber (Sec 3)

1 Rubber   3 Nut
2 Bracket   4 Bolts

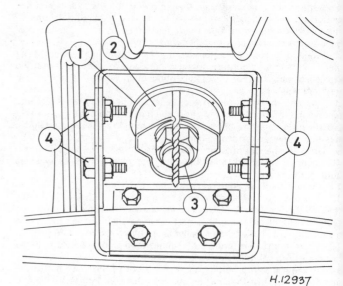

Fig. 7.6 Adjustment of bump stop with elliptical rubber
(Sec 3)

1 Bracket   3 Nut
2 Rubber   4 Bolts

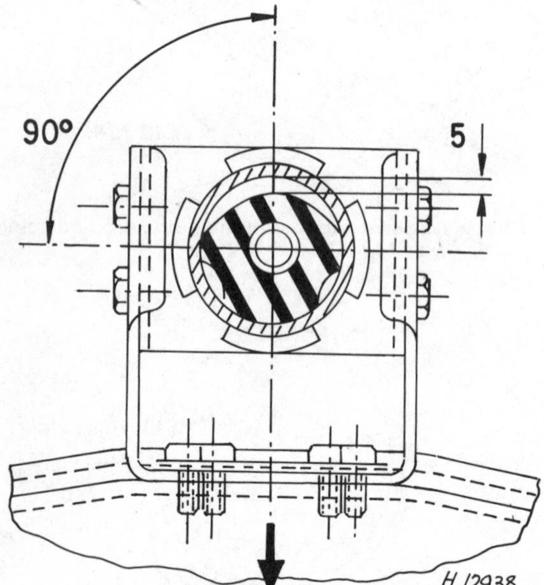

Fig. 7.7 Diagrammatic top view of elliptical rubber bump
stop adjustment – dimension in mm (Sec 3)

FRONT

90°

5

H.12938

4 Unscrew and remove the bolts securing the anti-roll bar links to the underbody, and withdraw the links from the brackets.
5 Pull out the spring plate securing the flexible brake hose to the torque tube. Do not disconnect the rigid brake line from the flexible hose.
6 Release the rigid brake line support, and also unclip the rear brake compensator supply line from the underbody.
7 Unbolt the compensator spring from the torque tube, and remove the compensator from the underbody, but do not disconnect the hydraulic lines.
8 Unbolt the hydraulic line three-way union from the top of the rear axle casing, but do not disconnect the hydraulic lines.
9 Unscrew and remove one of the nuts securing the front seat reinforcement bar to the underbody. Loosen the remaining nut, and swivel the bar to one side of the torque tube.
10 At the front of the torque tube, unscrew the bolts securing the ball

4 Propeller shaft (Estate models) – removal, inspection and refitting

1 Chock the front wheels, then jack up the rear of the vehicle and support on axle stands positioned on the underbody.
2 Unscrew fully the handbrake cable adjustment nuts (see Chapter 9 if necessary).
3 Move the front seats fully forwards, and remove the centre console. Unhook the handbrake inner cables from the equaliser.

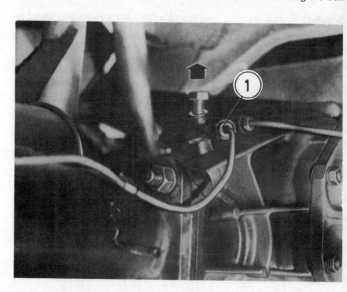

Fig. 7.8 Unbolting the three-way union (1) from the rear
axle (Sec 4)

cover halves to the rear of the gearbox. The bolts are socket-headed, so an Allen key will be required to remove them.

11 Using a trolley jack, raise the rear axle slightly, then unscrew and remove both rear shock absorber lower mounting bolts.

12 Unscrew the nuts securing the rear of the torque tube to the rear axle.

13 Unscrew the nut from the torque tube stay bar front mounting bolt (photo).

14 Lower the rear axle sufficiently to allow the rear wheels to clear the rear wheel arches.

15 Support the torque tube stay bars on axle stands.

16 Move the rear axle rearwards until the front of the propeller shaft slips from the universal joint splines.

17 Remove the stay bar front mounting bolt, and withdraw the torque tube forwards from the rear axle.

18 Extract the spring from inside the rear of the propeller shaft, and put it in a safe place. Also remove the rubber gaiter.

19 Withdraw the propeller shaft rearwards from the torque tube.

20 Unbolt the torque tube ball cover halves, and remove the O-ring (photo).

21 Clean the propeller shaft and examine it for wear and damage, especially at the splines, and at the centre, where it is supported in the needle bearing. Mount the shaft between centres, and use a dial test indicator to check the run-out on the centre bearing shoulder – it should not exceed 0.2 mm (0.008 in).

22 Similarly examine the torque tube for wear and damage. With the tube mounted between centres, the run-out at the centre should not exceed 2.0 mm (0.079 in).

23 Commence refitting by applying grease to the torque ball. Locate the O-ring, reassemble the cover halves, then insert and tighten the bolts to the specified torque.

24 Grease the propeller shaft splines and centre bearing shoulder. Fit the rear spring and rubber gaiter, making sure that the gaiter locates in the shaft groove.

25 Slide the rear of the propeller shaft onto the rear axle pinion shaft, then locate the torque tube over the propeller shaft. Tighten the nuts to the specified torque.

26 Fit the stay bar front mounting bolt and tighten the nut.

27 Raise the front of the torque tube. Move the rear axle forwards, so that the propeller shaft engages the universal joint splines.

28 Insert and tighten the bolts securing the ball cover halves to the rear of the gearbox.

29 Fit and tighten the nuts securing the rear of the torque tube to the rear axle.

30 Check that the rear coil springs are correctly located in their cups. Raise the rear axle on the trolley jack.

31 Refit and tighten the rear shock absorber lower mounting bolts, together with the spacer washers (refer to Chapter 10 if necessary).

32 Refit the front seat reinforcement bar, and tighten the nuts.

33 Refit the hydraulic line three-way union, and tighten the bolt.

34 Refit the compensator and spring, and tighten the bolts.

35 Refit the brake lines and flexible hose.

36 Refit the anti-roll bar links to the underbody, and tighten the bolts.

37 Reconnect the handbrake cables, and adjust as described in Chapter 9.

38 Refit the centre console.

39 Grease the propeller shaft centre bearing and torque tube ball through the nipples provided.

40 Check, and if necessary top up, the rear axle oil level.

41 Lower the vehicle to the ground.

Fig. 7.9 Disconnecting the torque tube and propeller shaft from the rear of the gearbox (Sec 4)

1   Torque ball cover halves

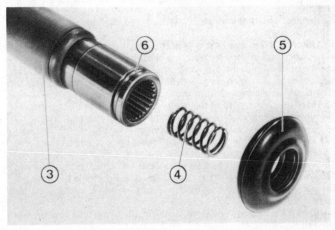

Fig. 7.10 Propeller shaft components (Sec 4)

3   Propeller shaft (rear end)   5   Rubber gaiter
4   Spring   6   Groove for gaiter

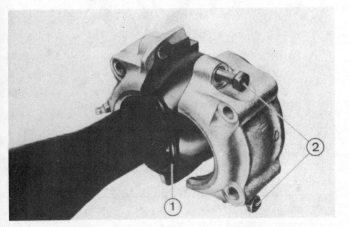

Fig. 7.11 Torque tube ball cover halves (Sec 4)

1   O-ring   2   Bolts

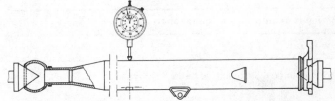

Fig. 7.12 Checking the torque tube for run-out (Sec 4)

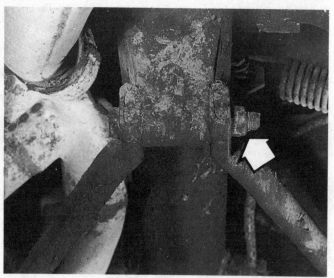

4.13 Torque tube stay bar front mounting bolt (arrowed)

4.20 Torque tube ball cover halves and O-ring

5 Propeller shaft centre bearing – removal and refitting

1 Before commencing work, it is necessary to obtain a tool for removing and refitting the bearing. Peugeot tool 8.0403 is shown in Fig. 7.13, and consists basically of a slide hammer fitted with a rocker which engages the bearing after inserting the tool. The tool also incorporates a guide plate and depth setting ring. although this tool ensures quick and accurate removal and refitting of the bearing, the use of a wooden or soft metal dowel rod will also achieve the same objective.

2 Remove the propeller shaft as described in Section 3 or 4, as applicable.

3 Unscrew the grease nipple from the centre of the tube.

4 Using a tape measure, determine the fitted position of the centre bearing in relation to the rear flange face of the tube. Since the bearing has a central lubrication groove, this dimension will be the distance to the grease nipple, less half the width of the bearing.

5 Drive the bearing out of the rear of the tube, using one of the tools described in paragraph 1. If using the special Peugeot tool, it is recommended that the bearing is first driven forwards slightly, in order to free it off. If this precaution is not taken, there is a risk of the tool rocker damaging the bearing track.

6 Wash the bearing in a suitable solvent, and check it for wear and damage. If the needle rollers are pitted, the bearing should be renewed. Temporarily fit the bearing on the propeller shaft, and check for excessive play.

7 To refit the bearing, first lubricate the inside of the tube with engine oil.

8 Dip the centre bearing in oil, then insert it in the tube and drive it to its correct position with the tool.

9 Refit and tighten the grease nipple.

10 Refit the propeller shaft with reference to Section 3 or 4, as applicable.

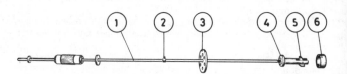

Fig. 7.13 Peugeot tool for removing and refitting the centre bearing (Sec 5)

1 Slide hammer
2 Depth setting ring
3 Guide plate
4 Support
5 Removal rocker
6 Guide bush

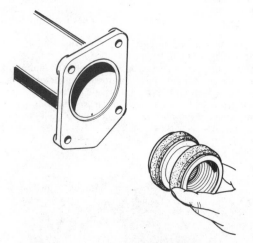

Fig. 7.14 Centre bearing removal (Sec 5)

6 Fault diagnosis – propeller shaft

Symptom	Reason(s)
Noise from final drive unit/rear axle	Lack of lubricant Worn bearings, crownwheel and pinion Worn centre bearing
Knock when taking up drive (Estate models only)	Worn universal joint bearings Lack of grease on torque ball

Chapter 8 Rear axle

Contents

Specifications

Type
Saloon ....

Estate ....

Unsprung final drive unit mounted on underbody, separate driveshafts with triple-pin spider constant velocity joints at each end
Conventional rigid rear axle, and torque tube propeller shaft

Final drive ratio ....

3.58 : 1, 3.89 : 1, or 4.22 : 1

Lubrication
Final drive lubricant type/specification:
  Except limited-slip differential ....
  Limited-slip differential ....
Capacity:
  Saloon ....
  Estate ....
Driveshaft CV joint lubricant type/specification ....

Gear oil, viscosity SAE 80W/90 (Duckhams Hypoid 80S)
Gear oil, viscosity SAE 90 (Duckhams Hypoid 90DL)

1.55 litres (2.7 pints)
1.6 litres (2.8 pints)
Special lubricant supplied in repair kit

Torque wrench settings
Final drive unit mounting:
  Two side mountings ....
  One top mounting ....
Rear hub carrier (Saloon models) ....
Driveshaft/hub nut (Saloon models) ....
Brake shoe backplate (Estate models) ....

Nm	lbf ft
38	28
95	70
50	37
280	207
50	37

1 General description

On Saloon models, the final drive unit is mounted on the rear suspension upper crossmember, with separate driveshafts transmitting the drive to hubs on the independent rear suspension arms. The driveshafts incorporate inner and outer constant velocity joints of the triple-pin spider type. On Estate models, the rear axle is of the rigid type, incorporating a torque tube with enclosed propeller shaft.

A limited-slip differential unit is fitted to certain models. It incorporates a slip cone and four pressure springs, which lock the differential gears when one roadwheel loses traction and attempts to spin.

Due to the need for specialised tooling, overhaul of the differential unit is not covered in this Chapter. Work of this nature should be entrusted to a Peugeot dealer or suitably-equipped engineering works.

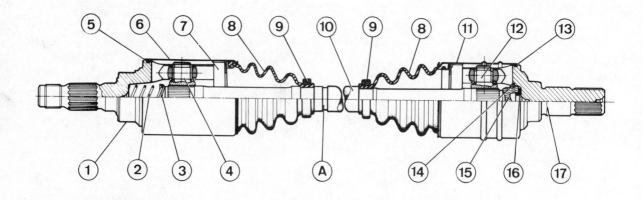

Fig. 8.1 Cross-section of a driveshaft fitted to Saloon models (Sec 1)

1 Stub axle and yoke (tulip)
2 Spring
3 Cup
4 Spider
5 O-ring

6 Cover
7 Spacer
8 Rubber bellows
9 Retaining ring

10 Driveshaft
11 Cover
12 Spider
13 O-ring

14 Stop ring
15 Stop
16 Spring washer
17 Yoke (tulip)

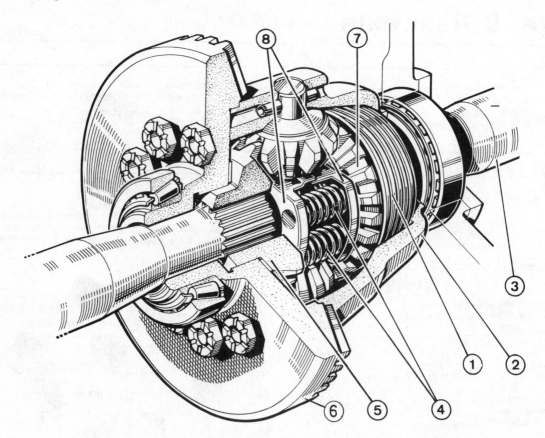

Fig. 8.2 Cutaway view of the limited-slip differential unit (Sec 1)

1 Slip cone
2 Crownwheel carrier
3 Driveshaft
4 Pressure springs

5 Differential sun gear –
   crownwheel side
6 Crownwheel

7 Differential sun gear – slip
   cone side
8 Pressure spring cages

2 Routine maintenance

Carry out the following procedures at the intervals given in Routine maintenance *at the front of this manual*

Check the oil level in the rear axle/final drive unit

1 With the vehicle over an inspection pit, or jacked up level and supported on axle stands, unscrew the filler plug from the rear axle/final drive unit (photos).
2 Using a short length of wire, check that the oil level is up to the bottom of the filler plug hole. If not, top up using the correct grade of oil. If constant topping-up is necessary, investigate the cause, and carry out repairs as required. Areas to check are driveshaft oil seals in Saloon models, and side tube gaskets on Estate models.

Check driveshaft rubber bellows (Saloon models)

3 Chock the front wheels, then jack up the rear of the car and support on axle stands. Clean the driveshaft rubber bellows and check them for deterioration and cuts.
4 If necessary, renew the rubber bellows.

Renew rear axle/final drive unit oil

5 With the vehicle over an inspection pit, or jacked up level and supported on axle stands, unscrew the filler and drain plugs, and allow the oil to drain into a suitable container.
6 Refit and tighten the drain plug.
7 Fill the rear axle/final drive unit with the correct grade and quantity of oil.
8 Refit and tighten the filler plug.

3 Final drive unit (Saloon models) – removal and refitting

1 Chock the front wheels. Jack up the rear of the car, and support on axle stands positioned beneath the rear suspension arms.
2 Remove the left-hand rear wheel.
3 Unscrew the filler and drain plugs, and drain the oil from the final drive unit into a suitable container. Refit and tighten the drain plug.
4 Unclip the brake hydraulic line and hose from the left-hand rear suspension arm.
5 On models with rear disc brakes, unclip the left-hand handbrake cable.
6 On models with rear drum brakes, remove the left-hand rear drum and disconnect the handbrake cable from the lever (refer to Chapter 9 if necessary).
7 Unscrew the socket-headed bolts securing the left-hand hub carrier to the rear suspension arm.
8 Lever the left-hand driveshaft, together with the hub and brake assembly, from the final drive unit, and rest it on an axle stand.
9 Where applicable, unbolt the brake compensator lever, and unhook the spring located to the left of the final drive unit.
10 Unbolt the exhaust mounting(s) from the final drive unit.
11 Unscrew the nuts securing the propeller shaft link tube to the final drive unit.
12 Support the final drive unit on a trolley jack.
13 Unscrew either the side mounting bolts (photo) or the lower link mounting bolt (according to type), then free the final drive unit from the link tube, making sure that the propeller shaft remains engaged with the gearbox output shaft.
14 Move the final drive unit to the left, and release it from the right-hand driveshaft. Support the driveshaft on an axle stand.
15 Lower the final drive unit, and withdraw it from under the car.
16 Examine the driveshaft oil seals in each side of the final drive unit for deterioration and signs of leakage, and if necessary, renew them. To do this, prise out the old seals, clean the seatings, then drive the new seals into position using a block of wood. Smear a little grease on the oil seal lips, final drive pinion splines and driveshaft splines. Make sure that the spring is positioned in the rear of the propeller shaft. Renew the pinion oil seal if necessary.
17 Refitting is a reversal of removal, but tighten all nuts and bolts to the specified torque. Where applicable, make sure that the lower link mounting bolt washers are correctly assembled, as shown in Fig. 8.3. Where a bump stop is fitted to the bottom of the link tube, adjust it as described in Chapter 7. Refill the final drive unit with the correct grade

2.1A Final drive unit filler plug (A) and drain (B) – Saloon models

2.1B Rear axle filler plug (A) and drain plug (B) – Estate models

3.13 Final drive unit side mounting bolt (arrowed)

and quantity of oil, and refit the filler plug. On completion, depress the brake pedal several times, in order to set the brake shoes or pads in the normal working position.

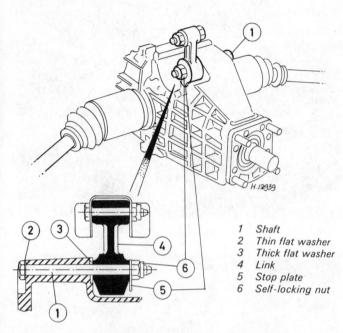

Fig. 8.3 Cross-section of link mounting for final drive unit (Sec 3)

1   Shaft
2   Thin flat washer
3   Thick flat washer
4   Link
5   Stop plate
6   Self-locking nut

4   Rear axle and differential unit (Estate models) – removal and refitting

1   Chock the front wheels. Jack up the rear of the car, and support on axle stands positioned under the rear jacking points. Remove both rear wheels.
2   Unscrew the rear axle filler and drain plugs, and drain the oil into a suitable container. Refit and tighten the drain plug.
3   With the handbrake released, remove the screws and withdraw the brake drums.
4   Disconnect the handbrake cables from the shoe operating levers. Remove the shoe steady springs, lever out the leading shoes, and use a small drift to drive the handbrake outer cables from the backplates. Unclip the cables from the axle tie-rods.
5   Disconnect the tension spring from the brake compensator and the bracket on the torque tube.
6   Fit a brake hose clamp to the flexible hose for the rear brakes.
7   Unscrew the union nut and disconnect the rigid brake pipe from the flexible hose, then detach the hose from the bracket on the torque tube.
8   Unscrew the nuts securing the anti-roll bar links to the rear underbody, then prise the links free.
9   Unbolt the Panhard rod from the rear axle casing.
10 Support the rear axle with a trolley jack.
11 Unscrew the shock absorber lower mounting nuts, and detach the shock absorbers from the rear axle.
12 Lower the rear axle until all tension is released from the coil springs, then lift the springs from their locations. Support the rear axle.
13 Unscrew and remove the bolt securing the front of the tie-rods to the torque tube.
14 Unscrew the nuts securing the torque tube to the front of the differential housing.
15 Lower the rear axle, then support the torque tube and withdraw the rear axle rearwards, making sure that the propeller shaft remains in

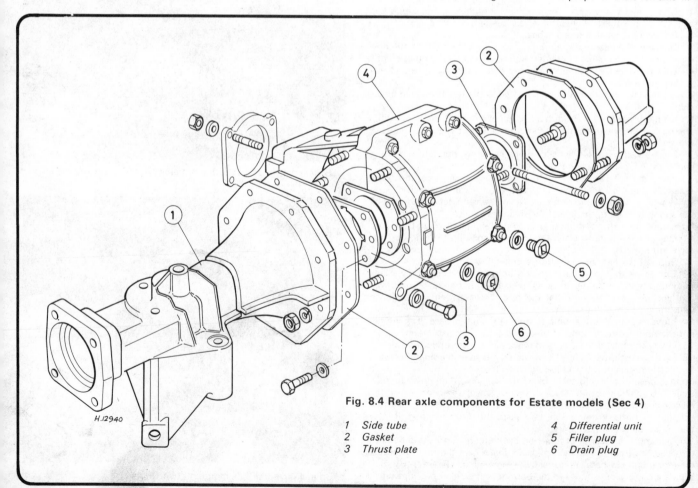

Fig. 8.4 Rear axle components for Estate models (Sec 4)

1   Side tube   4   Differential unit
2   Gasket   5   Filler plug
3   Thrust plate   6   Drain plug

engagement with the universal joint on the rear of the gearbox. Check also that the preload spring remains inside the rear of the propeller shaft.

16 To remove the differential unit, disconnect the rigid brake pipes and unscrew the nuts securing the side tubes. Recover the gaskets and side plates.

17 Refitting is a reversal of removal, but note the following additional points:

(a) Renew the side tube gaskets where removed
(b) Tighten all nuts and bolts to the specified torque
(c) On completion, refill the rear axle with the correct grade and quantity of oil, and refit the filler plug
(d) Bleed the rear brake hydraulic circuit (Chapter 9)

5 Driveshaft (Saloon models) – removal and refitting

1 Chock the front wheels, then jack up the rear of the car and support on axle stands. Remove the rear wheel on the side being worked on.
2 Using a trolley jack, raise the rear suspension arm without lifting the rear of the car off the axle stands.
3 Unclip the flexible brake hose from the rear suspension arm bracket, and also release the rigid brake line where applicable.
4 On models with rear disc brakes, unbolt the caliper and support it to one side.
5 On models with rear drum brakes, remove the drum, disconnect the handbrake cable from the shoe operating lever, and unclip the cable from the rear suspension arm.
6 The hub must now be held stationary while the hub nut is loosened. To do this, fit a length of metal bar to two wheel studs, with its end resting on the floor. Unscrew and remove the hub nut and washer, then remove the metal bar.
7 Using an Allen key through the hole in the drive flange, unscrew the socket-headed bolts securing the hub carrier to the rear suspension arm.

Drum brake models

8 Support the hub and brake shoe backplate assembly, then carefully lever the inner end of the driveshaft from the final drive unit, lower it, and support it on an axle stand. Be prepared for slight oil leakage from the final drive unit. Take care not to damage the rigid brake pipe leading to the rear wheel cylinder. An alternative method to remove the driveshaft is to screw two long bolts into the rear suspension arm from the inner side, to act as extractors by pressing against the inner face of the hub. If this method is used, a lever will not be required, and the bolts will also keep the hub suspended.
9 Using a suitable puller, press the driveshaft from the hub splines, and withdraw it inwards from the rear suspension arm.

5.13 Lock the hub nut at opposite points (arrowed)

Disc brake models

10 Carefully lever the inner end of the driveshaft from the final drive unit, and withdraw it, complete with the disc and backplate, outwards from the rear suspension arm.
11 Remove the backplate from the inner end of the the driveshaft.
12 Using a puller or press, separate the driveshaft from the hub splines.

All models

13 Refitting is a reversal of the removal procedure, but note the following additional points:

(a) Clean the driveshaft splines, then apply grease to the inner splines, and spray the outer splines with Molykote 321, or a similar molybdenum disulphide-based liquid
(b) Apply grease to the lips of the seals in the hub and final drive unit
(c) Renew spring washers and the hub nut
(d) Tighten all nuts and bolts to the specified torque
(e) After tightening the hub nut, lock it by punching the shoulder at opposite points into the grooves in the driveshaft stub (photo)
(f) On completion, check and if necessary top up the final drive oil level

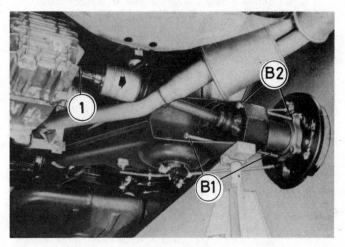

Fig. 8.5 Using two long bolts (B1 and B2) when removing the driveshaft on Saloon models (Sec 5)

1 Driveshaft inner splines

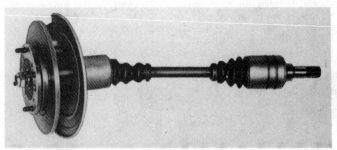

Fig. 8.6 Driveshaft and disc assembly (Sec 5)

6 Driveshaft (Saloon models) – overhaul

1 Mount the driveshaft vertically in a vice.
2 Bind some adhesive tape around the oil seal bearing face of the tulip to protect it from damage.
3 Using a pair of end cutters, carefully bend back the cover (Fig. 8.7).
4 Disengage the cover by lightly tapping with a soft-faced hammer (Fig. 8.8).
5 Remove the tulip by raising it vertically. On the wheel side joint, recover the spring and thrust cup.

Fig. 8.7 Bending back the end of the driveshaft cover (Sec 6)

Fig. 8.8 Releasing the cover from the tulip (Sec 6)

6   Slide the gaiter down on the shaft as far as possible.
7   Bind some adhesive tape around the bearing pack. This is a paired component, and must not be separated (Fig. 8.9).
8   Carefully remove as much grease as possible. **Do not** use any solvents.
9   Using a large vice or press, extract the bearing pack (Fig 8.10). Don't forget to hold the driveshaft or it will drop onto the floor. There is no need to remove the three punch marks on the shaft, as they will disappear during removal.
10 Remove the protector and rubber ring.
11 Dismantling the differential end side joint is similar to that for the wheel side.
12 Should both protectors need renewal, there is no need to remove both bearing packs. The protector for the second joint can be removed over the end of the first joint.
13 Remove the O-ring from the tulip, and then remove as much grease as possible from inside the tulip. **Do not** use any solvents.
14 If the differential side tulip needs attention because of wear or damage to the nylon stop, carefully cut this away using a sharp chisel.
15 Using a screwdriver, remove the retaining washer through the cut in the nylon stop.
16 Remove the punch marks from the washer using a small rotary file or stone.
17 Finally clean out the tulip really thoroughly, so that no traces of abrasive or metal are left behind.
18 Obtain the new protector assemblies and the correct amount of grease (130 gms per side joint).
19 To reassemble, first fit the gaiter and spacer together. Grease it and

Fig. 8.9 Wrap tape around the bearing pack (Sec 6)

Fig. 8.10 Pressing the driveshaft from the bearing pack (Sec 6)

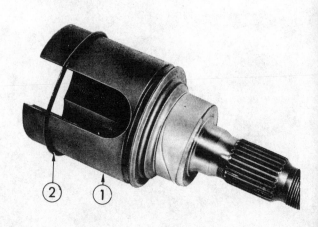

Fig. 8.11 Removing the O-ring (2) from the tulip (1) (Sec 6)

insert into the cover. Push the spacer in until it abuts.

20 Hold the shaft vertically in a vice, and slide on the retaining ring and previously-assembled protector.

21 Refit the bearing pack to the shaft, and using a tubular drift, drive it down the shaft until it abuts.

22 Check that the lower part of the bearing pack is flush with the bottom of the shaft groove.

23 Make three equidistant punch marks, spreading the splines on the shaft towards the hub of the bearing pack using a sharp centre-punch.

24 If the nylon stop has been removed, refit it to the interior of the tulip.

25 Insert the washer, and then make three equidistant punch marks to secure it inside the tulip.

26 Insert 180 gms of grease into each side joint. Spread the grease inside the tulip and gaiter.

27 Remove the adhesive tape from the bearing pack.

28 Place the cup and spring on the wheel end of the shaft.

29 Fit a new O-ring to the tulip, and then refit the tulip.

30 The tulip cover must now be crimped. For this, the use of a press will make life far easier. With the spacer held in position, bend over the lip using a hammer.

31 Fit the retaining ring to the gaiter. Slide a piece of welding wire or small electrician's screwdriver between the gaiter and shaft to release the air trapped. **Do not** puncture the gaiter.

32 To assemble the wheel side joint, insert the shaft to obtain a dimension of 88 mm (3.5 in) as shown in Fig. 8.12. Remove the metal rod without altering this position.

33 To assemble the differential side joint with the metal rod located under the gaiter, insert the shaft into the tulip until it abuts. Then remove the metal rod (Fig. 8.13).

34 Finally, check the operation of the joints by hand. They must slide freely.

7 Halfshaft (Estate models) – removal and refitting

1 Chock the front wheels. Jack up the rear of the car and support on axle stands. Remove the appropriate rear wheel.

2 With the handbrake released, remove the screws and withdraw the brake drum.

3 Disconnect the handbrake cable from the shoe operating lever.

4 Remove the shoe steady springs, then using a screwdriver, lever the leading shoe from the lower anchor and unhook the lower return spring. With the shoe to one side, use a small drift to drive the handbrake outer cable from the backplate.

5 Unclip the rigid brake hydraulic pipe from the rear axle casing.

6 Fit a brake hose clamp to the flexible hose for the rear brakes. Alternatively, it may be possible to restrict subsequent loss of fluid by tightening the brake fluid reservoir filler cap onto a thin piece of polythene.

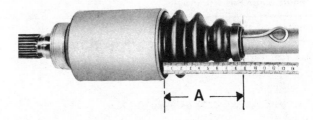

Fig. 8.12 Final assembly of wheel side joint (Sec 6)

A = 88 mm (3.5 in)

Fig. 8.13 Final assembly of differential side joint (Sec 6)

7 Unscrew the union nut and disconnect the rigid brake pipe from the rear wheel cylinder. Plug the end of the pipe.

8 Unscrew the nuts securing the backplate and bearing retainer to the rear axle (photo).

9 Withdraw the halfshaft from the rear axle. If it is tight, temporarily refit the wheel to the drive flange, and pull the wheel outwards to free the bearing outer track. Alternatively, a slide hammer may be attached to the drive flange. Remove the O-ring from the rear axle casing.

10 To remove the bearing and backplate, refer to Chapter 10.

11 Refitting is a reversal of removal, but note the following additional points:

(a) Clean the bearing seating inside the rear axle casing. Renew the O-ring, and dip it in rear axle oil before locating it in the mouth of the casing

(b) Tighten all nuts to the specified torque

(c) On completion, check and if necessary top up the final drive oil level

(d) Bleed the rear brake hydraulic circuit with reference to Chapter 9.

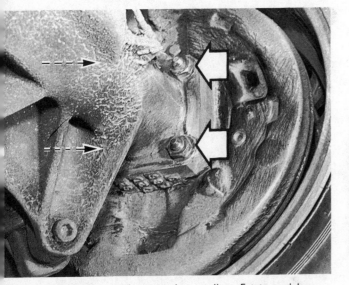

7.8 Backplate/bearing retainer nuts (arrowed) on Estate models

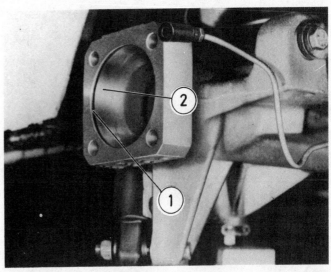

Fig. 8.14 O-ring (1) located in the rear axle casing (2) on Estate models (Sec 7)

8   Fault diagnosis – rear axle

Symptom	Reason(s)
Noise from rear axle	Insufficient lubricant Worn crownwheel and pinion Worn differential bearings
'Clonk' on acceleration and deceleration	Worn half shaft splines (Estate models) Worn driveshaft joints (Saloon models)

Chapter 9 Braking system

Contents

Specifications

Type .... Front disc brakes, rear drum or disc brakes, servo assistance.
Load-sensitive rear brake compensator. Cable-operated handbrake on rear wheels

Brake fluid type/specification .... Hydraulic fluid to SAE J1703 or DOT 3 (Duckhams Universal Brake and Clutch Fluid)

Disc brakes

Diameter:
    Front/rear .... 273 mm (10.75 in)
Disc thickness (new):
    Front, non-ventilated .... 12.75 mm (0.502 in)
    Front, ventilated .... 20.0 mm (0.788 in)
    Rear .... 12.0 mm (0.473 in)
Disc thickness (minimum after machining):
    Front, non-ventilated .... 11.25 mm (0.443 in)
    Front, ventilated .... 18.5 mm (0.729 in)
    Rear .... 11.0 mm (0.433 in)
Disc thickness (minimum before renewal):
    Front, non-ventilated .... 10.75 mm (0.424 in)
    Front, ventilated .... 18.0 mm (0.709 in)
    Rear .... 10.5 mm (0.414 in)
Disc thickness variation (maximum) .... 0.02 mm (0.0008 in)
Disc run-out (maximum):
    On vehicle .... 0.07 mm (0.003 in)
    On machining hub .... 0.05 mm (0.002 in)
Disc pad minimum lining thickness .... 2.5 mm (0.099 in)

Drum brakes

Drum internal diameter (new)	255 mm (10.047 in)
Drum internal diameter (maximum after machining)	256 mm (10.086 in)
Drum out-of-round (maximum):	
On vehicle	0.10 mm (0.004 in)
On machining hub	0.07 mm (0.003 in)
Maximum drum internal diameter variation, side-to-side	0.20 mm (0.008 in)
Shoe minimum lining thickness	1.0 mm (0.04 in)

Vacuum servo unit

Make/type	DBA or Teves
Diameter	229 mm (9.0 in)

Torque wrench settings

	Nm	lbf ft
Front/rear disc-to-hub bolts	50	37
Front caliper mounting bolts:		
Teves (with locking plate)	85	63
DBA	130	96

1 General description

The braking system is of hydraulic type, with discs at the front, and either drums or discs at the rear. The handbrake is cable-operated, on the rear wheels.

The hydraulic circuit consists of two independent sections, split front and rear, so that in the event of the failure of one section, the remaining section is still functional.

A load-sensitive rear brake compensator reduces the hydraulic pressure to the rear brakes, in order to prevent rear wheel lock-up under heavy applications of the brake pedal with the vehicle lightly loaded.

All models are fitted with a vacuum servo unit.

2 Routine maintenance

Carry out the following procedures at the intervals given in Routine maintenance *at the front of this manual.*

Check the brake fluid level

1 With the vehicle on level gound, check that the level of brake fluid in the reservoir on the master cylinder is at or near the maximum mark. Note that the level will drop slightly as the disc pad and brake shoe linings wear.

2 If necessary, top up the level with the specified brake fluid (photo). If frequent topping-up is required, the complete hydraulic circuit should be checked for leaks.

Check the hydraulic circuit for leaks and condition

3 Jack up the front and rear of the vehicle, and support on axle stands. Remove the front and rear wheels.

4 Check the hydraulic pipes and hoses with reference to Section 13.

5 Examine the master cylinder, rear brake compensator, disc calipers, wheel cylinders, and vacuum servo unit for damage, or leakage of brake fluid.

6 On completion, refit the wheels and lower the vehicle to the ground.

Check operation of the handbrake

7 Fully apply the handbrake, and check that the rear wheels are locked.

8 Check that the handbrake is fully applied between 4 and 7 notches on vehicles with rear drum brakes, and between 7 and 13 notches on vehicles with rear disc brakes. If not, adjust the handbrake as described in Section 18.

Renew the hydraulic brake fluid

9 Unscrew the filler cap from the brake fluid reservoir, and use a syringe to remove the fluid from both compartments.

10 Fill the reservoir with fresh hydraulic fluid, and proceed to bleed the system as described in Section 14. At least 5 or 6 depressions of the brake pedal will be necessary to clear the old fluid from each cylinder. Also bleed the clutch hydraulic circuit as described in Chapter 5.

2.2 Topping-up the brake fluid level

3 Disc pads (front) – inspection and renewal

1 Apply the handbrake, then jack up the front of the car and support on axle stands. Remove the front wheels.

2 Looking through the aperture at the front of each caliper, check the thickness of lining on each disc pad. To do this, turn the steering on full lock to the side being checked.

3 If the lining on any disc pad is worn below the specified minimum (indicated if the groove in the pad has disappeared), it will be necessary to renew all four front disc pads as follows.

DBA Caliper

4 Disconnect the wear warning light wire at the connector.

5 Extract the small clip and pull out the upper sliding key using pliers.

6 Using a lever against the front suspension strut, push the caliper outwards, then withdraw the outer pad after lifting it slightly to release the lower edge of the backing plate.

7 Push back the caliper, and withdraw the inner pad.

8 Clean away all dust and dirt from the caliper. Do not inhale the dust, as it may be injurious to health. Check for brake fluid leakage around the piston dust seal and, if evident, overhaul the caliper as described in Section 6. Check the brake disc for wear, and also check that the rubber bellows on the cylinder sliding rods are in good condition.

9 Clean the backs of the new disc pads, and apply a little anti-squeal brake grease. Also apply the grease to the lower pad locating lip on the caliper.

10 Using a block of wood, press the caliper piston fully into its cylinder.

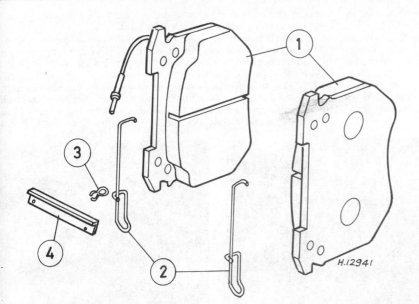

Fig. 9.1 DBA type front disc pads (Sec 3)

1 Disc pads	3 Clip
2 Anti-rattle springs	4 Sliding key

1 With the caliper pushed inwards, insert the inner pad (the one with
he pad wear wire), then push the caliper outwards and insert the outer
ad.
2 Check that the pads are correctly located on the caliper lip, then tap
n the upper sliding key to lock them. Fit the sliding key clip.
3 Reconnect the pad wear warning light wire.

Teves caliper

4 Disconnect the wear warning light wire at the connector (photo).
5 Extract the spring clip from the holes in the ends of the pad pins
photo).
6 Remove the pad pins and the anti-rattle spring (photos).
7 Using a lever against the front suspension strut, push the caliper
lightly outwards, then push the caliper inwards again. Withdraw the
nner pad (photo).
8 Push the caliper fully outwards. Disengage the outer pad from the
oss, and withdraw it from the caliper (photos).
9 Clean and check the caliper and disc as described in paragraph 8.
Check that the caliper piston cut-out is positioned as shown in Fig.
.3. A piece of card cut to the 20° angle may be used instead of the
pecial Peugeot tool (photo). If necessary, use internal expanding
irclip pliers to reposition the piston – do not use ordinary pliers on the
uter surface of the piston.

Fig. 9.2 Removing the DBA type front disc
pads (Sec 3)

1   Warning light wire
2   Clip
3   Sliding key
4   Pads
5   Suspension strut
6   Caliper

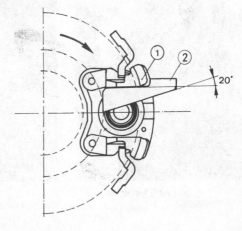

Fig. 9.3 Diagram showing correct position of Teves
front brake caliper piston cut-out (Sec 3)

1   Caliper   2   Setting tool
Arrow indicates forward rotation of disc

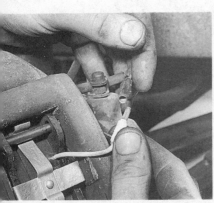

3.14 Disconnecting the pad wear warning
ight wire

3.15 Pad pin retaining spring clip (arrowed)

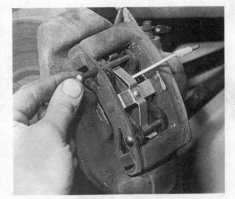

3.16A Removing the upper pad pin ...

20 Clean the backs of the new disc pads, and apply a little anti-squeal brake grease.

21 Using a block of wood, press the caliper piston fully into its cylinder.

22 With the caliper pushed outwards, insert the outer pad, and engage its backing plate with the boss.

23 Push the caliper inwards and insert the inner pad.

24 Insert one pad pin through the caliper and pads, then hold the anti-rattle spring in position (photo) and insert the second pad pin.

25 Fit the spring clip to the pad pins.

the bracket(s) from the caliper, and pull out the pad retaining fork.

6 Using pliers, withdraw both discs pads.

7 Using a screwdriver or similar tool in the central groove, turn th caliper piston clockwise 1/8th of a turn (45°). With a block of woo push the piston fully into its cylinder, then turn the piston 1/8th of turn (45°) anti-clockwise.

8 Clean away all dust and dirt from the caliper. Do not inhale th dust, as it may be injurious to health. Also clean the handbrak mechanism on the inside of the caliper. Check for brake fluid leakag around the piston dust seal and, if evident, overhaul the caliper a

3.16B ... lower pad pin, and anti-rattle spring (arrowed)

3.17 Removing the inner pad

3.18A Removing the outer pad. Note the cut-out (arrowed) ...

3.18B ... which engages with the boss (arrowed) on the caliper

3.19 Using a piece of card to check the position of the caliper piston cut-out

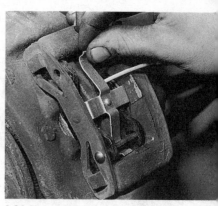
3.24 Fitting the anti-rattle spring

26 Feed the wear warning light wire under the spring clip loop, and press it into the connector.

DBA and Teves calipers

27 Repeat the operations on the opposite disc caliper.

28 Depress the footbrake pedal several times, in order to position the pads against the discs.

29 Check, and if necessary top up, the brake fluid level in the master cylinder reservoir.

30 Refit the front wheels and lower the car to the ground.

4 Disc pads (rear) – inspection and renewal

1 Chock the front wheels, then jack up the rear of the car and support on axle stands. Remove both rear wheels and release the handbrake.

2 Check the thickness of lining on each disc pad, and if worn below the specified minimum (indicated if the groove in the pad has disappeared), renew all four rear disc pads as follows.

3 Disconnect the wear warning light wire at the connector.

4 On late models, extract the small spring clip from the pad retaining fork. Unclip and remove the thrust spring plate. Unhook the ends of the damper spring. Pull out the pad retaining fork, and remove the damper spring from the caliper.

5 On early models, unclip and remove the thrust spring plate. Unbolt

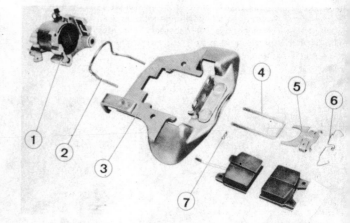
Fig. 9.4 Rear disc pad and caliper components (Sec 4)

1   Cylinder
2   Spacer rod
3   Caliper frame
4   Pad retaining fork
5   Thrust spring plate
6   Damper spring
7   Spring clip

described in Section 7. Examine the brake disc for scoring and, if excessive, renew the disc. Check that it is possible to slide the caliper in and out by hand.

9 It is recommended that the pad retaining fork and spring are renewed every time the pads are renewed.

10 Clean the backs of the new disc pads, and apply a little anti-squeal brake grease. Also apply the grease to the pad contact points on the caliper and pad retaining fork.

11 Push the caliper fully outwards, then insert the disc pads.

12 Refit the retaining fork components in reverse order. On later models, make sure that the ends of the damper spring engage the slots in the caliper.

13 Reconnect the wear warning light wire.

14 Repeat the operations on the opposite disc caliper.

15 Depress the footbrake pedal several times in order to position the pads against the discs. Check the handbrake travel, and if necessary adjust it as described in Section 18.

16 Check, and if necessary top up, the brake fluid level in the master cylinder reservoir.

5 Rear brake shoes – inspection and renewal

1 Chock the front wheels, then jack up the rear of the car and support on axle stands. Release the handbrake.

2 The lining thickness on the leading brake shoes may be checked without removing the brake drums. Prise out the plugs from the top front of the backplates, and use a torch to check the lining thickness (photo). If it is at, or near, the specified minimum, remove the drums and make a more thorough inspection.

3 Remove the rear wheels, then unscrew the cross-head screws and withdraw the brake drums. If the screws are tight, use an impact driver to remove them (photos). If the drum is tight on the brake shoes, prise out the plug from the lower rear of the backplate, and use a screwdriver to press in the handbrake operating lever. This will allow the lever to retract more. If the drum is still tight, back off the adjusting nuts on the handbrake cables.

4 On models where the lower shoe return spring is located behind the anchor plate, use a screwdriver to unhook and remove the spring (photo).

5 On models fitted with early DBA shoes, refer to Fig. 9.7 and check that the clearance 'a' is between 0.9 and 1.1 mm (0.035 and 0.043 in). If not, determine which components are worn, and renew them.

6 Unhook the upper shoe return spring (photo).

Girling brakes

7 Move the shoes apart as far as possible, and remove the automatic adjusting arm and spring.

8 Remove the spacer cup from the leading shoe.

9 Remove the automatic adjusting strut from the shoes.

10 Using pliers, depress and twist the steady spring cups through 90°. Remove the springs.

11 Remove the leading shoe. Remove the trailing shoe, and disconnect the handbrake cable.

Early DBA brakes

12 Remove the steady spring from the leading shoe. To do this, use a screwdriver or short length of dowel rod to unhook the bottom of the spring from the anchor plate.

13 Move the automatic adjusting lever towards the centre of the hub, then twist the leading shoe to release the adjusting lever from the link. Remove the leading shoe.

14 Disconnect the handbrake cable from its lever.

15 Remove the steady spring, and withdraw the trailing shoe together with the link.

16 Note how the levers and link are fitted to the brake shoes, then prise off the retaining clips and remove them.

Later DBA brakes

17 Remove the shoe steady springs, using a screwdriver or short length of dowel rod to unhook the springs from the anchor plates (photo).

18 Remove the leading shoe, and disconnect the lower return spring.

19 Disconnect the handbrake cable from its lever, then remove the trailing shoe, together with the link.

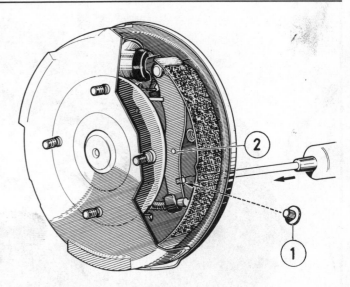

Fig. 9.5 Using a screwdriver to retract the rear brake shoes (Sec 5)

1 *Plug*   2 *Handbrake operating lever*

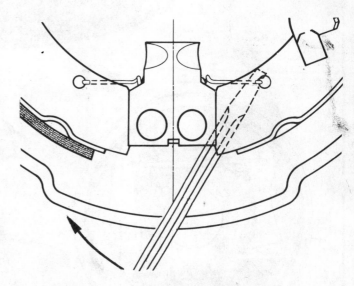

Fig. 9.6 Using a screwdriver to unhook the rear brake shoe lower return spring (Sec 5)

Fig. 9.7 Checking the clearance 'a' between the link (1) and lever (2) on early DBA rear brake shoes (Sec 5)

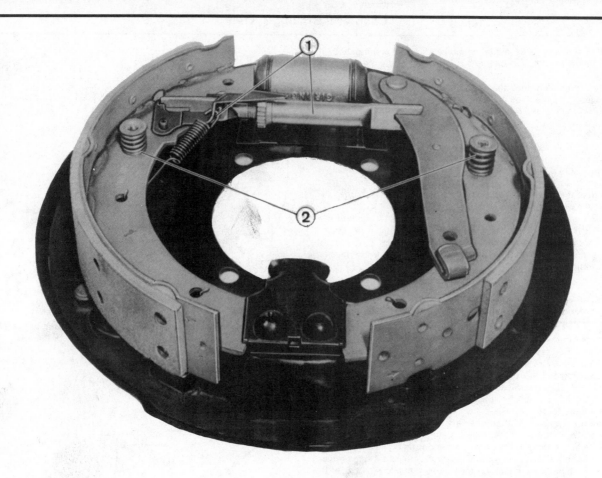

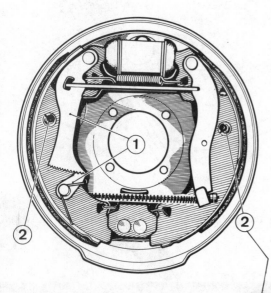

Fig. 9.9 Early DBA rear brake assembly (Sec 5)

1   *Automatic adjuster*   2   *Steady springs*

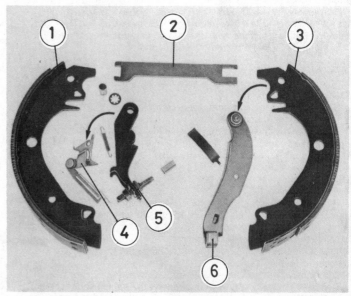

Fig. 9.10 Components of the later DBA rear brake assembly (Sec 5)

1 *Leading shoe*	4 *Control lever*	
2 *Strut*	5 *Automatic adjuster*	
3 *Trailing shoe*	6 *Handbrake operating lever*	

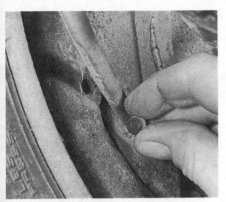

5.2 Removing the plug from the rear backplate to check the lining wear

5.3A Using an impact driver to remove the brake drum screws

5.3B Removing the brake drum

5.3C To retract the brake shoes, prise out this plug ...

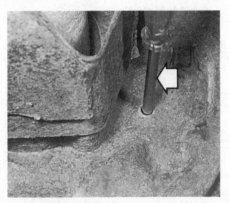

5.3D ... and insert a screwdriver (arrowed) against the handbrake operating lever

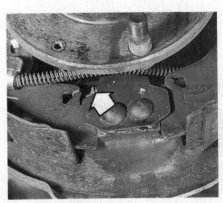

5.4 Lower shoe return spring (later DBA brakes)

5.6 Upper shoe return spring (later DBA brakes)

5.17 Shoe steady spring – arrowed (later DBA brakes)

20 Note how the levers and link are fitted to the brake shoes, then prise off the retaining clips and remove them. Disengage the adjuster lever spring.

All brakes

21 Brush the dust and dirt from the shoes, drum and backplate. Do not inhale it, as it may be injurious to health. Check for brake fluid leakage around the wheel cylinder dust seals and, if evident, overhaul the wheel cylinder as described in Section 9. Examine the brake drum for scoring and, if excessive, renew the drum, or have it reground as described in Section 10.

22 Smear a little brake grease onto the pressure pads on the backplate.

Later DBA brakes

23 Unscrew the special bolt from the self-adjusting lever, and thoroughly clean the nut and bolt. Check that the nut gently locks when turned clockwise, but locks firmly when turned anti-clockwise. Apply a little brake grease to the threads, then fully screw the bolt into the nut, and fit the plastic tube over the exposed thread. The tube is 17.0 mm (0.67 in) long on Saloon models, and 24.0 mm (0.95 in) long on Estate models.

24 Engage the adjuster arm in the nut groove and in the lever tab. Reconnect the spring.

25 Fit the adjuster lever to the new leading shoe, using new retaining clips. Note that on some early Estate models, the lever was fitted to the inner face of the shoe. This arrangement must be changed, by swapping the adjusters (or leading shoe assemblies) side for side between the left-hand and right-hand rear brakes.

26 Fit the handbrake lever to the new trailing shoe, locate the link, and lock by sliding the spring plate through the cut-out, and snapping the tab in the hole provided.

27 Locate the trailing shoe on the backplate, engage the handbrake cable, then refit the steady spring.

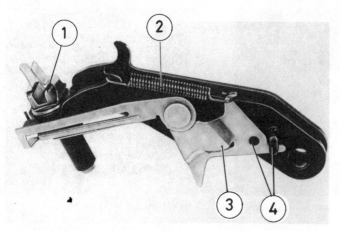

Fig. 9.11 Self-adjusting lever on the later DBA rear brake assembly (Sec 5)

1 Special bolt
2 Return spring
3 Control lever
4 Pivot and stop on lever

28 Except on later Estate models, locate the leading shoe and refit the steady spring. Fit the lower return spring, using a screwdriver to engage the hole in the shoe.
29 On later Estate models, engage the lower return spring before positioning the leading shoe on the backplate. Refit the steady spring.

Early DBA brakes

30 Fit the levers and link to the new shoes, using new retaining clips.
31 Locate the trailing shoe on the backplate, reconnect the handbrake cable, then refit the steady spring.
32 Locate the leading shoe on the backplate. Move the automatic adjusting lever towards the hub, then twist the shoe to engage it with the link. Lever down the pawl, and set the adjusting lever at the beginning of the serrations.
33 Refit the steady spring to the leading shoe.
34 Fit the lower return spring, using a screwdriver to engage the hole in the shoe.

Girling brakes

35 Locate the leading shoe on the backplate, and refit the steady spring. Engage the lower return spring with the hole in the leading shoe.

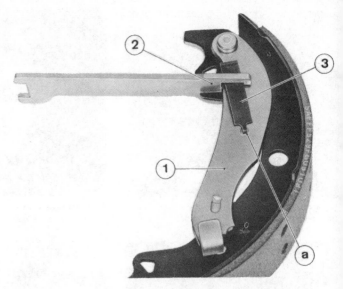

Fig. 9.12 Handbrake operating lever fitted to the trailing shoe – later DBA assembly (Sec 5)

1 Lever
2 Strut
3 Spring plate
a Location hole

36 Locate the trailing shoe on the backplate, and reconnect the handbrake cable. Refit the steady spring.
37 Reconnect the lower return spring, using a screwdriver to lever it.
38 Set the nut on the automatic adjusting strut so that there is 5.0 mm (0.2 in) of thread on the fork side of the nut. Fit the strut to the shoes. Note that the nut on the right-hand brake has a left-hand thread, and vice-versa.
39 Fit the spacer cup to the leading shoe, with its dome outside.
40 Engage the automatic adjusting arm on the strut fork, locate it on the spacer cup, then refit the spring behind the shoe web.

All brakes

41 Refit the upper shoe return spring (photos).
42 Refit the brake drums, followed by the rear wheels.
43 Depress the footbrake pedal several times in order to operate the automatic adjuster.
44 Adjust the handbrake as described in Section 18, and lower the car to the ground.

5.41A Later DBA self-adjusting mechanism, with fitted upper shoe return spring

5.41B View of later DBA rear brake shoes

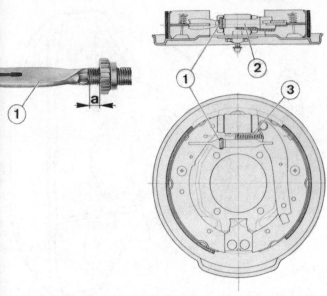

Fig. 9.13 Initial setting on Girling automatic adjusting strut
(Sec 5)

1 Adjusting nut and fork   3 Return spring
2 Pushrod   a = 5.0 mm (0.2 in)

6 Disc caliper (front) – removal, overhaul and refitting

1   Remove the front disc pads as described in Section 3.
2   Fit a brake hose clamp to the flexible hose connected to the caliper.
Alternatively, it may be possible to tighten the brake fluid reservoir filler
cap onto a thin piece of polythene sheet, in order to reduce the loss of
fluid when disconnecting the caliper.
3   Loosen only the flexible hose union connection at the caliper.
4   Where applicable, bend back the lockwasher. Unscrew the two
mounting bolts, withdraw the caliper from the disc, then unscrew the
caliper from the flexible hose. Plug the end of the hose.
5   Clean the exterior of the caliper.
6   On the DBA type, unbolt the caliper frame from the cylinder.
7   Prise the dust cover and ring from the end of the cylinder.
8   Withdraw the piston from the cylinder. If necessary, use air pressure
from a foot pump in the fluid inlet to force the piston out.
9   Prise the seal from inside the cylinder, taking care not to damage
the cylinder wall.
10 On the DBA type, remove the guides and rubber dust covers from
the housing. A stop plate (Fig. 9.15) is fitted to early models, and a
lockplate (Fig. 9.16) is fitted to later models.
11 On the Teves type, extract the damper spring from the cylinder.
12 Clean all the components, using methylated spirit or clean brake
fluid, then examine them for wear and damage. Check the piston and
cylinder surfaces for scoring, excessive wear, and corrosion, and if
evident, renew the complete caliper assembly. If the components are in
good condition, obtain a repair kit of rubber seals.
13 Dip the new seal in fresh brake fluid, then locate it in the cylinder
groove, using the fingers only to manipulate it.
14 Dip the piston in brake fluid, and insert it in the cylinder, twisting it
as necessary to locate it in the seal.

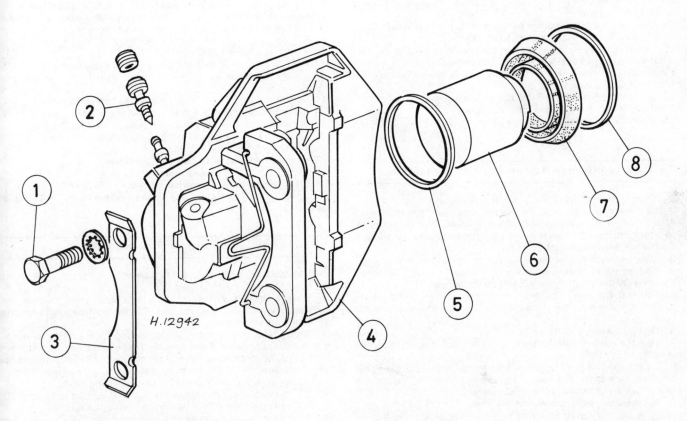

H.12942

Fig. 9.14 Teves front disc caliper (Sec 6)

1 Mounting bolt   3 Lockwasher   5 Piston seal   7 Dust cover
2 Bleed screw   4 Caliper assembly   6 Piston   8 Ring

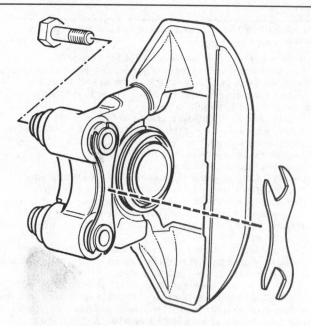

Fig. 9.15 DBA front disc caliper and stop plate (Sec 6)

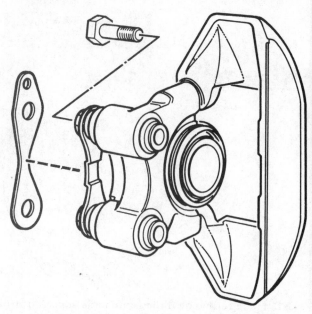

Fig. 9.16 DBA front disc caliper and lockplate (Sec 6)

15 Fit the dust cover and ring over the end of the piston and cylinder.
16 Lubricate the sliding guides with brake grease.
17 On the Teves type, refit the damper spring.
18 On the DBA type, refit the guides, rubber dust covers and plate. Refit the caliper frame and tighten the bolts.
19 To refit the caliper, first screw it onto the flexible hose, and locate it over the brake disc so that the hose is not twisted.
20 Clean the mounting bolt threads, and apply locking fluid where a lockwasher is not fitted.
21 Insert the bolts, and tighten to the specified torque. Where fitted, bend the lockwasher onto the bolt head flats.
22 Tighten the flexible hose union on the caliper. Check that the hose is clear of the strut and surrounding components and, if necessary, loosen the rigid pipe union on the body bracket, reposition the hose, and retighten the union.
23 Remove the brake hose clamp or polythene sheet.
24 Refit the disc pads, as described in Section 3.
25 Bleed the hydraulic system as described in Section 14.

7 Disc caliper (rear) – removal, overhaul and refitting

1 Remove the rear disc pads as described in Section 4.
2 Fit a brake hose clamp to the flexible hose leading to the caliper. Alternatively, it may be possible to tighten the brake fluid reservoir filler cap onto a thin piece of polythene sheet, in order to reduce the loss of fluid when disconnecting the caliper.
3 Unscrew the hydraulic line union connection at the caliper.
4 With the handbrake released, apply the caliper lever and disconnect the cable. Withdraw the outer cable from the bracket.
5 Unscrew the socket-headed mounting bolts, and withdraw the caliper from the disc, then plug the hydraulic line to prevent loss of fluid.
6 Clean the exterior of the caliper.
7 Turn the piston $1/8$th of a turn (45°) clockwise, then press it fully inwards.
8 Extract the spacer rod, and remove the cylinder from the frame. Note that early spacer rods are round in section, whereas later rods are oval – they are therefore not interchangeable.
9 Recover the plastic spacer from the frame.
10 Prise the dust covers and rings from the ends of the cylinder.
11 Withdraw the pistons from the cylinder. If necessary, use air pressure from a foot pump in the fluid inlet to force the pistons out.
12 Prise the seals from inside the cylinder, taking care not to damage the cylinder wall.
13 Clean all the components, using methylated spirit or clean brake

fluid, then examine them for wear and damage. Check the piston and cylinder surfaces for scoring, excessive wear, and corrosion, and if evident, renew the complete caliper assembly. If the components are in good condition, obtain a repair kit of rubber seals.
14 Dip the new seals in fresh brake fluid, then locate them in the cylinder grooves, using the fingers only to manipulate them.
15 Dip the pistons in brake fluid, and insert them in the cylinder. Before engaging the pistons, make sure that the ratchet teeth are aligned with the piston grooves. When completely entered, turn the direct piston $1/8$th of a turn (45°) anti-clockwise to engage the ratchet teeth.
16 Fit the dust covers and rings.
17 Lubricate the grooves in the cylinder with brake grease.
18 Locate the plastic spacer in the frame, then fit the cylinder and insert the spacer rod.
19 To refit the caliper, first locate it over the brake disc.
20 Clean the mounting bolt threads, and apply a little locking fluid. Insert the bolts, and tighten them securely.
21 Reconnect the handbrake cable to the bracket and lever.
22 Tighten the hydraulic line union.
23 Remove the brake hose clamp or polythene sheet.
24 Refit the disc pads as described in Section 4.
25 Bleed the hydraulic system as described in Section 14.
26 Check, and if necessary adjust, the handbrake as described in Section 18.

8 Brake disc – inspection, removal and refitting

1 Remove the disc pads as described in Section 3 or 4, as appropriate.
2 Using a dial gauge or feelers and a fixed block, check that the disc run-out is within the specified limit. Do not confuse wheel bearing endfloat with disc wear.
3 Check the condition of the disc for scoring. Light scoring is normal and may be removed by fitting genuine Peugeot disc pads, which have a thin coating of abrasive material for cleaning the disc during initial applications of the brake. If scoring is excessive, either renew the disc or have it reground within limits by an engineering works.
4 To remove a disc, first remove the hub as described in Chapter 10.
5 Mark the disc and hub in relation to each other.
6 Mount the hub in a soft-jawed vice, unscrew the bolts and separate the disc.
7 Refitting is a reversal of removal, but make sure that the disc-to-hub mating surfaces are clean, and apply a little locking fluid to the threads of the bolts, before inserting and tightening them to the specified torque.

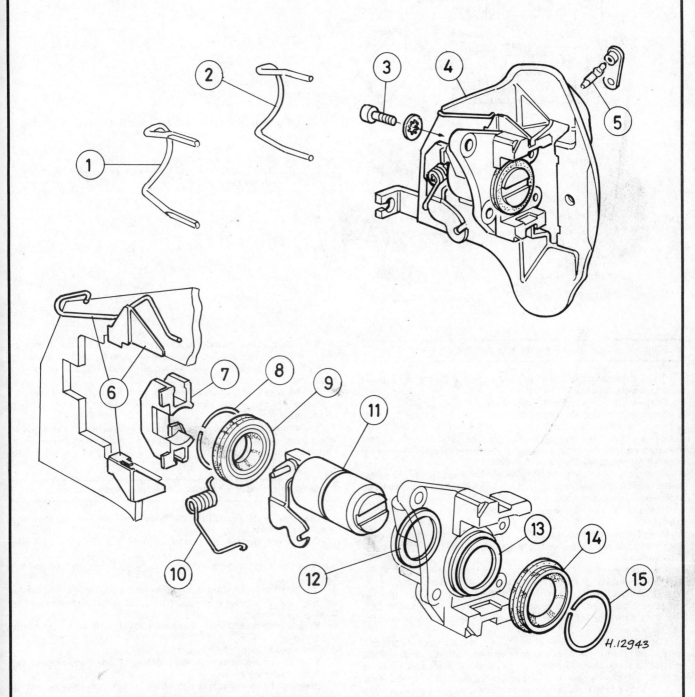

Fig. 9.17 Rear disc caliper components (Sec 7)

1	Spacer rod (late)	5	Bleed screw	9	Dust cover	13	Piston seal
2	Spacer rod (early)	6	Caliper spring kit	10	Handbrake return spring	14	Dust cover
3	Mounting bolt	7	Plastic spacer	11	Piston assembly	15	Ring
4	Caliper assembly	8	Ring	12	Piston seal		

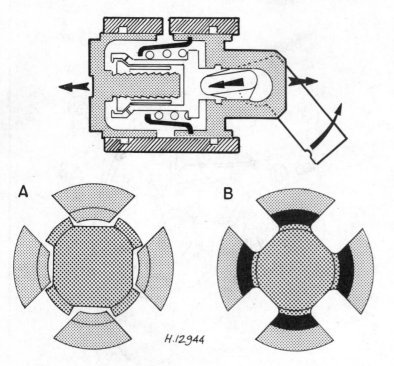

Fig. 9.18 Rear disc caliper handbrake self-adjusting mechanism (Sec 7)

A   Direct piston positioned for retraction
B   Direct piston turned $1/8$th of a turn (45°) to engage ratchet teeth

H.12944

9 Rear wheel cylinder – removal, overhaul and refitting

1   Chock the front wheels, then jack up the rear of the car and support on axle stands. Release the handbrake.
2   Remove the rear wheel and brake drum.
3   Note the location of the brake shoe upper return spring, then unhook and remove it.
4   Pull the handbrake lever on the trailing shoe fully forwards, so that the upper ends of the shoes are clear of the wheel cylinder. Wedge the lever in this position with a block of wood.
5   Fit a brake hose clamp to the flexible hose supplying the wheel being worked on. Alternatively, tighten the brake fluid reservoir cap onto a thin piece of polythene sheet.
6   Unscrew the hydraulic pipe union nut from the rear of the wheel cylinder.
7   Unscrew the two mounting bolts, and withdraw the wheel cylinder from the backplate. Take care not to spill any brake fluid on the brake shoe linings.
8   Clean the exterior of the wheel cylinder.
9   Prise the rubber dust covers from the wheel cylinder body.
10 Extract the pistons, seals, and return spring, keeping each component identified for location. On the Girling type, prise the seals from the piston grooves. On the DBA type, the seals are loose, and the return spring may have end seatings.
11 Check the surfaces of the cylinder bore and pistons for scoring and corrosion and, if evident, renew the complete wheel cylinder. If the components are in good condition, discard the seals and obtain a repair kit, which will contain all the necessary renewable components.
12 Clean the pistons and cylinder with methylated spirit or clean brake fluid, then dip each component in fresh brake fluid and reassemble in the reverse order to dismantling, making sure that the lips of the seals face into the cylinder. When completed, wipe clean the outer surfaces.
13 Clean the backplate and refit the wheel cylinder, using a reversal of the removal procedure.
14 Make sure that the brake hose clamp or polythene sheet is removed, then bleed the hydraulic system as described in Section 14.

10 Rear brake drum – inspection and renovation

1   Whenever the brake drums are removed, inspect them for wear and damage.

2   If the drums are grooved, owing to failure to renew worn linings, or after a very high mileage has been covered, then it may be possible to regrind them, providing the maximum internal diameter is not exceeded.
3   Even if only one drum is in need of grinding, both drums must be reground to the same size in order to maintain even braking characteristics.
4   The drums should be checked for excessive out-of-round wear, which may cause brake judder. If outside the specified limits, either renew or regrind the drums.

11 Master cylinder – removal, overhaul and refitting

1   Unscrew the filler cap from the brake fluid reservoir (photo), and draw out the fluid using a syringe.
2   Disconnect the clutch master cylinder supply hose from the reservoir.
3   Prise the reservoir from the brake master cylinder, and remove the seals.
4   Unscrew the union nuts securing the rigid brake lines to the master cylinder, and pull out the lines. Cap the pipe ends to prevent loss of fluid.
5   Unscrew the mounting nuts and withdraw the master cylinder from the servo unit.
6   Clean the exterior of the master cylinder.
7   Prise the circlip from the mouth of the cylinder, and remove the washer. Unscrew the stop pin.
8   Remove the primary and secondary piston components, noting their locations. If necessary, tap the cylinder on a block of wood.
9   Clean all the components in methylated spirit. Check the surfaces of the cylinder bore and pistons for scoring and corrosion, and, if evident, renew the complete master cylinder. If the components are in good condition, remove and discard the seals and obtain a repair kit, which will contain all the necessary renewable components. Note that genuine Peugeot kits include the pistons in addition to the seals.
10 Dip the new seals in fresh brake fluid, and fit them to the pistons, using the fingers only to manipulate them.
11 Reassemble the master cylinder in the reverse order to dismantling, and make sure that the circlip is fully engaged with the groove in the mouth of the cylinder.
12 Refitting is a reversal of removal, but on completion, bleed the complete hydraulic system as described in Section 14.

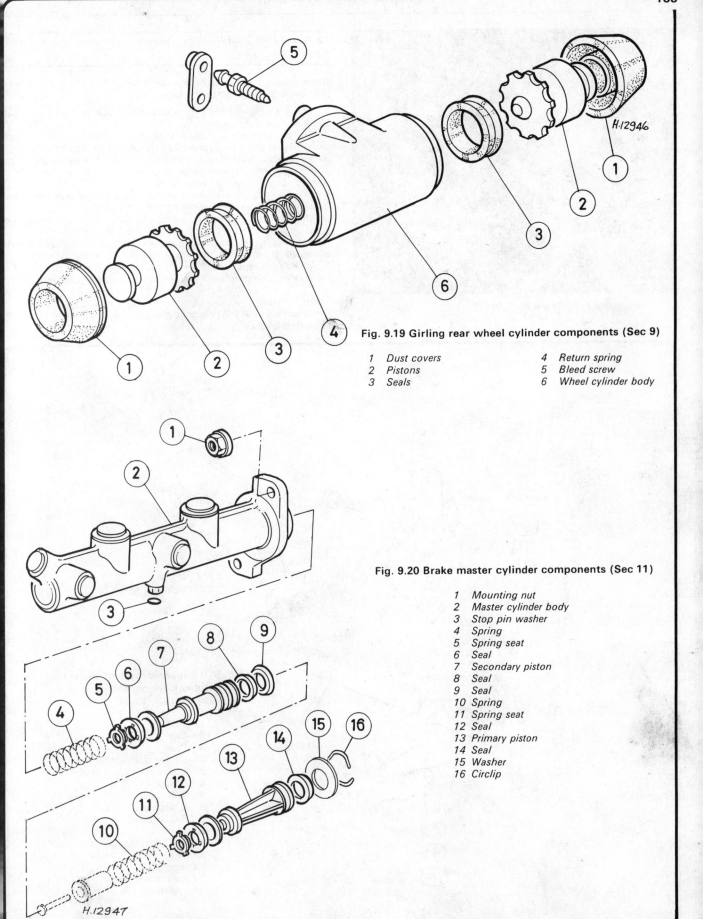

Fig. 9.19 Girling rear wheel cylinder components (Sec 9)

1 Dust covers   4 Return spring
2 Pistons   5 Bleed screw
3 Seals   6 Wheel cylinder body

Fig. 9.20 Brake master cylinder components (Sec 11)

1 Mounting nut
2 Master cylinder body
3 Stop pin washer
4 Spring
5 Spring seat
6 Seal
7 Secondary piston
8 Seal
9 Seal
10 Spring
11 Spring seat
12 Seal
13 Primary piston
14 Seal
15 Washer
16 Circlip

H.12946

H.12947

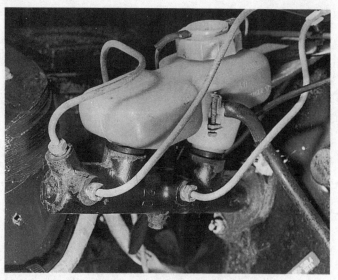

11.1 Brake master cylinder and fluid reservoir

12 Rear brake compensator – removal, refitting and adjustment

Note: *A twin brake hydraulic pressure gauge will be required to adjust the compensator on Estate models*

1   Chock the front wheels, then jack up the rear of the vehicle and support on axle stands.
2   The compensator is located on the rear underbody, inboard from the left-hand rear wheel (photos). First unhook the actuating spring.
3   Remove the brake fluid reservoir filler cap, and tighten it down onto a thin piece of polythene sheet, in order to reduce the loss of fluid when disconnecting the hydraulic pipes.
4   Unscrew the union nuts and disconnect the rigid hydraulic pipes from the compensator. Plug the ends of the pipes.
5   Unscrew the mounting bolts or nuts, and withdraw the compensator.
6   Refitting is a reversal of removal, but bleed the hydraulic system as described in Section 14, and adjust the compensator as follows.
7   With the vehicle at kerb weight (including the spare wheel and a full tank of fuel), position it over an inspection pit or on ramps.

Saloon models
8   Attach a 5 kg (11 lb) weight to the compensator lever on the notch beneath the spring.

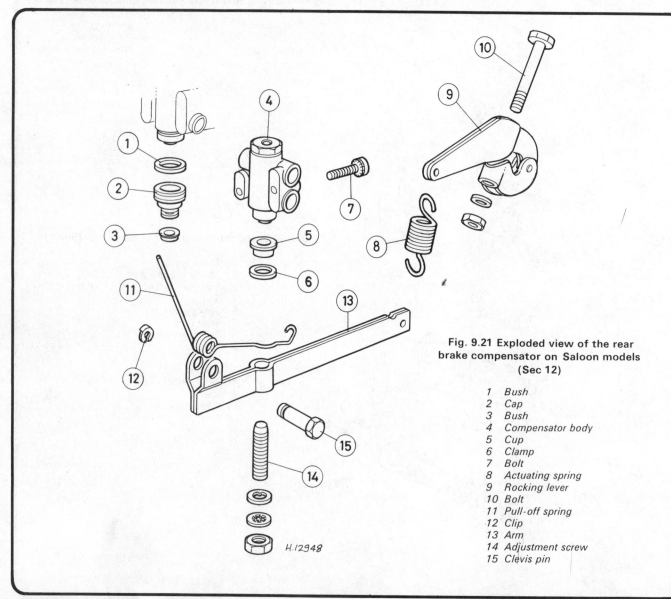

Fig. 9.21 Exploded view of the rear brake compensator on Saloon models (Sec 12)

1   Bush
2   Cap
3   Bush
4   Compensator body
5   Cup
6   Clamp
7   Bolt
8   Actuating spring
9   Rocking lever
10 Bolt
11 Pull-off spring
12 Clip
13 Arm
14 Adjustment screw
15 Clevis pin

H.12948

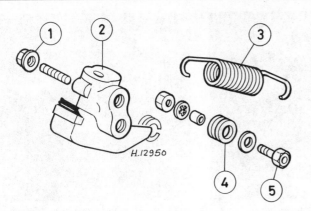

Fig. 9.22 Rear brake compensator on Estate models (Sec 12)

1 Mounting nut
2 Body
3 Control spring
4 Pivot wheel
5 Bolt

9   Fully push in the compensator piston.
10 Select a 0.8 mm (0.032 in) feeler blade for disc brake models, and a 1.3 to 1.8 mm (0.051 to 0.071 in) feeler blade for drum brake models.
11 Loosen the locknut, and using a screwdriver, adjust the screw so that the correct feeler blade is a firm sliding fit between the piston and lever. Tighten the locknut. If the fuel tank is empty, increase the feeler blade thickness by 0.2 mm (0.008 in).
12 Remove the weight.

Estate models

13 A twin brake hydraulic pressure gauge is required to adjust the compensator on Estate models. If this is not available, the vehicle should be taken to a Peugeot garage for the adjustment.
14 Connect one pressure gauge to the bleed screw port on one front caliper, then connect the remaining gauge to the bleed screw port on one rear wheel cylinder or caliper, as applicable.
15 Bleed the pressure gauge, then have an assistant apply the brake pedal to obtain a pressure of 60 bar (870 lbf/in²) in the front circuit. The pressure in the rear circuit should be 43 ± 1 bar (623 ± 15 lbf/in²) with an empty fuel tank, or 45 ± 1 bar (652 ± 15 lbf/in²) with a full fuel tank.
16 If adjustment is necessary, reposition the spring fixed point away from the compensator to increase the pressure, or towards the compensator to decrease the pressure.
17 With the brake pedal released, refit the bleed screws, and if necessary bleed the relevant calipers.

13 Flexible and rigid hydraulic lines – inspection and renewal

1   Examine all the unions for signs of leakage. Check the flexible hoses for leaks, fraying and chafing.
2   The rigid brake pipes must be examined carefully and methodically. Clean them with a wire brush, and check for signs of dents, corrosion or other damage. Where the depth of corrosion is significant, the pipes should be renewed. This is most likely in those areas underneath the vehicle body where the pipes are exposed and unprotected.
3   If any section of pipe or hose is to be removed, first unscrew the brake fluid reservoir filler cap, then place a piece of polythene sheeting over the reservoir neck and secure using a strong elastic band. This will minimise brake fluid loss when the pipe or hose is removed.
4   Brake pipe removal is usually quite straightforward. The union nuts at each end are undone, and the pipe unclipped from the body. Where the union nuts are exposed, they may be quite tight, and should first be soaked with penetrating oil. If the nuts cannot be loosened with an open-ended spanner, a special brake union spanner should be used, or alternatively a pair of self-locking grips may be used.
5   To remove a flexible hose, unscrew the union nut(s) securing the rigid brake pipe(s), then pull out the retaining clip(s) and withdraw the hose from the bracket(s) (photos). If a front hose is being removed, it can now be unscrewed from the brake caliper.
6   Brake pipes can be obtained individually or in sets from most accessory shops or garages, with the end flares and union nuts in place. The pipe is then bent to shape, using the old pipe as a guide.
7   Fitting the pipes and hoses is a reversal of the removal procedure. Make sure that the hoses are not kinked when in position, and that the

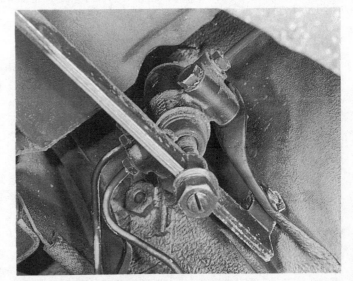

12.2A Rear brake compensator (Saloon model)

12.2B Rear brake compensator (Estate model)

pipes are secure in their clips. After fitting, remove the polythene sheeting and bleed the brake hydraulic system as described in the next Section.

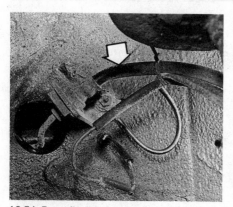

13.5A Front flexible brake hose (arrowed) and body bracket

13.5B Rear flexible brake hose (arrowed) (Saloon model)

13.5C Rear flexible brake hose (Estate model)

14 Hydraulic system – bleeding

1   If the master cylinder has been removed and refitted, then the complete system (both front and rear circuits) must be bled. If a component of one circuit has been disturbed, and there has been only minimal loss of fluid, then only that particular circuit need be bled.

2   Before bleeding the rear hydraulic circuit on Saloon models, position a 5 mm (0.2 in) thick spacer (such as an open-ended spanner) between the rear brake compensator piston and adjustment lever. If the rear wheels are not supporting the weight of the car, insert a thicker spacer, so that the piston is fully in its housing.

3   If the complete system is being bled, bleed the rear right-hand brake, followed by the rear left-hand brake, the front left-hand brake, and the front right-hand brake.

4   Unless the pressure bleeding method is being used, do not forget to keep the fluid level in the master cylinder reservoir topped up, to prevent air from being drawn into the system, which would make any work done worthless.

5   Before commencing operations, check that all system hoses and pipes are in good condition, with all unions tight and free from leaks.

6   Take great care not to allow hydraulic fluid to come into contact with the vehicle paintwork, as it is an effective paint stripper. Wash off any spilled fluid immediately with cold water.

7   Before commencing work, destroy the vacuum in the servo unit by giving several applications of the brake pedal in quick succession.

Bleeding – two-man method

8   Gather together a clean jar and a length of rubber or plastic tubing which will be a tight fit on the brake bleed screws.

9   Engage the help of an assistant.

10 Push one end of the bleed tube onto the first bleed screw, and immerse the other end in the jar, which should contain enough hydraulic fluid to cover the end of the tube.

11 Open the bleed screw one half a turn, and have your assistant depress the brake pedal fully, and slowly release it. Tighten the bleed screw at the end of each pedal downstroke, to obviate any chance of air or fluid being drawn back into the system.

12 Repeat this operation until clean hydraulic fluid, free from air bubbles, can be seen coming through into the jar. Tighten the bleed screw at the end of a pedal downstroke, and remove the bleed tube.

13 Bleed the remaining screws in a similar way.

Bleeding – using one-way valve kit

14 There are a number of one-man, one-way brake bleeding kits available from motor accessory shops. It is recommended that one of these kits is used wherever possible, as it will greatly simplify the bleeding operation, and also reduce the risk of air or fluid being drawn back into the system, quite apart from allowing one to do the work without the help of an assistant.

15 To use the kit, connect the tube to the bleed screw and open the screw one half a turn (photo).

16 Depress the brake pedal fully, and slowly release it. The one-way valve in the kit will prevent expelled air from returning at the end of each pedal downstroke. Repeat this operation several times to be sure of ejecting all air from the system. Some kits include a translucent

container, which can be positioned so that the air bubbles can actually be seen being ejected from the system.

17 Tighten the bleed screws, remove the tube and repeat the operations on the remaining brakes.

18 On completion, depress the brake pedal. If it still feels spongy, repeat the bleeding operations as air must still be trapped in the system.

Bleeding – using a pressure bleeding kit

19 These kits too are available from motor accessory shops, and are usually operated by air pressure from the spare tyre.

20 By connecting a pressurised container to the master cylinder fluid reservoir, bleeding is then carried out by simply opening each bleed screw in turn and allowing the fluid to run out, rather like turning on a tap, until no air is visible in the expelled fluid.

21 By using this method, the large reserve of hydraulic fluid provides a safeguard against air being drawn into the master cylinder during bleeding, which often occurs if the fluid level in the reservoir is not maintained.

22 Pressure bleeding is particularly effective when bleeding 'difficult' systems, or when bleeding the complete system at time of routine fluid renewal.

All methods

23 When bleeding is completed, check and top up the fluid level in the master cylinder reservoir.

24 Check the feel of the pedal. If it feels at all spongy, air must still be present in the system, and further bleeding is indicated. Failure to bleed satisfactorily, after a reasonable period of the bleeding operation, may be due to worn master cylinder seals.

14.15 Loosening the bleed screw on a front brake caliper

ar calipers are resting on their nylon pads.
0 Progressively screw in the adjustment nuts on each cable by equal
mounts, until the rear caliper levers just lift from the nylon pads.
1 Check that the threaded ends of the adjustment ferrules on each
able project by equal amounts. If not, reposition the adjustment nuts,
en repeat the procedure given in paragraph 10.
2 Unscrew each adjustment nut by half a turn.
3 Fully apply the handbrake lever, and check that the lever travel is
etween 7 and 13 notches. With the lever off, check that both rear
heels turn freely.

ll models
4 Retighten the adjustment locknuts.
5 Lower the car to the ground.

9 Handbrake cables – renewal

Chock the front wheels, then jack up the rear of the car and support
 axle stands. Remove the rear wheels.
 Fully release the handbrake.
 On models with rear drum brakes, remove the rear brake shoes,
en use a small drift to drive the outer cables from the backplates.
 On models with rear disc brakes, disconnect the inner cables from
e caliper levers, and withdraw the outer cables from the brackets.
 Release the outer cables from the underbody clips and springs
hoto).
 Working inside the vehicle, remove the centre console, then
sconnect the cables from the equaliser (photo). On Estate models
ted with a bench seat, the equaliser is connected to the handbrake
ver by an additional cable.
 Withdraw the cables from under the vehicle.
 Fit the new cables, using a reversal of the removal procedure.
nally, adjust the cables as described in Section 18.

0 Brake pedal – removal and refitting

Remove the lower facia panel from the steering column, in order to
in access to the pedal bracket.
 Extract the spring clip, withdraw the clevis pin, and disconnect the
shrod from the pedal.
 Unscrew the self-locking nut from the pivot bolt, and remove the
rustwasher.
 Pull out the bolt and remove the brake pedal. If the bolt is fitted
om the right-hand side, it will also be necessary to remove the clutch
dal on manual gearbox models.
 Examine the pedal bushes for wear, and renew them if necessary.
 Refitting is a reversal of removal, but lightly grease the bushes and
evis pin, and renew the self-locking nut. Check, and if necessary
just, the stop-lamp switch as described in the next Section.

1 Stop-lamp switch – removal and refitting

Remove the lower facia panel below the steering column.
 Disconnect the wiring from the stop-lamp switch on the pedal
acket (photo).
 Unscrew the lower adjustment locknut, and remove the switch
om the pedal bracket.
 Refitting is a reversal of removal, but adjust the locknuts so that the
earance between the threaded shank and pedal is at least 1.5 mm
.06 in). Check that the stop-lamps operate correctly with the ignition
itched on.

Handbrake warning light switch – removal and refitting

Remove the centre console.
 With the handbrake applied, remove the mounting screw,
thdraw the switch and disconnect the wiring (photo).
 Refitting is a reversal of removal.

19.5 Handbrake cable retaining spring

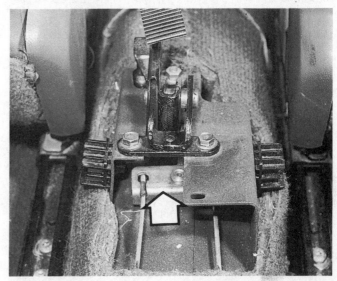
19.6 Handbrake inner cables and equaliser (arrowed)

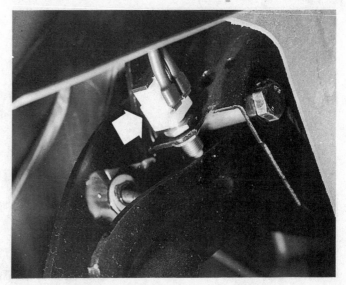
21.2 Brake stop-lamp switch (arrowed)

25 Discard brake fluid which has been expelled. It is almost certain to be contaminated with moisture, air and dirt, making it unsuitable for further use. Clean fluid should always be stored in an airtight container, as it absorbs moisture readily (hygroscopic) which lowers its boiling point, and could affect braking performance under severe conditions.

15 Vacuum servo unit – description and testing

1   A vacuum servo unit is fitted to the master cylinder, to provide power assistance to the driver when the brake pedal is depressed.
2   The unit operates by vacuum obtained from the induction manifold and comprises, basically, a booster diaphragm and a non-return valve.
3   The servo unit piston rod acts as the master cylinder pushrod. The driver's braking effort is transmitted through another pushrod to the servo unit piston and its built-in control system. The servo unit piston does not fit tightly into the container, but has a strong diaphragm to keep its edges in constant contact with the cylinder wall, so assuring an airtight seal between the two parts. The forward chamber is held under vacuum conditions created in the inlet manifold of the engine and, during periods when the brake pedal is not in use, the controls open a passage to the rear chamber, so placing it under vacuum. When the brake pedal is depressed, the vacuum passage to the rear chamber is cut off and the chamber opened to atmospheric pressure. The consequent rush of air pushes the servo piston forward in the vacuum chamber and operates the main pushrod to the master cylinder. The controls are designed so that assistance is given under all conditions and, when the brakes are not required, vacuum in the rear chamber is established when the brake pedal is released. Air from the atmosphere entering the rear chamber is passed through a small air filter.
4   Operation of the servo can be checked in the following way. With the engine off, depress the brake pedal several times. The pedal travel should remain the same.
5   Depress the brake pedal fully and hold it down. Start the engine and feel that the pedal moves down slightly.
6   Hold the pedal depressed with the engine running. Switch off the engine, holding the pedal depressed. The pedal should not rise nor fall.
7   If the foregoing tests do not prove satisfactory, check the servo vacuum hose and non-return valve for security and leakage. The valve and rubber grommet may be renewed by prising them from the servo body (photo).
8   If the brake servo operates properly in the test, but still gives less effective service on the road, the air filter through which air flows into the servo should be inspected. A dirty filter will limit the formation of a difference in pressure across the servo diaphragm.
9   The servo unit itself cannot be repaired, and therefore a complete renewal is necessary if the measures described are not effective.

16 Vacuum servo air filter – renewal

1   Remove the right-hand lower facia panel.
2   Reach up behind the footpedals, and pull the dust excluder off the servo onto the pushrod. If the dust excluder is supplied with the new air filter as a kit, disconnect the pushrod from the pedal and remove the excluder.

3   Using a scriber or similar tool, pick out the filter, and cut it remove it if not renewing the dust excluder.
4   Fit the new air filter, using a reversal of the removal procedure. not renewing the dust excluder, cut the new filter radially befo locating it on the pushrod.

17 Vacuum servo unit – removal and refitting

1   Remove the master cylinder as described in Section 11.
2   Disconnect the vacuum hose from the non-return valve on t servo unit (photo).
3   Disconnect the pushrod from the brake pedal by extracting the sp pin and the clevis pin.
4   Unscrew the mounting nuts from inside the vehicle, then withdra the servo unit into the engine compartment. Remove the gasket.
5   Adjustment of the servo output pushrod is not possible on t Teves version. On the DBA version, adjustment is possible, and t pushrod projection from the face of the unit should be 9.0 mm (0. in).
6   Refitting is a reversal of removal, but fit a new gasket and full tighten the mounting nuts. Finally, with the brake pedal release check that the clearance between the stop-lamp switch thread shank and pedal is at least 1.5 mm (0.06 in). If necessary, loosen t locknuts, adjust the switch, then tighten the locknuts.

18 Handbrake – adjustment

1   The handbrake is normally kept adjusted by the action of t automatic adjusters on the rear brake shoes (drum brakes) or re caliper pistons (disc brakes). However, the cables may require perioc adjustment to compensate for cable stretch.
2   With the engine idling, depress the brake pedal hard several time This will ensure that the brake linings are in the normal adjuste position. Switch off the engine.
3   Chock the front wheels, then jack up the rear of the car and suppe on axle stands. Release the handbrake.
4   Working beneath the vehicle, loosen the locknuts at the front e of the outer cables (photo).

Rear drum brake models
5   Screw in the adjustment nuts on each cable by equal amoun until the rear brake shoe linings are just touching the drums. It shou still be possible to turn the rear wheels by hand, although slig resistance should be apparent.
6   Check that the threaded ends of the adjustment ferrules on ea cable project by equal amounts. If not, reposition the adjustment nu then repeat the procedure given in paragraph 5.
7   Unscrew each adjustment nut by half a turn.
8   Fully apply the handbrake lever, and check that the level travel between 4 and 7 notches. With the lever off, check that both re wheels turn freely.

Rear disc brake models
9   Check that, with the handbrake lever released, both levers on t

15.7 Removing the non-return valve from the servo

1.7.2 Disconnecting the vacuum hose

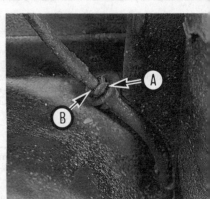

18.4 Handbrake cable adjustment nut (A) and locknut (B)

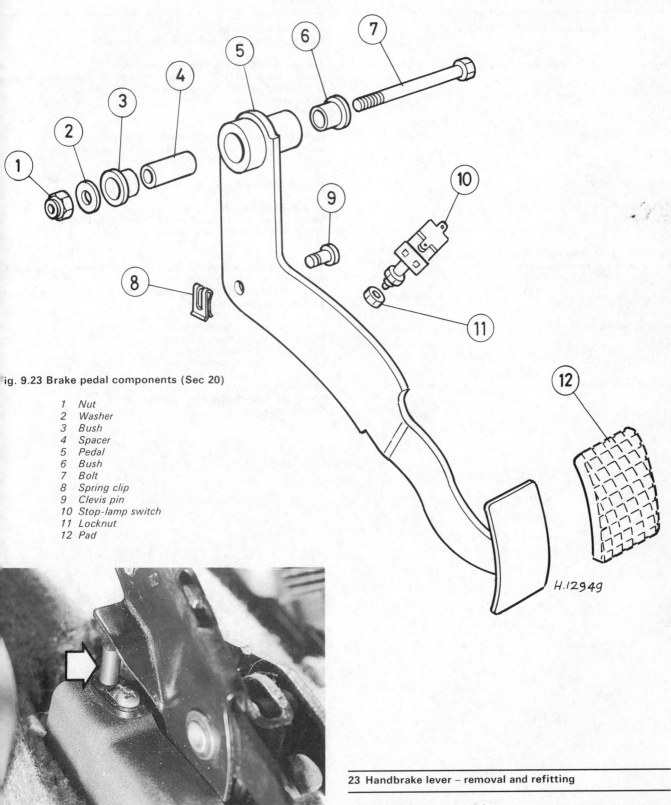

Fig. 9.23 Brake pedal components (Sec 20)

1   Nut
2   Washer
3   Bush
4   Spacer
5   Pedal
6   Bush
7   Bolt
8   Spring clip
9   Clevis pin
10 Stop-lamp switch
11 Locknut
12 Pad

H.1294g

22.2 Handbrake warning light switch (arrowed)

23 Handbrake lever – removal and refitting

1   Remove the centre console.
2   With the handbrake released, disconnect the handbrake cable(s).
3   Unscrew the mounting bolts and nut, and remove the handbrake lever assembly from the floor.
4   Refitting is a reversal of removal, but adjust the handbrake as described in Section 18.

24 Fault diagnosis – braking system

Symptom	Reason(s)
Pedal travels a long way before the brakes operate	Air in hydraulic system Rear drum brake self-adjusting mechanism faulty
Stopping ability poor, even though pedal pressure is firm	Linings, discs or drums badly worn or scored One or more wheel cylinder or caliper pistons seized, resulting in some brake shoes/pads not pressing against the drums/discs Brake linings contaminated with oil Faulty servo unit
Vehicles veers to one side when the brakes are applied	Brake linings on one side contaminated with oil Hydraulic wheel cylinder/caliper on one side partially or fully seized A mixture of lining materials fitted between sides
Pedal feels spongy	Air in hydraulic system
Pedal feels springy when the brakes are applied	New brake linings not bedded in Master cylinder or rear brake backplate mounting bolts loose Excessive wear of discs or brake drums
Pedal travels right down with little or no resistance, and brakes are virtually non-operative	Leak in hydraulic system, resulting in lack of pressure for operating wheel cylinder/caliper pistons If no signs of leakage are apparent, the master cylinder internal seals are failing to sustain pressure
Binding, juddering, overheating	Rear brake shoes fitted incorrectly Broken rear brake shoe return spring Disc/drum distorted Handbrake cable(s) seized
Lack of servo assistance	Vacuum hose leaking Non-return valve defective or incorrectly fitted Servo internal fault

Chapter 10 Suspension and steering

Contents

Specifications

Front suspension

Type .... Independent, McPherson struts, coil springs, radius arms, anti-roll bar
Coil spring free length:
    Standard – without air conditioning .... 575 mm (22.7 in)
    Standard – with air conditioning .... 553 mm (21.8 in)
    Heavy duty – without air conditioning .... 485 mm (19.1 in)
    Heavy duty – with air conditioning .... 498 mm (19.6 in)
Hub bearing lubricant type/specification .... Multi-purpose lithium-based grease (Duckhams LB 10)

Rear suspension

Type:
    Saloon models .... Independent, trailing arms, coil springs, telescopic shock absorbers, anti-roll bar

    Estate models .... Rigid axle, coil springs, telescopic shock absorbers, Panhard rod, anti-roll bar on most models

Coil spring free length:
    Standard .... 419 mm (16.5 in)
    Heavy duty .... 413 mm (16.3 in)

Steering

Type .... Rack and pinion, steering column and intermediate shaft, power assistance on some models

Lubrication:
    Steering rack lubricant type/specification .... Lithium-based molybdenum disulphide grease (Duckhams LBM 10)
    Power steering fluid capacity .... 0.7 litres (1.2 pints)
    Power steering fluid type/specification .... Dexron II ATF (Duckhams D-Matic)

Steering (cont)

Turns lock to lock:
Manual steering	4.5
Power-assisted steering	3.0 or 3.4

Front wheel alignment (at kerb weight):

Toe-in:
Saloon models	3.0 ± 1.0 mm (0.118 ± 0.04 in)
Estate (except GTI)	3.5 ± 1.0 mm (0.138 ± 0.04 in)
Estate (GTI)	2.0 ± 1.0 mm (0.079 ± 0.04 in)

Camber:
Saloon models	−0°45′ ± 30′
Estate (except GTI)	−0°30′ ± 30′
Estate (GTI)	−0°55′ ± 30′

Castor:
Saloon models	2°40′ ± 30′
Estate models	2° ± 30′

Steering axis inclination:
Saloon models	9°15′ ± 30′
Estate (except GTI)	9° ± 30′
Estate (GTI)	9°25′ ± 30′

Rear wheel alignment (Saloon models):
Toe-in	3.0 ± 1.0 mm (0.118 ± 0.04 in)
Camber	−1° ± 30′

Roadwheels

Type	Pressed-steel or light alloy

Size:
Steel	5½J14 FH 4.30 or 4.23
Alloy – Saloon (except GTI)	6J14 FHH 20
Alloy – Saloon (GTI)	6J15 FHH 25
Alloy – Estate (except GTI)	5½J14 FHH 30
Alloy – Estate (GTI)	6J14 FHH 20

Tyres

Size	175 R14S, 185/70 R14T, 185 R14S, 195/70 R14T, 195/60 R15H, or 205/70 R14S

Pressures – bar (lbf/in²):	Front	Rear
175 R14S	1.8 (26)	2.0 (29)
185/70 R14T	1.8 (26)	2.1 (30)
185 R14S	1.9 (28)	2.1 (30)
195/70 R14T	1.9 (28)	2.3 (33)
195/60 R15S	2.0 (29)	2.1 (30)
205/70 R14S	2.0 (29)	2.2 (32)

Torque wrench settings

Front suspension	Nm	lbf ft
Lower balljoint housing nut (early Saloon)	45	33
Lower balljoint housing (later, Saloon, and Estate)	170	125
Lower balljoint nut (later Saloon, and Estate)	45	33
Suspension strut upper mounting bolts	10	7
Shock absorber cover nut	80	59
Shock absorber piston rod nut	45	33
Lower suspension arm pivot pin	45	33
Anti-roll bar link bolt	45	33
Radius arm nut	45	33
Wheel nuts – steel wheels	60	44
Wheel nuts – alloy wheels	95	70

Rear suspension		
Hub nut	250	185
Crossmember nuts (Saloon)	65	48
Trailing arm pivot bolt	55	41
Hub carrier/backplate (Estate)	55	41
Shock absorber upper mounting (Saloon)	12.5	9
Shock absorber lower mounting (Saloon)	45	33
Shock absorber upper and lower mountings (Estate)	57.5	42

Steering		
Track rod end to steering arm	35	26
Track rod locknut	45	33
Intermediate shaft couplings	25	18
Steering gear	33	24
Track rod inner balljoint	50	37
Power-assisted steering ram	50	37
Power-assisted steering pump union	25	18

1 General description

The front suspension is of independent type, incorporating McPherson struts with integral shock absorbers, and coil springs. The lower ends of the suspension struts are attached to the suspension arms by balljoints, and vertical movement is controlled by radius arms. An anti-roll bar is fitted.

On Saloon models, the rear suspension is of independent type, incorporating trailing arms, coil springs, telescopic shock absorbers and an anti-roll bar. The trailing arms are attached to a lower crossmember, and an upper crossmember accommodates the shock absorbers upper mountings and coil spring seats.

On Estate models, a live axle is fitted, being supported at the front by the torque tube. Lateral movement is controlled by a Panhard rod. Coil springs, telescopic shock absorbers and an anti-roll bar are fitted.

Rack-and-pinion steering is fitted, incorporating a steering column and intermediate shaft. Power-assisted steering is fitted to some models.

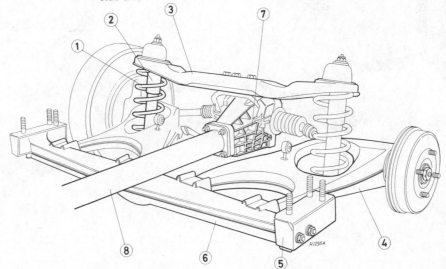

Fig. 10.1 Front suspension components (Sec 1)

1 Rear crossmember
2 Front suspension strut and stub axle
3 Front lower suspension arm
4 Radius arm
5 Front crossmember

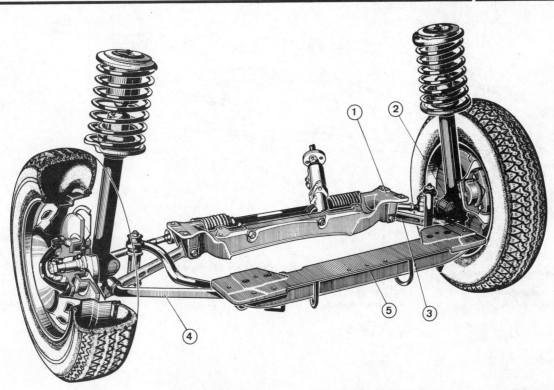

Fig. 10.2 Rear suspension components on Saloon models (Sec 1)

1 Coil spring
2 Shock absorber
3 Upper crossmember
4 Trailing arm
5 Support
6 Lower crossmember
7 Final drive unit
8 Propeller shaft link tube

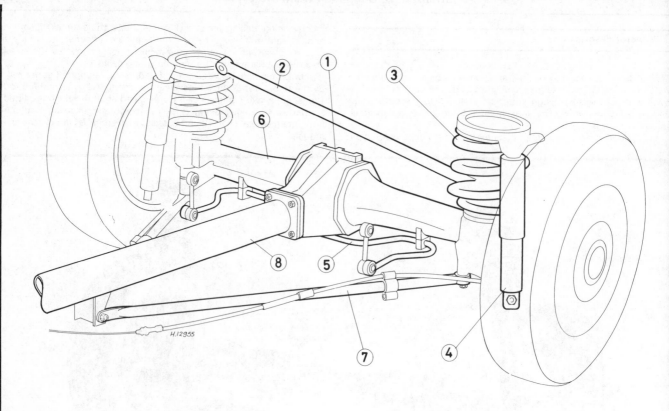

Fig. 10.3 Rear suspension components on Estate models (Sec 1)

1	Final drive unit	3	Coil spring	5	Anti-roll bar	7	Tie-bar
2	Panhard rod	4	Shock absorber	6	Rear axle	8	Torque tube

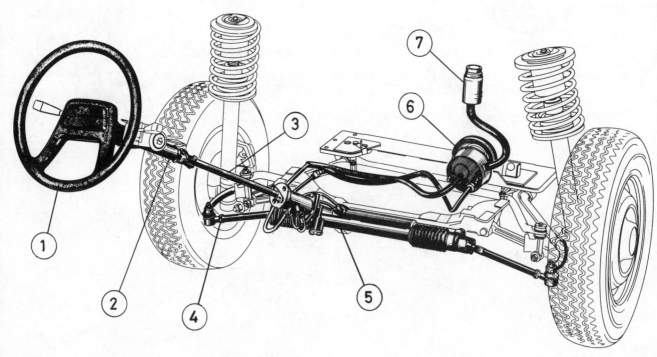

Fig. 10.4 Steering components – LHD shown, RHD similar (Sec 1)

1	Steering wheel	3	Intermediate shaft	5	Steering gear	7	Power steering fluid
2	Steering column	4	Track rod	6	Power steering pump		reservoir

Routine maintenance

Carry out the following procedures at the intervals given in Routine maintenance *at the front of this manual.*

Check tyre condition and pressures

1 With the vehicle supported on axle stands, check that the tyre tread on each tyre is not worn below the legal limit.
2 Check all tyres for damage, and for any flints or nails embedded in the tread.
3 With the (kerb) weight of the vehicle on the tyres, check and adjust the tyre pressures.

Check power steering fluid level

4 Visually check the power steering system pipes and hoses for signs of leakage.
5 The fluid level must be checked with the fluid cold, at least two or three hours after switching the engine off.
6 If necessary, top up the reservoir on the right-hand side of the engine to the 'Cold' ('Froid') mark. On completion, tighten the filler cap onto the reservoir.

Check front hub bearing adjustment

7 Jack up the front of the vehicle and support on axle stands.
8 Grip the top and bottom of the tyre, and attempt to rock the wheel. If movement within the bearing is perceptible, adjust it with reference to Section 8.

Check suspension and steering balljoints

9 With the vehicle raised, attempt to move the front lower suspension arms up and down. If there is any noticeable movement within a balljoint, renew it.
10 Similarly check the steering track rod end balljoints for wear.

Check suspension rubber bushes

11 With the vehicle raised, check all suspension rubber bushes for damage and deterioration, including anti-roll bar, shock absorber, and Panhard rod mountings.

Check shock absorbers

12 Check the action of each shock absorber by pressing down on the appropriate corner of the vehicle. After quickly releasing the vehicle, the body should rise, then stabilise. If there are several oscillations, the shock absorber should be renewed.

Check power steering pump drivebelt

13 Inspect the pump drivebelt for cracking, glazing or fraying, and renew if necessary, as described in Section 25 or Chapter 2.
14 Check the pump drivebelt tension, and adjust if necessary, as described in Section 25.

3 Front anti-roll bar – removal and refitting

1 Apply the handbrake, then jack up the front of the vehicle and support on axle stands.
2 Unscrew and remove the bolts securing the anti-roll bar links to the lower suspension arms (photo).
3 Support the anti-roll bar, then unscrew and remove the front mounting bolts and withdraw the bar from under the vehicle (photo). Recover the clamps and spacers.
4 Remove the rubber bushes from the anti-roll bar.
5 Disconnect the links from each end of the anti-roll bar. On some models, a vertically-positioned nut together with spacer and rubber bushes is used, whereas on other models, a horizontally-positioned bolt is used.
6 Refitting is a reversal of removal, but delay tightening the nuts and bolts until the weight of the vehicle is on the suspension. Refer to the torque wrench settings quoted in the Specifications Section at the start of this Chapter.

4 Front suspension strut – removal, overhaul and refitting

1 Apply the handbrake, then jack up the front of the vehicle and support on axle stands positioned under the body channel sections. Remove the appropriate front wheel.
2 Unscrew the brake caliper mounting bolts, withdraw the caliper from the disc, and support it to one side on an axle stand without straining the flexible hydraulic hose. There is no need to remove the disc pads, or to disconnect the hydraulic hose. On some models, the caliper mounting bolts may be locked with locktabs, which must be bent back before loosening the bolts.
3 Unscrew the nut securing the steering track rod end to the hub carrier arm, then use an extractor tool to release the track rod end.
4 Unscrew the pivot pin nut from the inner end of the lower suspension arm (photo). Using a wooden mallet, drive the pivot pin rearwards to release the splined section beneath the head, and remove it.
5 Unscrew and remove the bolt securing the anti-roll bar link to the lower suspension arm.
6 Unscrew the nut securing the radius arm to the lower suspension arm. Remove the cup and rubber bush.
7 Release the lower suspension arm from the crossmember and radius arm.
8 Support the front suspension strut with a trolley jack.
9 Working inside the engine compartment, unscrew the three bolts from the strut upper mounting.
10 Lower the trolley jack, and withdraw the strut from under the front wing (photo).
11 Clean away all external dirt from the strut and coil spring.

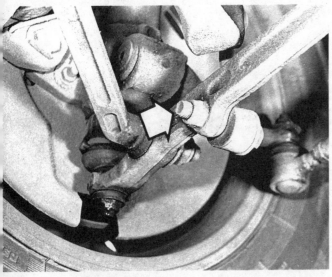

3.2 Anti-roll bar link bolt (arrowed)

3.3 Anti-roll bar front mounting (arrowed)

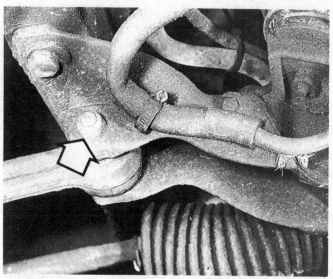

4.4 Lower suspension arm inner pivot pin (arrowed)

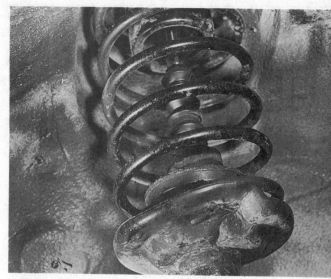

4.10 Front suspension strut viewed from under the front wing

12 Fit spring compressors to the coil spring, and tighten them evenly until the spring is released from the upper mounting.
13 Unscrew the piston rod nut, if necessary using a screwdriver to hold the rod stationary.
14 Remove the washer, rebound limiter, bearing assembly, cup and spring seat.
15 Remove the coil spring. The spring can remain in the compressed state, ready for refitting to the strut. If the spring is to be renewed, release the compressors very gently and evenly, until they can be removed and fitted to the new spring.
16 If necessary, remove the gaiter and bump stop from the piston rod. Note the location of each component to ensure correct refitting.
17 Check the strut for signs of fluid seepage at the piston rod seal. Temporarily refit the upper mounting to the piston rod, and, with the bottom of the strut gripped in a vice, fully extend and retract the piston rod. If the resistance is not firm and even in both directions, or if there are signs of leakage or damage, the strut must be renewed or overhauled.
18 To overhaul the strut, first mount it vertically in a vice.
19 Unscrew the nut and withdraw the shock absorber, while keeping the cylinder in the strut.
20 Withdraw the cylinder, and tap the compensator valve from the bottom of it.
21 Drain the fluid from the strut. Lever off the rebound stop.

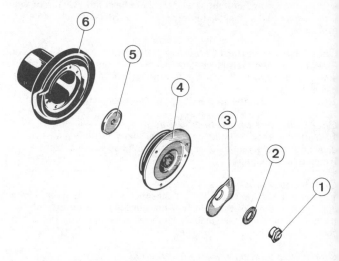

Fig. 10.5 Front suspension strut upper mounting components (Sec 4)

1   Piston rod nut   4   Bearing assembly
2   Washer   5   Cup
3   Rebound limiter   6   Spring seat

Fig. 10.6 Withdrawing the shock absorber cylinder from the front suspension strut (Sec 4)

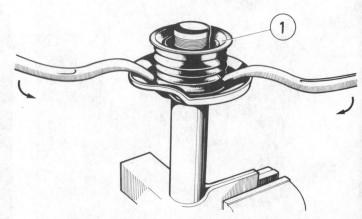

Fig. 10.7 Levering off the rebound stop (1) (Sec 4)

22 Clean the components thoroughly, and renew the parts indicated in Fig. 10.8.
23 Fit the rebound stop, engaging its slots, and using a suitable lubricant if necessary on the strut screw threads.
24 Drive the new compensator valve into the cylinder, using a hide or wooden mallet.
25 Insert the cylinder in the strut, then pour in 3.35 cc of suitable fluid – consult your Peugeot dealer.
26 Insert the shock absorber slowly, being careful not to damage the seal.
27 Fit the upper bearing 3.0 mm (0.118 in) below the upper edge of the strut.
28 Smear the upper seal with the above-mentioned fluid, and locate it on the bearing. Similarly fit the rod seal.
29 Refit and tighten the nut, using a crowfoot spanner and torque wrench to tighten it to the specified torque.
30 Pull out the piston rod as far as possible.
31 Refit the gaiter and bump stop.
32 Locate the coil spring (compressed) on the strut.
33 Refit the cup and spring seat, bearing assembly, rebound limiter and washer, and a new piston rod nut. Tighten the nut to the specified torque.
34 Carefully release the spring compressors, making sure that the coil spring locates correctly in the seatings. Push the rubber gaiter over the shock absorber retaining nut.
35 Lift the front suspension unit into position under the front wing, and support it on a trolley jack.
36 With the rebound limiter parallel with the vehicle centre-line, insert the three strut upper mounting bolts, and tighten them to the specified torque. Where applicable, fit the earth lead to the outer bolt.
37 Fit the lower suspension arm onto the radius arm. Refit the rubber bush and cup, and screw on the nut finger-tight.
38 Insert the bolt through the anti-roll bar link and lower suspension arm, and screw on the nut finger-tight.
39 Locate the lower suspension arm in the crossmember, and insert the pivot pin from the rear without engaging the splined section. Screw on the nut finger-tight.
40 Fit the steering track rod end to the hub carrier arm. Screw on the nut and tighten to the specified torque.
41 Refit the brake caliper and tighten the mounting bolts to the specified torque given in Chapter 9. Bend over the locktabs where applicable.
42 Apply the brake pedal several times to reset the disc pads.
43 Refit the front wheel and lower the vehicle to the ground (photo).
44 Move the vehicle a few yards backwards and forwards to settle the suspension, then drive in the lower suspension arm pivot pin to engage the splines, and tighten the nut to the specified torque. Also tighten the anti-roll bar link bolt and radius arm nut to the specified torque.

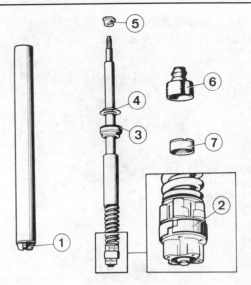

Fig. 10.8 Shock absorber overhaul components (Sec 4)

1 Compensator valve assembly
2 Sealing ring
3 Bearing seal
4 Rod seal
5 Upper nut
6 Gaiter
7 Cover nut

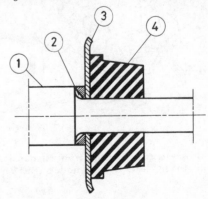

4.43 Tightening the wheel nuts

5 Front radius arm – removal and refitting

1 Apply the handbrake, then jack up the front of the vehicle and support on axle stands. Remove the appropriate front wheel.
2 Unscrew and remove the bolt securing the anti-roll bar link to the lower suspension arm.
3 Unscrew the nut securing the radius arm to the lower suspension arm (photo). Remove the cup and rubber bush.
4 Unscrew the pivot pin nut from the inner end of the lower suspension arm. Using a wooden mallet, drive the pivot pin rearwards to release the splined section beneath the head, and remove it.
5 Release the lower suspension arm from the crossmember and radius arm.
6 Unscrew the front nut from the radius arm. Remove the cup and rubber bush.
7 Withdraw the radius arm from the front bracket.
8 Remove the inner rubber bushes, cups and thrust washers.
9 Examine the rubber bushes for damage and deterioration, and renew them if necessary.
10 Refitting is a reversal of removal, but check that the thrustwashers and cups are located as shown in Fig. 10.9, and delay tightening the nuts and bolts until the weight of the vehicle is on the suspension.

Fig. 10.9 Cross-section of radius arm components (Sec 5)

1 Radius arm
2 Thrustwasher
3 Cap
4 Rubber bush

5.3 Radius arm rear nut (arrowed)

6 Front lower suspension arm – removal and refitting

1   Apply the handbrake, then jack up the front of the vehicle and support on axle stands. Remove the appropriate front wheel.
2   Unscrew and remove the bolt securing the anti-roll bar link to the lower suspension arm.
3   Unscrew the nut securing the radius arm to the lower suspension arm. Remove the cup and rubber bush.
4   Unscrew the pivot pin nut from the inner end of the lower suspension arm. Using a wooden mallet, drive the pivot pin rearwards to release the splined section beneath the head, and remove it.

5   Release the lower suspension arm from the crossmember and radius arm.
6   On early Saloon models having a vehicle identification number (VIN) up to 1.341.364, unscrew the lower balljoint housing nut from the arm, together with the grease nipple. Unscrew the ball securing nut, then tap the arm from the bottom of the strut. Use a puller if necessary.
7   On later Saloon models, and all Estate models, unscrew the lower balljoint nut, and use a balljoint separator tool to release the arm.
8   Refitting is a reversal of removal, but delay tightening the radius arm, anti-roll bar link, and inner pivot nuts and bolts until the weight of the vehicle is on the suspension. On early Saloon models, grease the balljoint through the grease nipple.

7 Front lower suspension balljoint – renewal

1   Remove the front suspension strut as described in Section 4.
2   Remove the lower suspension arm with reference to Section 6.

Early Saloon models (up to VIN 1.341.364)
3   Unclip the balljoint boot from the groove in the lower suspension arm.
4   Remove the ball and lower half-bearing from the arm.
5   Remove the upper half-bearing from the arm.
6   Clean the balljoint cavity in the lower suspension arm, and obtain a balljoint repair kit. This will include a rubber boot and clip, upper and lower half-bearings, ball, ball nut, housing nut, and grease nipple.
7   Grease the half-bearings and ball, then locate them in the lower suspension arm.
8   Fit the rubber boot in the groove, and secure with the clip.

Later Saloon models, and all Estate models
Note: *To unscrew the balljoint housing, a special tool will be required, but it may be possible to use a home-made alternative – refer to paragraph 11.*
9   Mount the strut in a vice.
10 Bend back the tabs of the lockwasher.

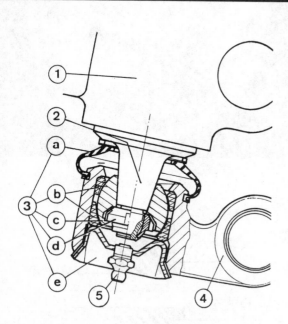

Fig. 10.10 Cross-section through front suspension lower balljoint on early Saloon models (Sec 7)

1	Strut	c	Ball
2	Ball pin	d	Nut
3	Balljoint assembly:	e	Housing nut
a	Rubber boot	4	Lower suspension arm
b	Half-bearings	5	Grease nipple

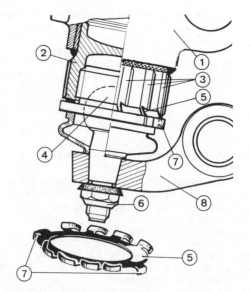

Fig. 10.11 Cross-section through front suspension lower balljoint on later Saloon, and Estate models (Sec 7)

1	Strut	5	Lockwasher
2	Internally-threaded balljoint housing	6	Self-locking nut
3	Locking splines	7	Locating lugs
4	Balljoint	8	Lower suspension arm

11 A special tool is now required in order to unscrew the balljoint housing. If Peugeot tool 8.0616 F (Fig. 10.12) cannot be obtained from a Peugeot garage or tool hire agent, a similar tool may be made from metal tubing or an old box spanner.

12 Using the special tool, unscrew the balljoint housing from the bottom of the strut – considerable force will be required.

13 Clean the cavity in the strut, and obtain a new balljoint housing and lockwasher.

14 Apply a little grease to the threads of the new balljoint housing. Locate the new lockwasher on the balljoint housing, with the special tabs in the cut-outs.

15 Insert the balljoint housing into the strut, and tighten, using the special tool, to the specified torque – considerable force will be required.

All models

16 Refit the front suspension strut and lower suspension arm, with reference to Sections 4 and 6 respectively.

---

8 Front hub bearings – renewal

1 Apply the handbrake, then jack up the front of the vehicle and support on axle stands. Remove the appropriate front wheel.

2 Unscrew the brake caliper mounting bolts, withdraw the caliper from the disc, and support it to one side on an axle stand without straining the flexible hydraulic hose. There is no need to remove the disc pads, or to disconnect the hydraulic hose. On some models, the caliper mounting bolts may be locked with locktabs, which must be bent back before loosening the bolts.

3 Carefully tap the hub cap from the hub (photo), and prise the O-ring seal from the groove.

4 Unscrew the hub nut, and remove the special thrust washer.

5 Withdraw the front hub, taking care to catch the inner race as it comes off the stub axle. If the other inner race remains on the stub axle,

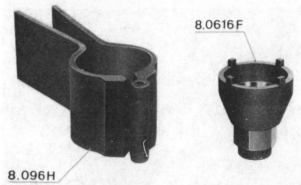

8.0616 F

8.096H

Fig. 10.12 Tool for removing the later front lower suspension balljoint (Sec 7)

use a puller to remove it. Prise out the oil seal, and remove it from the hub.

6 Using a soft metal drift, drive the outer tracks from the hub.

7 Scoop the grease from the hub, and clean all the components. Obtain a new hub nut and oil seal in addition to the new bearings. Check that the stub axle threads are not damaged.

8 Smear a little grease on the outer track seatings inside the hub.

9 Using suitable diameter metal tubing, press or drive the bearing outer tracks fully into the hub.

10 Fit the inner race, then drive in the oil seal squarely using a block of wood, until flush with the edge of the hub.

11 Apply some grease in the cavity between the bearing outer tracks, and smear a little grease on the oil seal lips.

12 Locate the front hub on the stub axle, together with the remaining inner race, and push the assembly fully into position.

13 Fit the thrustwasher, followed by the new hub nut.

14 Tighten the hub nut to 40 Nm (30 lbf ft), at the same time rotating the hub to settle the bearings.

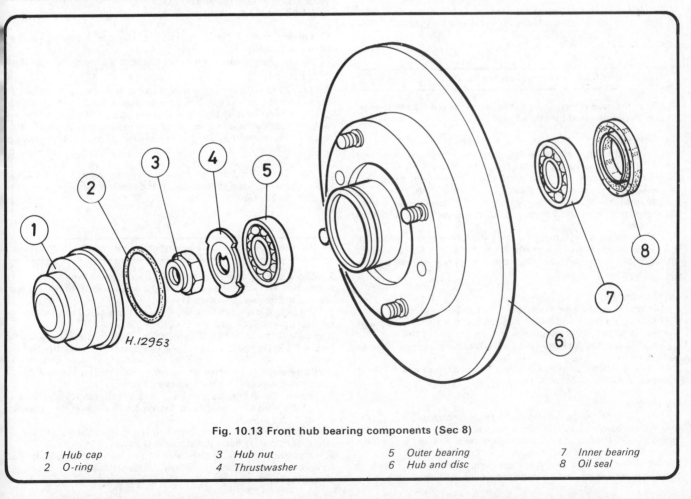

H.12953

Fig. 10.13 Front hub bearing components (Sec 8)

1 Hub cap	3 Hub nut	5 Outer bearing	7 Inner bearing
2 O-ring	4 Thrustwasher	6 Hub and disc	8 Oil seal

8.3 Removing the front hub cap

15 Loosen the hub nut, then re-tighten to 10 Nm (7 lbf ft).
16 Loosen the hub nut a further 45° ($^1/_8$ th of a turn), then lock the nut by punching the shoulder into the groove in the stub axle. Using a screwdriver, check that it is possible to move the thrustwasher side to side beneath the hub nut.
17 Fit the O-ring seal, then tap the hub cap onto the hub.
18 Refit the brake caliper, and tighten the mounting bolts to the specified torque given in Chapter 9. Bend over the locktabs where applicable.
19 Apply the brake pedal several times to reset the disc pads.
20 Refit the front wheel and lower the vehicle to the ground.

9 Rear anti-roll bar – removal and refitting

1 Chock the front wheels. Jack up the rear of the vehicle and support on axle stands. Remove the rear wheels.

Saloon models

2 Unscrew the anti-roll bar-to-rear suspension arm link nuts, and remove the cups and rubber bushes (photo).
3 Unscrew the nuts and remove the clamp plates from the rubber mountings on the underbody (photo).
4 Unhook the rear brake compensator spring. Release the links from the suspension arms, and withdraw the anti-roll bar from one side of the vehicle.
5 Unbolt the links and remove the cups and rubber bushes. Mark the rear brake compensator arm in relation to the bar to ensure correct operation of the compensator, then unscrew the bolt and remove the arm.

Estate models

6 Unbolt the anti-roll bar links from the underbody (photo).
7 Unscrew the nuts and bolts, and remove the clamp plates and spacers from the rubber mountings on the bottom of the rear axle (photo). Lower the anti-roll bar, and withdraw it from under the vehicle.
8 Unbolt the links from the anti-roll bar, and remove the rubber mounting bushes.

All models

9 Check the mounting rubbers for damage and deterioration, and renew them as necessary. On Estate models, the link bushes may be renewed separately by using metal tubing, thick washers and a long bolt and nut to remove and fit them.
10 Refitting is a reversal of removal, but delay tightening the mounting bolts until the weight of the vehicle is on the suspension.

10 Rear coil springs (Saloon models) – removal and refitting

1 Before commencing work, it is recommended that the guide pins described in Chapter 7, Section 3 are obtained in order to support the rear crossmember. Long bolts and washers may be used instead.
2 Chock the front wheels, then jack up the rear of the vehicle and support on axle stands positioned on the underbody. Remove the rear wheels.
3 Unscrew the nut and release the exhaust tailpipe mounting.
4 Unscrew and remove the nuts and bolts securing the anti-roll bar mountings to the underbody.
5 Unbolt the exhaust front silencer heat shield from the underbody.
6 Where applicable, unbolt the bump stop and bracket from the bottom of the propeller shaft link tube and crossmember.
7 Support the final drive unit on a trolley jack, then unscrew either the side mounting bolts or lower link mounting bolt, and lower the final drive unit so that the link tube rests on the rear crossmember.
8 Loosen, but do not remove, the nuts of the rear suspension arm pivot pins.
9 Support the rear crossmember with a trolley jack.
10 Working inside the car, remove the rear seat to give access to the rear crossmember mounting nuts (photo). Unscrew the front nut on each side, then lift the tab washers and remove the centre plug. Screw the guide pins or long bolts into the rear crossmember threaded holes. Leave the tommy bars in the guide pins to support the rear crossmember.
11 Unscrew the rear nuts, remove the tab washers, then lower the rear crossmember until the tommy bars or washers contact the floor.
12 Support the two rear suspension arms with a trolley jack and length of wood.
13 Using an Allen key, unscrew and remove the rear shock absorber lower mounting bolts.
14 Open the bootlid, remove the plastic covers, and unscrew the rear shock absorber upper mounting nuts.
15 Withdraw the shock absorbers down through the rear suspension arms.
16 Lower the rear suspension arms until the rear coil springs can be lifted out (photo).
17 Refitting is a reversal of removal, but note the following additional points:

(a) Check that the upper rubber spring seats are correctly located in the upper suspension crossmember
(b) When refitting the lower crossmember mounting nuts, check that flat washers are located under the tab washers. After tightening the nuts, bend up the tab washers to lock the nuts
(c) Where fitted, centralise the bump stop with reference to Chapter 7, Section 3
(d) Delay tightening the suspension arm pivot pins and anti-roll bar mountings until the weight of the vehicle is on the suspension

11 Rear coil springs (Estate models) – removal and refitting

1 Chock the front wheels, then jack up the rear of the vehicle and support on axle stands positioned on the underbody. Remove the rear wheels and release the handbrake.
2 Unscrew and remove the bolts securing the anti-roll bar links to the underbody, and withdraw the links from the brackets.
3 Pull out the spring plate securing the flexible brake hose to the torque tube. Do not disconnect the rigid brake line from the flexible hose.
4 Release the rigid brake line support, also unclip the rear brake compensator supply line from the underbody.
5 Unbolt the compensator spring from the torque tube, and the compensator from the underbody, but do not disconnect the hydraulic lines.
6 Unbolt the hydraulic line three-way union from the top of the rear axle casing, but do not disconnect the lines.
7 Unscrew and remove one of the nuts securing the front seat reinforcement bar to the underbody. Loosen the remaining nut and swivel the bar to one side of the torque tube.

9.2 Rear anti-roll bar lower mounting (Saloon models)

9.3 Rear anti-roll bar mounting on the underbody (Saloon models)

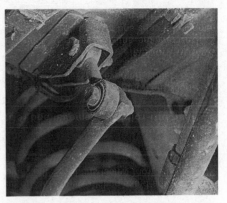

9.6 Rear anti-roll bar mounting on the underbody (Estate models)

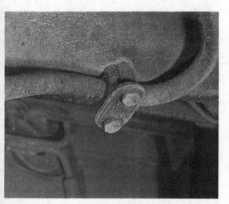

9.7 Rear anti-roll bar mounting on the rear axle (Estate models)

10.10 Rear crossmember mounting nuts (Saloon models)

10.16 Rear coil spring (Saloon models)

8   Using a trolley jack, raise the rear axle slightly, then unscrew and remove both rear shock absorber lower mounting bolts.

9   Lower the rear axle until the rear coil springs can be lifted out (photo).

10 Refitting is a reversal of removal, but tighten all nuts and bolts to the specified torque. Make sure that the coil spring ends locate correctly in the seatings.

12 Rear suspension trailing arms (Saloon models) – removal and refitting

1   Remove the appropriate driveshaft as described in Chapter 8, Section 5.

2   Unscrew the nut securing the anti-roll bar link to the rear suspension arm, and remove the cups and rubber bushes.

3   Position a trolley jack directly beneath the coil spring and shock absorber, and raise the arm slightly.

4   Unscrew and remove the pivot bolts from the front of the suspension arm (photo). Prise the arm from the crossmember.

5   Open the bootlid, remove the plastic covers, and unscrew the rear shock absorber upper mounting nut.

6   Lower the rear suspension arm, and remove the coil spring.

7   Unbolt the shock absorber from the suspension arm.

8   Refitting is a reversal of removal, but delay tightening the pivot bolts until the weight of the vehicle is on the suspension. Make sure that the coil spring seat is correctly located in the crossmember.

13 Rear shock absorber – removal and refitting

1   Chock the front wheels, then jack up the rear of the vehicle and

support on axle stands. Remove the appropriate rear wheel.

2   Position a trolley jack under the outer end of the trailing arm (Saloon models), or under the rear axle (Estate models). Raise the jack slightly, so that the shock absorber is not fully extended.

3   Using an Allen key, unscrew and remove the shock absorber lower mounting bolt, noting which way round it is fitted (photos).

4   On Saloon models, open the bootlid, remove the plastic cover, and unscrew the shock absorber upper mounting nut (photo). The shock absorber may then be withdrawn downwards through the trailing arm.

5   On Estate models, unbolt the shock absorber upper mounting bracket from the body (photo) and withdraw the shock absorber downwards, then unbolt the shock absorber from the bracket.

6   Examine the mounting rubbers for damage and deterioration, and renew them if necessary. Use metal tubing, washers and a long bolt to renew the mounting rubber in the eye of the shock absorber.

7   Refitting is a reversal of removal, but tighten the nuts and bolts to the specified torque.

14 Panhard rod (Estate models) – removal and refitting

1   Chock the front wheels, then jack up the rear of the vehicle and support on axle stands.

2   Unscrew and remove the bolt securing the Panhard rod to the rear axle.

3   Unscrew and remove the bolt securing the Panhard rod to the underbody, and remove the rod from under the vehicle.

4   Examine the mounting bushes for damage and deterioration. If necessary, the bushes may be renewed using metal tubing, washers and a long bolt to extract and fit them.

5   Refitting is a reversal of removal, but delay tightening the mounting bolts until the weight of the vehicle is on the suspension.

11.9 Rear coil spring (Estate models)

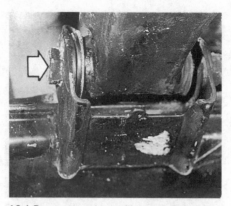

12.4 Rear suspension trailing arm pivot bolt
– arrowed (Saloon models)

13.3A Rear shock absorber lower mounting
on Saloon models ...

13.3B ... and Estate models

13.4 Rear shock absorber upper mounting
on Saloon models

13.5 Rear shock absorber upper mounting
on Estate models (arrowed)

15 Rear hub bearings (Saloon models) – renewal

Note: *Refer to the preliminary note in Section 16*

1   Remove the driveshaft as described in Chapter 8, Section 5.

Rear disc brake models
2   Using a suitable puller, press the hub/drive flange from the hub bearings.
3   Where the bearing inner track and oil seal have remained on the hub, pull off the track using a suitable puller. To fit the puller, it is advantageous to unbolt the disc first. Mark the disc in relation to the hub, so that it may be refitted in the same position.

Rear drum brake models
4   Since the hydraulic brake line is still attached to the rear wheel cylinder, and the brake shoes and backplate are suspended, it is not possible to use a puller from the inside to push out the hub. If it is preferred not to disturb the hydraulic circuit, a metal plate must be bolted to the inside face of the bearing carrier (see Fig. 10.16), and a puller attached to the hub from the outside. The plate is then used as a reaction base when pulling the hub from the bearings.
5   With the hub removed, remove the bolts and withdraw the bearing carrier from the backplate. Refit the bolts to retain the backplate in position.
6   Refer to paragraph 3 if the bearing inner track has remained on the hub.

Early models (to VIN 1.214.586)
7   Mount the bearing carrier in a soft-jawed vice, and unscrew the bearing retaining nut using a tool to engage the special slots. A tool may be made from metal tubing for this purpose.
8   Remove the oil seals and bearing race.

Later models (VIN 1.214.587 on)
9   Prise the oil seals from the bearing carrier.
10 Extract the bearing retaining circlip.

All models
11 Support the bearing carrier on a vice.
12 Using a soft metal drift on the inner track, drive the bearing outer track from the bearing carrier.
13 Clean all the components, and examine them for wear and damage. Obtain new oil seals in addition to the new bearing. On early models, it is recommended that the bearing retaining nut is also renewed.

Early models
14 Press the oil seal in the bearing retaining nut, using a metal tube or block of wood.
15 Insert the bearing outer track and inner race in the bearing carrier. Using a metal tube, drive the outer track fully into position.
16 Fit the bearing retaining nut, and tighten to 250 Nm (185 lbf ft). Stake the edge of the nut to lock it.
17 Press the outer oil seal in the bearing carrier, using a metal tube or block of wood.

Later models
18 Insert the bearing in the carrier. Using a metal tube on the outer track, drive the bearing fully into position.
19 Refit the retaining circlip in its groove.
20 Make sure that the inner tracks are located in the bearing, then press in the inner and outer oil seals, using a metal tube or block of wood.

Rear disc brake models
21 Where applicable, refit the brake disc with reference to Chapter 9.
22 Support the hub bearing inner track on a metal tube, then press or drive the hub into position.

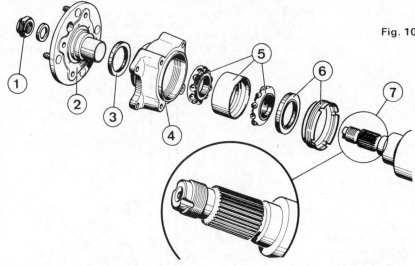

Fig. 10.14 Rear hub bearing components on early Saloon models (Sec 15)

1   Hub nut
2   Hub
3   Outer oil seal
4   Hub carrier
5   Bearing
6   Bearing retaining nut and oil seal
7   Stub axle (with straight-cut splines)

Fig. 10.15 Rear hub bearing components on later Saloon models (Sec 15)

1   Hub nut
2   Hub
3   Outer oil seal
4   Hub carrier
5   Bearing
6   Circlip
7   Inner oil seal
8   Stub axle (with helical-cut splines)

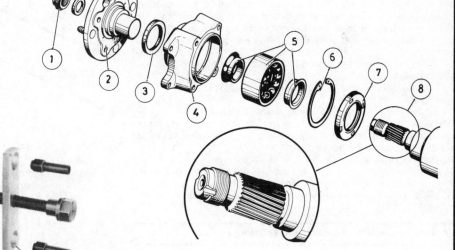

Fig. 10.16 Removing the hub on rear drum brake Saloon models (Sec 15)

1   Bolts supporting hub carrier
2   Reaction plate
3   Bolts
4   Extension
5   Puller plate
6   Nuts
7   Puller bolt

23 At this stage, then run-out of the brake disc may be checked by mounting the hub carrier in a vice. Refer to Chapter 9 for more details. If necessary, the disc may be re-positioned in relation to the hub, in order to obtain the correct run-out.

Rear drum brake models
24 Locate the bearing carrier in the brake backplate, after temporarily removing the supporting bolts.
25 Insert the hub in the bearing and, using a long bolt, washers and nut, draw the hub fully into the bearing.

All models
26 Refit the driveshaft with reference to Chapter 8, Section 5.

16 Rear hub bearings (Estate models) – renewal

Note: *Premature failure of the rear hub bearings can be caused by heavy electrical current flow, as a result of a poor earth return of the battery negative lead. Radial lines on the bearing outer track are an indication of this condition, and where evident, the negative lead-to-body connection should be cleaned and tightened when renewing the bearings*

1 Remove the halfshaft as described in Chapter 8, Section 7.
2 Support the bearing stop ring in a vice, then use a sharp cold chisel to make a 5.0 mm (0.2 in) groove across the stop ring.
3 Cut the lip from the bearing oil seal.
4 Using a suitable puller (long), draw the stop ring from the halfshaft. Alternatively, the stop ring may be drilled or chiselled free, but if this method is used, care must be taken not to damage the halfshaft.
5 Remove the bearing, using the puller or levers. Remove the brake backplate.
6 Clean the halfshaft and backplate. Obtain a new bearing, oil seal and stop ring.
7 Dip the new oil seal in engine oil, and press it squarely into the bearing by hand.
8 Locate the backplate and bearing on the halfshaft.
9 Position a metal tube against the bearing inner track, and mount the assembly on a vice. Tie the backplate to the drive flange to prevent it being trapped by the bearing.
10 Press or drive the halfshaft fully into the bearing.
11 Similarly fit the stop ring against the bearing, noting that the removal recess should be towards the bearing.
12 Refit the halfshaft with reference to Chapter 8, Section 7.

17 Steering wheel – removal and refitting

1 Set the front wheels in the straight-ahead position.
2 Prise out the steering wheel centre pad, then use a socket to unscrew the retaining nut (photo).
3 Mark the hub in relation to the inner column, then pull off the steering wheel. If it is tight, a rocking action may release it from the splines.
4 Refitting is a reversal of removal, but check that the steering wheel is correctly centred with the front wheels straight-ahead. Tighten the nut while holding the steering wheel rim.

18 Steering column and lock – removal and refitting

1 Remove the steering wheel as described in Section 17.
2 Remove the lower trim panel from under the steering column.
3 Mark the universal joint at the base of the column in relation to the intermediate shaft, then unscrew and remove the clamp bolt (photo).
4 Remove the combination switches as described in Chapter 12.
5 Disconnect the ignition switch wiring multi-plugs.
6 Unscrew the mounting nuts from the upper and lower brackets, and withdraw the steering column from the universal joint (photos).
7 If necessary, the intermediate shaft can be removed by unscrewing the pinch-bolt(s) and removing the universal joint(s) or flexible coupling where applicable (photo). Mark the joints in relation to their corresponding shafts before disconnecting them. The rubber grommet

may also be unbolted from the bulkhead.
8 To remove the steering lock, unscrew the retaining bolt, then, with the ignition key aligned with the small arrow between the 'A' and 'M' positions, depress the plunger in the housing and withdraw the lock.
9 Refitting is a reversal of removal.

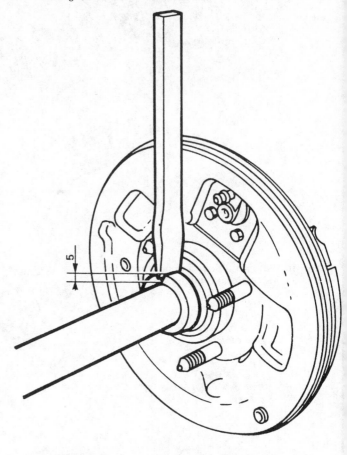

Fig. 10.17 Using a cold chisel to cut the rear hub bearing stop ring on Estate models (Sec 16)

Fig. 10.18 Fitting a new rear hub bearing oil seal on Estate models (Sec 16)

17.2 Steering wheel retaining nut

18.3 Steering column lower universal joint – clamp bolt arrowed

18.6A Steering column upper mounting nuts (arrowed) ...

18.6B ... and lower mounting nuts

18.7 Intermediate shaft-to-power steering gear flexible coupling

19 Steering gear – removal and refitting

1   Apply the handbrake. Jack up the front of the vehicle and support on axle stands.
2   On power-assisted steering models, drain the fluid by unscrewing the feed and return pipe unions at the steering gear (photo). If the fluid is to be re-used, keep it in a clean container. Also unscrew the steering ram nut (photo).
3   Remove both front wheels.
4   Unscrew the steering track rod end nuts on each side, then use a balljoint splitter to release the track rod ends.

5   Unscrew the pinch-bolt from the intermediate shaft lower universal joint or flexible coupling.
6   Unscrew and remove the two mounting bolts.
7   Withdraw the steering gear from the intermediate shaft sufficiently to mark the two shafts in relation to each other to ensure correct reassembly.
8   Separate the shafts, and withdraw the steering gear from under the vehicle.
9   Refitting is a reversal of removal, but tighten all nuts and bolts to the specified torque, and checktk the front wheel alignment on completion. On power-assisted steering models, refill the fluid reservoir with reference to Section 24.

19.2A Feed and return pipes (arrowed) on the power steering gear

19.2B Power steering ram mounting nut

20 Steering gear – overhaul

The steering gear should normally have a very long life before any wear becomes evident, provided that damage has not occurred to the rubber bellows, resulting in inadequate lubrication.

In view of the special tools and gauges required to overhaul the steering gear, it is recommended that when the need for this arises, the unit should be changed for a new or factory reconditioned one rather than dismantle the old one.

21 Track rod end – removal and refitting

1   Apply the handbrake. Jack up the front of the vehicle and support on axle stands. Remove the appropriate front wheel.
2   Loosen the locknut on the track rod.
3   Unscrew the track rod end nut (photo), and use a balljoint splitter tool to separate the taper from the steering arm.
4   Unscrew the track rod end from the track rod, noting the number of turns necessary to remove it.
5   Screw the new track rod end in the track rod the number of turns noted in paragraph 4. If both track rod ends are being renewed, set them to the initial dimension shown in Fig. 10.19.
6   Clean the taper surfaces, then fit the balljoint to the steering arm and tighten the nut to the specified torque. If the balljoint taper pin turns, so preventing the nut from being tightened, use a jack or lever under the track rod end to force the pin in its conical seat.
7   Tighten the track rod locknut.
8   Refit the wheel and lower the car to the ground.
9   Check the front wheel alignment as described in Section 26.

22 Steering rack bellows – renewal

1   Remove the relevant track rod end as described in Section 21.
2   On the left-hand side of power steering models, remove the track rod as described in Section 23, and also disconnect the power steering ram from the rack by unscrewing the nut.
3   Release the clips from each end of the bellows and withdraw the bellows from the steering gear.
4   Fit the new bellows using a reversal of the removal procedure, with reference also to Sections 21 and 23 as applicable. Check that the bellows is not twisted before tightening the clips.

23 Track rod – removal and refitting

1   Remove the track rod end as described in Section 21.
2   Loosen both bellows clips, except on the left-hand side of power steering models, where the joint cover should be removed. On all other models, prise the bellows from the steering gear.
3   Unscrew the balljoint from the rack. The Peugeot tool for this is shown in Fig. 10.20, and if necessary a similar tool may be made from steel plate. Alternatively, use a pair of grips.
4   Withdraw the track rod and recover the lockwashers.
5   Refitting is a reversal of removal, but fit new lockwashers where applicable, and tighten the inner balljoint and track rod end nut to the specified torque. Check the front wheel alignment as described in Section 26.

24 Power steering fluid – draining and refilling

1   With the engine switched off, disconnect the battery negative lead.
2   Unscrew the filler cap from the reservoir.
3   Unscrew the union nut and disconnect the high-pressure pipe from the rear of the power steering pump. Drain the fluid into a clean container.
4   Turn the steering slowly from lock to lock several times in order to remove remaining fluid.
5   Refit the high-pressure pipe, and tighten the union nut.

21.3 Track rod end nut (arrowed)

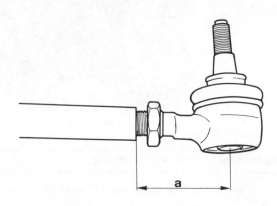

Fig. 10.19 Track rod end initial setting dimension (Sec 21)

a = 55.0 mm (2.17 in)

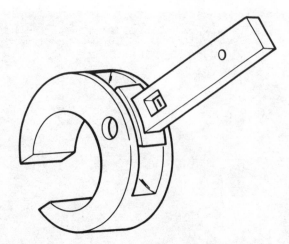

Fig. 10.20 Peugeot tool for unscrewing the track rod inner balljoint (Sec 23)

The arm pivots on the C-plate in order to grip the balljoint

6 Pour fresh fluid into the reservoir to the 'Hot' ('Chaud') level, then turn the steering slowly from lock to lock several times. If necessary, top up the fluid to the 'Cold' ('Froid') level.
7 Connect the battery negative lead and start the engine.
8 With the engine idling, move the steering slowly from lock to lock while topping-up the fluid to the 'Cold' ('Froid') level.
9 When the level no longer drops, switch off the engine and refit the filler cap.

25 Power steering pump – removal and refitting

1 Unscrew the filler cap from the reservoir.
2 Position a container beneath the pump. Unscrew the high-pressure pipe union nut, and also disconnect the low-pressure pipe from the rear of the pump (photos). Drain the fluid and disconnect the supply hose.
3 Loosen the tension adjustment bolt, push the pump towards the engine, and disconnect the drivebelt from the pulley (photos). Note that, on some models, it is necessary to unbolt the pulley from the pump.
4 Remove the tension bolt and spacer.
5 Unscrew and remove the pivot bolt and spacer, and withdraw the power steering pump from the engine (photo). On some models, it may be necessary to unbolt the mounting bracket. On fuel injection models, it will be necessary to remove the air filter.
6 If necessary, unbolt the tension link and reservoir bracket from the engine (photos).
7 If it is required to renew the pump drivebelt, the cooling fan drivebelt must first be removed, as described in Chapter 2.
8 Refitting is a reversal of removal, but tension the drivebelt as follows. Adjust the pump so that the deflection of the belt, under firm thumb pressure, midway between the pulleys, is approximately 12.5 mm (0.5 in) – do not over-tension. Refill the system with fresh fluid, with reference to Section 24.

Fig. 10.21 Power steering fluid reservoir level marks (Sec 24)

25.2A Disconnecting the power steering pump high-pressure pipe ...

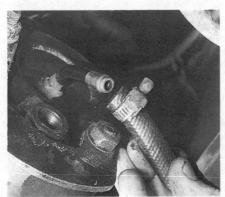

25.2B ... and low-pressure return pipe

25.3A Loosen the power steering pump tension bolt ...

25.3B ... and disconnect the drivebelt

25.5 Removing the power steering pump

25.6A Pump tension link-to-engine bolt

25.6B Removing the power steering fluid reservoir and bracket

26 Steering angles and front wheel alignment

1   Accurate front wheel alignment is essential to provide good steering and roadholding characteristics, and to ensure slow and even tyre wear. Before considering the steering angles, check that the tyres are correctly inflated, that the front wheels are not buckled, the hub bearings are not worn or incorrectly adjusted, and that the steering linkage is in good order, without slackness or wear at the joints.
2   Wheel alignment consists of four factors:
Camber is the angle at which the road wheels are set from the vertical, when viewed from the front or rear of the vehicle. Positive camber is the angle (in degrees) that the wheels are tilted outwards at the top from the vertical.
Castor is the angle between the steering axis and a vertical, when viewed from each side of the vehicle. Positive castor is indicated when the steering axis is inclined towards the rear of the vehicle at its upper end.
Steering axis inclination is the angle, when viewed from the front or rear of the vehicle, between vertical and an imaginary line drawn between the top and bottom strut mountings.
Toe is the amount by which the distance between the front inside edges of the roadwheel rims differs from that between the rear inside edges. If the distance between the front edges is less than that at the rear, the wheels are said to toe-in. If the distance between the front inside edges is greater than that at the rear, the wheels toe-out.

Note: *Camber, castor and steering axis inclination are set during production, and cannot be adjusted. Where the angles differ from those specified, suspect collision damage or severe wear in the steering or suspension components*

3   To check the front wheel alignment, first make sure that the lengths of both track rods are equal, when the steering is in the straight-ahead position. Adjust if necessary by releasing the track rod locknuts and turning the track rods. Reposition the bellows if necessary, so that it is not twisted.
4   Obtain a tracking gauge. These are available in various forms from accessory stores, or one can be fabricated from a length of steel tubing, suitably cranked to clear the sump and bellhousing, and having a setscrew and locknut at one end.
5   With the gauge, measure the distance between the two wheel inner rims (at hub height) at the rear of the wheel. Push the vehicle forwards to rotate the wheel through 180° (half a turn), and measure the distance between the wheel inner rims, again at hub height, at the front of the wheel. This last measurement should differ from the first by the appropriate toe-in figure (see Specifications).
6   Where the toe-in is found to be incorrect, release the track rod locknuts, and turn the track rods equally. Note that one turn of the track rod will make a 3.0 mm (0.118 in) difference in the wheel alignment. Tighten the locknuts before checking the alignment again, and reposition the bellows if necessary.

27 Wheels and tyres – general care and maintenance

Wheels and tyres should give no real problems in use provided that a close eye is kept on them with regard to excessive wear or damage. To this end, the following points should be noted.

Ensure that tyre pressures are checked regularly and maintained correctly. Checking should be carried out with the tyres cold and not immediately after the vehicle has been in use. If the pressures are checked with the tyres hot, an apparently high reading will be obtained owing to heat expansion. Under no circumstances should an attempt be made to reduce the pressures to the quoted cold reading in this instance, or effective underinflation will result.

Underinflation will cause overheating of the tyre owing to excessive flexing of the casing, and the tread will not sit correctly on the road surface. This will cause a consequent loss of adhesion and excessive wear, not to mention the danger of sudden tyre failure due to heat build-up.

Overinflation will cause rapid wear of the centre part of the tyre tread coupled with reduced adhesion, harsher ride, and the danger of shock damage occurring in the tyre casing.

Regularly check the tyres for damage in the form of cuts or bulges, especially in the sidewalls. Remove any nails or stones embedded in the tread before they penetrate the tyre to cause deflation. If removal of a nail *does* reveal that the tyre has been punctured, refit the nail so that its point of penetration is marked. Then immediately change the wheel and have the tyre repaired by a tyre dealer. Do *not* drive on a tyre in such a condition. In many cases a puncture can be simply repaired by the use of an inner tube of the correct size and type. If in any doubt as to the possible consequences of any damage found, consult your local tyre dealer for advice.

Periodically remove the wheels and clean any dirt or mud from the inside and outside surfaces. Examine the wheel rims for signs of rusting, corrosion or other damage. Light alloy wheels are easily damaged by 'kerbing' whilst parking, and similarly steel wheels may become dented or buckled. Renewal of the wheel is very often the only course of remedial action possible.

The balance of each wheel and tyre assembly should be maintained to avoid excessive wear, not only to the tyres but also to the steering and suspension components. Wheel imbalance is normally signified by vibration through the vehicle's bodyshell, although in many cases it is particularly noticeable through the steering wheel. Conversely, it should be noted that wear or damage in suspension or steering components may cause excessive tyre wear. Out-of-round or out-of-true tyres, damaged wheels and wheel bearing wear/maladjustment also fall into this category. Balancing will not usually cure vibration caused by such wear.

Wheel balancing may be carried out with the wheel either on or off the vehicle. If balanced on the vehicle, ensure that the wheel-to-hub relationship is marked in some way prior to subsequent wheel removal so that it may be refitted in its original position.

General tyre wear is influenced to a large degree by driving style – harsh braking and acceleration or fast cornering will all produce more rapid tyre wear. Interchanging of tyres may result in more even wear, but this should only be carried out where there is no mix of tyre types on the vehicle. However, it is worth bearing in mind that if this is completely effective, the added expense of replacing a complete set of tyres simultaneously is incurred, which may prove financially restrictive for many owners.

Front tyres may wear unevenly as a result of wheel misalignment. The front wheels should always be correctly aligned according to the settings specified by the vehicle manufacturer.

Legal restrictions apply to the mixing of tyre types on a vehicle. Basically this means that a vehicle must not have tyres of differing construction on the same axle. Although it is not recommended to mix tyre types between front axle and rear axle, the only legally permissible combination is crossply at the front and radial at the rear. When mixing radial ply tyres, textile braced radials must always go on the front axle, with steel braced radials at the rear. An obvious disadvantage of such mixing is the necessity to carry two spare tyres to avoid contravening the law in the event of a puncture.

In the UK, the Motor Vehicles Construction and Use Regulations apply to many aspects of tyre fitting and usage. It is suggested that a copy of these regulations is obtained from your local police if in doubt as to the current legal requirements with regard to tyre condition, minimum tread depth, etc.

28 Fault diagnosis – suspension and steering

Symptom	Reason(s)
Car pulls to one side	Worn front suspension lower balljoint Incorrect tyre pressures
Excessive pitching or rolling	Weak shock absorbers
Wheel wobble or vibration	Unbalanced wheels Damaged wheels Worn wheel bearings
Excessive tyre wear	Incorrect wheel alignment Worn front suspension lower balljoint Unbalanced wheels
Stiff steering	Seized track rod end balljoint Loss at steering gear lubricant Low tyre pressures
Excessive movement of steering wheel	Worn track rod end balljoint Worn rack and pinion

Chapter 11 Bodywork and fittings

Contents

1 General description

The bodyshell is of one-piece design, with the front and rear sections designed to crumple in a controlled manner, and absorb the impact of a crash. The central passenger compartment forms a safety cell.

The complete body is given an extensive anti-corrosion treatment during manufacture, including stone-chip protection and wax injection. Peugeot guarantee the body against perforation as a result of corrosion for a period of six years, provided the car is given periodic inspections by a Peugeot dealer.

The heater uses heat from the engine coolant to heat the passenger compartment, and coolant flow is controlled by a thermostatic valve. The heater flaps are activated by vacuum rams via the control panel. The system uses engine vacuum from the inlet manifold, and a vacuum reservoir is provided on the left-hand side of the engine compartment (photo).

2 Maintenance – bodywork and underframe

The general condition of a vehicle's bodywork is the one thing that significantly affects its value. Maintenance is easy but needs to be regular. Neglect, particularly after minor damage, can lead quickly to further deterioration and costly repair bills. It is important also to keep watch on those parts of the vehicle not immediately visible, for instance the underside, inside all the wheel arches and the lower part of the engine compartment.

The basic maintenance routine for the bodywork is washing – preferably with a lot of water, from a hose. This will remove all the loose solids which may have stuck to the vehicle. It is important to flush these off in such a way as to prevent grit from scratching the finish. The wheel arches and underframe need washing in the same way to remove any accumulated mud which will retain moisture and

tend to encourage rust. Paradoxically enough, the best time to clean the underframe and wheel arches is in wet weather when the mud is thoroughly wet and soft. In very wet weather the underframe is usually cleaned of large accumulations automatically and this is a good time for inspection.

Periodically, except on vehicles with a wax-based underbody protective coating, it is a good idea to have the whole of the underframe of the vehicle steam cleaned, engine compartment included, so that a thorough inspection can be carried out to see what minor repairs and renovations are necessary. Steam cleaning is available at many garages and is necessary for removal of the accumulation of oily grime

1.3 Heater control vacuum reservoir

which sometimes is allowed to become thick in certain areas. If steam cleaning facilities are not available, there are one or two excellent grease solvents available, such as Holts Engine Cleaner or Holts Foambrite, which can be brush applied. The dirt can then be simply hosed off. Note that these methods should not be used on vehicles with wax-based underbody protective coating or the coating will be removed. Such vehicles should be inspected annually, preferably just prior to winter, when the underbody should be washed down and any damage to the wax coating repaired using Holts Undershield. Ideally, a completely fresh coat should be applied. It would also be worth considering the use of such wax-based protection for injection into door panels, sills, box sections, etc, as an additional safeguard against rust damage where such protection is not provided by the vehicle manufacturer.

After washing paintwork, wipe off with a chamois leather to give an unspotted clear finish. A coat of clear protective wax polish, like the many excellent Turtle Wax polishes, will give added protection against chemical pollutants in the air. If the paintwork sheen has dulled or oxidised, use a cleaner/polisher combination such as Turtle Extra to restore the brilliance of the shine. This requires a little effort, but such dulling is usually caused because regular washing has been neglected. Care needs to be taken with metallic paintwork, as special non-abrasive cleaner/polisher is required to avoid damage to the finish. Always check that the door and ventilator opening drain holes and pipes are completely clear so that water can be drained out (photos). Bright work should be treated in the same way as paint work. Windscreens and windows can be kept clear of the smeary film which often appears by the use of a proprietary glass cleaner like Holts Mixra. Never use any form of wax or other body or chromium polish on glass.

3 Maintenance – upholstery and carpets

Mats and carpets should be brushed or vacuum cleaned regularly to keep them free of grit. If they are badly stained remove them from the vehicle for scrubbing or sponging and make quite sure they are dry before refitting. Seats and interior trim panels can be kept clean by wiping with a damp cloth and Turtle Wax Carisma. If they do become stained (which can be more apparent on light coloured upholstery) use a little liquid detergent and a soft nail brush to scour the grime out of the grain of the material. Do not forget to keep the headlining clean in the same way as the upholstery. When using liquid cleaners inside the vehicle do not over-wet the surfaces being cleaned. Excessive damp could get into the seams and padded interior causing stains, offensive odours or even rot. If the inside of the vehicle gets wet accidentally it is worthwhile taking some trouble to dry it out properly, particularly where carpets are involved. *Do not leave oil or electric heaters inside the vehicle for this purpose.*

4 Minor body damage – repair

The photographic sequences on pages 214 and 215 illustrate the operations detailed in the following sub-sections.
Note: *For more detailed information about bodywork repair, the Haynes Publishing Group publish a book by Lindsay Porter called The Car Bodywork Repair Manual. This incorporates information on such aspects as rust treatment, painting and glass fibre repairs, as well as details on more ambitious repairs involving welding and panel beating.*

Repair of minor scratches in bodywork

If the scratch is very superficial, and does not penetrate to the metal of the bodywork, repair is very simple. Lightly rub the area of the scratch with a paintwork renovator like Turtle Wax New Color Back, or a very fine cutting paste like Holts Body + Plus Rubbing Compound to remove loose paint from the scratch and to clear the surrounding bodywork of wax polish. Rinse the area with clean water.

Apply touch-up paint, such as Holts Dupli-Color Color Touch or a paint film like Holts Autofilm, to the scratch using a fine paint brush; continue to apply fine layers of paint until the surface of the paint in the scratch is level with the surrounding paintwork. Allow the new paint at least two weeks to harden: then blend it into the surround-

ing paintwork by rubbing the scratch area with a paintwork renovator or a very fine cutting paste, such as Holts Body + Plus Rubbing Compound or Turtle Wax New Color Back. Finally, apply wax polish from one of the Turtle Wax range of wax polishes.

Where the scratch has penetrated right through to the metal of the bodywork, causing the metal to rust, a different repair technique is required. Remove any loose rust from the bottom of the scratch with a penknife, then apply rust inhibiting paint, such as Turtle Wax Rust Master, to prevent the formation of rust in the future. Using a rubber or nylon applicator fill the scratch with bodystopper paste like Holts Body + Plus Knifing Putty. If required, this paste can be mixed with cellulose thinners, such as Holts Body + Plus Cellulose Thinners, to provide a very thin paste which is ideal for filling narrow scratches. Before the stopper-paste in the scratch hardens, wrap a piece of smooth cotton rag around the top of a finger. Dip the finger in cellulose thinners, such as Holts Body + Plus Cellulose Thinners, and then quickly sweep it across the surface of the stopper-paste in the scratch; this will ensure that the surface of the stopper-paste is slightly hollowed. The scratch can now be painted over as described earlier in this Section.

Repair of dents in bodywork

When deep denting of the vehicle's bodywork has taken place, the first task is to pull the dent out, until the affected bodywork almost attains its original shape. There is little point in trying to restore the original shape completely, as the metal in the damaged area will have stretched on impact and cannot be reshaped fully to its original contour. It is better to bring the level of the dent up to a point which is about $\frac{1}{8}$ in (3 mm) below the level of the surrounding bodywork. In cases where the dent is very shallow anyway, it is not worth trying to pull it out at all. If the underside of the dent is accessible, it can be hammered out gently from behind, using a mallet with a wooden or plastic head. Whilst doing this, hold a suitable block of wood firmly against the outside of the panel to absorb the impact from the hammer blows and thus prevent a large area of the bodywork from being 'belled-out'.

Should the dent be in a section of the bodywork which has a double skin or some other factor making it inaccessible from behind, a different technique is called for. Drill several small holes through the metal inside the area – particulary in the deeper section. Then screw long self-tapping screws into the holes just sufficiently for them to gain a good purchase in the metal. Now the dent can be pulled out by pulling on the protruding heads of the screws with a pair of pliers.

The next stage of the repair is the removal of the paint from the damaged area, and from an inch or so of the surrounding 'sound' bodywork. This is accomplished most easily by using a wire brush or abrasive pad on a power drill, although it can be done just as effectively by hand using sheets of abrasive paper. To complete the preparation for filling, score the surface of the bare metal with a screwdriver or the tang of a file, or alternatively, drill small holes in the affected area. This will provide a really good 'key' for the filler paste.

To complete the repair see the Section on filling and re-spraying.

Repair of rust holes or gashes in bodywork

Remove all paint from the affected area and from an inch or so of the surrounding 'sound' bodywork, using an abrasive pad or a wire brush on a power drill. If these are not available a few sheets of abrasive paper will do the job just as effectively. With the paint removed you will be able to gauge the severity of the corrosion and therefore decide whether to renew the whole panel (if this is possible) or to repair the affected area. New body panels are not as expensive as most people think and it is often quicker and more satisfactory to fit a new panel than to attempt to repair large areas of corrosion.

Remove all fittings from the affected area except those which will act as a guide to the original shape of the damaged bodywork (eg headlamp shells etc). Then, using tin snips or a hacksaw blade, remove all loose metal and any other metal badly affected by corrosion. Hammer the edges of the hole inwards in order to create a slight depression for the filler paste.

Wire brush the affected area to remove the powdery rust from the surface of the remaining metal. Paint the affected area with rust inhibiting paint like Turtle Rust Master; if the back of the rusted area is accessible treat this also.

Before filling can take place it will be necessary to block the hole in some way. This can be achieved by the use of aluminium or plastic mesh, or aluminium tape.

Aluminium or plastic mesh or glass fibre matting, such as the Holts Body + Plus Glass Fibre Matting, is probably the best material to use for a large hole. Cut a piece to the approximate size and shape of the hole to be filled, then position it in the hole so that its edges are below the level of the surrounding bodywork. It can be retained in position by several blobs of filler paste around its periphery.

Aluminium tape should be used for small or very narrow holes. Pull a piece off the roll and trim it to the approximate size and shape required, then pull off the backing paper (if used) and stick the tape over the hole; it can be overlapped if the thickness of one piece is insufficient. Burnish down the edges of the tape with the handle of a screwdriver or similar, to ensure that the tape is securely attached to the metal underneath.

Bodywork repairs – filling and re-spraying

Before using this Section, see the Sections on dent, deep scratch, rust holes and gash repairs.

Many types of bodyfiller are available, but generally speaking those proprietary kits which contain a tin of filler paste and a tube of resin hardener are best for this type of repair, like Holts Body + Plus or Holts No Mix which can be used directly from the tube. A wide, flexible plastic or nylon applicator will be found invaluable for imparting a smooth and well contoured finish to the surface of the filler.

Mix up a little filler on a clean piece of card or board – measure the hardener carefully (follow the maker's instructions on the pack) otherwise the filler will set too rapidly or too slowly. Alternatively, Holts No Mix can be used straight from the tube without mixing, but daylight is required to cure it. Using the applicator apply the filler paste to the prepared area; draw the applicator across the surface of the filler to achieve the correct contour and to level the filler surface. As soon as a contour that approximates to the correct one is achieved, stop working the paste – if you carry on too long the paste will become sticky and begin to 'pick up' on the applicator. Continue to add thin layers of filler paste at twenty-minute intervals until the level of the filler is just proud of the surrounding bodywork.

Once the filler has hardened, excess can be removed using a metal plane or file. From then on, progressively finer grades of abrasive paper should be used, starting with a 40 grade production paper and finishing with 400 grade wet-and-dry paper. Always wrap the abrasive paper around a flat rubber, cork, or wooden block – otherwise the surface of the filler will not be completely flat. During the smoothing of the filler surface the wet-and-dry paper should be periodically rinsed in water. This will ensure that a very smooth finish is imparted to the filler at the final stage.

At this stage the 'dent' should be surrounded by a ring of bare metal, which in turn should be encircled by the finely 'feathered' edge of the good paintwork. Rinse the repair area with clean water, until all of the dust produced by the rubbing-down operation has gone.

Spray the whole repair area with a light coat of primer; either Holts Body + Plus Grey or Red Oxide Primer – this will show up any imperfections in the surface of the filler. Repair these imperfections with fresh filler paste or bodystopper, and once more smooth the surface with abrasive paper. If bodystopper is used, it can be mixed with cellulose thinners to form a really thin paste which is ideal for filling small holes. Repeat this spray and repair procedure until you are satisfied that the surface of the filler, and the feathered edge of the paintwork are perfect. Clean the repair area with clean water and allow to dry fully.

The repair area is now ready for final spraying. Paint spraying must be carried out in a warm, dry, windless and dust free atmosphere. This condition can be created artificially if you have access to a large indoor working area, but if you are forced to work in the open, you will have to pick your day very carefully. If you are working indoors, dousing the floor in the work area with water will help to settle the dust which would otherwise be in the atmosphere. If the repair area is confined to one body panel, mask off the surrounding panels; this will help to minimise the effects of a slight mis-match in paint colours. Bodywork fittings (eg chrome strips, door handles etc) will also need to be masked off. Use genuine masking tape and several thicknesses of newspaper for the masking operations.

Before commencing to spray, agitate the aerosol can thoroughly, then spray a test area (an old tin, or similar) until the technique is mastered. Cover the repair area with a thick coat of primer; the thickness should be built up using several thin layers of paint rather than one thick one. Using 400 grade wet-and-dry paper, rub down the sur-

face of the primer until it is really smooth. While doing this, the work area should be thoroughly doused with water, and the wet-and-dry paper periodically rinsed in water. Allow to dry before spraying on more paint.

Spray on the top coat using Holts Dupli-Color Autospray, again building up the thickness by using several thin layers of paint. Start spraying in the centre of the repair area and then, with a single side-to-side motion, work outwards until the whole repair area and about 2 inches of the surrounding original paintwork is covered. Remove all masking material 10 to 15 minutes after spraying on the final coat of paint.

Allow the new paint at least two weeks to harden, then, using a paintwork renovator or a very fine cutting paste such as Turtle Wax New Color Back or Holts Body + Plus Rubbing Compound, blend the edges of the paint into the existing paintwork. Finally, apply wax polish.

Plastic components

With the use of more and more plastic body components by the vehicle manufacturers (eg bumpers, spoilers, and in some cases major body panels), rectification of more serious damage to such items has become a matter of either entrusting repair work to a specialist in this field, or renewing complete components. Repair of such damage by the DIY owner is not really feasible owing to the cost of the equipment and materials required for effecting such repairs. The basic technique involves making a groove along the line of the crack in the plastic using a rotary burr in a power drill. The damaged part is then welded back together by using a hot air gun to heat up and fuse a plastic filler rod into the groove. Any excess plastic is then removed and the area rubbed down to a smooth finish. It is important that a filler rod of the correct plastic is used, as body components can be made of a variety of different types (eg polycarbonate, ABS, polypropylene).

Damage of a less serious nature (abrasions, minor cracks etc) can be repaired by the DIY owner using a two-part epoxy filler repair material like Holts Body + Plus or Holts No Mix which can be used directly from the tube. Once mixed in equal proportions (or applied direct from the tube in the case of Holts No Mix), this is used in similar fashion to the bodywork filler used on metal panels. The filler is usually cured in twenty to thirty minutes, ready for sanding and painting.

If the owner is renewing a complete component himself, or if he has repaired it with epoxy filler, he will be left with the problem of finding a suitable paint for finishing which is compatible with the type of plastic used. At one time the use of a universal paint was not possible owing to the complex range of plastics encountered in body component applications. Standard paints, generally speaking, will not bond to plastic or rubber satisfactorily, but Holts Professional Spraymatch paints to match any plastic or rubber finish can be obtained from dealers. However, it is now possible to obtain a plastic body parts finishing kit which consists of a pre-primer treatment, a primer and coloured top coat. Full instructions are normally supplied with a kit, but basically the method of use is to first apply the pre-primer to the component concerned and allow it to dry for up to 30 minutes. Then the primer is applied and left to dry for about an hour before finally applying the special coloured top coat. The result is a correctly coloured component where the paint will flex with the plastic or rubber, a property that standard paint does not normally possess.

5 Major body damage – repair

The construction of the body is such that great care must be taken when making cuts, or when renewing major members, to preserve the basic strength and geometry of the structure, for safety reasons. In addition, the heating of certain areas, particularly during welding, is not advisable.

In view of the specialised knowledge necessary for this work, and the alignment jigs and special tools frequently required, the owner is advised to consult a specialist body repairer or Peugeot dealer.

6 Bonnet – removal and refitting

1   Open the bonnet and support with the stay.
2   Using a pencil, mark the position of the hinges on the bonnet.
3   Unbolt the braided earth lead where fitted.
4   Place some cloth beneath the rear corners of the bonnet.

5 With the help of an assistant, support the weight of the bonnet, then unscrew the hinge bolts and remove the bonnet from the vehicle (photo).
6 Refitting is a reversal of removal, but check that the bonnet is central within its aperture. If necessary, loosen the hinge bolts and move it within the elongated holes to reposition it. Check for closure and adjust the bonnet locks and strikers if necessary.

7 Bonnet locks and cable release – removal and refitting

1 Remove the steering column lower cowl and lower facia panel.
2 Unbolt the release handle, and unclip the cable (photo).
3 Remove the headlamp units (Chapter 12).
4 Disconnect the cables, and unbolt the locks (photo).
5 Unclip and remove the cables. The primary cable leads from the release handle to the right-hand lock, and the secondary cable interconnects the two locks.
6 Refitting is a reversal of removal, but finally apply a little grease to the jaws of each lock (photo).

8 Front grille – removal and refitting

1 Using a screwdriver through the slots in the radiator grille, remove the cross-head screws.
2 Lift the front grille from its location (photo).
3 Refitting is a reversal of removal.

9 Bumpers – removal and refitting

Front bumper
1 Unscrew the bolts securing the side brackets to the valance.
2 Remove the parking/direction indicator lamps with reference to Chapter 12.

3 Unscrew the nuts securing the centre brackets to the valance (photo), and withdraw the bumper from the vehicle.
4 Refitting is a reversal of removal.

Rear bumper
5 Where applicable, unscrew the bolts securing the bumper side sections to the valance.
6 On Estate models, remove both rear light clusters.
7 Unbolt the main brackets from the valance and withdraw the bumper. If necessary, unbolt the brackets from the bumper (photos).
8 Refitting is a reversal of removal.

10 Door – removal and refitting

1 Drive out the roll pin from the door check strap, where this is separate from the hinge.
2 Where applicable, remove the twin panel and disconnect the central locking and loudspeaker wiring.
3 Support the door in the fully-open position by placing blocks, or a jack and a pad of rag, under its lower edge.
4 Either drive out the hinge pivot pins (after removing the plastic caps) or unbolt the hinges (photo).
5 Withdraw the door from the vehicle.
6 Refitting is a reversal of removal, but where necessary adjust the striker to ensure correct closure of the door (photo).

11 Door trim panel – removal and refitting

1 On models with manually-operated windows, fully close the window and note the position of the winder handle.
2 Using a piece of cloth, release the winder handle clip and withdraw the handle. Remove the spacer (photos).
3 On early models, slide the escutcheon from the interior handle (photo).

6.5 Removing the bonnet

7.2 Bonnet release handle (arrowed)

7.4 Bonnet lock

7.6 Apply a little grease to the bonnet locks

8.2 Removing the front grille

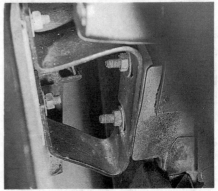
9.3 Front bumper bracket

1

This photographic sequence shows the steps taken to repair the dent and paintwork damage shown above. In general, the procedure for repairing a hole will be similar; where there are substantial differences, the procedure is clearly described and shown in a separate photograph.

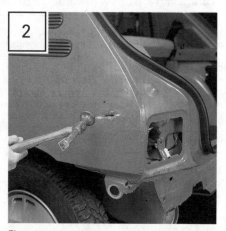

2

First remove any trim around the dent, then hammer out the dent where access is possible. This will minimise filling. Here, after the large dent has been hammered out, the damaged area is being made slightly concave.

3

Next, remove all paint from the damaged area by rubbing with coarse abrasive paper or using a power drill fitted with a wire brush or abrasive pad. 'Feather' the edge of the boundary with good paintwork using a fine grade of abrasive paper.

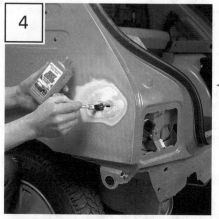

4

Where there are holes or other damage, the sheet metal should be cut away before proceeding further. The damaged area and any signs of rust should be treated with Turtle Wax Hi-Tech Rust Eater, which will also inhibit further rust formation.

5

For a large dent or hole mix Holts Body Plus Resin and Hardener according to the manufacturer's instructions and apply around the edge of the repair. Press Glass Fibre Matting over the repair area and leave for 20-30 minutes to harden. Then ...

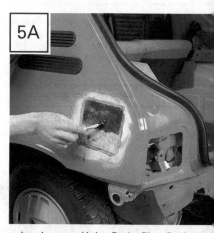

5A

... brush more Holts Body Plus Resin and Hardener onto the matting and leave to harden. Repeat the sequence with two or three layers of matting, checking that the final layer is lower than the surrounding area. Apply Holts Body Plus Filler Paste as shown in Step 5B.

5B

For a medium dent, mix Holts Body Plus Filler Paste and Hardener according to the manufacturer's instructions and apply it with a flexible applicator. Apply thin layers of filler at 20-minute intervals, until the filler surface is slightly proud of the surrounding bodywork.

5C

For small dents and scratches use Holts No Mix Filler Paste straight from the tube. Apply it according to the instructions in thin layers, using the spatula provided. It will harden in minutes if applied outdoors and may then be used as its own knifing putty.

6

Use a plane or file for initial shaping. Then, using progressively finer grades of wet-and-dry paper, wrapped round a sanding block, and copious amounts of clean water, rub down the filler until glass smooth. 'Feather' the edges of adjoining paintwork.

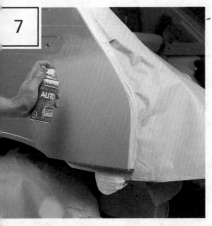

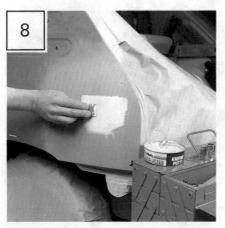

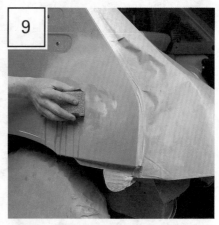

Protect adjoining areas before spraying the whole repair area and at least one inch of the surrounding sound paintwork with Holts Dupli-Color primer.

Fill any imperfections in the filler surface with a small amount of Holts Body Plus Knifing Putty. Using plenty of clean water, rub down the surface with a fine grade wet-and-dry paper – 400 grade is recommended – until it is really smooth.

Carefully fill any remaining imperfections with knifing putty before applying the last coat of primer. Then rub down the surface with Holts Body Plus Rubbing Compound to ensure a really smooth surface.

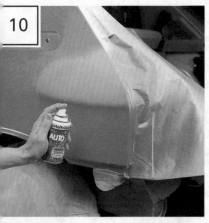

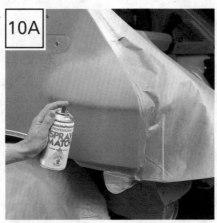

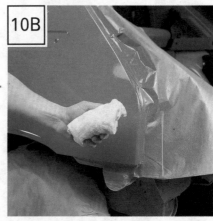

Protect surrounding areas from overspray before applying the topcoat in several thin layers. Agitate Holts Dupli-Color aerosol thoroughly. Start at the repair centre, spraying outwards with a side-to-side motion.

If the exact colour is not available off the shelf, local Holts Professional Spraymatch Centres will custom fill an aerosol to match perfectly.

To identify whether a lacquer finish is required, rub a painted unrepaired part of the body with wax and a clean cloth.

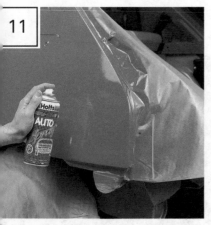

If no traces of paint appear on the cloth, spray Holts Dupli-Color clear lacquer over the repaired area to achieve the correct gloss level.

The paint will take about two weeks to harden fully. After this time it can be 'cut' with a mild cutting compound such as Turtle Wax Minute Cut prior to polishing with a final coating of Turtle Wax Extra.

When carrying out bodywork repairs, remember that the quality of the finished job is proportional to the time and effort expended.

9.7A Rear bumper bracket

9.7B Bolt (arrowed) securing bracket to rear bumper

10.4 Door hinge incorporating check strap

10.6 Adjusting the rear door striker

11.2A Using a piece of cloth to release the clip on the window winder handle

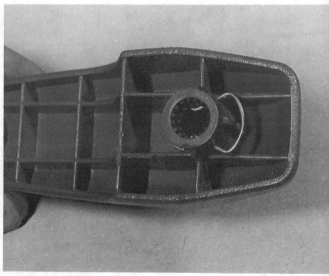

11.2B Window winder handle and clip

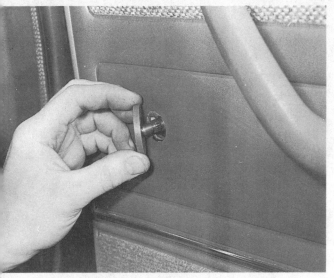

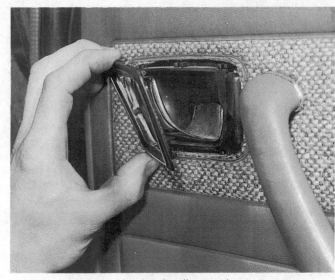

11.2C Removing the spacer for the window winder handle

11.3 Removing the interior door handle escutcheon

4 Slide the cover from the locking knob (photo).
5 Remove the screws from the armrest, then withdraw it. On later models, also remove the interior handle cover (photos).
6 On later models, remove the panel centre screws (photo).
7 Using a wide-bladed screwdriver or special removal tool, release the panel clips from the inner door, and withdraw the trim panel (photos).
8 Refitting is a reversal of removal, but first make sure that the clips are correctly located in the panel.

12 Door – dismantling and reassembly

1 Remove the trim panel as described in Section 11, then carefully peel off the plastic sheeting (photos).
2 Pull off the locking knob (photo).
3 To remove the outer handle, unscrew the nuts and remove the retaining plate. Disconnect the operating rod and withdraw the handle from the outside (photos).

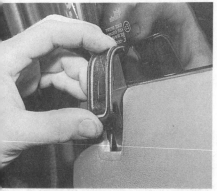

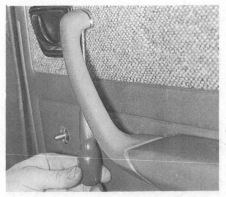

11.4 Removing the locking knob cover

11.5A On early models, remove the upper screw ...

11.5B ... lower screws ...

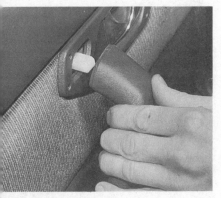

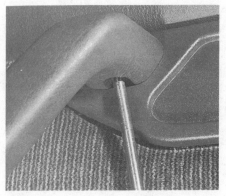

11.5C ... and armrest

11.5D On later models, remove the screws ...

11.5E ... armrest ...

11.5F ... and interior handle cover

11.6 Door trim panel centre screw removal

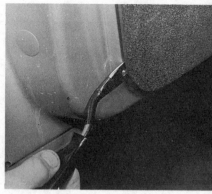
11.7A Prise the clips free ...

11.7B ... and remove the door trim panel

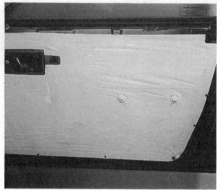
12.1A Door panel plastic sheeting

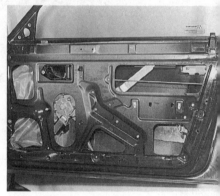
12.1B View of the door with the plastic sheeting removed

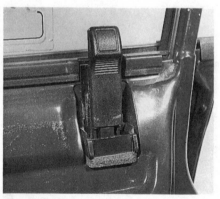
12.2 Removing the locking knob

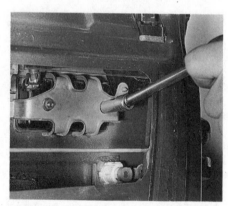
12.3A Unscrew the nuts ...

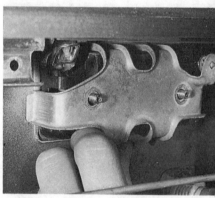
12.3B ... remove the retaining plate ...

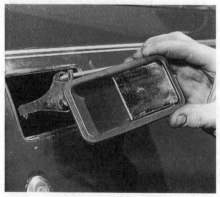
12.3C ... and withdraw the outer door handle

12.4 Inner door handle

12.5A Pull out the spring clip ...

To remove the inner handle, drill out the retaining rivet, disconnect the rod and withdraw the handle (photo).

To remove the private lock, pull out the spring clip and disconnect the rod (photos).

To remove the window regulator, disconnect the wiring plug where electric windows are fitted, then unscrew the mounting nuts, slide the lifting arm(s) from the channel, and withdraw the regulator through the access panel (photos).

To remove the door lock, disconnect the operating rods, then unscrew the Torx screws retaining the lock (photo).

8 To remove the central locking unit on cars so equipped, unscrew the mounting bolts, disconnect the wiring and withdraw the unit (photos).

9 To remove the door glass, unbolt the side channels (photo). Tilt the glass and withdraw it upwards.

10 Reassembly of the door is a reversal of removal. When refitting the door glass, adjust the side channels so that the glass moves smoothly without excessive play.

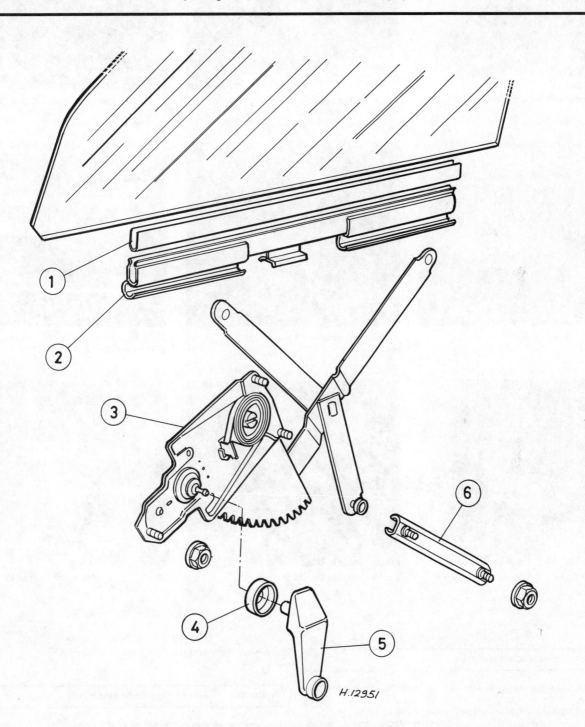

H.12951

Fig. 11.1 Front door window regulator components – manually operated window (Sec 12)

1 Packing	3 Regulator	5 Handle
2 Window channel	4 Spacer	6 Guide

12.5B ... and withdraw the private lock

12.6A Disconnecting the wiring from the electric window motor

12.6B Window regulator and mounting nut

12.6C Electric window motor

12.6D Rear door window regulator mounting nuts

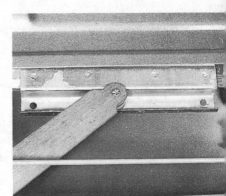

12.6E Regulator lifting arm and window glass channel

12.7 Door lock – Torx screws arrowed

12.8A Unscrew the bolts ...

12.8B ... and remove the control locking unit

13 Bootlid – removal and refitting

1   Open the bootlid, and use a pencil to mark the position of the hinges.
2   Disconnect the wiring to the rear number plate lights.
3   Have an assistant support the bootlid, then unscrew the bolts and lift it from the vehicle (photo).
4   To remove the hydraulic stay, disconnect the upper socket, and unhook the piston rod from the lower mounting (photo).
5   Refitting is a reversal of removal, but check that the bootlid is central within its aperture. If necessary, loosen the hinge bolts and move it within the elongated holes to reposition it. Adjust the striker if necessary, so that the lock engages it correctly.

14 Bootlid – dismantling and reassembly

1   Prise the trim from the inside of the bootlid.
2   Working from inside the bootlid, pull out the spring clip and withdraw the private lock (photos).
3   Unbolt and remove the lock (photo).
4   Refitting is a reversal of removal, but adjust the lock so that the bootlid weatherstrip is compressed sufficiently to prevent entry of water. Adjust the striker if necessary so that the lock engages correctly.

12.9 A door glass side channel retaining bolt

13.3 Bootlid hinge bolts

13.4 Bootlid stay (arrowed)

14.2A Pull out the spring clip (arrowed) ...

14.2B ... and withdraw the private lock

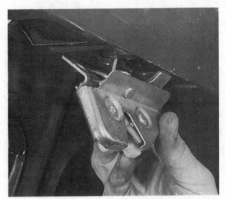

14.3 Removing the bootlid lock

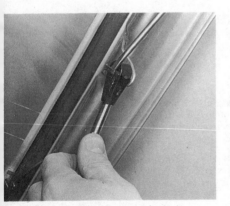

15.3A Disconnecting the strut from the tailgate ...

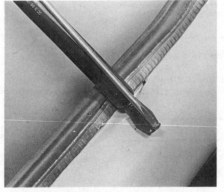

15.3B ... and body

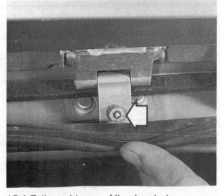

15.4 Tailgate hinge – Allen key bolt (arrowed)

15 Tailgate – removal and refitting

1 Support the tailgate in the open position.
2 Disconnect the wiring for the rear number plate lights.
3 Note which way round the hydraulic struts are fitted, then disconnect them by prising out the plastic clips with a small screwdriver. The struts may also be disconnected from the body (photo).
4 With the help of an assistant, pull back the weatherstrip, and use an Allen key to unscrew the bolts securing the hinges to the brackets (photo). Withdraw the tailgate from the vehicle.
5 If necessary, remove the trim and unscrew the nuts to remove the rubber guides (photos).
6 Refitting is a reversal of removal, but adjust the striker if necessary,

so that the lock lever engages it correctly (photo).

16 Tailgate – dismantling and reassembly

1 Using a wide-bladed screwdriver or special tool (photo), prise the trim from the inside of the tailgate.
2 Remove the rear window wiper motor as described in Chapter 12.
3 Unbolt the lock and disconnect the operating rod by prising it out (photo).
4 Unscrew the pinch-bolt and disconnect the operating rod from the private lock (photo).
5 Reassembly is a reversal of dismantling, but adjust the operating rod to ensure correct movement of the lock lever.

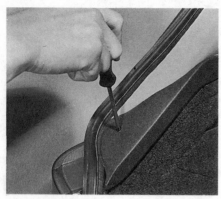

15.5A Removing the trim ...

15.5B ... for access to the rubber guide

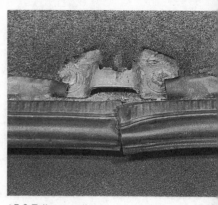

15.6 Tailgate striker

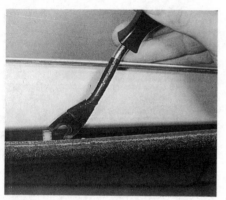

16.1 Prising off the tailgate trim

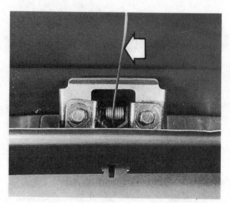

16.3 Tailgate lock – operating rod arrowed

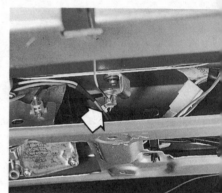

16.4 Operating rod and pinch-bolt (arrowed) on the tailgate private lock

17 Windscreen and rear window glass removal and refitting – general

Removal and fitting of the windscreen and rear window glass is a specialist job, requiring the use of equipment not normally available to the home mechanic, and therefore it is recommended that the work is entrusted to a windscreen replacement company or Peugeot dealer.

18 Seats – removal and refitting

Front seats
1   Move the seat fully forwards, and remove the rear sliding track mounting Torx belts (photo).
2   Move the seat fully rearwards, and remove the front sliding track mounting bolts.
3   Remove the seat from the vehicle.

Rear seat
4   Press the rear seat cushion down and rearwards to disengage it from the central mounting bracket, then lift it forwards (photos).
5   Bend up the tabs retaining the bottom of the backrest, then lift the backrest from the upper hooks (photos).

Front and rear seats
6   Refitting is a reversal of removal.

18.1 Front seat rear mounting Torx bolts

18.4A Disconnecting the rear seat cushion ...

18.4B ... from the mounting bracket

8.5A Rear seat backrest lower mounting tab (arrowed) ...

18.5B ... and upper hook

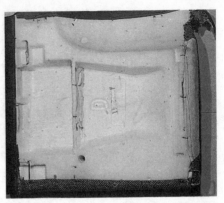

18.5C Rear view of the backrest

19 Sunroof – general

1 The sunroof fitted to some models is electrically operated, with a control switch on the centre console. The electric motor operates a gear on a cable rack, which opens and closes the sunroof.
2 Access to the electric motor is gained through the boot.
3 It is recommended that removal and refitting, and any adjustments to the sunroof, be entrusted to a Peugeot dealer.

20 Exterior mirror – removal and refitting

Manually operated

1 Remove the door trim panel as described in Section 11.
2 Carefully prise off the plastic cover (photo).

3 Remove the foam seal (photo).
4 Support the mirror, then unscrew the screws and withdraw the mirror from the door (photo).
5 Refitting is a reversal of removal.

Electrically operated

6 Remove the door trim panel as described in Section 11.
7 Carefully prise off the plastic cover (photo).
8 Peel back the door inner sheeting, and disconnect the mirror wiring plug.
9 Support the mirror, then unscrew the screws and withdraw the mirror from the door while feeding through the wiring (photos).
10 If necessary, the glass may be removed using a thin screwdriver through the hole in the housing. Turn the inner glass retaining clip by to-and-fro action (photos).
11 Refitting is a reversal of removal.

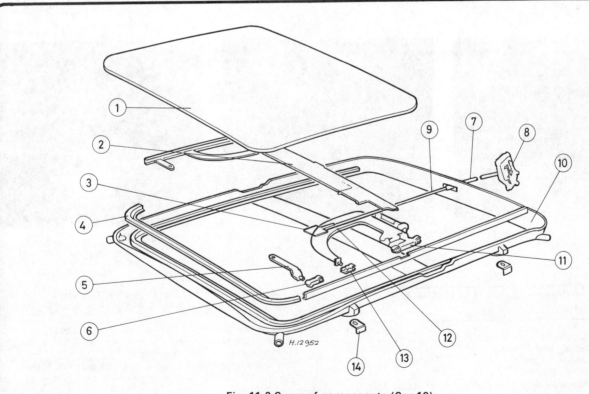

H.12952

Fig. 11.2 Sunroof components (Sec 19)

1 Sliding panel	5 Front slider support	9 Guide rail	12 Side moving crossmember
2 Centre moving crossmember	6 Front slider	10 Side rail	13 Intermediate slide
3 Operating rack cable	7 Control cable sleeve	11 Rear rocker and slide	14 Frame securing bracket
4 Front trim piece	8 Electric motor		

20.2 Remove the plastic cover ...

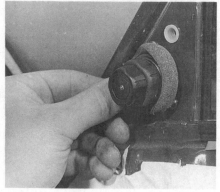

20.3 ... foam seal ...

20.4A ... then unscrew the screws ...

20.4B ... and withdraw the manually
operated exterior mirror

20.7 Remove the plastic cover ...

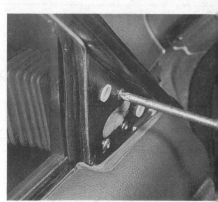

20.9A ... unscrew the screws ...

20.9B ... and withdraw the electrically
operated exterior mirror

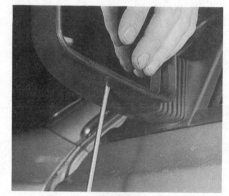

20.10A Using a screwdriver to release the
internal clip ...

20.10B ... and remove the mirror glass

21 Facia panel and centre console (pre-1986 models) – removal and refitting

1   Remove the instrument panel (Chapter 12).
2   Remove the digital clock (Chapter 12).
3   Prise out the air vents (photo).
4   Remove the radio (Chapter 12).
5   Unscrew the screws and withdraw the radio surround (photos). Disconnect the wiring from the cigar lighter.
6   Pull the knob from the gearstick, then prise out and remove the gaiter (photo).
7   Move the front seats forwards, and unscrew the centre console rear mounting screws after prising out the plugs (photos).
8   Unscrew the centre console front mounting screws and the facia centre panel screws. Remove the centre panel (photos).
9   Remove the front door window and sunroof switches from the centre console.
10 Withdraw the cover from the handbrake lever (photo).
11 Lift the centre console over the handbrake lever and remove the console from inside the vehicle (photo).
12 Remove the air ducting from in front of the gearstick (photo).
13 Prise out the plastic check strap from the front of the glovebox (photo).
14 Unclip and remove the glovebox (photos).
15 Remove the screws from each side of the heater control panel.
16 Remove the steering wheel and column cowls (Chapter 10).
17 Remove the headlamp beam adjuster from the lower facia panel.
18 Unbolt the lower facia panel and disconnect the instrument illumination rheostat and ignition key illumination bulb (photos).

21.3 Removing the air vents

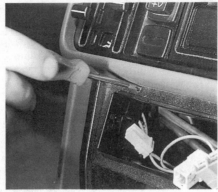
21.5A Unscrew the screws ...

21.5B ... and withdraw the radio surround

21.6 Removing the gearstick gaiter

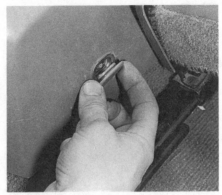
21.7A Remove the plugs ...

21.7B ... and unscrew the centre console rear mounting screws (Saloon model shown)

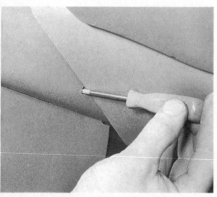
21.8A Unscrew the front screws ...

21.8B ... and facia centre panel screws ...

21.8C ... and remove the centre panel

21.10 Removing the handbrake lever cover

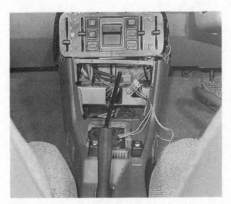
21.11 Centre console front section ready for removal

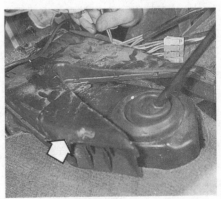
21.12 Air ducting (arrowed)

19 Lift out the ashtray (photo).
20 Pull off the heater control levers (photos).
21 Remove the hazard warning and lighting switches (Chapter 12).
22 Remove the screws and lift off the heater control panel (photos).
23 Remove the glovebox illumination lamp switch (Chapter 12), and remove the facia printed circuit board (photos).
24 Remove the fusebox and steering column switches (Chapter 12).
25 Prise the covers from the facia panel mounting screws, and remove the screws. Three bolts are located along the front of the facia, and two beneath the facia.
26 Withdraw the facia from one side of the vehicle, and at the same time disconnect the air vent ducts.
27 Refitting is a reversal of removal, but adjust the glovebox catch position if necessary (photo).

22 Centre console and heater control panel (1986-on models) – removal and refitting

1 Remove the electric window switches from the rear of the centre console (Chapter 12).
2 Remove the screws from the steering column lower cowl, and suspend the cowl leaving the wiring attached.
3 Unbolt and remove the glovebox (photo).
4 Remove the ashtray.
5 Remove the radio (Chapter 12).
6 Remove the screws and withdraw the blanking plate (photos).
7 Withdraw the radio surround (photo).
8 Unscrew the centre console-to-heater control panel bolts (photo).

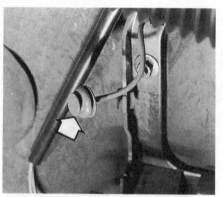
21.13 Glovebox checkstrap (arrowed)

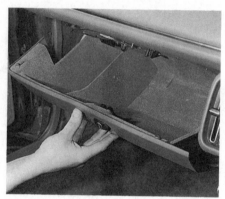
21.14A Removing the glovebox

21.14B Plastic clips on the bottom of the glovebox

21.14C Glovebox hinge points (arrowed)

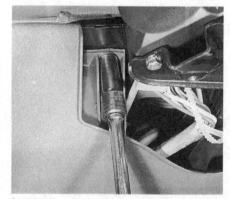
21.18A Unbolt the lower facia panel ...

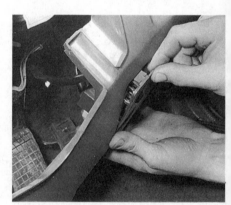
21.18B ... and disconnect the instrument illumination rheostat

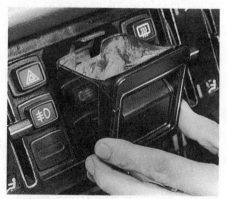
21.19 Removing the ashtray

21.20A Removing the heater control lever ...

21.20B ... from the control quadrant (arrowed)

21.22A Heater control panel screw removal

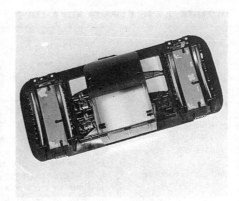
21.22B Rear view of the heater control panel

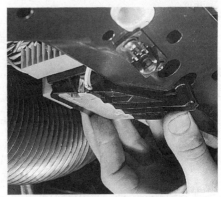
21.23A Removing the glovebox lamp and facia printed circuit board

21.23B Disconnecting the wiring from the facia printed circuit board

21.27 Glovebox catch

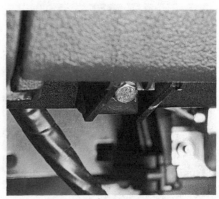
22.3 Glove box mounting bolt

22.6A Remove the screws ...

22.6B ... and withdraw the blanking plate

22.7 Removing the radio surround

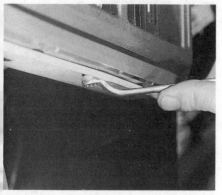
22.8 Unscrewing the centre console-to-heater control panel bolts

22.9A Prise out the plastic cover ...

22.9B ... and unscrew the heater control panel screw

9 Prise out the plastic cover and unscrew the screw located above the air vents (photos).
10 Pull the knob from the gear lever (photo).
11 Pull the grip from the handbrake lever (photo).
12 Remove the screw behind the ashtray (photo).
13 Remove the front electric window switches (if fitted) and disconnect the wiring (photo).
14 Prise up the rear of the gear lever surround, then release the front clips (photos).
15 Remove the cover at the rear of the centre console, and unscrew the screws (photo).
16 Remove the front mounting screws, then withdraw the centre console from the vehicle (photos).
17 Remove the mounting screws, and withdraw the heater control

panel (photo). Disconnect the wiring and the vacuum pipes, after noting their locations.
18 Refitting is a reversal of removal.

23 Facia panel (1986-on models) – removal and refitting

1 Disconnect the battery negative lead.
2 Remove the instrument panel (Chapter 12).
3 Prise out the plastic cover above the centre vents.
4 Remove the ashtray.
5 Remove the steering wheel (Chapter 10).
6 Remove the radio (Chapter 12)

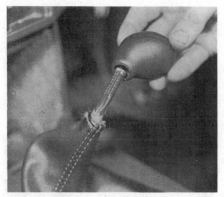
22.10 Removing the gear lever knob

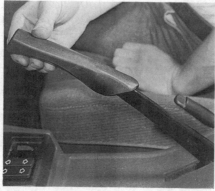
22.11 Removing the handbrake lever grip

22.12 Removing the screw behind the ashtray

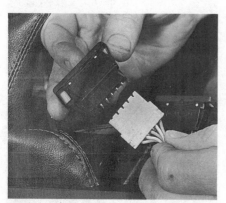
22.13 Disconnect the wiring from the front electric window switch

22.14A Lifting the rear of the gear lever surround

22.14B Releasing the front of the gear lever surround

22.15 Removing the centre console rear cover (Estate model shown)

22.16A Centre console front mounting screws (arrowed)

22.16B Removing the centre console rear section

22.17 Withdrawing the heater control panel

7   Unscrew the two upper screws and lift the radio surround from the lower tabs.
8   Open the glovebox, then squeeze in the sides and disconnect the rod (if fitted) to remove it.
9   Remove the upper screw, the screw in the ashtray aperture, and the three lower screws, and withdraw the heater control panel.
10 Identify the heater vacuum pipes for location, then disconnect them. Similarly disconnect the wiring plugs.
11 Remove the switches from the right-hand side of the facia panel by removing the two screws and disconnecting the wiring.
12 Remove the steering column lower cowl and the lower facia panel. Disconnect the headlamp height control and the instrument illumination rheostat.
13 Disconnect the glovebox illumination light and switch, and where fitted, the passenger compartment temperature sensor.
14 Pull out the side air vents, and if fitted, the loudspeaker grilles.
15 Prise out the facia centre front cover.
16 Release the speedometer cable and wiring harnesses.
17 Unscrew the mounting screws and nuts. There are two upper nuts at the front corners, one screw at the centre front, two side bottom

screws, and three screws along the bottom.
18 Lift the facia panel from the centre tab, and withdraw it from one side of the vehicle.
19 Refitting is a reversal of removal, but in particular, make sure that the wiring harness is located correctly.

24 Heater matrix – removal and refitting

1   Drain the cooling system as described in Chapter 2.
2   Remove the glovebox.
3   Remove the steering column and pedal bracket as described in Chapters 9 and 10.
4   Disconnect the heater valve control cable (photo).
5   Loosen the clips and disconnect the coolant hoses from the matrix (protect the carpets from spilled coolant).
6   Unscrew the mounting bolt and withdraw the matrix from the heater.
7   Refitting is a reversal of removal, but fill the cooling system with reference to Chapter 2.

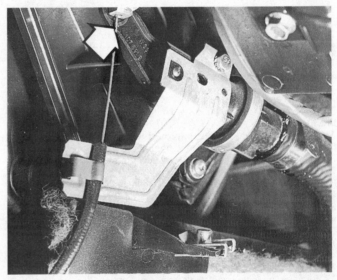

24.4 Heater valve and control cable (arrowed)

Fig. 11.3 Disconnecting the coolant hoses from the heater matrix (Sec 24)

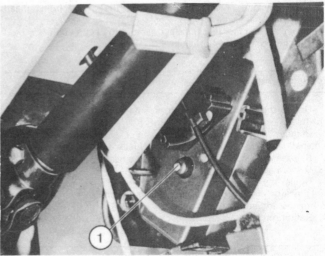

Fig. 11.4 Heater matrix mounting bolt (1) – left-hand drive vehicle shown (Sec 24)

Fig. 11.5 Removing the heater matrix (Sec 24)

25 Heater – removal and refitting

1   Disconnect the battery negative lead.
2   Drain the cooling system (Chapter 2).

Pre-1986 models
3   Remove the glovebox, lower facia panel, and steering column lower cowl.
4   Disconnect the heater hoses (protect the carpet from spillage).
5   Unscrew the heater side flange upper bolts.
6   Identify and disconnect the heater vacuum pipes.
7   Disconnect the heater wiring plugs (photo).
8   Pull off the heater control knobs, then remove the screws and withdraw the heater control panel without disconnecting the wiring.
9   Unscrew the heater mounting bolts from the crossmember, and the mounting nuts on the bulkhead (photo).
10 Disconnect the air ducts and remove the heater unit.
11 Refitting is a reversal of removal.

1986-on models
12 Remove the facia panel as described in Section 23.
13 Unbolt the facia support crossmember.
14 Remove the glovebox illumination lamp.
15 Disconnect the air ducts from the top of the heater.
16 Unscrew the side support bolts.
17 Disconnect the lower air ducting.
18 Disconnect the heater hoses (protect the carpet from spilled coolant), and the vacuum pipes.
19 Unscrew the mounting bolts and remove the heater unit.
20 Refitting is a reversal of removal.

26 Heater blower – removal and refitting

1   Unclip the hydraulic brake pipes from the left-hand side of the bulkhead.
2   Remove the heater blower cover. The cover is made of very brittle material, and care must be taken not to break it.
3   Release the air duct from the heater blower.
4   Disconnect the wiring plug.
5   Unclip the heater blower and withdraw it from the bulkhead. On fuel injection models, the throttle housing and air box may be removed to provide additional working room.
6   Refitting is a reversal of removal.

27 Air conditioning system – description and precautions

1   When an air conditioning system is fitted, it is necessary to observe special precautions whenever dealing with any part of the system, its associated components and any items within the engine and heating compartment that necessitate disconnection of the system.
2   The refrigeration circuit contains a liquid gas (Freon), and it is therefore dangerous to disconnect any part of the system without specialised knowledge and equipment. If for any reason the system must be disconnected (engine removal for example), entrust this task to your Peugeot dealer or a refrigeration engineer.
3   The refrigerant gas must not be allowed to come in contact with a naked flame, or a poisonous gas will be created. Do not allow the fluid to come in contact with the skin or eyes.
4   The system consists of a compressor (belt-driven by the engine), a condenser (located in front of the radiator), a receiver/dryer, and an evaporator (located in the passenger compartment). A blower fan forces air through the evaporator to provide cooled air inside the passenger compartment.

28 Air conditioning system – maintenance

1   Regularly inspect the condition of hoses and the security of connections.
2   A sight glass is located on top of the receiver/dryer chamber. If bubbles are evident immediately after switching on the system, a fluid leak is indicated.
3   Keep the fins of the condenser free from flies and dirt, and keep the compressor drivebelt in good condition and correctly tensioned (the procedure is similar to that for the drivebelt given in Chapter 2).
4   Water dripping or collecting on the floor under the car is quite normal, and is the result of condensation.
5   Run the system for a few minutes each week when it is not in regular use.

29 Seat belts – removal and refitting

1   To remove the front seat belts, remove the trim from the centre pillar, then unbolt the inertia reel. Also unbolt the upper guide and rear mounting (photos).
2   Unbolt the front stalk from the body.
3   To remove the rear seat belts, remove the trim from the luggage compartment, then unbolt the inertia reel (photo). Also unbolt the upper guide and rear mounting.
4   Unbolt the stalk from the body.
5   Refitting is a reversal of removal – ensure that all mountings are tightened securely.

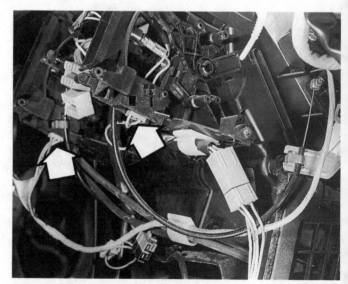

25.7 Heater wiring plugs (arrowed)

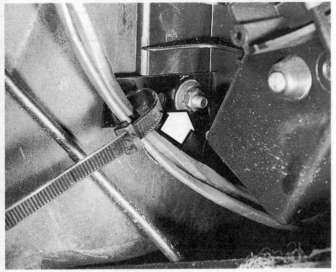

25.9 Heater mounting nut (arrowed)

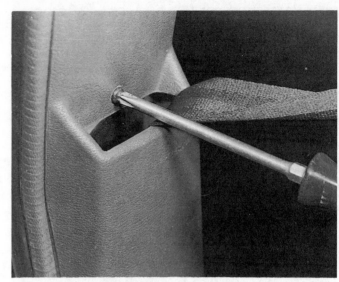

29.1A Removing the centre pillar trim on an Estate model ...

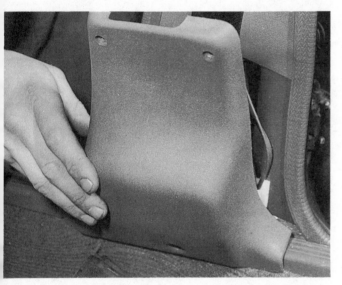

29.1B ... and on a Saloon model

29.1C Front seat belt inertia reel

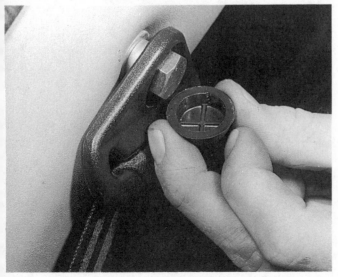

29.1D Remove the cap for access to ...

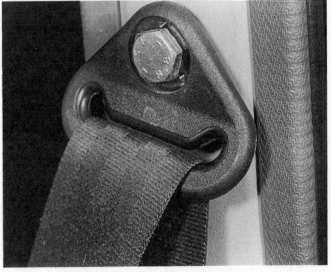

29.1E ... the front seat belt upper guide bolt

29.1F Front seat belt rear mounting

29.3 Rear seat belt inertia reel

Chapter 12 Electrical system

Contents

Specifications

System type
12 volt negative earth, battery, alternator, and pre-engaged starter motor

Battery
Rating .... 300 amps (rapid discharge rate to −18°C)
Maximum charging rate .... 6.0 amps

Alternator
Rating – carburettor models .... 500 watts
Rating – fuel injection models .... 750 watts
Minimum brush length .... 5.0 mm (0.20 in) beyond holder

Starter motor
Type .... Pre-engaged
Minimum brush length .... 10.5 mm (0.41 in)

Wiper blades
Front and rear .... Champion X-4503

Fuses

No	Circuit protected	Rating (amps)
1	Rear foglamps	7.5
2	Rear view mirrors, sunroof, electric windows, glovebox, parcel tray, automatic transmission gear selector, clock illumination, heated seats	25
3	Windscreen wash/wipe, heated rear window and exterior mirror relay, direction indicators, map reading lamp, courtesy mirror, temperature control	20
4	Hazard warning	15
5	Clock, horns, rear interior lamp, bootlamp, cigar lighter, central door locking, front interior lamp delay, radio	20
6	Spare	25
7	Front interior lamp, central door locking	15
8	Reverse lamp, automatic transmission inhibitor switch	15
9	Heated rear window and exterior mirror	25
10	Heater motor	10
11	Stop-lamps, instrument panel	15
12	Instrument panel illumination rheostat	7.5
12A	Facia panel and switch illumination, front parking lamps, 'lights-on' warning, warning lamps, rear lamps, number plate lamps	7.5
15 or 12B	RH tail lamp	7.5
13	LH tail lamp	7.5
14	Radio	7.5

Bulbs

	Wattage
Front direction indicator	21
Front parking	5
Side marker	4
Rear direction indicator	21
Stop-lamp	21
Tail lamp	5
Rear foglamp	21
Reversing lamp	21
Headlamp	55/60
Glovebox	5
Interior lamps	5

Torque wrench settings

	Nm	lbf ft
Starter motor	20	15
Alternator mounting bolt	45	33

1 General description

The electrical system is of 12 volt negative earth type, and the major components are a battery, a belt-driven alternator, and a pre-engaged starter motor.

The alternator has an integral regulator, which varies the output according to demand from the battery and electrical equipment.

The electrical system has many semi-conductor components, which may be permanently damaged if excessive current is passed through them, or if their supply leads are connected the wrong way round. It is therefore recommended that the battery is disconnected when working on the system, and that particular care is exercised to ensure correct electrical connections.

2 Routine maintenance

Carry out the following procedures at the intervals given in Routine maintenance *at the front of this manual*

Check battery electrolyte level (where applicable)

1 Remove the battery cell covers, and check the electrolyte level as described in Section 3.

Check functioning of lights

2 Check that the headlight main and dipped beams function correctly. Also check the parking lights, rear lights, and indicator lights

3 Battery – maintenance

1 The battery may be of conventional or low-maintenance type depending upon the date of production of the car.

2 With conventional batteries, check the electrolyte level regularly and add purified water to the cells so that the electrolyte level is 10. mm (0.4 in) above the tops of the plates.

3 With low-maintenance batteries, the electrolyte level should only require checking after the first four years, and every two year thereafter.

4 Never attempt to add acid to a battery – this could prove dangerous. If electrolyte must be added to make up for spillage caused by careless removal of the battery, always have the job done by you dealer or battery specialist.

5 Keep the battery terminals smeared with petroleum jelly to protec them against corrosion.

6 Any corrosion occurring on the battery platform or surrounding bodywork should be treated immediately to neutralise it. Apply sodium

bicarbonate or household ammonia, wash off and then paint the affected areas.

7 The battery will not normally require charging from the mains supply, but if only very short journeys are made, with much use being made of the starter and electrical accessories, then a regular charge from an outside source may be required.

8 An indication of the state of charge of a battery can be obtained by checking the electrolyte in each cell, using a hydrometer. The specific gravity range of the electrolyte, at a temperature of 20°C, is as follows:

Fully-charged – 1.280
Half-charged – 1.200
Flat – 1.120

9 Before charging the battery, remove it from the car as described in the next Section.

10 Connect the leads correctly, and make sure that no sparks or naked flames are allowed near the battery during charging, as the hydrogen being produced by the battery could cause an explosion.

4 Battery – removal and refitting

1 The battery is located in the front left-hand corner of the engine compartment.

2 Loosen the terminal clamp nut and disconnect the negative battery lead, then similarly disconnect the positive battery lead. Position the leads to one side, away from the battery.

3 Unscrew the clamp bolt (photo) or nuts, and lift the battery carefully from the engine compartment. On some models, the clamp is fitted to the base of the battery, but on others, the clamp fits over the top of the battery.

4 Refitting is a reversal of removal, but smear the terminals with petroleum jelly on completion. Connect the positive battery lead first, followed by the negative lead.

5 Alternator – description and testing

1 The alternator is of the rotating field coil design, with an integral voltage regulator. The output windings are wound on the stator, and the field windings are wound on the rotor. A diode rectifier is incorporated in the alternator to provide direct current for charging the battery.

2 To prevent damage to the alternator semi-conductor components, do not run the engine with the alternator or battery leads disconnected, do not connect the battery leads the wrong way round, and always disconnect both battery leads before charging it. If using electric welding equipment on the vehicle, disconnect both the battery and alternator leads.

3 To test the alternator, first check that the battery is in good condition, the drivebelt is correctly tensioned, and the alternator wiring is secure.

4 Connect a voltmeter across the battery terminals, then run the engine at 3000 rpm. The recorded voltage should be between 13.3 and 14.8 volts. Repeat the test with all accessories and lights on, and check that the voltage is still within the same limits. If not, the alternator voltage regulator is faulty, and should be renewed.

5 If the alternator is still inoperative, remove the brushes and, using an ohmmeter, check that the resistance of the rotor windings is between 3 and 5 ohms. If not, the windings are faulty.

6 Alternator – removal and refitting

1 Disconnect the battery negative lead.

2 Loosen the pivot and adjustment bolts, swivel the alternator towards the engine, then remove the drivebelt from the pulley.

3 Unscrew the nut and disconnect the main cable from its terminal. Also disconnect the warning lamp wire (photo).

4 Remove the adjustment bolt and spacer. If necessary, the adjustment link may be unbolted from the cylinder head or block as applicable (photos).

5 Remove the pivot bolt, and lift the alternator from the engine (photo).

4.3 Battery clamp

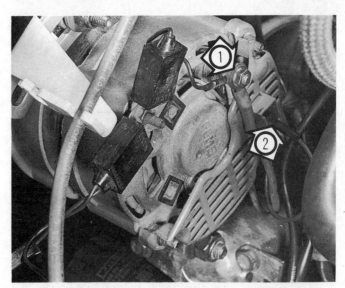
6.3 Alternator main cable (1) and warning lamp wire (2)

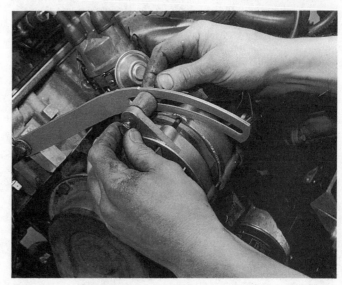
64A Removing the alternator adjustment bolt and spacer

6.4B Alternator adjustment link removal

6.5 Removing the alternator pivot bolt

6   Refitting is a reversal of removal, but tension the drivebelt as described in Chapter 2.

7   Alternator – brush renewal

Note: *Several different alternators have been fitted to the model range. This Section describes brush renewal for the Femsa alternator, but the procedure for other types is similar*

1   With the alternator removed from the engine, unscrew the nuts and remove the plastic cover. Remove the spacers (photos).
2   Unscrew and remove the bolt retaining the resistor bar to the alternator (photo). Loosen the nut at the other end of the bar, and swivel the bar outwards.
3   Disconnect the wiring from the 'C' terminal on the brush holder (photo).
4   Note the location of the second wire on the brush holder, then remove the screw and withdraw the brush holder (photos).
5   Check the condition of the slip rings. If they are blackened, clean them with a fuel-moistened rag. If they are deeply scored or grooved, then the alternator is probably well-worn and should be renewed.
6   Check the length of the carbon brushes (photo). If less than the specified minimum length, the brush holder must be renewed.
7   Reassembly is a reversal of dismantling.

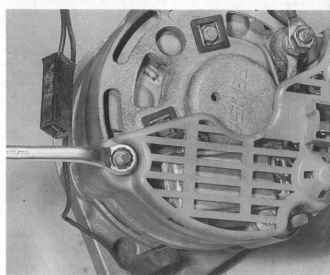

7.1A Unscrew the nuts ...

8   Starter motor – description and testing

1   The starter motor is located on the rear left-hand side of the engine, and is bolted to the gearbox. It is of the pre-engaged type, where the drive pinion is brought into mesh with the starter ring gear on the flywheel/driveplate before the main current is applied.
2   When the starter switch is operated, current flows from the battery to the solenoid, which is mounted on the top of the starter motor body. The plunger in the solenoid moves inwards, so causing a centrally-pivoted lever to push the drive pinion into mesh with the starter ring gear. When the solenoid plunger reaches the end of its travel, it closes an internal contact, and full starting current flows to the starter field coils. The armature is then able to rotate the crankshaft, so starting the engine.
3   A special freewheel clutch is fitted to the starter drive pinion, so that, as soon as the engine fires and starts to operate on its own, it does not drive the starter motor.
4   When the starter switch is released, the solenoid is de-energised, and a spring moves the plunger back to its rest position. This operates

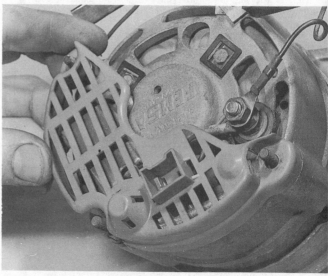

7.1B ... and remove the plastic cover ...

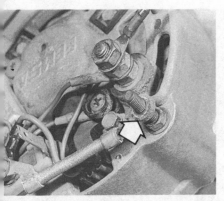

7.1C ... and spacers (arrowed)

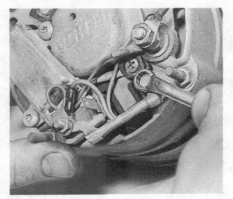

7.2 Unscrewing the resistor bar bolt

7.3 Brush holder terminal and wiring (arrowed)

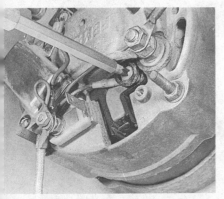

7.4A Removal of the second wire from the brush holder

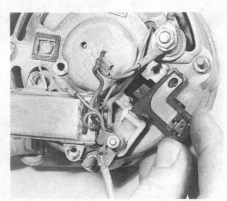

7.4B Removing the brush holder

7.6 Carbon brushes (arrowed) and brush holder

the pivoted lever, to withdraw the drive pinion from engagement with the starter ring gear.

5   If the starter motor fails to turn the engine when the switch is operated, there are four possible reasons why:

(a)   The battery is discharged or faulty
(b)   The electrical connections between switch, solenoid, battery and starter motor are somewhere failing to pass the necessary current from the battery, through the starter, to earth
(c)   The solenoid has an internal fault
(d)   The starter motor is electrically defective

6   To check the battery, switch on the headlights. If they dim after a few seconds, the battery is discharged. If they glow brightly, next operate the ignition/starter switch. If the headlights dim, this indicates that power is reaching the starter motor, but failing to turn it. If the starter turns very slowly, go on to the next check.

7   If the headlights remain bright when the switch is operated, then power is not reaching the starter motor. Check all connections from the battery to the solenoid for security. Check that the earth cable between the engine and body is also connected securely.

8   If the solenoid clicks when the switch is operated, the starter motor must have an internal fault.

9   To check that current is reaching the starter motor, connect a voltmeter to the solenoid-to-motor terminal, and operate the switch. If current is available, the starter motor must be removed for further investigation.

9   Starter motor – removal and refitting

1   Disconnect the battery negative lead.
2   Disconnect the wiring from the solenoid terminals (photo).
3   On fuel injection models, unbolt the bracket from the front of the starter motor.

4   Unscrew the mounting bolts, and withdraw the starter motor from the gearbox (photos).
5   Where fitted, remove the cover plate from the gearbox aperture (photo).
6   Refitting is a reversal of removal.

9.2 Starter motor solenoid terminals and wiring

9.4A Unscrew the bolts (arrowed) ...

9.4B ... and remove the starter motor

9.4C Starter motor unit

9.5 Removing the starter motor cover plate

10 Starter motor – overhaul

1   Full overhaul of the starter motor is a specialist job, and best entrusted to an auto electrician.
2   Exploded views of the Ducellier and Paris-Rhône starter motors are shown in Figs. 12.1 and 12.2 respectively. Bosch and Valeo types may also be fitted.

11 Fuses and relays – general

1   The main fusebox is located in the right-hand rear corner of the engine compartment. Access to the fuses and relays is gained by removing the cover (photo).

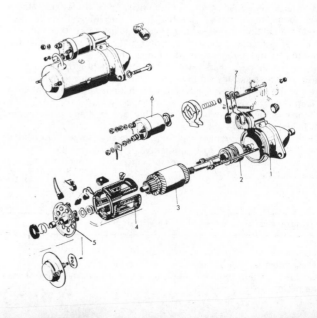

Fig. 12.1 Exploded view of the Ducellier starter motor (Sec 10)

1   Drive end housing
2   Drive pinion
3   Armature
4   Field coils
5   Brush endplate
6   Solenoid
7   Actuating lever

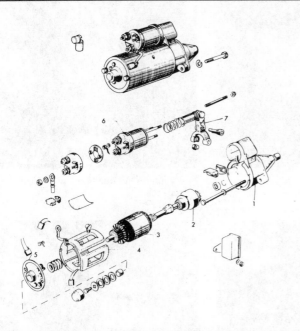

Fig. 12.2 Exploded view of the Paris-Rhône starter motor (Sec 10)

1 Drive end housing   5 Brush endplate
2 Drive pinion   6 Solenoid
3 Armature   7 Actuating lever
4 Field coils

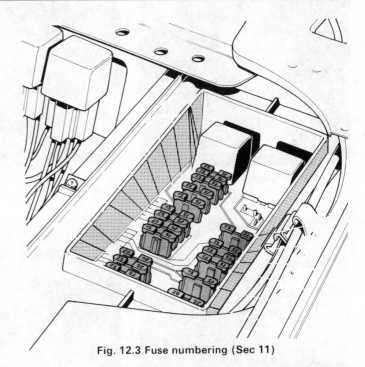

Fig. 12.3 Fuse numbering (Sec 11)

*Refer to Specifications Section
for details*

The circuit protected by each fuse are given in the Specifications section, and the fuse numbers are indicated in Fig. 12.3.

On fuel injection models, two additional fuses are located in the heater control panel, behind the ashtray (photo). One is for the fuel pump (15 amps), and the other is a spare.

Should a fuse blow, replace it only with one of identical rating and, if the new one blows again immediately, trace and rectify the cause, which may be a short-circuit.

The blade-type fuses may be removed by pulling them directly from the fuseboard (photo). On some models, a removal tool is provided with the vehicle.

The relays are located either on the fuseboard or behind the lower facia panel (photos).

2 Switches – removal and refitting

As a safety precaution, always disconnect the battery negative lead before removing a switch. Reconnect the lead after refitting the switch.

Facia and centre console switches

2 Carefully prise the switch from the panel (photo).

3 Disconnect the wiring plug. If there is a chance that the wiring plug will fall back through the switch aperture, retain the plug with tape or string.

4 Refitting is a reversal of removal.

Electrically-operated mirrors switch (1986-on models)

5 Carefully prise the switch from the door trim panel (photo).

6 Disconnect the wiring plugs and remove the switch.

7 Refitting is a reversal of removal.

Glovebox illumination lamp switch

8 Remove the glovebox (Chapter 11).

9 Prise the switch from its location, and disconnect the wiring (photo).

10 Refitting is a reversal of removal.

Courtesy light switch

11 Unscrew the mounting screw, and ease the switch from its location hole (photo).

12 Tape the wire to the door pillar, then disconnect it and remove the switch.

13 Refitting is a reversal of removal.

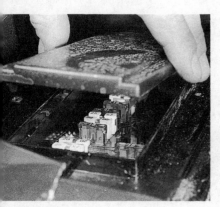

1.1 Removing the fusebox cover

11.3 Fuses located behind the ashtray – fuel injection models
A Fuel pump   B Spare

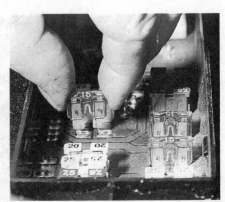

11.5 Removing a fuse

11.6A Removing a relay from the fuseboard

11.6B Relay mounted beneath the headlamp load adjuster bracket

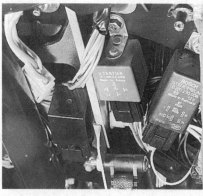

11.6C Relays mounted behind the lower facia panel

12.2A Removing the rear window locking switch ...

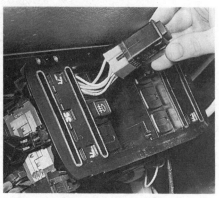

12.2B ... the hazard warning switch (pre-1986 models) ...

12.2C ... the rear foglamp switch (1986-on models) ...

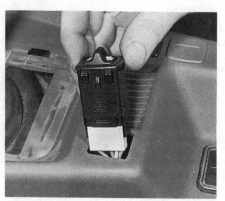

12.2D ... the front left-hand electric window switch (pre-1986 models) ...

12.2E ... and the rear left-hand electric window switch (1986-on models)

12.5 Electrically operated mirror switch removal (1986-on models)

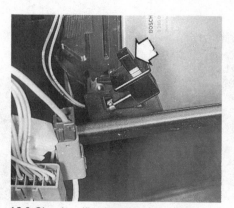

12.9 Glovebox illumination lamp switch (arrowed)

12.11 Courtesy light switch removal

Steering column combination switches

14 Remove the steering wheel (Chapter 10).
15 Unscrew the screws and remove the steering column lower cowl. On pre-1986 models, pull out the switch cover from the cowl (photos).
16 Unscrew the mounting bolts, disconnect the wiring plug and remove the switch (photos).
17 Refitting is a reversal of removal.

Luggage compartment illumination lamp switch

18 Remove the trim panel from the left-hand side of the luggage compartment.
19 Prise the switch from its location, and disconnect the wiring (photo).
20 Refitting is a reversal of renewal.

13 Cigar lighter – removal and refitting

1 Disconnect the battery negative lead.
2 Remove the radio as described in Section 28.
3 Remove the upper screws and lift out the radio surround.
4 Disconnect the wiring, and unclip the cigar lighter from the surround (photo).
5 Refitting is a reversal of removal.

14 Digital clock – removal and refitting

1 Disconnect the battery negative lead.

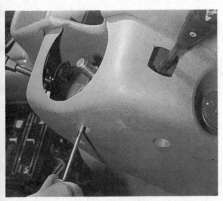
12.15A Remove the lower screw ...

12.15B ... pull out the switch cover (arrowed) ...

12.15C ... and remove the lower cowl (pre-1986 models)

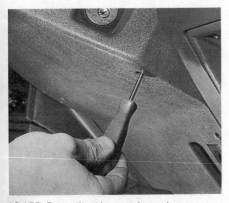
12.15D Removing the steering column lower cowl on 1986-on models

12.16A Unscrew the bolts (arrowed) ...

12.16B ... and remove the steering column combination switch (pre-1986 models)

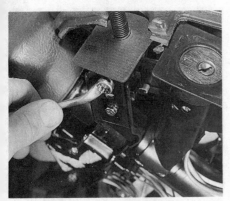
12.16C Steering column combination switch removal (1986-on models)

12.16D Wiring plug (arrowed) on the combination switch (1986-on models)

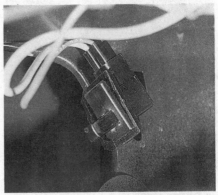
12.19 Luggage compartment illumination lamp switch removal

Pre-1986 models

2   Carefully prise the clock from the facia panel (photos).
3   Disconnect the wiring and remove the clock.

1986-on models

4   Prise the clock from the heater control panel.
5   Disconnect the wiring and remove the clock.

All models

6   Refitting is a reversal of removal. It will of course be necessary to reset the time.

---

15 Instrument illumination rheostat – removal and refitting

1   Disconnect the battery negative lead.
2   Unclip the support panel from the lower facia panel.
3   Disconnect the wiring from the rheostat, then depress the plastic clips and remove the rheostat (photo).
4   Refitting is a reversal of removal.

---

16 Instrument panel – removal and refitting

1   Disconnect the battery negative lead.
2   Remove the steering wheel (Chapter 10). Though not essential, this will provide improved working room.
3   Using a small screwdriver through the small holes each side of the instrument panel, depress the plastic clips to release the panel (photo).
4   Withdraw the instrument panel sufficiently to disconnect the speedometer cable and wiring plugs (photos).
5   Remove the instrument panel from its location (photos).
6   Refitting is a reversal of removal. The speedometer cable is automatically engaged as the instrument panel is inserted and the guide pins enter their holes.

17 Instrument panel – dismantling and reassembly

1   Pull the rubber knobs from the trip recorder and clock.
2   Disconnect the printed circuit from the tachometer or clock.
3   Unscrew the speedometer screws, the temperature gauge nuts, the fuel gauge nuts, and the rear casing nuts, noting the location of the spring washers.
4   Using a screwdriver, release the clips and remove the front face.
5   Carefully lever off the gauge needles, and remove the rear assembly.
6   To remove the speedometer, release the plastic or metal retainer and withdraw the unit.
7   To remove the gauges, release the retaining plate and withdraw them.
8   To remove the tachometer, first remove the oil temperature and level gauge printed circuit as applicable, then prise off the retaining plate.
9   To remove the clock, release it from the two posts.
10 To remove the buzzer (where fitted), pull the rubber caps from the two pins and withdraw the unit.
11 Reassembly is a reversal of dismantling, but refit the clock hands at 12 o'clock. The remaining hands can only be fitted in one position.

---

18 Speedometer cable – removal and refitting

1   Jack up the front of the vehicle and support on axle stands.
2   Unscrew the retaining bolt and withdraw the cable from the gearbox.
3   Remove the instrument panel as described in Section 16.
4   Prise the grommet from the bulkhead, then remove the cable.
5   Refitting is a reversal of removal.

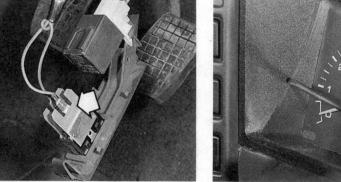

13.4 Cigar lighter removal

14.2A Prise out the digital clock ...

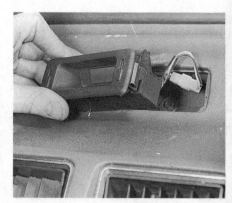

14.2B ... and remove from the facia (pre-1986 models)

15.3 Instrument illumination rheostat (arrowed)

16.3 Method of releasing the instrument panel clips

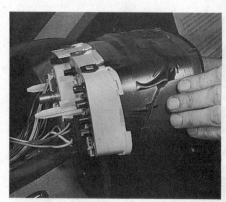

16.4A Instrument panel removal (pre-1986 models)

16.4B Instrument panel removal (1986-on models)

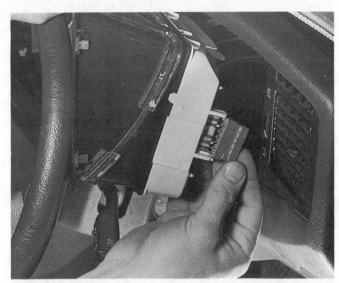
16.4C Disconnecting a wiring plug from the instrument panel

16.5A Instrument panel connections (pre-1986 models)

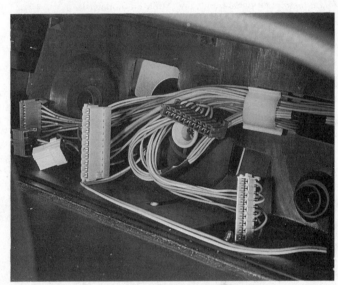
16.5B Instrument panel connections (1986-on models)

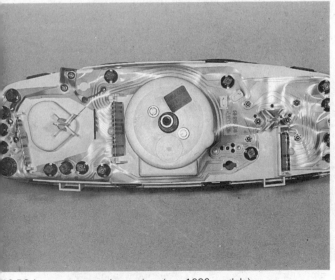
16.5C Instrument panel rear view (pre-1986 models)

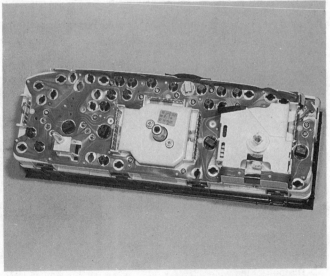
16.5D Instrument panel rear view (1986-on models)

16.5E Instrument panel front view (1986-on models)

Fig. 12.4 Instrument panel front face removal (Sec 17)

1   Plastic clips

19 Bulbs (exterior) – renewal

Headlamps

1   Pull the wiring connector from the rear of the headlamp (photo).
2   Remove the rubber protector (photo).
3   Release the spring clips and extract the bulb (photos).
4   Fit the new bulb, taking care not to touch the glass. If necessary, clean the glass with methylated spirit before fitting. Refitting is a reversal of removal – make sure that the 'TOP' mark on the rubber protector is uppermost (photo).

Front parking and direction indicator lamp

5   Reach under the front wheel arch and squeeze together the plastic 'ears' on the inner end of the lamp (photo).
6   Release the lamp from the bumper by unhooking the outer post.
7   Unclip the appropriate bulbholder, then depress and twist the bulb to remove it (photo). Refitting is a reversal of removal.

Rear lamp cluster (Saloon)

8   Unscrew the plastic nuts from inside the luggage compartment, and remove the inner cover (photo).
9   Withdraw the lamp unit, and separate the bulbholder by releasing the plastic clips (photo).
10 Depress and twist the appropriate bulb to remove it (photo).

Refitting is a reversal of removal.
11 If necessary, the bulbholder and printed circuit board may be removed by disconnecting the wiring plug (photo).

Rear lamp cluster (Estate)

12 Open the tailgate, then unscrew the upper mounting screw and withdraw the rear lamp cluster (photo).
13 Prise up the tabs, and separate the bulbholders (photos).
14 Depress and twist the appropriate bulb to remove it (photo). Refitting is a reversal of removal.

Rear number plate lamp

15 On Saloon models, use a small screwdriver to depress the end clip on the lamp lens, then withdraw the lamp. Unclip the bulbholder, then depress and twist the bulb to remove it (photo).
16 On Estate models, use a small screwdriver to prise off the lamp lens, then depress and twist the bulb to remove it (photos).
17 Refitting is a reversal of removal.

Side marker lamp

18 Prise out the lens (photo).
19 Prise out the rubber grommet, making sure that the bulbholder does not fall back inside the wing (photo).
20 Hold the bulbholder, then depress and twist the bulb to remove it (photo). Refitting is a reversal of removal.

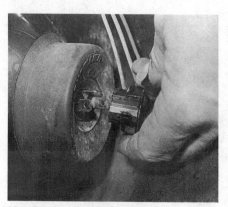

19.1 Disconnect the wiring ...

19.2 ... remove the rubber protector ...

19.3A ... release the spring clips ...

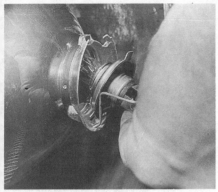

19.3B ... and extract the headlamp bulb

19.4 'TOP' mark (arrowed) must be uppermost on the rubber protector

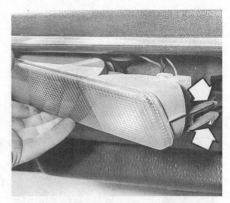

19.5 Plastic 'ears' (arrowed) on the front parking and direction indicator lamp

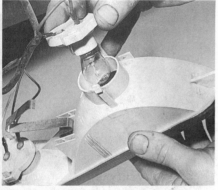

19.7 Removing a front direction indicator lamp bulb

19.8 Removing the rear lamp cluster inner cover (Saloon)

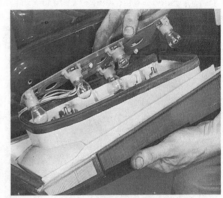

19.9 Rear lamp cluster bulbholder removal (Saloon)

19.10 Removing a rear lamp cluster bulb (Saloon)

19.11 Disconnecting the rear lamp cluster wiring plug (Saloon)

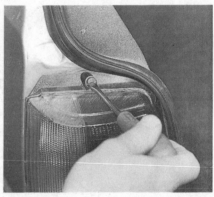

19.12 Rear lamp cluster upper mounting screw removal (Estate)

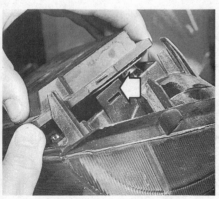

19.13A Prise up the tabs (arrowed) ...

19.13B ... and remove the bulbholder (Estate)

19.14 Removing a rear lamp cluster bulb (Estate)

19.15A Withdraw the number plate lamp ...

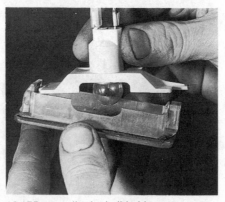

19.15B ... unclip the bulbholder ...

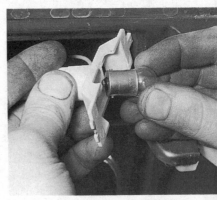

19.15C ... and remove the bulb (Saloon models)

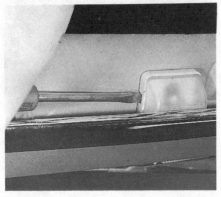

19.16A Prise off the number plate lamp lens ...

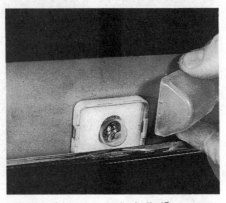

19.16B ... for access to the bulb (Estate models)

19.18 Remove the side marker lens ...

19.19 ... rubber grommet and bulbholder ...

19.20 ... and extract the bulb

20 Bulbs (interior) – renewal

Roof lamp
1 Using a thin screwdriver, depress the plastic ear at one end of the lamp, then remove the lamp (photo).
2 Extract the festoon-type bulb from the metal contacts (photo).
3 If necessary, unclip the lamp surround (photo).

Map reading lamp
4 Using a screwdriver, rock the lamp to release the tongues.
5 Withdraw the lamp and remove the bulb.

Luggage compartment and glovebox lamps
6 Prise out the lens (photos).
7 Extract the festoon-type bulb from the metal contacts.

Instrument panel warning lamps
8 Remove the instrument panel as described in Section 16.
9 Twist the bulbholders and remove them (photo).

Fig. 12.5 Removing the roof lamp and map reading lamp (Sec 20)

1   Plastic ears   2   Retaining tongues

10 Pull the wedge-type bulbs from the bulbholders (photo).

Facia switch

11 Prise out the switch button (photo).
12 Using plastic or rubber tubing, pull out the wedge-type bulb (photo).

Ignition switch illumination bulb

13 Remove the lower facia panel (Chapter 11).
14 Pull out the bulbholder and remove the bulb (photo).

Heater control panel illumination bulb (pre-1986 models)

15 Remove the heater control panel with reference to Chapter 11.
16 Extract the wedge-type bulb from the bulbholder (photo).

Heater control/coinbox/ashtray illumination bulb (1986-on models)

17 Remove the heater control panel with reference to Chapter 11.
18 Remove the bulbholder and extract the bulb (photos).

Digital clock (1986-on models)

19 Remove the digital clock as described in Section 14.
20 Twist and remove the bulbholder, then extract the wedge-type bulb (photo).

All interior lamps/bulbs

21 Refitting is a reversal of removal.

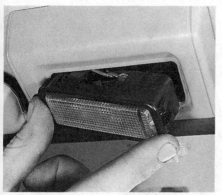
20.1 Roof lamp removal

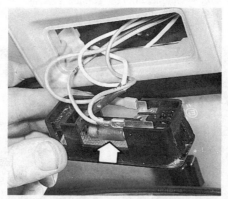
20.2 Roof lamp bulb location (arrowed)

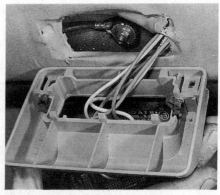
20.3 Roof lamp surround removal

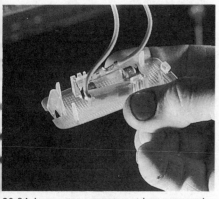
20.6A Luggage compartment lamp removal

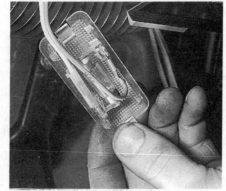
20.6B Glovebox lamp removal

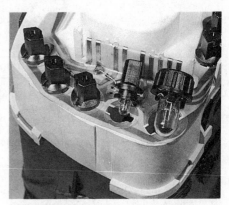
20.9 Instrument panel warning lamp bulbholder removal

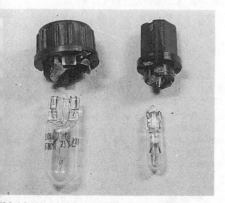
20.10 Warning lamp bulb removal from bulbholders

20.11 Remove the switch button ...

20.12 ... and use tubing to remove the bulb

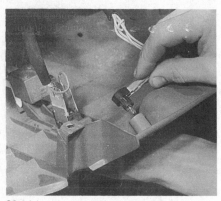

20.14 Ignition switch illumination bulb removal

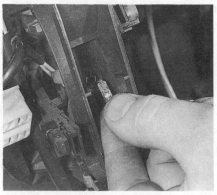

20.16 Heater control panel bulb removal (pre-1986 models)

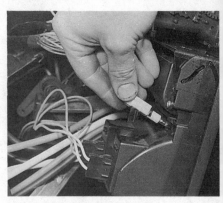

20.18A Coinbox bulb removal

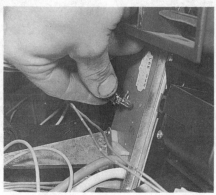

20.18B Heater control illumination bulb removal (1986-on models)

20.20 Digital clock bulb removal (1986-on models)

21 Headlamp unit – removal and refitting

1   Remove the headlamp bulb as described in Section 19.
2   Unclip the headlamp surround (photo).
3   Unhook the tension spring from the body bracket (photo).
4   Disconnect the earth wire, where fitted.
5   Prise the inner pivot socket from its ball, and disconnect the outer socket (photos).
6   Withdraw the headlamp unit, and at the same time disconnect the load correction servo.
7   Unhook the tension spring from the unit (photo).
8   Refitting is a reversal of removal, but check and if necessary adjust the beam alignment as described in Section 22 (photo).

22 Headlamp beam alignment

1   It is recommended that the headlamp beam alignment is carried out by a Peugeot dealer, or a service station having the necessary optical beam setting equipment.
2   As a temporary measure, the load adjuster should be set to its basic position, and the main beams aligned parallel to the ground by focusing on a wall.
3   Horizontal movement is adjusted by the screw located behind the headlamp, and vertical movement by the load adjuster mounting (photos).
4   Holts Amber Lamp is useful for temporarily changing the headlight colour to conform with the normal usage on Continental Europe.

23 Headlamp beam load adjuster – general

1   A sealed hydraulic beam adjusting device is fitted, so that the headlamp beams may be adjusted independently from the normal basic setting, to compensate for variations in the vehicle loading.

2   The device consists of a master control and control knob, two servo units, and connecting tubing.
3   To remove the master control, first pull off the control knob (photo).
4   On Saloon models, remove the lower facia panel, then unbolt the master control mounting bracket (photos).
5   On Estate models, remove the steering column lower cowl, then detach the master control by removing the screws (photo).
6   To remove the servo units, release the headlamp tension springs, then unlock the plastic mountings (photo).
7   Refitting is a reversal of removal.

24 Horn unit – removal and refitting

1   Remove the front grille as described in Chapter 11.
2   Disconnect the battery negative lead.
3   Disconnect the wiring, and unbolt the horn unit from its mounting (photo).
4   Refitting is a reversal of removal.

25 Wiper blades and arms – removal and refitting

1   Whenever the wiper blades fail to clean the screen the blades or their rubber inserts should be renewed.
2   To remove a blade, pull the arm from the glass, then depress the clip and release the blade from the arm (photos).
3   Before removing a wiper arm, stick some masking tape on the glass to indicate its rest position.
4   Flip up the cover, unscrew the nut, and pull the arm from the spindle (photos). It may be necessary to rock the arm slightly to release it from the spindle splines.
5   Refitting is a reversal of removal.

21.2 Headlamp surround removal

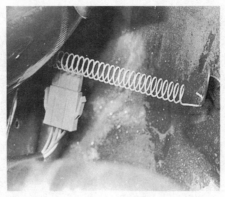
21.3 Headlamp tension spring

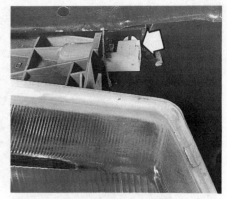
21.5A Headlamp inner pivot socket (arrowed)

21.5B Disconnecting the headlamp outer socket (arrowed)

21.7 Tension spring connection to the headlamp

21.8 Headlamp refitted in its location

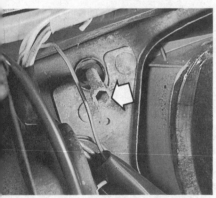
22.3A Horizontal headlamp adjustment screw (arrowed)

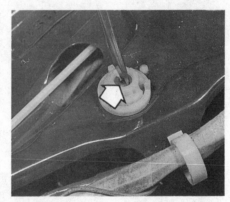
22.3B Vertical headlamp adjustment screw (arrowed)

23.3 Pull off the control knob ...

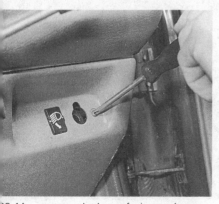
23.4A ... remove the lower facia panel on Saloon models ...

23.4B ... unscrew the bolts ...

23.4C ... and remove the headlamp adjuster mounting bracket

23.5 Headlamp adjuster on Estate models

23.6 Headlamp adjuster servo unit

24.3 Horn unit location

25.2A Removing early type wiper blade

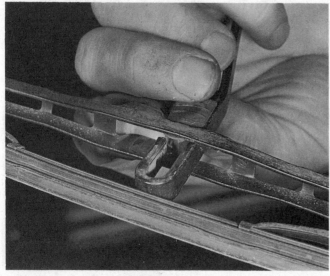

25.2B Removing later type wiper blade

25.4A Unscrew the spindle nut ...

25.4B ... and remove the wiper arm

26 Windscreen wiper motor and linkage – removal and refitting

1   Remove the wiper blades and arms as described in Section 25.
2   Remove the screws and withdraw the fresh air inlet grille. Disconnect the washer tubes (photos).
3   Remove the remaining screws and withdraw the intermediate plate (photos).
4   Disconnect the wiring from the wiper motor (photo).

5   Unbolt the support brackets and main crossmember (photos), and withdraw the complete linkage.
6   The wiper motor may be separated from the linkage by disconnecting the operating rod from the crank lever, then unbolting the unit.
7   Refitting is a reversal of removal, but make sure that the washer tubes are clipped to the air inlet grille.

27 Tailgate wiper motor (Estate models) – removal and refitting

1   Remove the wiper blade and arm, as described in Section 25.
2   Remove the tailgate trim panel, with reference to Chapter 11.
3   Disconnect the wiring plug and unbolt the earth wire (photo).
4   Unscrew the spindle nut and recover the washers.
5   Unscrew the mounting bolts (photo) and remove the motor assembly from the tailgate. Note the location of the mounting rubbers and spacers.
6   Refitting is a reversal of removal.

28 Radio, speakers and aerial – removal and refitting

Note: *On later models, the radio is security-coded. This means that if the electrical supply is disconnected (for example disconnecting the battery), a coded number must be entered by depressing the number buttons before the radio can be switched on again*

1   Disconnect the battery negative lead.
2   Insert radio removal tools, or thin rods, into the holes on each side of the radio, and depress to release the clips (photo).
3   Withdraw the radio sufficiently to disconnect the wiring plug, speaker plugs and aerial lead (photo).
4   To remove a front speaker, first pull the weatherstrip away from the front door pillar near the speaker only. Remove the screws and

26.2A Remove the screws ...

26.2B ... and withdraw the fresh air inlet grille

26.2C Washer tube connection on the inlet grille

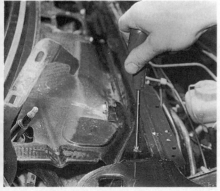

26.3A Remove the screws ...

26.3B ... and withdraw the intermediate plate

26.4 Windscreen wiper motor and wiring plug (arrowed)

26.5A Windscreen wiper linkage support bracket and bolt

26.5B Windscreen wiper linkage main crossmember bolt

27.3 Tailgate wiper motor wiring plug

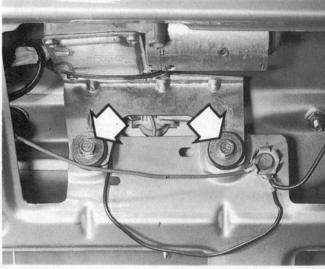

27.5 Tailgate wiper motor mounting bolts (arrowed)

withdraw the speaker panel, then disconnect the wiring (photos).

5 To remove a rear speaker, unscrew the mounting screws, withdraw the speaker and disconnect the wiring (photos).

6 Access to the aerial mounting nut is gained by removing the roof lamp as described in Section 20 (photo).

7 Refitting of all components is a reversal of removal.

29 Heated rear screen – general

1 To prevent damage to the elements of the heated rear window, observe the following precautions:

   (a) *Clean the interior surface of the glass with a damp cloth or chamois leather, rubbing in the direction that the elements run*

   (b) *Avoid scratching the elements with rings on the fingers or contact with articles in the luggage compartment*

   (c) *Do not stick adhesive labels over the elements*

2 Should the element be broken, it can be repaired using a conductive silver paint, without the need to remove the glass from the window.

3 The paint is available from many sources, and should be applied with a soft brush to a really clean surface. Use two strips of masking tape as a guide to the thickness of the element to be repaired.

4 Allow the new paint to dry thoroughly before switching the heater on.

5 On cars fitted with heated exterior rear view mirrors, the mirror heating element is switched on when the rear screen switch is operated.

30 Washer system – general

1 The washer system arrangement varies according to model. Some models have just a windscreen washer, others incorporate the headlamp washer with the windscreen, and Estate models have a tailgate washer system, which is either incorporated with the windscreen system or separate.

2 The windscreen washer reservoir is located next to the battery, on the left-hand side of the engine compartment. Where the tailgate washer reservoir is separate, it is located on the left-hand side of the luggage compartment (photos).

3 Adjustment of the washer jets is carried out by inserting a pin in the jet nozzle, and moving it to obtain the desired jet pattern on the screen

28.2 Inserting the radio removal rods

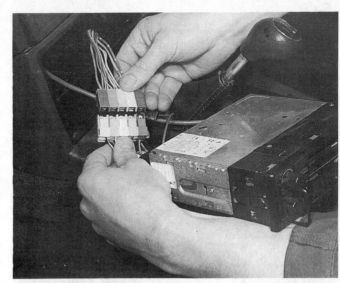
28.3 Disconnecting the radio wiring

28.4A Pull out the weatherstrip ...

28.4B ... remove the screws ...

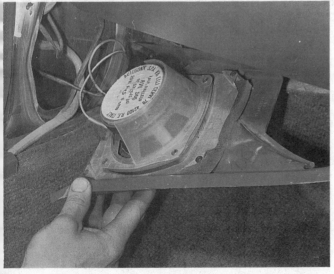
28.4C ... and withdraw the speaker panel

28.5A Remove the screws ...

28.5B ... and withdraw the rear speaker

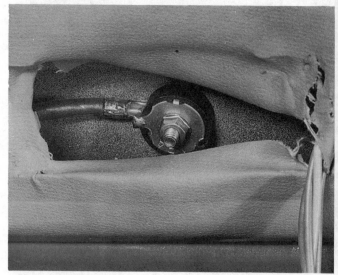

28.6 Aerial mounting nut

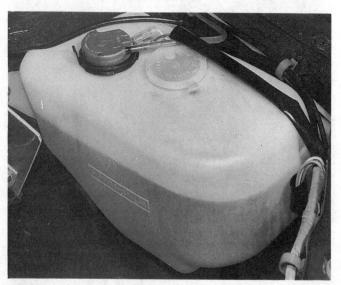

30.2A Windscreen washer reservoir

30.2B Tailgate washer reservoir

31 Central locking system – general

1   On models fitted with central door locking, it is possible to lock all doors, including the boot or tailgate, simply by locking the driver's door.

2   The system uses electric actuators to move the door lock mechanisms. The actuators can be removed by dismantling the doors, boot or tailgate as described in Chapter 11.

3   On some models, the fuel filler flap is also incorporated in the system.

4   An electronic control unit sends the opening and closing information to the actuators in the doors and fuel filler flap (photo).

5   In the event of failure of the system, the doors, boot and tailgate may be locked and unlocked manually using the key or locking knob.

6   To operate the fuel filler flap manually, remove the trim from the rear

luggage compartment, and move the actuator rod by hand (photo).

32 Dim-dip lighting – general

1   All models manufactured from late 1986 are fitted with a dim-dip lighting system, which essentially prevents the vehicle from being driven with the sidelights alone switched on.

2   When the ignition is switched on with the sidelights also switched on, the relay is energised, closing the internal contacts and supplying current to the dipped beam circuit via the resistor. This causes the dip filaments in the headlamps to be illuminated at one-sixth dipped beam brightness. The relay winding is earthed through the headlamp main beam filaments, so that the relay is de-energised when the main beam is switched on.

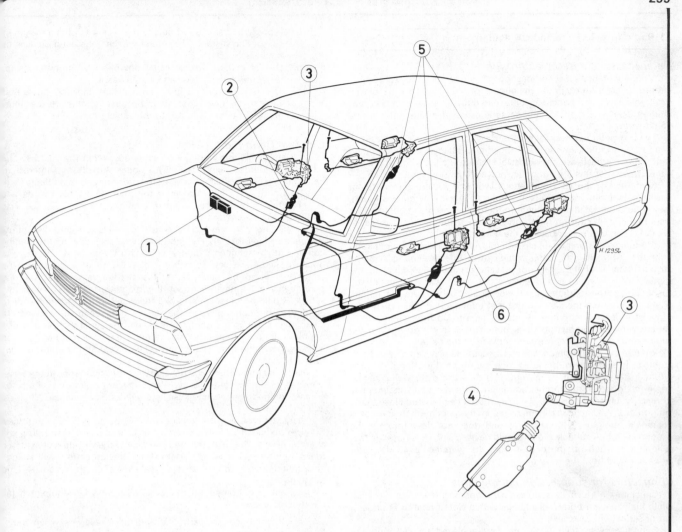

Fig. 12.6 Central door locking system (Sec 31)

1 Control unit
2 Actuator (with switch)
3 Door lock (driver's side)
4 Actuator rod
5 Actuators (without switches)
6 Door lock (passenger side)

31.4 Central locking system electronic control unit

31.6 Fuel filler flap actuator rod – arrowed (trim removed)

33 Radio interference and CB equipment

Radio/cassette case breakthrough

Magnetic radiation from dashboard wiring may be sufficiently intense to break through the metal case of the radio/cassette player. Often this is due to a particular cable routed too close and shows up as ignition interference on AM and cassette play and/or alternator whine on cassette play.

The first point to check is that the clips and/or screws are fixing all parts of the radio/cassette case together properly. Assuming good earthing of the case, see if it is possible to re-route the offending cable – the chances of this are not good, however, in most cars.

Next release the radio/cassette player and locate it in different positions with temporary leads. If a point of low interference is found, then if possible fix the equipment in that area. This also confirms that local radiation is causing the trouble. If re-location is not feasible, fit the radio/cassette player back in the original position.

Alternator interference on cassette play is now caused by radiation from the main charging cable which goes from the battery to the output terminal of the alternator, usually via the + terminal of the starter motor relay. In some vehicles this cable is routed under the dashboard, so the solution is to provide a direct cable route. Detach the original cable from the alternator output terminal and make up a new cable of at least 6 mm² cross-sectional area to go from alternator to battery with the shortest possible route. *Remember – do not run the engine with the alternator disconnected from the battery.*

Ignition breakthrough on AM and/or cassette play can be a difficult problem. It is worth wrapping earthed foil round the offending cable run near the equipment, or making up a deflector plate well screwed down to a good earth. Another possibility is the use of a suitable relay to switch on the ignition coil. The relay should be mounted close to the ignition coil; with this arrangement the ignition coil primary current is not taken into the dashboard area and does not flow through the ignition switch. A suitable diode should be used since it is possible that at ignition switch-off the output from the warning lamp alternator terminal could hold the relay on.

Connectors for suppression components

Capacitors are usually supplied with tags on the end of the lead, while the capacitor body has a flange with a slot or hole to fit under a nut or screw with washer.

Connections to feed wires are best achieved by self-stripping connectors. These connectors employ a blade which, when squeezed down by pliers, cuts through cable insulation and makes connection to the copper conductors beneath.

Chokes sometimes come with bullet snap-in connectors fitted to the wires, and also with just bare copper wire. With connectors, suitable female cable connectors may be purchased from an auto-accessory shop together with any extra connectors required for the cable ends after being cut for the choke insertion. For chokes with bare wires, similar connectors may be employed together with insulation sleeving as required.

VHF/FM broadcasts

Reception of VHF/FM in an automobile is more prone to problems than the medium and long wavebands. Medium/long wave transmitters are capable of covering considerable distances, but VHF transmitters are restricted to line of sight, meaning ranges of 10 to 50 miles, depending upon the terrain, the effects of buildings and the transmitter power.

Because of the limited range it is necessary to retune on a long journey, and it may be better for those habitually travelling long distances or living in areas of poor provision of transmitters to use an AM radio working on medium/long wavebands.

When conditions are poor, interference can arise, and some of the suppression devices described previously fall off in performance at very high frequencies unless specifically designed for the VHF band. Available suppression devices include reactive HT cable, resistive distributor caps, screened plug caps, screened leads and resistive spark plugs.

For VHF/FM receiver installation the following points should be particularly noted:

(a) Earthing of the receiver chassis and the aerial mounting is important. Use a separate earthing wire at the radio, and scrape paint away at the aerial mounting.

(b) If possible, use a good quality roof aerial to obtain maximum height and distance from interference generating devices on the vehicle.

(c) Use of a high quality aerial downlead is important, since losses in cheap cable can be significant.

(d) The polarisation of FM transmissions may be horizontal, vertical, circular or slanted. Because of this the optimum mounting angle is at 45° to the vehicle roof.

Citizens' Band radio (CB)

In the UK, CB transmitter/receivers work within the 27 MHz and 934 MHz bands, using the FM mode. At present interest is concentrated on 27 MHz where the design and manufacture of equipment is less difficult. Maximum transmitted power is 4 watts, and 40 channels spaced 10 kHz apart within the range 27.60125 to 27.99125 MHz are available.

Aerials are the key to effective transmission and reception. Regulations limit the aerial length to 1.65 metres including the loading coil and any associated circuitry, so tuning the aerial is necessary to obtain optimum results. The choice of a CB aerial is dependent on whether it is to be permanently installed or removable, and the performance will hinge on correct tuning and the location point on the vehicle. Common practice is to clip the aerial to the roof gutter or to employ wing mounting where the aerial can be rapidly unscrewed. An alternative is to use the boot rim to render the aerial theftproof, but a popular solution is to use the 'magmount' – a type of mounting having a strong magnetic base clamping to the vehicle at any point, usually the roof.

Aerial location determines the signal distribution for both transmission and reception, but it is wise to choose a point away from the engine compartment to minimise interference from vehicle electrical equipment.

The aerial is subject to considerable wind and acceleration forces. Cheaper units will whip backwards and forwards and in so doing will alter the relationship with the metal surface of the vehicle with which it forms a ground plane aerial system. The radiation pattern will change correspondingly, giving rise to break-up of both incoming and outgoing signals.

Interference problems on the vehicle carrying CB equipment fall into two categories:

(a) Interference to nearby TV and radio receivers when transmitting.

(b) Interference to CB set reception due to electrical equipment on the vehicle.

Problems of break-through to TV and radio are not frequent, but can be difficult to solve. Mostly trouble is not detected or reported because the vehicle is moving and the symptoms rapidly disappear at the TV/radio receiver, but when the CB set is used as a base station any trouble with nearby receivers will soon result in a complaint.

It must not be assumed by the CB operator that his equipment is faultless, for much depends upon the design. Harmonics (that is, multiples) of 27 MHz may be transmitted unknowingly and these can fall into other user's bands. Where trouble of this nature occurs, low pass filters in the aerial or supply leads can help, and should be fitted in base station aerials as a matter of course. In stubborn cases it may be necessary to call for assistance from the licensing authority, or, if possible, to have the equipment checked by the manufacturers.

Interference received on the CB set from the vehicle equipment is fortunately, not usually a severe problem. The precautions outlined previously for radio/cassette units apply, but there are some extra points worth noting.

It is common practice to use a slide-mount on CB equipment enabling the set to be easily removed for use as a base station, for example. Care must be taken that the slide mount fittings are properly earthed and that first class connection occurs between the set and slide-mount.

Vehicle manufacturers in the UK are required to provide suppression of electrical equipment to cover 40 to 250 MHz to protect TV and VHF radio bands. Such suppression appears to be adequately effective at 27 MHz, but suppression of individual items such as alternators, dynamos, clocks, stabilisers, flashers, wiper motors, etc, may still be necessary. The suppression capacitors and chokes available from auto-electrical suppliers for entertainment receivers will usually give the required results with CB equipment.

Other vehicle radio transmitters

Besides CB radio already mentioned, a considerable increase in the use of transceivers (ie combined transmitter and receiver units) has taken place in the last decade. Previously this type of equipment was fitted mainly to military, fire, ambulance and police vehicles, but a large business radio and radio telephone usage has developed.

Generally the suppression techniques described previously will suffice, with only a few difficult cases arising. Suppression is carried out to satisfy the 'receive mode', but care must be taken to use heavy duty chokes in the equipment supply cables since the loading on 'transmit' is relatively high.

34 Fault diagnosis – electrical system

Symptom	Reason(s)
No voltage at starter motor	Battery discharged Battery defective internally Battery terminals loose or earth lead not securely attached to body Loose or broken connections in starter motor circuit Starter motor switch or solenoid faulty
Voltage at starter motor – faulty motor	Starter brushes badly worn, sticking, or brush wires loose Commutator dirty, worn or burnt Starter motor armature faulty Field coils earthed
Starter motor noisy or rough in engagement	Pinion or flywheel gear teeth broken or worn Starter motor retaining bolts loose
Alternator not charging*	Drivebelt loose and slipping, or broken Brushes worn, sticking, broken or dirty Brush springs weak or broken

If all appears to be well but the alternator is still not charging, take the car to an automobile electrician for checking of the alternator

Symptom	Reason(s)
Battery will not hold charge for more than a few days	Battery defective internally Electrolyte level too low or electrolyte too weak due to leakage Plate separators no longer fully effective Battery plates severely sulphated Drivebelt slipping Battery terminal connections loose or corroded Alternator not charging properly Short in lighting circuit causing continual battery drain
Ignition light fails to go out, battery runs flat in a few days	Drivebelt loose and slipping, or broken Alternator faulty
Fuel gauge gives no reading	Fuel tank empty Electric cable between tank sender unit and gauge earthed or loose Fuel gauge case not earthed Fuel gauge supply cable interrupted Fuel gauge unit broken
Fuel gauge registers full all the time	Electric cable between tank unit and gauge broken or disconnected
Horn fails to operate	Blown fuse Cable or cable connection loose, broken or disconnected Horn has an internal fault
Horn emits intermittent or unsatisfactory noise	Cable connections loose Horn incorrectly adjusted
Lights do not come on	If engine not running, battery discharged Light bulb filament burnt out or bulbs broken Wire connections loose, disconnected or broken Light switch shorting or otherwise faulty
Lights come on but fade out	If engine not running, battery discharged
Lights give very poor illumination	Lamp glasses dirty Reflector tarnished or dirty Lamps badly out of adjustment Incorrect bulb with too low wattage fitted Existing bulbs old and badly discoloured Electrical wiring too thin not allowing full current to pass
Lights work erratically, flashing on and off, especially over bumps	Battery terminals or earth connections loose Contacts in light switch faulty

34 Fault diagnosis – electrical system (cont)

Symptom	Reason(s)
Wiper motor fails to work	Blown fuse
	Wire connections loose, disconnected or broken
	Brushes badly worn
	Armature worn or faulty
	Field coils faulty
Wiper motor works very slowly and takes excessive current	Commutator dirty, greasy or burnt
	Drive to spindles bent or unlubricated
	Drive spindle binding or damaged
	Armature bearings dry or unaligned
	Armature badly worn or faulty
Wiper motor works slowly and takes little current	Brushes badly worn
	Commutator dirty, greasy or burnt
	Armature badly worn or faulty
Wiper motor works but wiper blades remain static	Linkage disengaged or faulty
	Drive spindle damaged or worn
	Wiper motor gearbox parts badly worn

Wiring diagrams commence overleaf

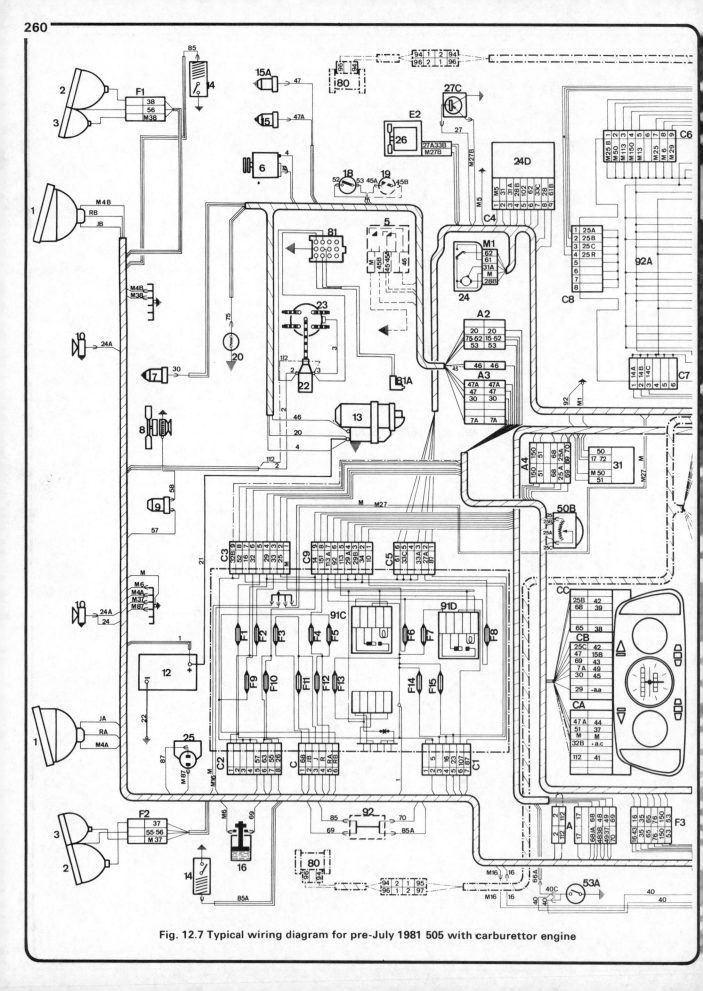

Fig. 12.7 Typical wiring diagram for pre-July 1981 505 with carburettor engine

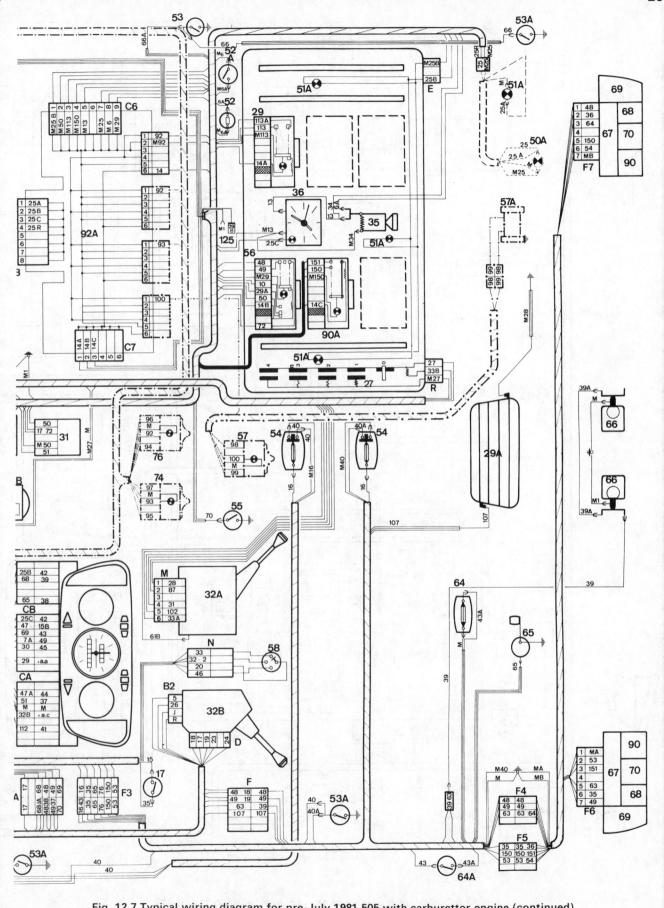

Fig. 12.7 Typical wiring diagram for pre-July 1981 505 with carburettor engine (continued)

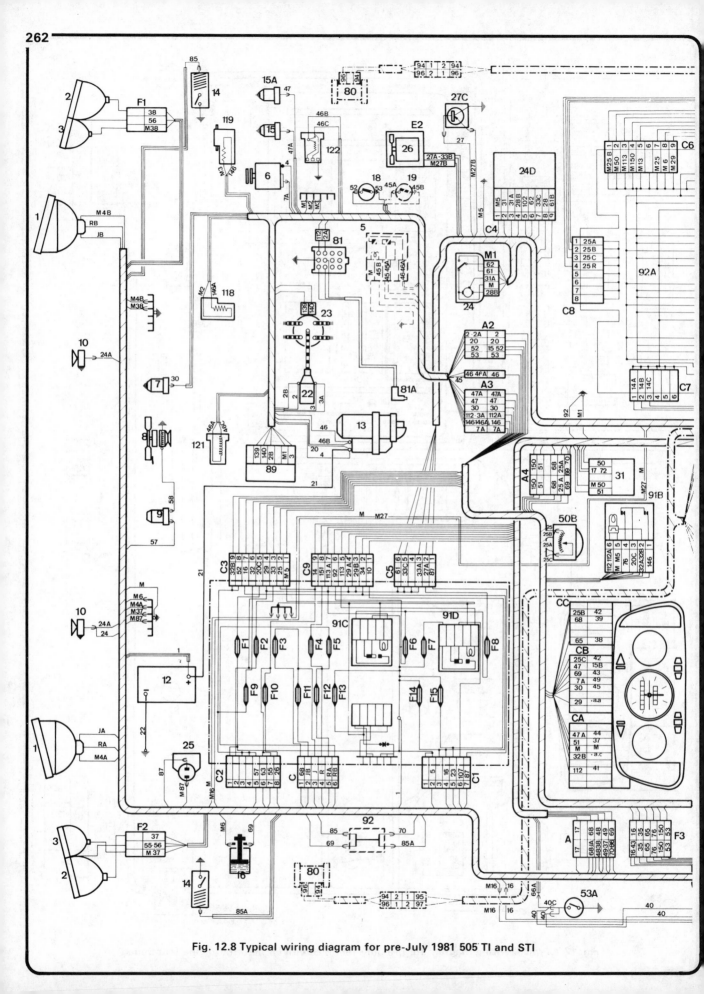

Fig. 12.8 Typical wiring diagram for pre-July 1981 505 TI and STI

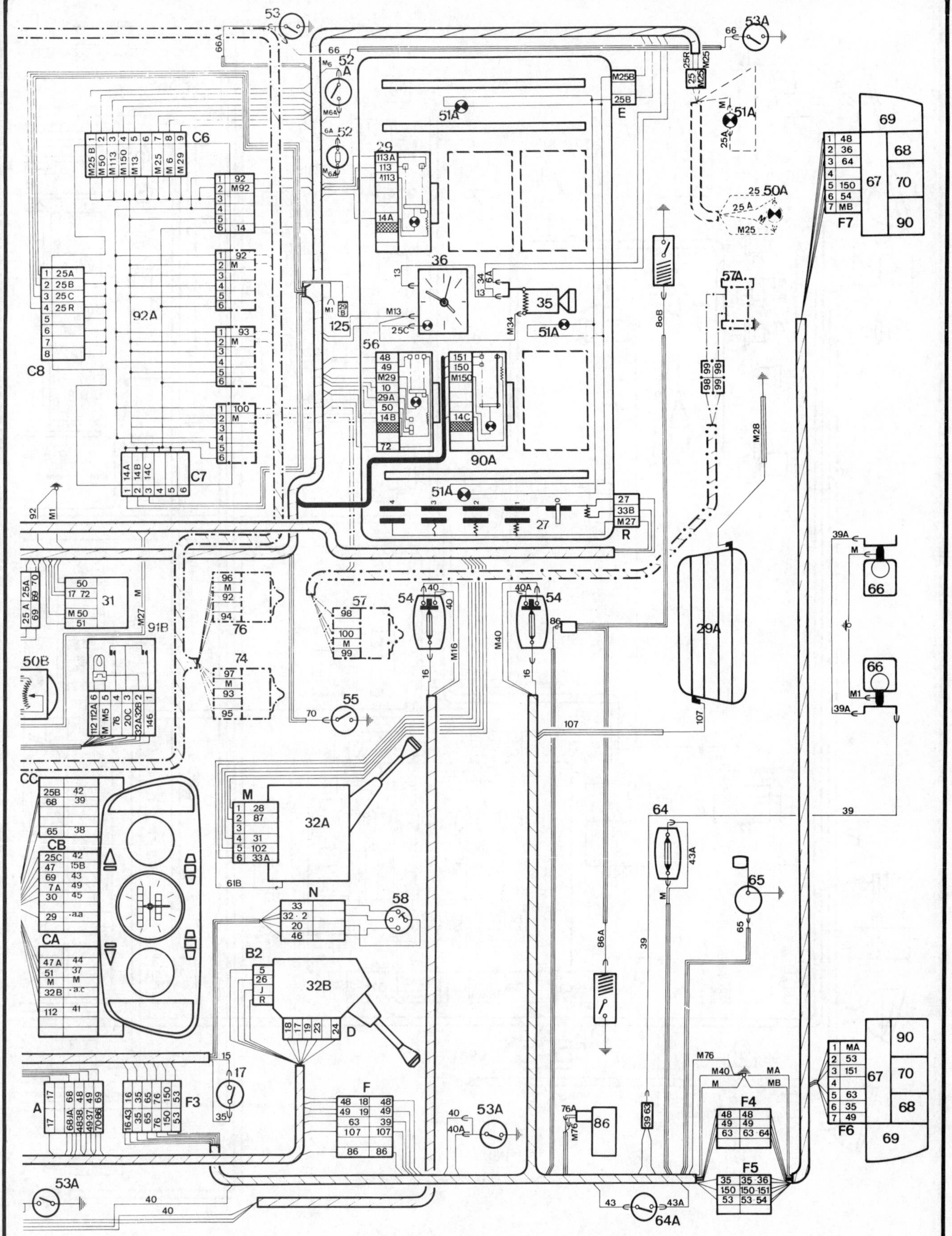

Fig. 12.8 Typical wiring diagram for pre-July 1981 505 TI and STI (continued)

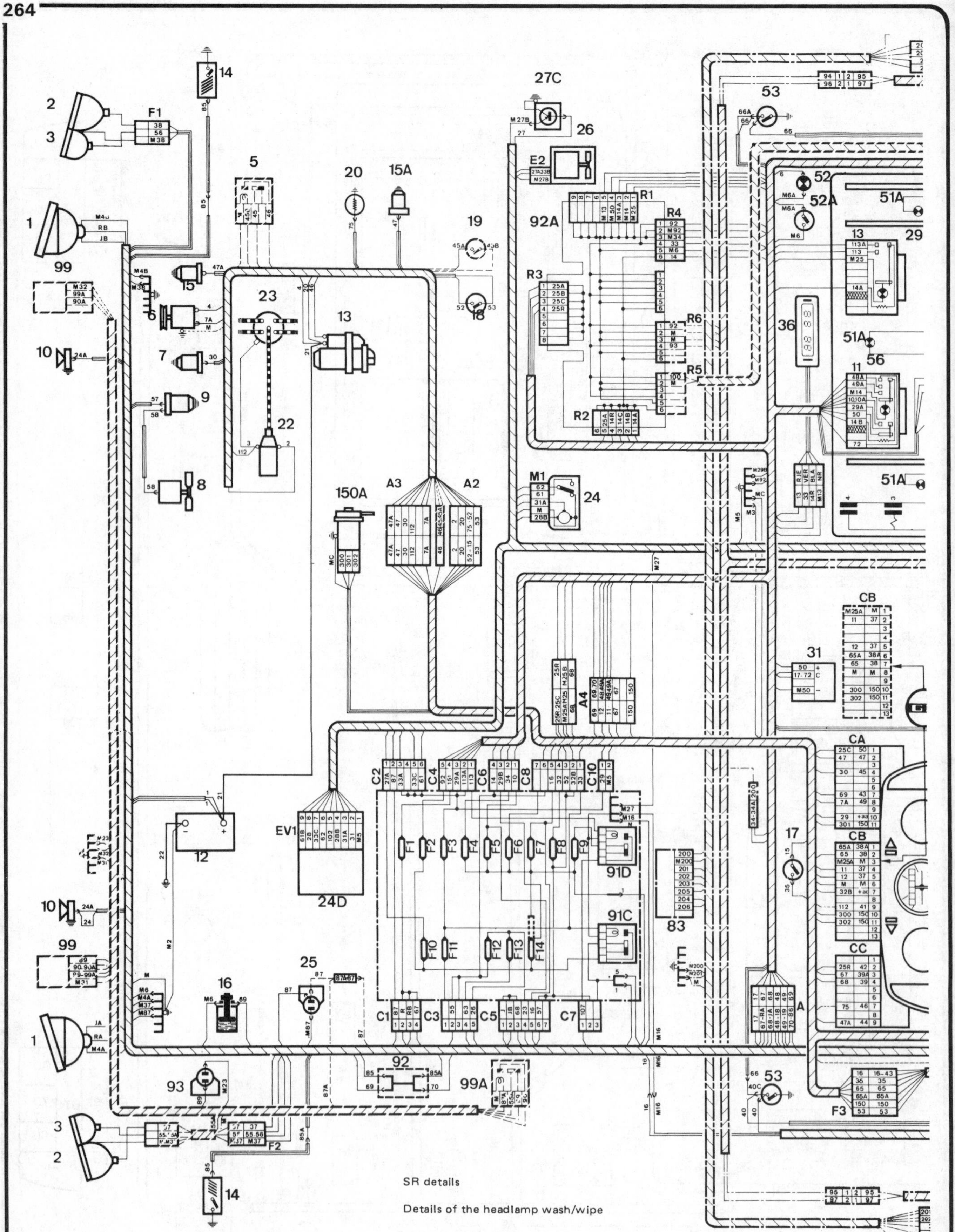

Fig. 12.9 Typical wiring diagram for July 1981-on 505 with carburettor engine

SR details

Details of the headlamp wash/wipe

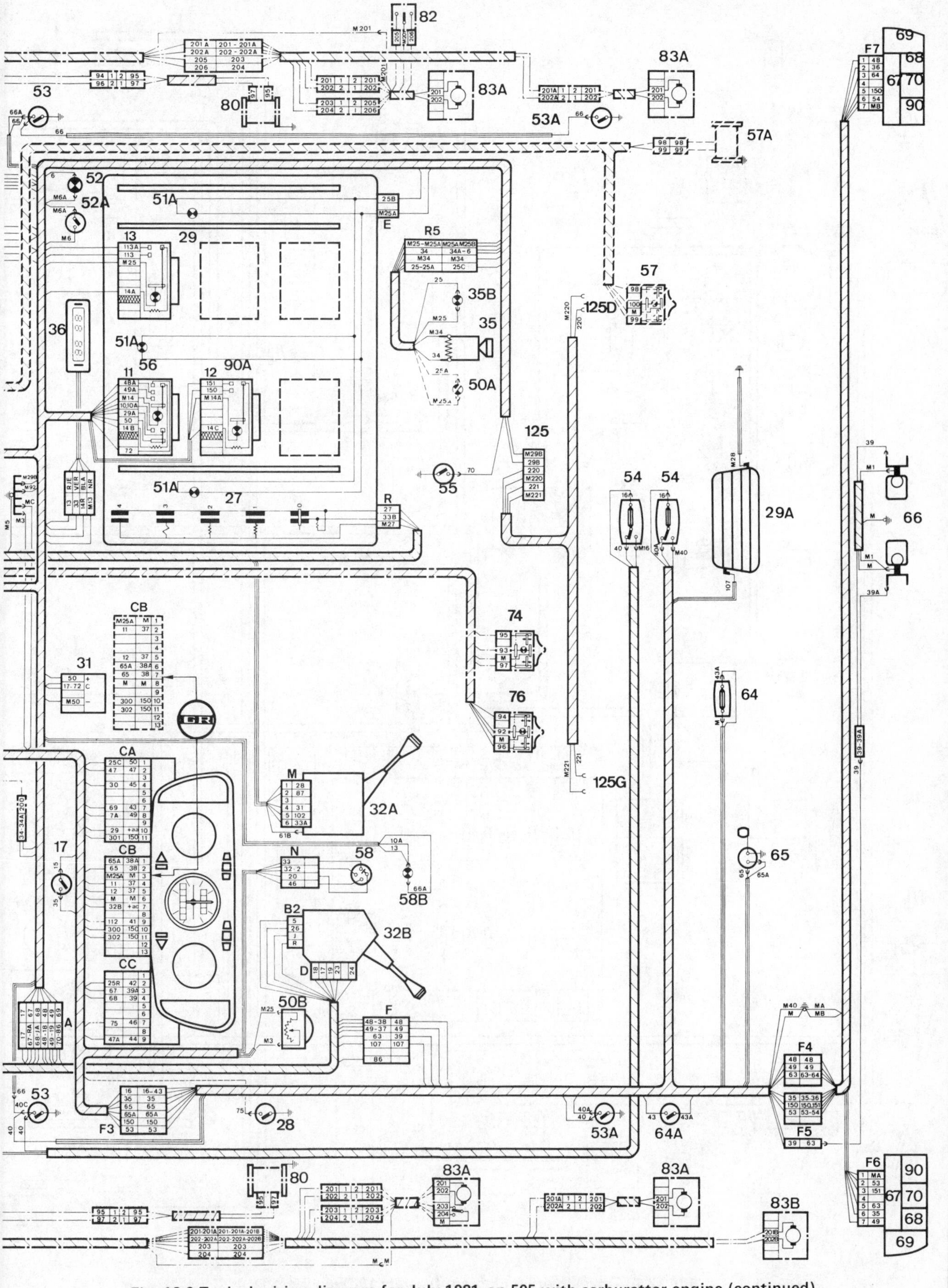

Fig. 12.9 Typical wiring diagram for July 1981-on 505 with carburettor engine (continued)

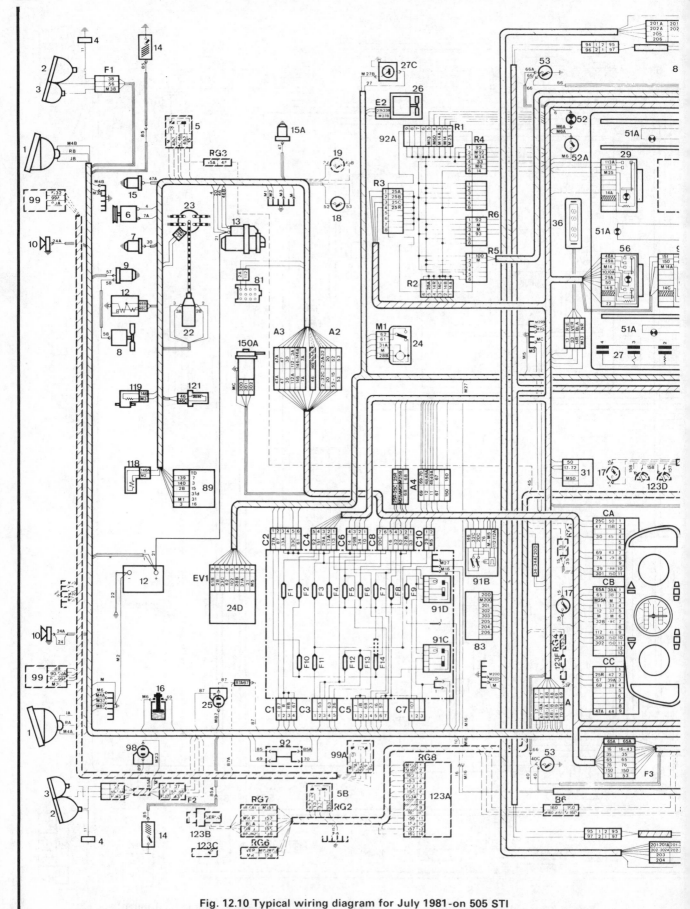

Fig. 12.10 Typical wiring diagram for July 1981-on 505 STI

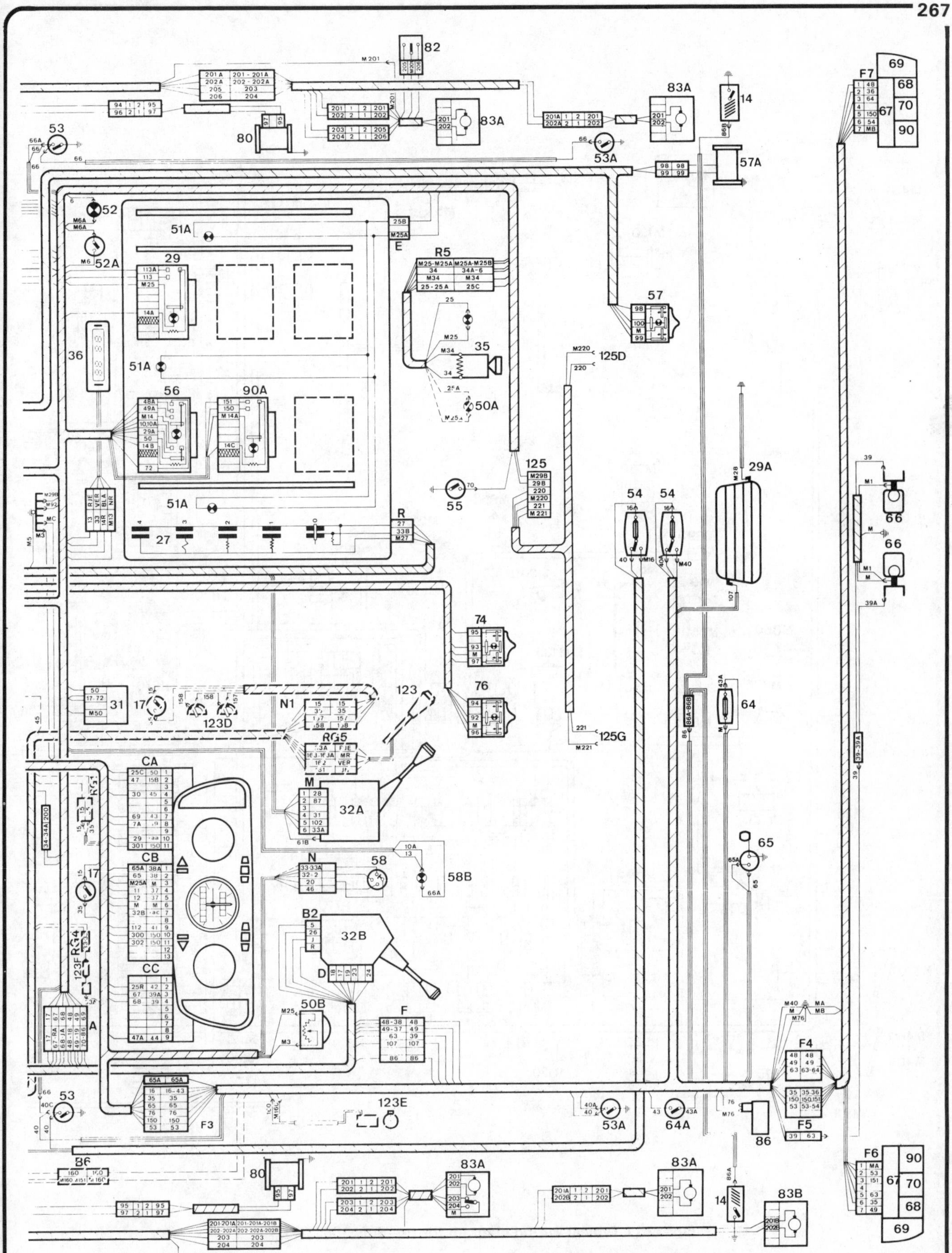

Fig. 12.10 Typical wiring diagram for July 1981-on 505 STI (continued)

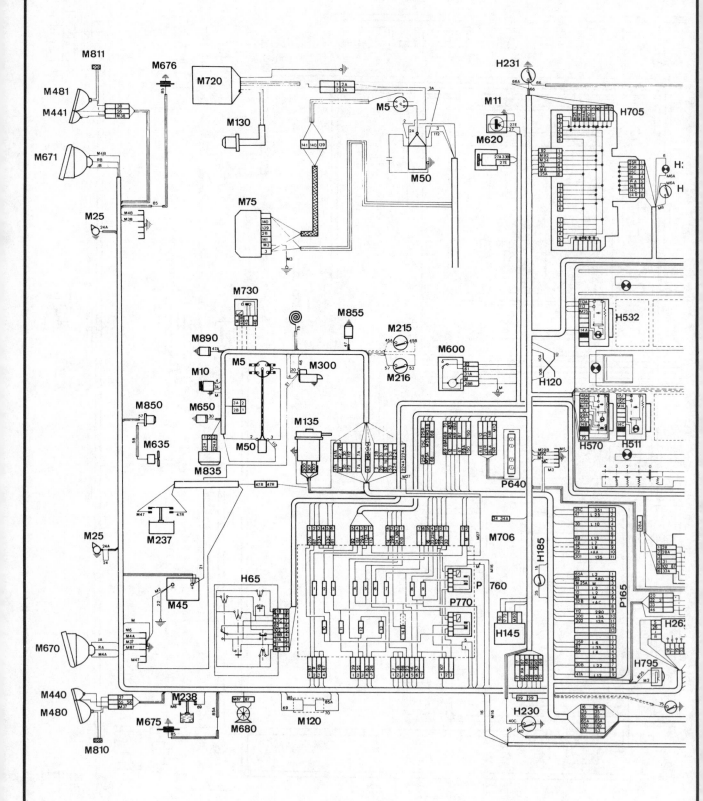

Fig. 12.11 Typical wiring diagram for pre-July 1985 505 SR

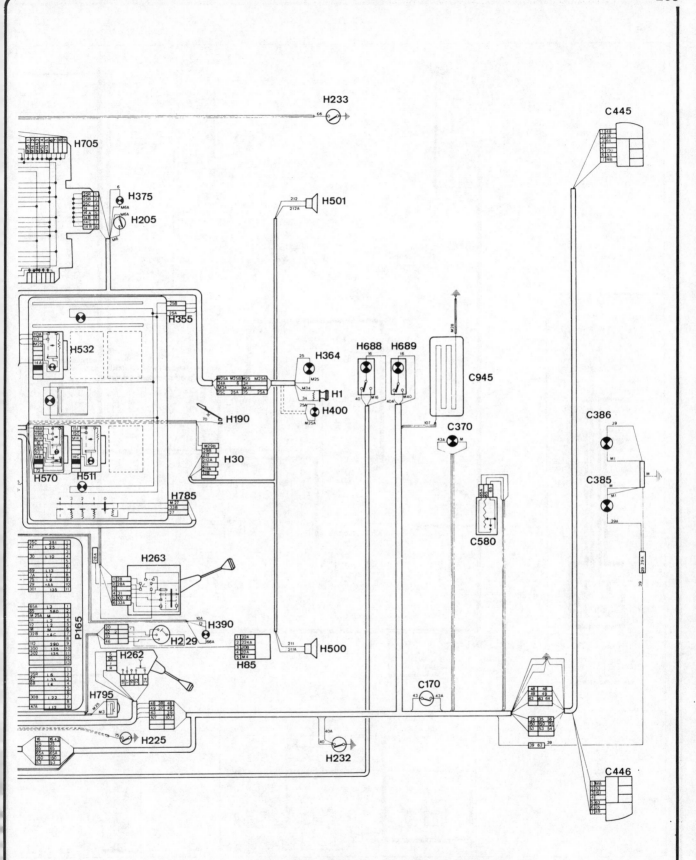

Fig. 12.11 Typical wiring diagram for pre-July 1985 505 SR (continued)

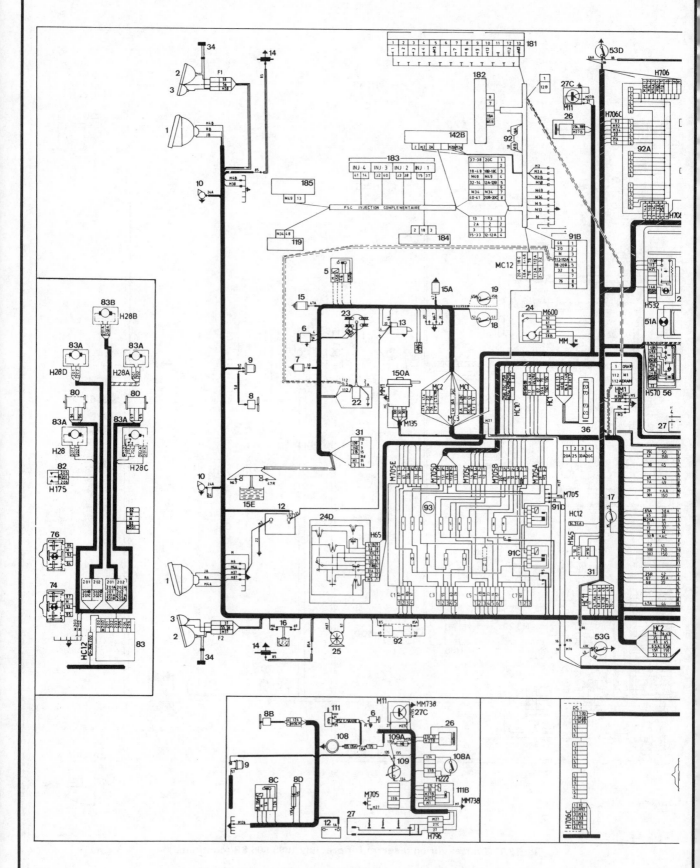

Fig. 12.12 Typical wiring diagram for pre-July 1985 505 GTI

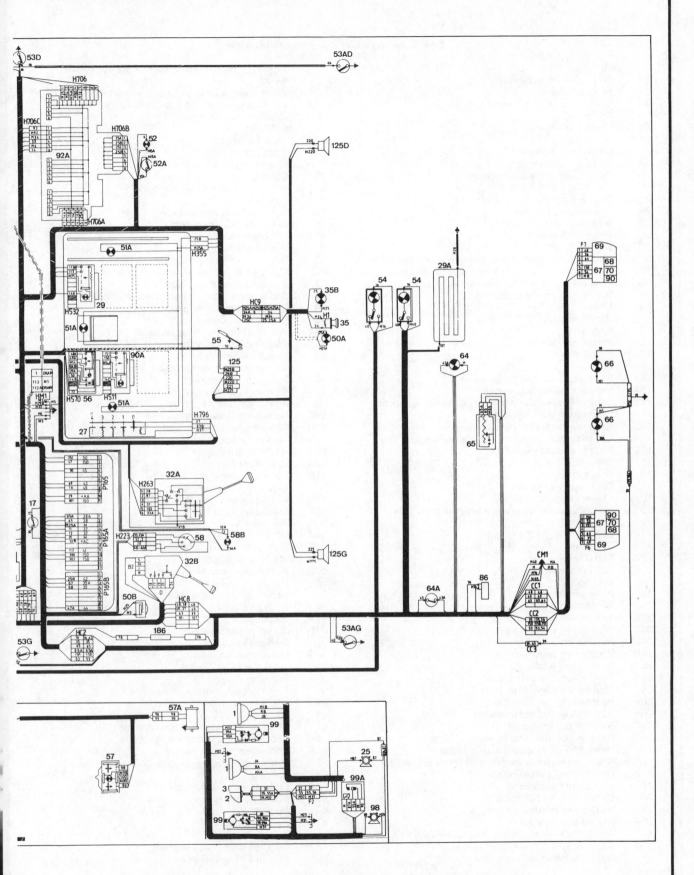

Fig. 12.12 Typical wiring diagram for pre-July 1985 505 GTI (continued)

Key to wiring diagrams – up to July 1985

1	Headlight
2	Front direction indicator
3	Front sidelight
4	Direction indicator repeater
5	Starter relay
5A	Neutral safety relay
6	Alternator
7	Oil pressure switch
7A	Oil level indicator
7B	Control box, oil level indicator
7C	Checking diode, oil level indicator
8	Electro-magnetic fan or electric fan
8A	Disengaging fan relay
8B	Air conditioning electric fan
8C	Electric fan relay
8D	Diodes
9	Temperature switch, fan clutch or electric fan
9A	Temperature switch, fan clutch, cooling system
9B	Temperature switch, fan clutch, lube system
9C	Sender unit, oil temperature gauge
10	Horn
11	Headlight relay
12	Battery
12A	Battery cut-out
13	Starter motor
14	Brake pads
15	Sender unit, coolant temperature
15A	Switch, coolant temperature
15B	Coolant temperature warning light switch or coolant temperature warning light
15C	Resistor, coolant temperature gauge
15D	Checking diode, coolant temperature warning light
15E	Switch, coolant level
16	Brake fluid reservoir
17	Stop switch
18	Reversing light switch
19	Starter safety cut-out
20	Idling cut-out or carburettor resistance
21	Regulator
22	Coil
22A	Coil relay
22B	Coil resistor
22C	Coil resistor relay
23	Distributor
23A	Pulse generator
24	Windscreen wiper
24A	Windscreen wiper relay
24B	Windscreen wiper timer
24C	Rear window wiper
24D	Windscreen wiper unit
25	Windscreen washer pump
25A	Rear window washer pump
26	Heating/ventilation fan, front
26A	Rear heating/ventilation fan
26B	Heating/ventilation fan switch
26C	Air conditioning blower
26D	Relay, air conditioning blower
27	Heating/ventilation switch or rheostat
27A	Rheostat resistor or heating/ventilation fan resistor
27B	Rear heating/ventilation switch
27C	Air conditioning control unit
28	Choke warning light switch
29	Heated rear window switch
29A	Heated rear window
30	Windscreen wiper/windscreen washer switch
30A	Rear window wiper/washer switch
31	Direction indicator flasher unit
32	Lighting – windscreen wiper/windscreen washer switch
32A	Windscreen wiper/windscreen washer switch
32B	Lighting/direction indicator/horn control switch
33	Headlight flasher relay
34	Sidelights
35	Cigar lighter, front
35A	Cigar lighter, rear
35B	Illumination, cigar lighter
36	Clock
37	Direction indicator repeater light
38	Fuel gauge
38A	Warning light, low fuel level
39	Main beam warning light
39A	Dip beam warning light
40	Hazard warning light
41	Rev counter
42	Sidelight warning light
43	Brake safety warning light
43A	Brake safety warning light checking diode
44	Coolant temperature gauge
45	Oil pressure warning light
45A	Warning light, oil temperature
45B	Warning light, oil pressure and temperature
46	Choke warning light
47	Oil and water warning light
48	Preheater warning light
49	Charge/discharge warning light
50	Instrument panel lighting
50A	Gearchange gate light
50B	Rheostat, gearchange gate light
50C	Switch lighting
51	Heater lighting
51A	Console lighting
51B	Console lighting rheostat
52	Glove compartment light
52A	Glove compartment light switch
53	Front door switch
53A	Rear door switch
54	Interior lighting
54A	Light under facia panel
54B	Map reading light
54C	Illumination, courtesy mirror
55	Handbrake switch
56	Hazard warning light switch
57	Sunroof switch
57A	Sunroof motor
57E	Locking relay, sunroof
58	Steering lock
58B	Ignition switch light
59	Preheat – starter switch
59A	Preheater plugs
60	Pump cut-out motor or solenoid valve
61	Preheater warning light switch
62	Preheater relay
63	Direction indicator and horn control
64	Boot or rear compartment lighting
64A	Boot lid or tailgate switch
65	Fuel gauge tank unit with or without low fuel warning
65A	External tank unit resistor
65B	Rheostat, fuel gauge
66	Number plate light
67	Reversing lights
68	Stop-light
68B	Stop/tail lamp (twin filament)
69	Rear direction indicator

Key to wiring diagrams – up to July 1985 (continued)

70	Tail lamp	111	Idling speed compensation solenoid valve
71	Tailgate switch	111A	Air conditioning shut off pressure switch
72	Door mounted light	118	Control pressure regulator
73	Left-hand relay window winder switch	119	Additional air control
73A	Locking relay, LH rear window winder	120	Sensor plate switch
74	Window winder switch, LH front	121	Cold starting injector
74A	Locking relay, LH front window winder	122	Thermal time switch
75	Interlock, rear window winder	123	Speed regulator switch
76	Window winder switch, RH front	123A	Speed regulator electronic unit
76A	Locking relay, RH front window winder	123B	Speed regulator servo
77	Window winder switch, RH rear	123C	Speed regulator safety switch
77A	Locking relay, RH rear window winder	123D	Speed regulator disengagement switch
78	Left-hand window winder rear switch	123E	Speed regulator pick-up
79	Right-hand window winder rear switch	123F	Speed regulator fuse
80	Window winder motor	123G	Safety relay speed regulator
80A	Window winder relay	123H	Vacuum capsule
81	Diagnostic socket	123I	Safety relay
81A	TDC sensor, diagnostic socket	123J	Main switch, speed regulator
82	Door lock switch	125	Radio connection
83	Control box, central door locking	125D	Radio speaker, front RH
83A	Actuator, door lock	125G	Radio speaker, front LH
83B	Actuator, fuel filler flap	125AD	Radio speaker, rear RH
86	Fuel pump	125AG	Radio speaker, rear LH
86A	Primary fuel pump	125E	Connector, radio speaker
87	Solenoid valve	129	Speed sensor
87A	Solenoid valve control switch	142	Tachymetric relay, fuel cut-off on overrun
88	Ignition pick-up	142A	Relay, fuel injection cut-off on overrun
89	Electronic unit or amplifier module	142B	Control unit, for delay of fuel injection cut-off
90	Rear foglights	150	Warning light, economy
90A	Rear foglight switch	150A	Vacuum pick-up
90B	Rear foglight warning light	151	Switch, water detector
91	Relay	151A	Warning light, water detector switch
91B	Tachymetric relay	152	Connector, front foglamps
91C	Accessory relay	152A	Switch, front foglamps
91D	Heated rear window relay	152B	Relay, front foglamps
92	Connecting terminal	170	Relay ignition system
92A	Connection board	171	Calculator, ignition advance
93	Services connection board	172	Control unit, knock detector
93A	Fusebox No 1	172A	Knock detector
93B	Fusebox No 2	173	Warning light, LED, knock detector
94	Conductive tailgate stay	174	Relay, capsule venting
95	Brake servo vacuum switch	175	Electronic relay
96	Brake pedal travel switch	180	Relay, fuel injection system
97	Headlight washer/wiper switch	181	Calculator, fuel injection system
98	Headlight washer pump	182	Airflow sensor
99	Headlight wiper motor	183	Injector
99A	Headlight wiper relay	184	Throttle switch unit
100	Pressure drop indicator	185	Temperature sensor, engine
101	Tachograph	190	Sensor, fuel pressure
102	Flasher light	191	Sensor, turbocharger excess pressure
102A	Flasher light switch	192	Gauge, turbocharger pressure
103	Centre interior light	195	100 mbar switch – turbo full-load control, turbo injection intercooler
103A	Centre interior light switch		
104	Feed warning light	196	Switch, advance curve selector
104A	Feed warning light switch	197	Resistor, full-load circuit (turbo injection intercooler)
105	Air fan	200	Control unit, voice synthesizer
105A	Air fan switch	200A	Filter
106	Warning bell	201	Test button, voice synthesizer
106A	Warning bell switch	210	Trip computer
107	Electrical plug	211	Display control
108	Compressor clutch	212	Fuel flow sensor
108A	Compressor clutch switch	213	Digital display
108B	Relay, compressor clutch	M	Earth
109	Thermostat	+P	Supple from the battery
109A	Protection diode, thermostat	+aa	Accessory supply
110	Constant pressure unit	+ac	Supply from the ignition switch

Not all items are fitted to all models
The wires are not colour-coded

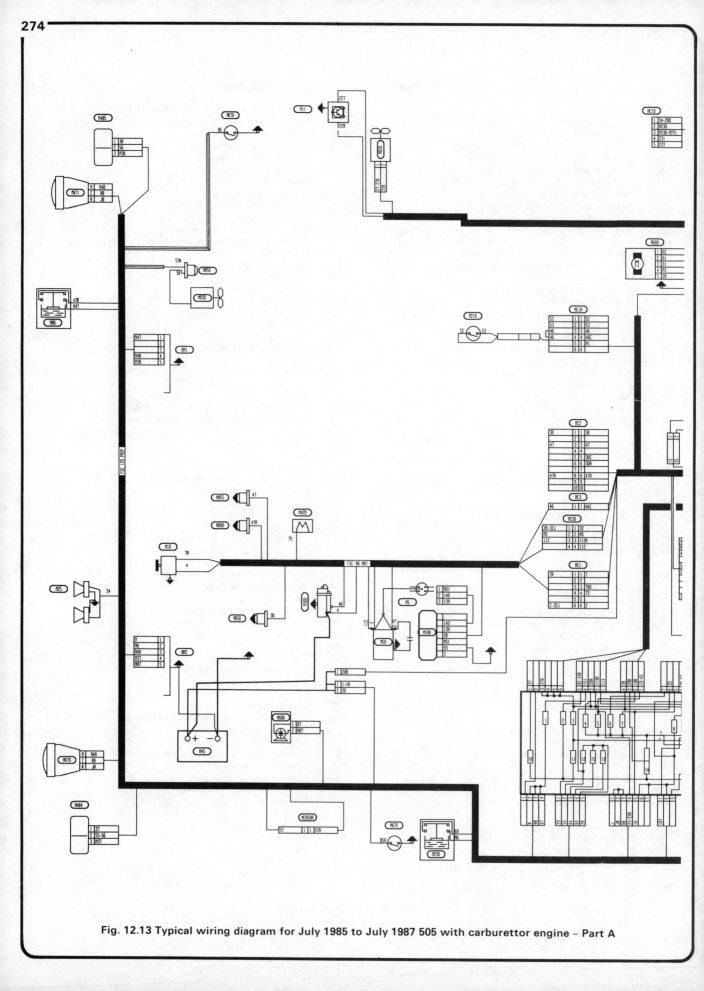

Fig. 12.13 Typical wiring diagram for July 1985 to July 1987 505 with carburettor engine – Part A

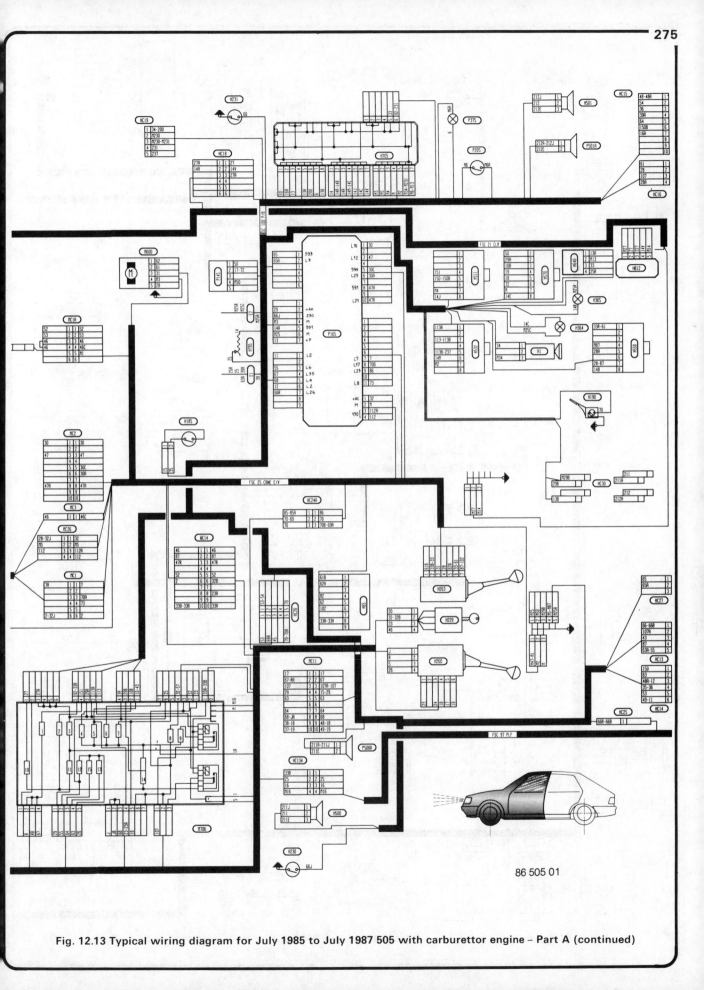

Fig. 12.13 Typical wiring diagram for July 1985 to July 1987 505 with carburettor engine – Part A (continued)

86 505 01

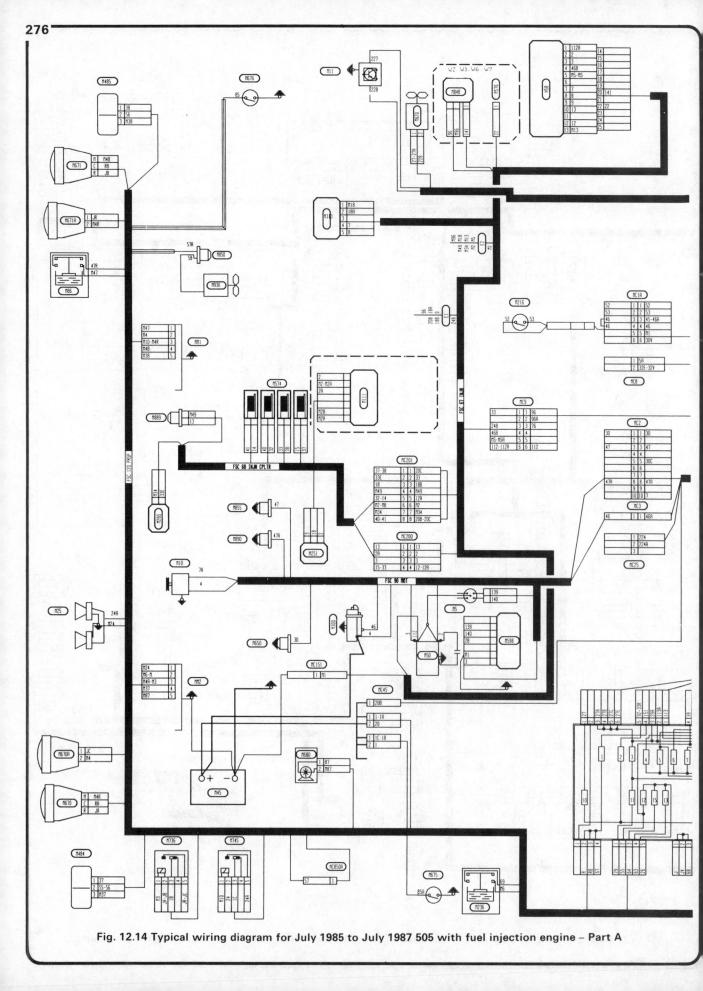

Fig. 12.14 Typical wiring diagram for July 1985 to July 1987 505 with fuel injection engine – Part A

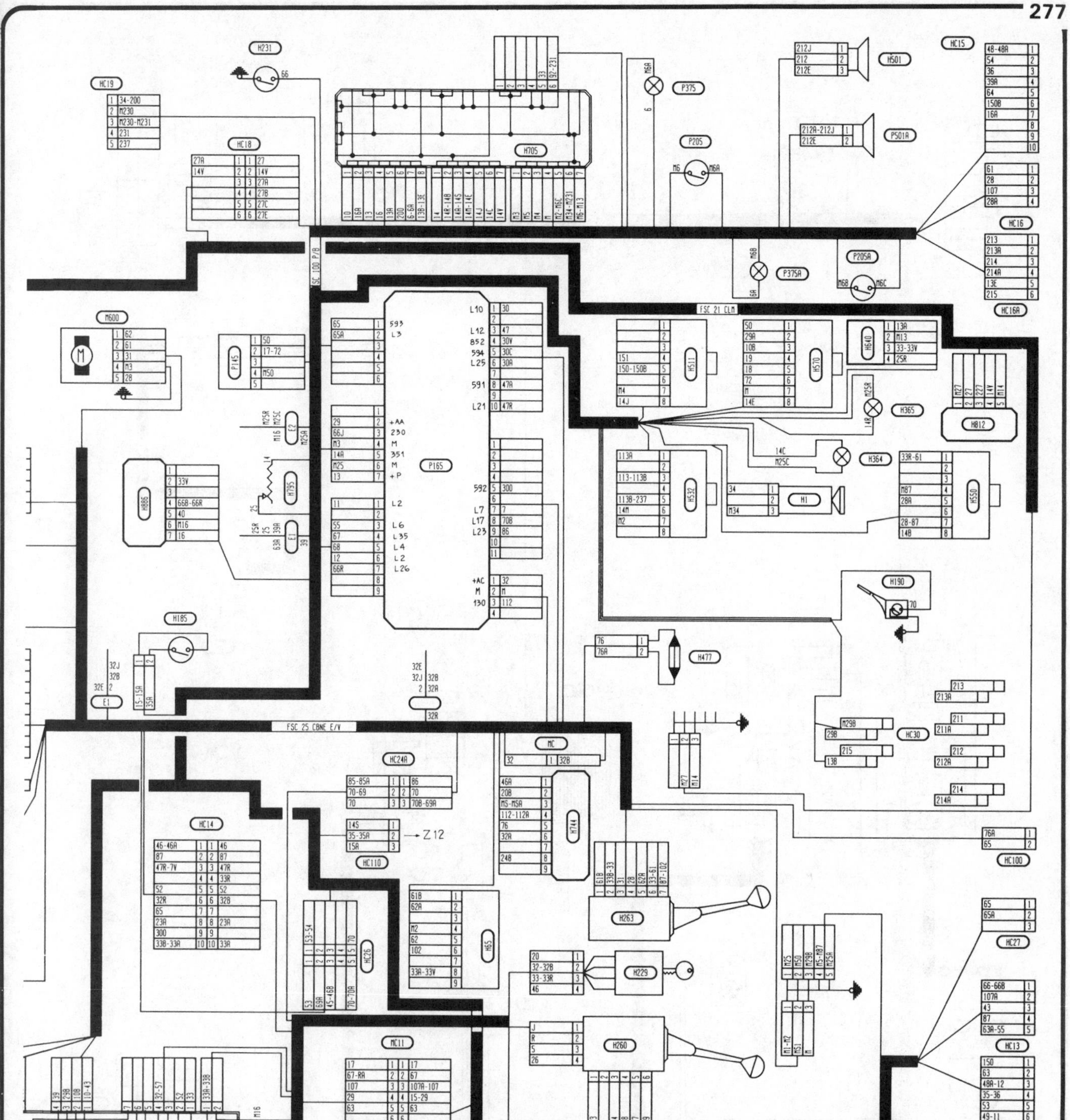

Fig. 12.14 Typical wiring diagram for July 1985 to July 1987 505 with fuel injection engine – Part A (continued)

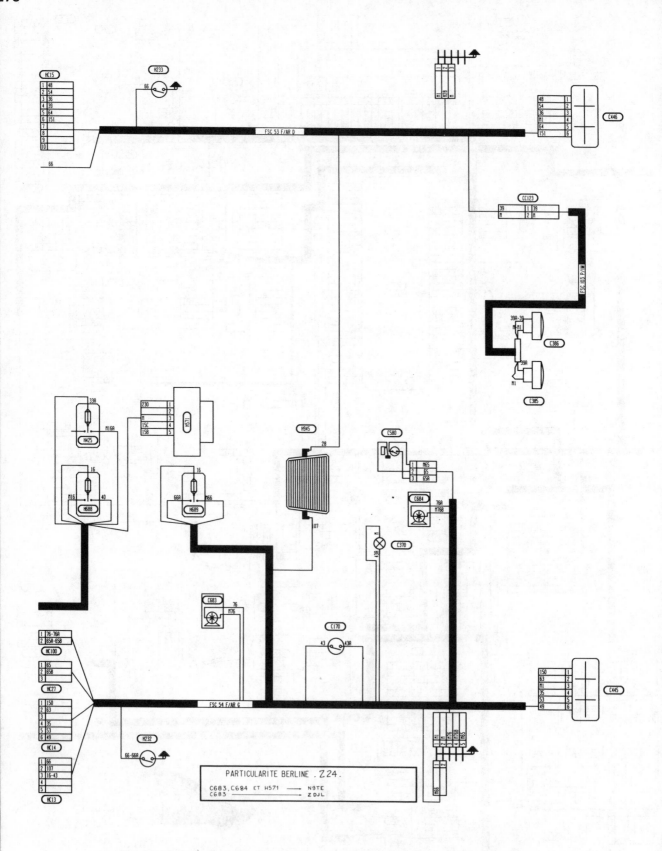

Fig. 12.15 Typical wiring diagram for July 1985 to July 1986 505 Saloon – Part B

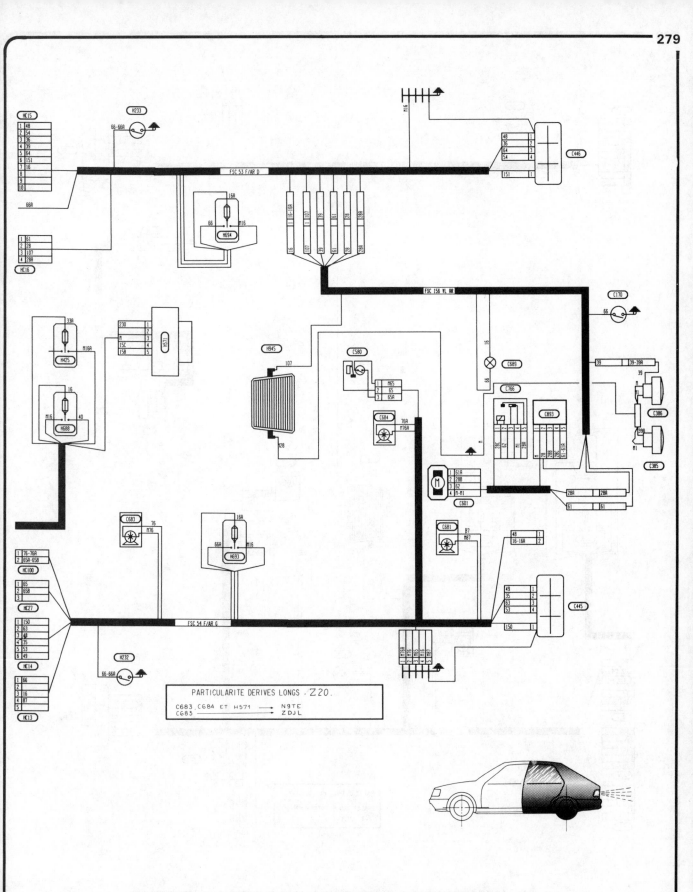

Fig. 12.16 Typical wiring diagram for July 1985 to July 1986 505 Estate – Part B

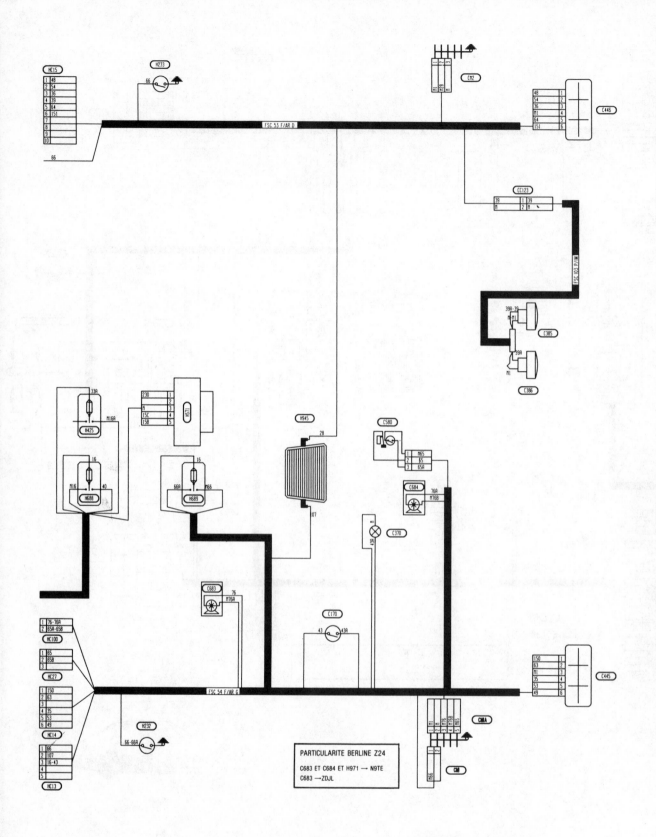

Fig. 12.17 Typical wiring diagram for July 1986-on 505 Saloon – Part B

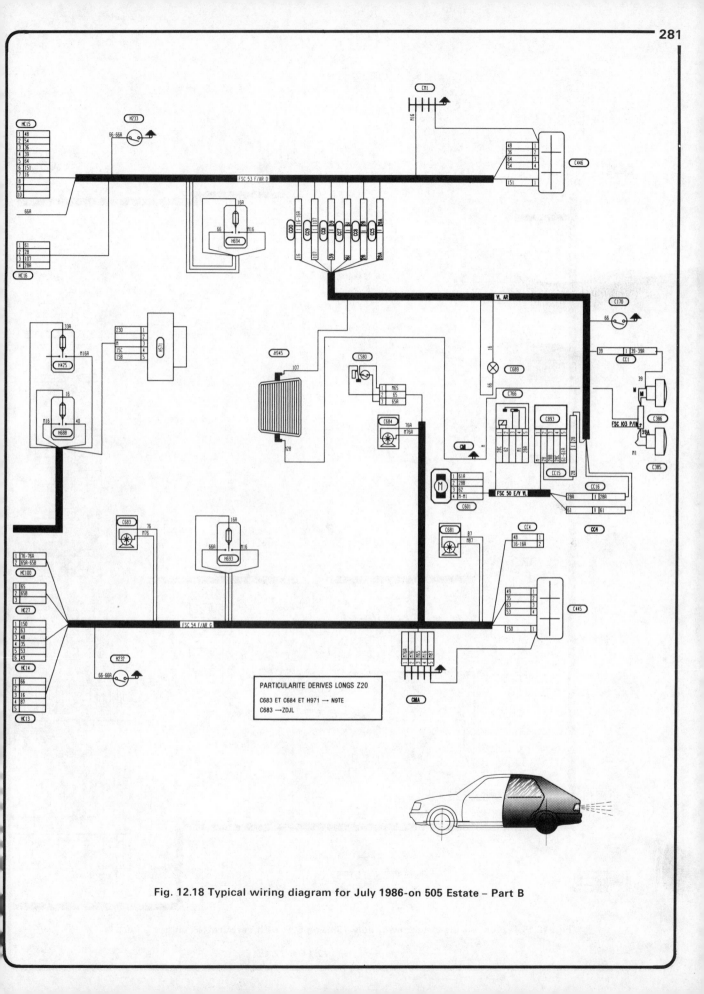

Fig. 12.18 Typical wiring diagram for July 1986-on 505 Estate – Part B

PARTICULARITE DERIVES LONGS Z20

C683 ET C684 ET H971 → N9TE

C683 →ZDJL

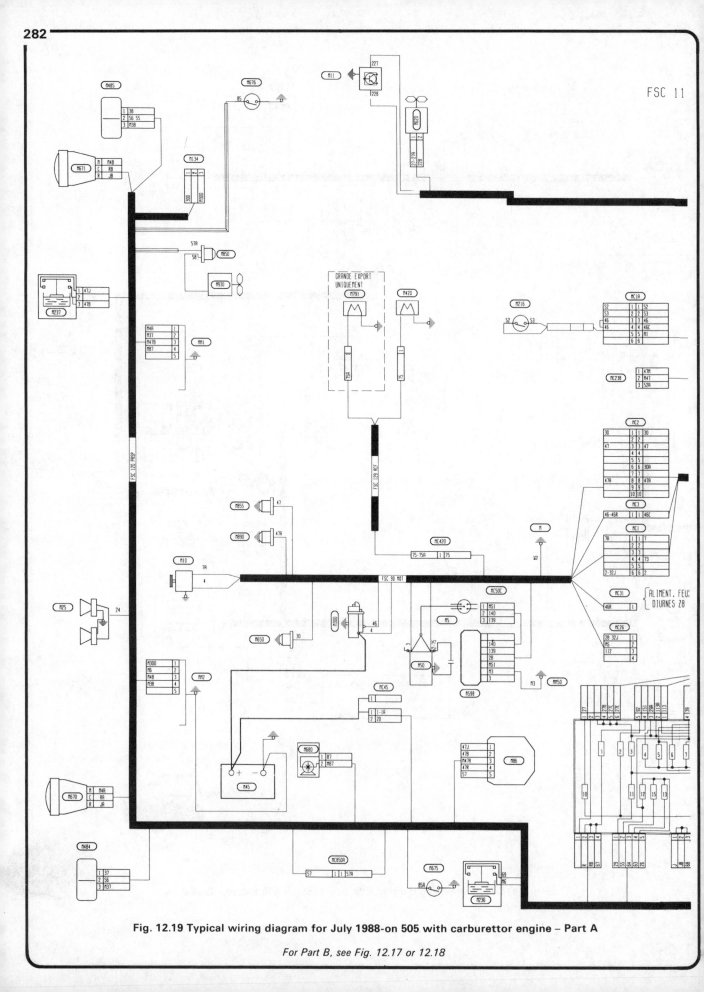

Fig. 12.19 Typical wiring diagram for July 1988-on 505 with carburettor engine – Part A

For Part B, see Fig. 12.17 or 12.18

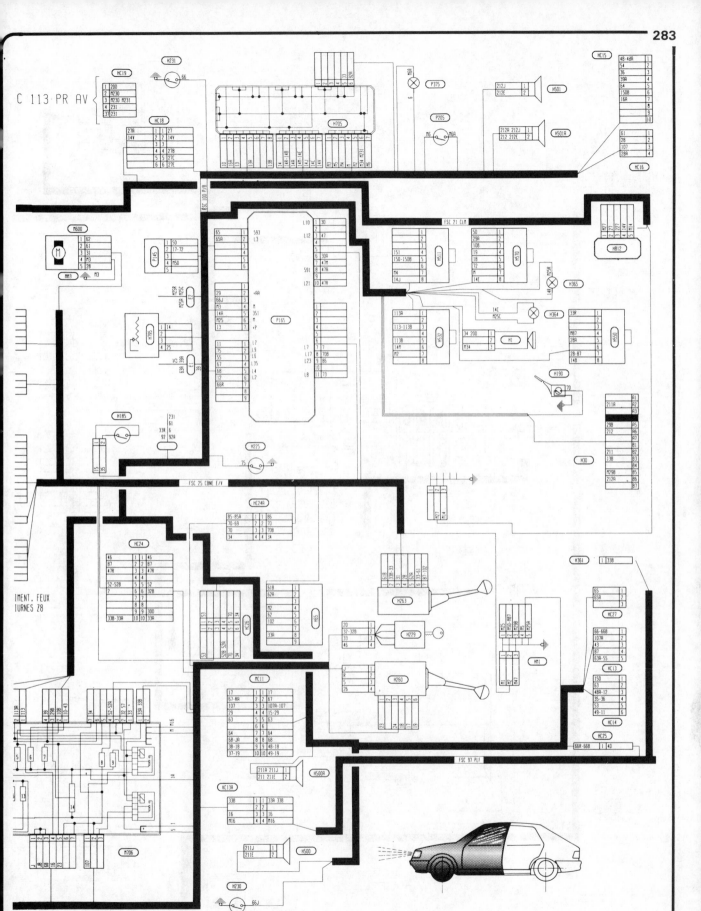

Fig. 12.19 Typical wiring diagram for July 1988-on 505 with carburettor engine – Part A (continued)

For Part B, see Fig. 12.17 or 12.18

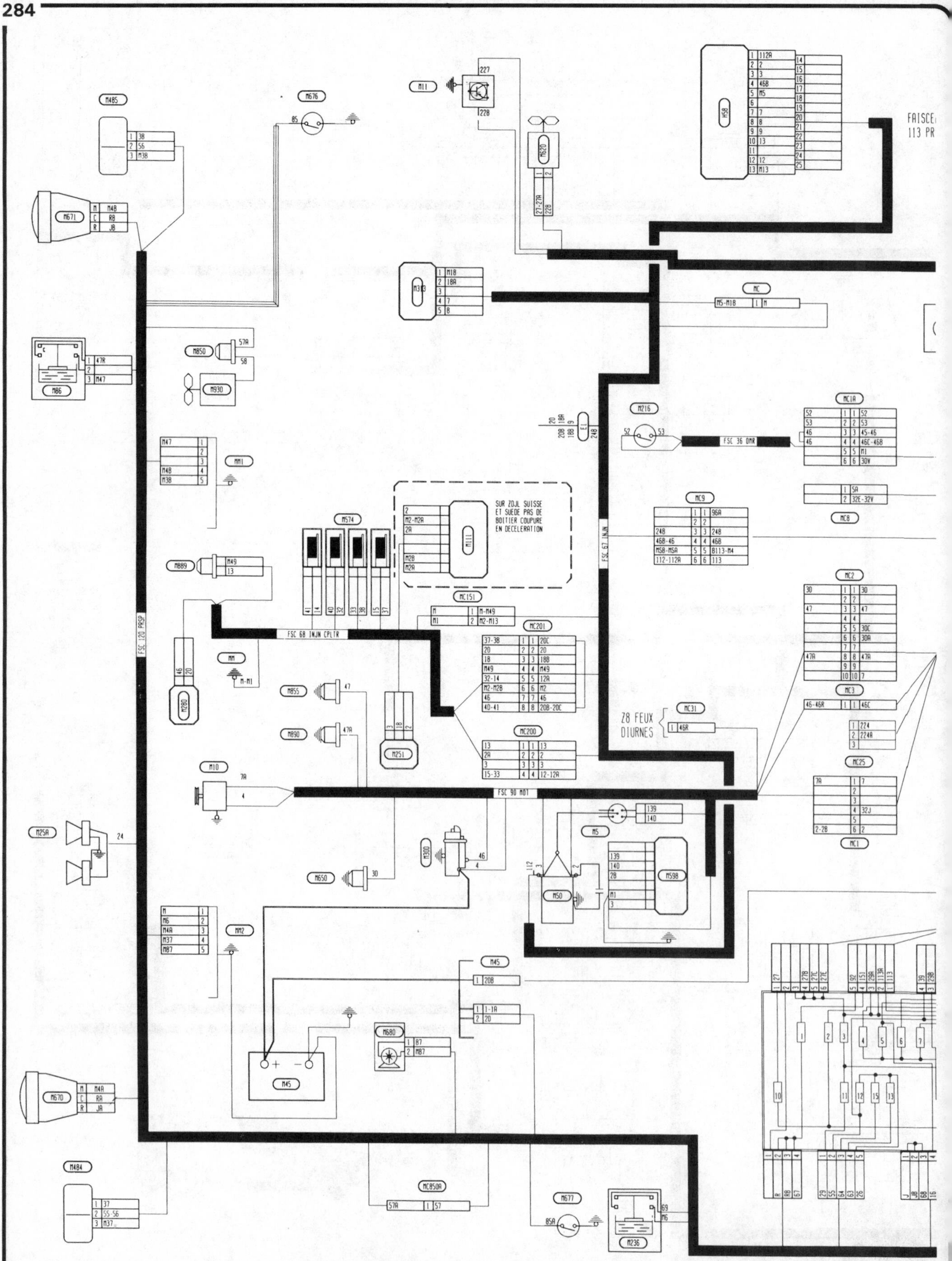

Fig. 12..20 Typical wiring diagram for July 1988-on 505 with fuel injection engine – Part A

For Part B, see Fig. 12.17 or 12.18

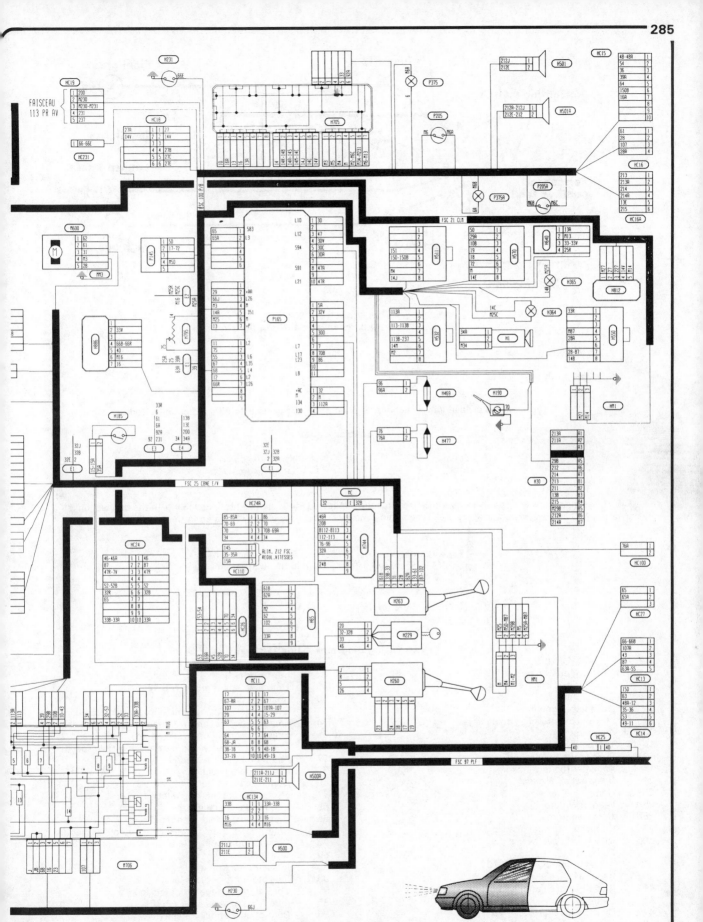

Fig. 12.20 Typical wiring diagram for July 1988-on 505 with fuel injection engine – Part A (continued)

For Part B, see Fig. 12.17 or 12.18

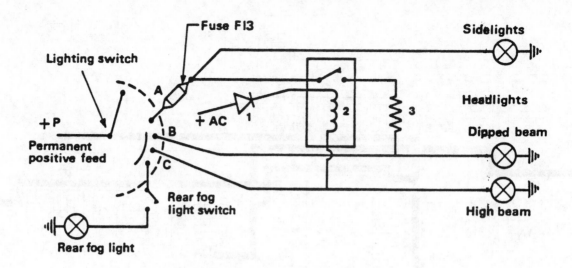

Fig. 12.21 Wiring diagram for dim-dip lighting

The vehicle is divided into 4 sections. Section codes are given before the component code.

Section codes

M	Engine	H	Passenger compartment
P	Facia	C	Luggage area

For connections between harnesses the Section codes, followed by C, are used to indicate where the connection is eg MC indicates a connector between the engine and facia harnesses which is located in the engine compartment

For earthing points the Section code is followed by M eg CM indicates an earthing point in the luggage area

Key to wiring diagrams – July 1985 on

Component codes		Component codes	
1	Cigar lighter, front	49	Unit, fuse board group (FBG)
3	Cigar lighter, rear	50	Ignition coil
5	Distributor, ignition	53	Control box, exhaust emission, for pilot carburettor
9	Idling actuator (idling solenoid)	54	Emission control unit (ignition advance modulator)
10	Alternator	55	Emission control unit (idle retard)
11	Transistor, heater blower control (power transistor)	56	Control unit, automatic transmission (idle speed)
13	Strut (earth connection)	57	Alarm unit, theft protection
14	Ammeter (battery charge)	58	Control unit, injection
20	Radio aerial, electric	60	Control unit, air conditioning
25	Horn	61	Electronic unit, brake antilock
25A	Horn, low note	65	Control unit, screenwiper
25B	Horn, high note	66	Control box, power steering
27	Connector, towing attachment	75	Control unit, ignition, or pick-up amplifier module
28	Dimmer, dipped beams	76	Detector unit, bulb failure
30	Radio	80	Cruise control unit
35	Actuator, fuel output (VP15)	85	Indicator unit, oil level
40	Radio balance control, front	86	Indicator unit, coolant level
41	Radio balance control, front/rear	90	Control unit, central door locking
45	Battery	95	Infra red signal receiver (PLIP)
47	Diodes unit	96	Control unit, knock detector
48	Unit, electric pump group (EPG)	97	Thermostat unit (passenger compartment)

Key to wiring diagrams – July 1985 on (continued)

Component codes

110	Control unit, preheater
111	Control unit, fuel cut-off on overrun
112	Control unit, fuel flow (trip computer)
113	Electronic control unit, advance (Diesel)
114	Control box, coolant temperature, air conditioning
115	Preheater plug
120	Terminal connector
121	Buzzer (P4, warning, coolant temperature, oil pressure, charge warning light)
122	Buzzer, direction indicator (P4)
125	Audible warning, seat belt
126	Audible warning (key in the ignition/steering lock with the driver's door open)
127	Audible warning, excessive speed
128	Audible warning (lights on, door open or 'STOP' warning lamp on)
130	TDC sensor
131	Altitude sensor
132	Knock detector
133	Sensor, engine speed
134	Sensor, absolute pressure (Diesel)
135	Sensor, potentiometer (econoscope vacuum)
136	Sensor, demisting the rear glass
137	Pressure sensor, inlet manifold
138	Pressure sensor, speedometer cable
140	Speed sensor, speedometer cable
141	Speed sensor, trip computer
142	Sensor, oil pressure
143	Sensor, No 1 cylinder
144	Sensor, diesel injector needle lifted
145	Direction indicator flasher unit
146	Antilock sensor, LH front wheel
147	Antilock sensor, RH front wheel
148	Antilock sensor, LH rear wheel
149	Antilock sensor, RH rear wheel
150	Air temperature sensor (air conditioning)
151	Load sensor (Diesel)
155	Pilot carburettor
160	Battery isolator
165	Instrument panel
167	Connector, emission control setting
169	Switch, starter/preheater
170	Switch, luggage compartment lamp
171	Switch, enrichment (LPG)
175	Switch, door lock
176	Switch, vacuum (LPG)
177	Switch, LH front lock (door open detector)
178	Switch, RH front lock (door open detector)
179	Switch, LH rear lock (door open detector)
180	Switch, RH rear lock (door open detector)
181	Switch, luggage compartment lock (lid open detector)
182	Switch, bonnet lock (bonnet open detector)
185	Switch, stop lamps
186	Switch, brake pedal travel
190	Switch, handbrake
195	Switch, low pressure (Freon)
196	Switch, mean pressure (Freon)
200	Thermal switch (Freon)
205	Switch, glovebox lamp
210	Switch, seat belt
211	Switch, display (trip computer)
215	Switch, starter inhibitor
216	Switch, reverse lamps
217	Switch, reverse lamps/starter inhibitor
220	Switch, heating/ventilation fan
221	Switch, heating/ventilation fan (rear)
225	Switch, choke warning light

Component codes

229	Switch, ignition/steering lock
230	Door switch, LH front
231	Door switch, RH front
232	Door switch, LH rear
233	Door switch, RH rear
234	Control switch, audible warning (ignition key 'in')
235	Switch, brake fluid pressure drop
236	Switch, brake fluid level
237	Switch, coolant level
238	Switch, water sensing, fuel system
239	Switch, washer bottle level
240	Limit switch, sunroof
241	Switch on accelerator pedal (idle speed)
242	Switch, idle speed
243	Switch, power take-off (P4)
247	Switch, rear differential lock
248	Switch, front differential lock
249	Switch, windscreen wiper lockout (P4)
250	Disengaging switch, cruise control (brake)
250A	Disengaging switch, cruise control (clutch)
251	Throttle switch (idling + full load)
252	Level switch, brake antilock
260	Control, lighting/direction indicators/horn
261	Control, lighting/screen wiper/screen wash
262	Control, lighting/screen wiper/direction indicator/horn
263	Control, screen wiper/wash
264	Control, lighting/horn
265	Control, direction indicator/horn
266	Switch, cruise control
267	Switch, cruise control/direction indicator
268	Switch, flasher unit (P4)
269	Switch, lighting/blackout (P4)
270	Switch, windscreen wiper (P4)
275	Control, driver's seat position
276	Control, rear view mirror LH
277	Control, rear view mirror RH
280	Supplementary air device (cold start)
281	Corrector, fuel reheating
285	Capacitor, coil positive
286	Capacitor, direction indicator flasher unit
290	Tachometer
295	Compressor
296	Compressor, air horn
300	Starter motor
301	Vapour relief valve (LPG)
302	Diode, relay protection
303	Diode, rear foglamps
304	Protection diode, electronic control unit
305	Checking diode, coolant temperature warning light
306	Checking diode, brake warning light
307	Diode, air conditioning control
308	Diode, lighting dimmer
309	Diode, electric fan
310	Diode, compressor
311	Diode, roof lamp
312	Diode, speech synthesizer
313	Flow sensor
329	Solenoid valve, cruise control deceleration
330	Solenoid valve, air conditioning
331	Solenoid valve, EGR (pilot carburettor)
332	Solenoid valve, opening the carburettor throttle valve
333	Solenoid valve, injection cut-off on overrun
334	Solenoid, emission control advance modulator
335	Solenoid, exhaust emission
336	Solenoid, carburettor breather
337	Main solenoid, brake antilock

Component codes

338	Control solenoid, brake antilock
340	Solenoid, pump stop
344	Solenoid, turbine fan
345	Solenoid valve, fast idle stabiliser
346	Solenoid, canister
347	Solenoid, cruise control
348	Advance solenoid, diesel
349	Solenoid valve, temperature control
350	Switches, illumination
351	Illumination, instrument panel
355	Illumination, heating/ventilation control
360	Illumination, console
361	Courtesy lamp
364	Illumination, cigar lighter
365	Illumination, ashtray
370	Illumination, luggage compartment (or tailgate)
375	Illumination, glovebox
380	Illumination, engine compartment
385	Illumination, number plate LH
386	Illumination, number plate RH
390	Illumination, ignition switch/steering lock
395	Floor illumination, driver's side
396	Floor illumination, passenger's side
397	Sill illumination, driver's side
398	Sill illumination, passenger side
400	Illumination, gear selector lever
410	Clutch, compressor
420	Idling cut-off, carburettor
425	Map reading lamp
440	Sidelamp LH
441	Sidelamp RH
445	Tail lamp cluster LH
446	Tail lamp cluster RH
452	Marker lamp, LH rear
453	Marker lamp, RH rear
455	Door marker lamp LH
456	Door marker lamp RH
457	Front foglamp RH
458	Front foglamp LH
460	Rear foglamp LH
461	Rear foglamp RH
462	Reverse lamp
463	Stop-lamp
464	Reverse lamp + foglamp (rear)
465	Suppressor filter, tachometer
466	Fuse holder (+ accessories, brake antilock)
467	Fuse holder (for warning light, brake antilock)
468	Fuse holder (power circuit, brake antilock)
469	Fuse holder Lambda sensor heater
470	Fuses (fusebox)
471	Fuse holder (radio)
472	Fuse holder (locks)
473	Fuse holder (dipped beams)
474	Fuse holder (speech synthesizer)
475	Fuse holder (carburettor heater)
476	Fuse holder (cruise control)
477	Fuse holder, supply pump
478	Flashing lamps, priority
479	Fuse holder (pump, brake antilock)
480	Direction indicator lamp, LH front
481	Direction indicator lamp, RH front
482	Direction indicator lamp, LH rear
483	Direction indicator lamp, RH rear
484	Side lamp/direction indicator, LH front
485	Side lamp/direction indicator, RH front
486	Suppression filter, speech synthesizer
487	Fuse holder (control unit, fuel output VP15)

Component codes

488	Fuse holder (control unit, advance regulator VP15)
489	Fuse holder, cooling fan group (CFG)
490	Impulse generator (speed)
491	Rotating lamp
500	Loudspeaker, LH front
501	Loudspeaker, RH front
502	Loudspeaker, LH rear
503	Loudspeaker, RH rear
505	Hour meter (P4)
510	Switch, front foglamps
511	Switch, rear foglamps
512	Switch, auxiliary driving lamp
513	Switch, siren
514	Switch, rotating lamp
515	Switch, rheostat, instrument panel illumination
516	Switch, parking lights
517	Switch, general (military P4)
518	Test switch, oil, coolant or charging fault (P4)
519	Switch, horn (P4)
520	Switch, window winder (driver's)
521	Switch, window winder (passenger's)
521A	Switch, passenger's window winder
522	Switch, window winder, LH rear
523	Switch, window winder, RH rear
524	Switch, window winder, LH rear (in rear compartment)
525	Switch, window winder, RH rear (in rear compartment)
526	Child safety switch, rear window winders
527	Switch, main/dip beams (P4)
530	Switch, sunroof
532	Switch, heated rear window
535	Switch, driver's seat heating
536	Switch, passenger's seat heating
540	Switch, preheater
545	Switch, central roof lamp
548	Test switch, brake wear warning light
549	Diagnostic switch, diesel
550	Switch, rear screen wiper
552	Switch, headlamp wiper
555	Switch, fuel supply warning light
556	Switch, police horn
557	Switch, rotating lamp
558	Switch, air fan
560	Switch, warning bell
565	Switch, pressure drop
566	Switch, air conditioning control
567	Switch, cruise control
570	Switch, hazard warning
571	Test switch
572	Switch, lamps (police)
574	Injectors
575	Cold start injector
576	Information display, injection control box
580	Fuel tank unit
590	Map reading lamp
591	Indicator, coolant temperature
592	Gauge, turbocharger pressure
593	Fuel gauge
594	Gauge, engine oil temperature
595	Gauge, engine oil pressure
598	Electronic control unit, ignition
600	Motor, screen wiper
601	Motor, window wiper, rear
605	Wiper motor, headlamp LH
606	Wiper motor, headlamp RH
607	Motor, heater control flap

Key to wiring diagrams – July 1985 on (continued)

Component codes		Component codes	
610	Motor, sunroof	735	Relay, main beams
615	Motor, LH front window winder	736	Relay, auxiliary driving lamps
616	Motor, RH front window winder	737	Relay, dipped beams
617	Motor, LH rear window winder	738	Relay, heating/ventilation fan, fast speed
618	Motor, RH rear window winder	740	Relay, coil
620	Motor, heating/ventilation fan	741	Relay, coil resistance
625	Actuator, LH front door lock	742	Relay, cold start control
626	Actuator, RH front door lock	743	Relay, compressor
627	Actuator, LH rear door lock	744	Tachymetric relay or pump control relay
628	Actuator, RH rear door lock	745	Relay, air horn compressor
629	Actuator, luggage compartment lock	746	Tachymetric relay (cut-off on overrun)
630	Motor, fuel filler flap lock	747	Relay, CLT
635	Motor, engine cooling fan	748	Relay, ECU, exhaust emission
636	Motor, air conditioning fan	749	Relay, cold cut-off
640	Clock	750	Relay, front foglamps
645	Pressure switch, brake servo	751	Relay, rear foglamps
646	Pressure switch, power steering	752	Relay, compressor cut-off (105°)
647	Pressure switch, air conditioning cut-out	753	Relay, pump, brake antilock
650	Oil pressure switch	754	Relay, power circuit, brake antilock
651	Vacuum-pressure switch	755	Relay, headlamp wiper
652	Pressure switch, turbocharger cut-out	756	Relay, headlamp wiper timer
653	Fuel throttle enrichment switch	757	Relay, advance curve selection
654	Advance curve selection switch	760	Relay, heated rear window
660	Trip computer	761	Relay, rear electric window
660A	Keyboard, trip computer	762	Relay, front electric window
660B	Display, trip computer	763	Relay, sunroof
669	Potentiometer, throttle	764	Relay, sunroof tilt + central locking
669A	Potentiometer, accelerator pedal (Diesel)	765	Relay, front screen wiper
670	Headlamp LH	766	Relay, rear window wiper
671	Headlamp RH	767	Relay, warning light occultation (P4)
672	Headlamp blackout (P4)	770	Relay, accessories
673	Driving lamp LH	771	Relay, visual warning
674	Driving lamp RH	772	Relay, two-speed (mixture control)
675	Brake pads, LH front	773	Relay, carburettor heater
676	Brake pads, RH front	775	Relay, starter motor isolator
677	Brake pads, LH rear	776	Relay, cruise control disengagement
678	Brake pads, RH rear	777	Relay, pilot carburettor supply
679	Vacuum pump, cruise control	778	Relay, scavenge pump
680	Washer pump, front	780	Relay, lighting dimmer
681	Washer pump, rear	781	Relay, excessive speed
682	Washer pump, headlamp	782	Relay, ignition supply
683	Fuel supply pump	783	Relay, injection supply
684	Scavenge pump	784	Relay, trip computer/cruise control/speech synthesizer information
685	Coolant pump, heater matrix		
686	Hydraulic pump, brake anti-lock	785	Relay, brake warning (Australia)
688	Interior lamp, front	786	Resistor, coil
689	Interior lamp, rear	787	Resistor, heating/ventilation fan
690	Interior lamp, centre	788	Resistor, two-speed cooling fan
691	Interior lamp, LH front	789	Resistor, lighting dimmer
692	Interior lamp, RH front	790	Heater, diesel fuel
693	Interior lamp, LH rear	791	Heater, carburettor
694	Interior lamp, RH rear	793	Resistor, preheater (P4)
697	PLIP	794	Resistor, injection matching
700	Pressure switch	795	Rheostat, instrument illumination
705	Connector board	800	Regulator, voltage
706	Services connector board	801	Regulator, control pressure
710	Battery supply socket	810	Side repeater flasher LH
720	Diagnostic socket	811	Side repeater flasher RH
721	Test socket (injection)	812	Rheostat, temperature display
723	Front foglamp LH	814	Rear view mirror LH
724	Front foglamp RH	815	Rear view mirror RH
729	Relay, emission control	817	Heated seat, front LH
730	Relay, starter motor	818	Heated seat, front RH
731	Relay, preheater	820	Bell
732	Relay, fan clutch	829	Servo, power steering
733	Relay, electric fan motor	830	Servo, cruise cotrol
734	Relay, hour meter (P4)	832	Sensor, evaporator

Key to wiring diagrams – July 1985 on (continued)

Component codes

833	Sensor, blown air
834	Sensor, interior air temperature
835	Sensor, oil level
836	Sensor, fuel flow (trip computer)
837	Sensor, coolant level
838	Sensor, mixture regulator
840	Sensor high temperature
841	Siren
845	Speech synthesizer
846	Sensor, body temperature (exhaust)
847	Sensor, passenger compartment temperature regulation
848	Lambda sensor
849	Sensor, external air temperature
850	Thermal switch, cooling fan (coolant)
852	Thermal switch, transmission oil
853	Thermal switch, 18°C (coolant temperature)
855	Thermal switch, coolant
861	Thermal switch, 40°C (coolant temperature)
862	Thermal switch, 60°C (coolant temperature)
865	Thermostat, electronic (air conditioning)
870	Thermal time switch (cold start opening)
880	Tachograph
885	Timer switch, seat belt
886	Timer switch, interior lamp
887	Timer switch, headlamp wash
888	Sender unit, oil temperature gauge
889	Temperature sender unit, injection
890	Sender unit, coolant temperature gauge
891	Temperature sender unit, electronic (heating/ventilation)
892	Sender unit, engine oil temperature
893	Timer switch, rear screen wiper
893A	Timer switch, windscreen wiper
894	Temperature sender unit, controlling cooling fan motors by ECU (liquid cooling)
895	Sender unit, exhaust emission
896	Thermal resistor, inlet air temperature
897	Tester, anti-lock
898	Sender unit, oil pressure
899	Test unit, variable power steering
929	Proportioning valve, cruise control
930	Fan, electromagnetic clutch
935	Fan, heating/ventilation
936	Fan, heating/ventilation, rear
945	Heated rear window
950	Fan
955	Ram, driver's seat
960	Fan, air conditioning

965	Cold start flap
970	Voltmeter
+AA	Supply from accessories terminal
+AC	Supply from ignition switch
BL	Screened cable
+D	Supply from starter motor
L1	Warning lamp, seat belt
L2	Warning lamps, direction indicator
L3	Warning lamp, low fuel level
L4	Warning lamp, main beams
L5	Warning lamp, hazard warning
L6	Warning lamp, side/tail lamps 'on'
L7	Warning lamp, no battery charge
L8	Warning lamp, preheater
L9	Warning lamp, choke control
L10	Warning lamp, oil pressure
L11	Warning lamp, oil and coolant
L12	Warning lamp, coolant temperature
L13	Warning lamp, brake safety
L14	Warning lamp, rear foglamps
L15	Warning lamp, fuel supply
L16	Warning lamp, 'stop'
L17	Warning lamp, brake fluid/stop-lamps
L18	Warning lamp, sidelamp failure
L19	Warning lamp, tail lamp failure
L20	Warning lamp, screenwash level
L21	Warning lamp, coolant level
L22	Warning lamp, engine oil level
L23	Warning lamp, brake pad wear
L24	Manual test switch, instrument panel
L25	Warning lamp, oil temperature
L26	Warning lamp, 'door open'
L27	Warning lamp, tail lamp or rear foglamp failure
L30	Warning lamp, rear differential lock
L31	Warning lamp, front differential lock
L32	Warning lamp, knock detector
L33	Warning lamp, diagnosis
L34	Warning lamp, water in fuel
L35	Warning lamp, dipped beams
L36	Warning lamp, trailer direction indicator
L37	Warning light, power take-off (P4)
L38	Warning lamp, catalytic converter
L39	Warning lamp, brake anti-lock alert
M	Earth connections
+P	Supply from battery

Not all items are fitted to all models

The wires are not colour-coded

Index